Conversations Abou†

'Reflexivity' is defined as the regular exercise of the mental ability, shared by all normal people, to consider themselves in relation to their (social) contexts and vice versa. Hence it is crucial in mediating between what actors themselves are most concerned to achieve in society and the social constraints and enablements that they confront as they try to realize their concerns. Their reflexive 'internal conversations' are the means through which they deliberate about what course of action to take. Focusing fully on this phenomenon, this book discusses three main questions associated with this subject in detail.

1 What are the social conditions leading people to practice reflexivity in different ways?
2 What part do our internal reflexive deliberations play in designing the courses of action we take: subordinate to habitual action or not?
3 If 'reflexivity' is not a homogeneous practice for all people at all times, does it show significant variations over history?

In addressing these questions, contributors engage critically with the most relevant studies, by thinkers such as G. H. Mead, C. S. Peirce, J. Habermas, N. Luhmann, U. Beck, A. Giddens and P. Bourdieu. Most contributors are leading Pragmatists or Critical Realists, associated with the 'Reflexivity Forum': an informal, international and inter-disciplinary group.

This combination of reference to influential writers of the past and the best of modern theory has produced a fascinating book that is essential reading for all students with a serious interest in social theory and two of its main problems – how structure and agency are linked and what is the relationship between human subjectivity and the objective social context.

Margaret S. Archer is Professor of Sociology at the University of Warwick. She has published 25 books in the area of Social Theory, with particular emphasis on social ontology, emergent properties and the problem of linking structure and agency.

Ontological Explorations
Other titles in this series:

Conversations About Reflexivity

Edited by Margaret S. Archer

 Routledge
Taylor & Francis Group

LONDON AND NEW YORK

First published 2010
by Routledge
2 Park Square, Milton Park, Abingdon, Oxon, OX14 4RN

Simultaneously published in the USA and Canada
by Routledge
711 Third Avenue, New York, NY 10017

Routledge is an imprint of the Taylor & Francis Group, an informa business

© 2010 Margaret S. Archer for selection and editorial material; individual
chapters, the contributors

Typeset in Goudy by
Pindar NZ, Auckland, New Zealand

First issued in paperback in 2013

British Library Cataloguing in Publication Data
A catalogue record for this book is available from the British Library

Library of Congress Cataloging-in-Publication Data
A catalog record has been requested for this book

ISBN13: 978-0-415-73307-6 (pbk)
ISBN13: 978-0-415-55852-5 (hbk)
ISBN13: 978-0-203-86755-6 (ebk)

Contents

Illustrations

Figures

Tables

Contributors

Margaret S. Archer received her Ph.D. from the London School of Economics and has been Professor of Sociology at the University of Warwick, UK, since 1979. She is the past editor of *Current Sociology* and past president of the International Sociological Association. Her previous books include *Culture and Agency* (1988), *Realist Social Theory* (1995), *Being Human* (2000), *Structure, Agency and the Internal Conversation* (2003) and *Making Our Way Through the World* (2007).

Pierpaolo Donati is Professor of Sociology, University of Bologna, Italy. He is the past president of the Italian Sociological Association; Director of the Centre for Social Policy Studies and Social Health, University of Bologna, Director of the 'National Observatory on the Family' and editor of the journal, *Sociologia e Politiche Sociali*. His main recent publications include *Teoria Relazionale della Società* (1992), *La cittadinanza societaria* (2000), *La cultura civile in Italia: fra stato, mercato e privato sociale* (2002), *Il capitale sociale degli italiani. Le radici familiari, comunitarie e associative del civismo* (2008), and *Teoria Relazionale della Società* (2009).

Vincent Colapietro is Liberal Arts Research Professor in the Department of Philosophy at Pennsylvania State University. He received his M.A. and Ph.D. from Marquette University, Wisconsin, (while his M.A. thesis was on Dewey, his dissertation was on Peirce). His books include *Peirce's Approach to the Self* (1989) and *Fateful Shapes of Human Freedom* (2003). He has written especially on the central figures in American pragmatism and themes related to their unique contribution to philosophical inquiry (meaning, agency, practice, and art).

Helena Flam received her Fil.Kand. in Sweden and her Ph.D. at Columbia University. She has been Professor of Sociology in Leipzig, Germany, since 1993. Her publications in the sociology of emotions include *The Emotional Man and the Problem of Collective Action* (2000), *Soziologie der Emotionen* (2002) and *Emotions and Social Movements* (2005). She is a co-founder of the Emotions Network of the European Sociological Association.

Pablo Garcia-Ruiz is Associate Professor of Sociology, University of Zaragoza, Spain; Ph. D. University of Navarra, Spain; M. Sc. Management Science, IESE Business School, University of Navarra; Postdoctoral Research Scholar at the London School of Economics. His newest book *Repensar el consumo* (2009) deals with the social conditions of consumption patterns.

Andrea M. Maccarini is Professor of Sociology in the Department of Sociology, University of Padua, Italy. He is a member of the editorial board of the journals *Comparative Sociology* and *Italian Journal of Sociology of Education*. His main research interests are social theory, the sociology of culture and the sociology of education (both education policy and socialisation processes).

Adam Mrozowicki is lecturer at the Institute of Sociology, University of Wrocław, Poland, and Postdoctoral Research Fellow of the Foundation for Polish Science (2009–2011). He defended his Ph.D. thesis at the Centre for Sociological Research at the Catholic University of Leuven, Belgium. He has published in the *European Journal of Industrial Relations*, *Qualitative Sociology Review* and in edited books on cultural identities and trade union revitalisation.

Alistair Mutch is Professor of Information and Learning at Nottingham Trent University, UK. A historian by training, he received his Ph.D. in rural history from Manchester. He has published on the relationship between organisations, information and technology in leading US and European journals such as *Organization Studies* and *Organization Science*.

Douglas Porpora is Professor of Sociology at Drexel University, Philadelphia. He has written widely on social theory and on what he calls 'macro-morality', that is, issues of genocide, war, and torture. His books include *How Holocausts Happen: The US in Central America* (1992), *Landscapes of the Soul: The Loss of Moral Meaning in American Life* (2001), and with Margaret Archer and Andrew Collier *Transcendence: Critical Realism and God* (2004). He is now writing a book on the Iraq war.

Riccardo Prandini is Associate Professor in the Department of Sociology, University of Bologna, Italy. He is Editorial Secretary of *Sociologia e Politiche Sociali*. His publications include *Le radici fiduciarie del legame sociale* (1998), (ed.) *La realtà del sociale: sfide e nuovi paradigmi* (2004), with P. Donati (eds) *Buone pratiche e servizi innovativi per la famiglia* (2006), *La cura della famiglia e il mondo del lavoro* (2008), with L. Martignani (eds), *Cultura riflessiva e politiche sociali* (2008), and, with A.M. Maccarini, E. Morandi (eds), *Realismo sociologico* (2008).

Carlos Rodriguez-Lluesma earned his PhD in Organizations from Stanford University, he is Assistant Professor of Organizational Behavior at IESE Business School in Zaragoza. Professor Rodriguez-Lluesma has published two books and several papers on management in national and international journals.

Andrew Sayer is Professor of Social Theory and Political Economy in the Department of Sociology at Lancaster University, UK. His books include *Method in Social Science: A Realist Approach* (1992), *The New Social Economy* (with R.A.Walker, 1992), *Radical Political Economy: A Critique* (1995), *Realism and Social Science* (2000) and *The Moral Significance of Class* (2005). He is currently finishing a book on lay normativity and ethics called, *Why Things Matter: Social Science, Values and Ethical Life*.

Wesley Shumar is Professor of Anthropology and the Department Head of the Department of Culture and Communication at Drexel University, Philadelphia. His research focuses on higher education and online educational communities. He is author of *College for Sale: A Critique of the Commodification of Higher Education* (1997) and co-editor of two books, *Structure and Agency in the Neoliberal University* (2008) and *Building Virtual Communities* (2002).

Frédéric Vandenberghe is Professor in Sociology at the University Institute of Rio de Janeiro (IUPERJ) in Brazil. He works at the intersection of German social philosophy, Anglo-Saxon social theory and French sociological theory. He is the author of *La sociologie de Georg Simmel* (2001), *Complexités du posthumanisme. Trois essais dialectiques sur la sociologie de Bruno Latour* (2006), *A Philosophical History of German Sociology* (2009) and *Teoria social realista. Um dialogo franco-britanico* (2009).

Norbert Wiley has a M.A. in philosophy and sociology from the University of Notre Dame, Indiana, and a Ph.D. in sociology from Michigan State University. His main book is *The Semiotic Self* (1994). His current project is a book on inner speech. He and his wife, Christine Chambers, received an award from the United States Congress for their activities in the gay-lesbian rights movement.

1   Introduction

The reflexive re-turn

Margaret S. Archer

That eleven social theorists of different persuasions – mainly pragmatist and realist – should sit down for a week of intensive exchanges* on reflexivity and then
produce this collective volume gives pause (some would bridle at saying 'cause')
for an exercise in reflexivity itself. Already, the writing of this first sentence has
entailed reflexive practice: self-monitoring for choice of the appropriate word
('pause' or 'cause') because, as William James observed, we welcome some words
as more closely expressing our 'premonitionary notions' and discard others (1890:
281–4); self-awareness that 'causality' must be used cautiously in the academy;
and self-conscious recognition, through bending the choice of words back upon
myself and my intentions, that at the start I should choose the more neutral term
if I wish to get a conversation going on reflexivity.

This one sentence has also introduced the need for clarification amongst a
cluster of conceptual siblings: *reflex-responses*, *reflective* thoughts, and *reflexive*
processes. Most of us would agree that *reflex* action, in its purely autonomous
physiological form (the physical reflexes for which newborn babies are tested,
our knee-jerk reactions, or swallowing and blinking given appropriate stimuli),
are wholly inadequate – even as metaphors – for how we produce sentences or
utterances. However, does this also mean that the model of 'conditioned reflexes'
in the Pavlovian tradition is considered to be equally inappropriate? For example,
when introduced to someone, we often respond semi-automatically: 'Pleased to
meet you', '*Enchanté*', '*Encantada*', '*Piacere*' etc. Do these learnt and conventional
responses approximate to conditioned reflexes? Most of us would want to differentiate between animal 'conditioning' and human 'conventionality', precisely
because verbally we do not do the equivalent of 'salivating' and, more importantly,
because our local conventions are matters upon which we can both reflect and
about which we can be reflexive. In any case, we can agree that the interventions

* My thanks go to the ESRC for funding the Reflexivity Workshop (University of Warwick,
  17–21 September 2007), from which the informal Reflexivity Forum developed and attracted new
  'members' at the 38th annual conference of the International Institute of Sociology, Budapest, June,
  2008, some of whose work appears in this volume.

we make in a seminar and the sentences that eventually make up a book are not things we can be pre-conditioned to produce like Skinner's chickens pecking out a figure eight.

I have just said that these are distinguished from animal conditioning by our human ability to reflect upon or be reflexive about our conventionality, but what is the difference between the latter two? Human *reflection is the action of a subject towards an object*, as in a mathematician reflecting on an abstract problem. In the case of how to respond when introduced to a stranger, the object in question is a socio-linguistic convention. Whether or not we use it, we all have the capacity to reflect about the appropriateness of reproducing it and its implications. This does not require the knowledgeability of an Elias-style disquisition on the history of manners. For instance, collectively the young have clearly reflected that the conventional formality of their elders should be replaced by 'Hi' and '*Ciao*'. Equally, their elders have reflected, in comparison with their own elders, that signing off a letter as 'Your obedient servant' or, worse, 'Your humble servant', is outdated and false.

Circumstances, especially those of rapid change, can indeed prompt new reflections on protocol. Revolutions are always occasions promoting new forms of address which, reflectively in terms of their intended impact, can be deployed to metonymic effect: President de Gaulle began his speeches with '*Citoyennes, Citoyens*', deliberately playing on the continuity of 'his' Fifth Republic with *La République* and, possibly, not oblivious to making a polysemic appeal to the Second Sex. During today's cyber-revolution, the form of address and final salutation used in emailing show that globally 'we' have concluded that the conventions of the letter form do not transfer comfortably. As yet, a new set of email conventions has not been consolidated. Hence, we reflect upon appropriate openings, with some concluding *pro tem* that none at all is the safest policy, others reviving the unobjectionable Quaker practice of using someone's full name, but the increasingly ubiquitous opener 'Hi' seems to indicate that many have reflected upon the inappropriateness of addressing all and sundry as 'Dear' (in English).

Reflection can be directed at any object whatsoever; sometimes it is unavoidable – Is it safe to cross the road? Do they take credit cards here? – and sometimes it is done willingly – thinking out an argument or doing a crossword puzzle. The sale of puzzle-books at stations and airports rivals that of self-help manuals, so it appears that 'reflecting' is fun, just as 'reflexivity' can be (in idle fantasy), although the two are very different activities. The distinguishing feature of reflexivity is that it has the self-referential characteristic of 'bending-back' some thought upon the self, such that it takes the form of *subject-object-subject*.

Undoubtedly, reflection and reflexivity have fuzzy borders and can shift from one to the other. When attempting to make a device work, the question 'What next?' is indistinguishable from 'What do I do next with this?' and can segue into the fully reflexive 'Can I cope with this and do I really want to?' – more simply expressed as an expletive. Thus, utterances are not a good guide to reflexivity, which finds its home, I argue, in the 'internal conversation'. Take the earlier example of protocol, this time when about to be introduced to the local *nomenclatura*. My uttering the local protocol form for such a greeting *may* have involved an internal conversation about (a) an initial reluctance to pronounce the standard formula, given its literal meaning (which is as close to the reflex-response as things get), through (b) reflection upon the consequences of substituting an anodyne alternative (saying 'Hello'), to (c) a self-referential and truly reflexive consideration of such things as 'what will others think of me?', 'is this the best form of self-promotion?' and matters of self-concern and social-engagement ('do I really care sufficiently?'). Reflexivity always involves that mental and self-referential 'bending back' upon oneself of some notion, whose referent may be trivial or crucial.

Considerable conceptual confusion has been introduced by the title of Beck, Giddens and Lash's book *Reflexive Modernization* (1994), where the adjective implies *systemic reflexivity*, whilst the text deals with dangerous and uncontrolled 'side effects', given that Modernity has 'no brakes or a steering wheel' (p. 180). Why should a well-established term like 'reflexivity', with its stable denotations of self-monitoring and self-control, be used to refer to its precise opposite? That it does just that, Beck avows, without justifying this perverse usage:

> In pointed terms, the 'reflexivity' of modernity and modernization in my sense does not mean reflection on modernity, self-relatedness, the self-referentiality of modernity, nor does it mean the self-justification or self-criticism of modernity ... modernization *undercuts* modernization, unintended and unseen, and therefore also reflection-free. (p. 177)

In their 'Preface' to the book, the authors' best collective recommendation for using 'reflexivity' in this way is that 'the protracted debate about modernity and post-modernity has become wearisome'; thus, the 'idea of reflexive modernization, regardless of whether or not one uses that term as such, breaks the stranglehold which these debates have tended to place on conceptual innovation' (p. vi). We should not delay further over the wordplay of these authors.

In the history of ideas the salience of some concepts comes and goes – the 'body', 'climate' and 'ecology' are clear examples in social theory. Partly, this can be explained by a fallible taken-for-grantedness, which requires some radical re-problematization to re-insert a familiar concept in the current agenda of social theory (the rediscovery of the body through social 'body work' being a fairly recent example). Partly, too, waves of attention and inattention are artefacts of the relatively arbitrary disciplinary division of academic labour such that 'climate', once a major variable in early sociology, gradually became the preserve of natural science. Neither explanation works well for reflexivity and its idiosyncratic history within social theory; it has been articulated – neglected – 'rediscovered' – fallen into desuetude – and now 'rediscovered' again. However, no other discipline (with the partial exception of some forms of psychology) made reflexive mental activities its preserve and therefore this does not account for the discontinuous interest social theorists have taken in reflexivity over time. Perhaps this strange trajectory itself represents one of the conditions that made our exchanges possible at the Workshop: reflexivity really belongs to no particular school of thought, unlike other equally general concepts, of which 'interpretation' is the best example.

The chequered biography of reflexivity

Plato's characterization of reflexivity in the *Theaetetus* can be credited as the first conceptualization, where reflexivity is significantly regarded as practised through 'inner conversation' and to result in opinion formation, the latter surely not irrelevant to nascent sociology.

> I mean the conversation which the soul holds with herself in considering of anything. I speak of what I scarcely understand; but the soul when thinking appears to me to be just talking – asking questions of herself and answering them, affirming and denying. And when she has arrived at a decision, whether gradually or by sudden impulse, and has at last agreed, and does not doubt, that is called her opinion. I say, then, that to form an opinion is to speak, and opinion is a word spoken – I mean to oneself and in silence, not aloud or to another. (Plato, 1992, 189E-190A)

One reason why reflexivity's potential was declined was the generic place assigned to 'subjectivity' in the foundational traditions of sociology: with Durkheim (of the *Rules*) seeking, somewhat unsuccessfully, to banish it from the sociological domain; Marx largely restricting the subjective to his concerns with 'false consciousness'; and Weber, in principle the best predisposed, obscuring it under his fourfold typology of action. Arguably the type most relevant to reflexivity, value-rational action (*Wertrationalität*), was consigned to irrational action rather than to deliberatively designed courses of action intended to realize the values underpinning our ultimate concerns (Donati, 2008: 97–109).

Another reason for neglect was methodological. How was anyone to come by this self-knowledge? 'Introspection' had been accepted as its reliable source for two thousand years, based upon 'looking inwards' (*spect intra*). However, Kant had voiced his difficulties with introspection in 1804, when sociology was barely in *statu nascendi*. He maintained that our self-knowledge was an 'indubitable fact', but one that we were unable to explain. His problem with introspection was that it had to assume a split within the self such that we could simultaneously be both the observer and the observed – subject and object at the same time.

> That I am conscious of myself is a thought that already contains a twofold self, the I as subject and that I as object. How it might be possible for the I that I think to be an object (of intuition) for me, one that enables me to distinguish me from myself, is absolutely impossible to explain, even though it is an indubitable fact. (1804/1983:73)

On these Kantian grounds, Comte made a particularly forceful argument for introspection being 'null and void': 'The thinker cannot divide himself into two, of whom one reasons while the other observes him reason. The organ observed and the organ observing being, in this case, identical, how could observation take place?'(1975: 34–8).

To many, this seemed an irrefutable argument against introspection and, consequently, against our having any immediate knowledge of our mental activities. However, it is strictly an attack upon the observational model of self-awareness alone. It has no force at all for our other senses through which we can be both the observer and the observed simultaneously (especially when listening to our own voices). It is the eye alone that cannot see itself seeing and, as William James declared: 'The attempt at introspective analysis … is like seizing a spinning top to catch its motion, or turning up the gas quickly enough to see how the darkness looks'(1890: 243–4).

Moreover, John Stuart Mill's (1973: 64) riposte to Comte had many takers because it preserved the 'indubitable fact' that we have knowledge of our own mental activities. With one revision to the concept of introspection, rather than involving its complete overhaul or overthrow, he proposed to solve the subject-object problem by inserting a small time gap, such that what we were engaged in was *retrospection* rather than *introspection*. Thus, introspection could be absorbed into an unobjectionable study of memory, but in effect was thus handed over to psychologists such as Wundt and Titchener, without apparent sociological remainder or regret (Lyons, 1986: 15).

However, the rediscovery of reflexivity as inner dialogue – the achievement of the great America pragmatists – was based upon listening to ourselves and then responding inwardly rather than looking inward. In 1868, Peirce remarked, 'Thought, says Plato, is a silent speech of the soul with itself. If this be admitted, immense consequences follow; quite unrecognised, I believe, hitherto' (1867–71: 172). The first was that the reduction of the introspective process to a study of memory was entirely irrelevant. As Colapietro notes, for Peirce 'the principal function of internal reflection does not reside in taking stock of what we have already thought or in attempting to view what we are presently thinking; it resides in engaging in an inner dialogue – indeed an inner drama – and in judging the outcome of that dialogue or drama' (1989: 117) as a guide to action. Since intra-communication was directly related to determining people's future courses of action, the import of this mental activity was acknowledged in sociology for the first time.

The point of reflexivity – personal or social?

However, the 'reception' of reflexivity was simultaneously the occasion for division over it, perhaps responsible for squandering the patrimony of pragmatist insights for almost a century. If reflexivity was 'purposive', then whose purposes did it serve: those of the individual, those of society, or was it an attempt to balance the two? This, I have maintained, divided pragmatism itself, setting Peircian equipoise – his fine balancing of the social and the personal – against Meadean over-sociality (Archer, 2003: 64–90), although not all would agree with my interpretation (see

Vandenberghe Ch. 4). What seems less disputable is that theorists at the extremes of the continuum running from monadic individualism to socio-cultural determinism are those who would have declined to join our Workshop.

It is significant that theorists most closely attached to monadic individualism – Rational Choice theorists – are vaccinated against taking an interest in reflexivity. The origins of the Humean 'passions' remain 'mysterious' and in any case *de gustibus non est disputandum* (to any profit or avail). Thus, Rational Choice theory begins from individuals' fixed preference schedules and concerns itself exclusively with courses of action 'maximising' or 'satisficing' these preferences in order to leave their bearers 'better off' in terms of some indeterminate future 'utiles'. Instrumental rationality is the only name of the game and it is concerned with impersonal calculation rather than personalised deliberation. Equally, Rational Choice theorists' most intransigent opponents, and especially the greatest protagonist of cultural socialization – Bourdieu – maintained the same lack of interest in reflexivity. Once described by Lash as being the only cultural game in town, Bourdieu and his followers have undoubtedly and very successfully marginalized 'reflexive studies' to the profit of 'cultural studies'. All the same, because Bourdieu held that reflexivity could come to be practised by *homo academicus*, by collectively engaging in the academic critique pertaining to their 'field', he would not have been astonished at our gathering, though I doubt very much that he would have joined us.

In other words, the purpose of reflexivity is a question of no interest either to monadic individualists (who simply believe that we know our own minds) or to cultural determinists (who generically believe that our minds have been made up for us). It is theorists falling between these extremes who can be expected to take some interest in reflexive deliberations and to ask what or whose purpose they serve. They are the majority. However, it is not the case that those who attach more importance to structural and cultural factors as emergent, not holistic phenomena (for example, Critical Realists or Relational sociologists) have proportionately less interest in reflexivity or vice versa (Symbolic interactionists and Interpretivists scarcely use the concept).

Indeed, there has been something of a convergence between pragmatism and realism, at the empirical if not at the meta-theoretical level, allowing collaboration to triumph over the theoretical odds. On the pragmatist side, their traditional preoccupation with habitual action has been somewhat displaced. As a considerable over-simplification, the great American pragmatists identified two kinds of situations in which recourse was made to reflexive deliberation, in order to define a future course of action. First, problematic situations where the difficulties or obstructions confronted meant that the established repertoire of routine actions could not avail and internal deliberation had to take over from habit (Mead 1938: 79). Second, ones where the (impulsive and propulsive) 'I' was at variance with the guidelines of habitual action. In both cases, the promptings of habit had to be overcome, as in Peirce's famous Courtroom analogy in which the (mental) Counsel advocating change had to overcome the 'critical self's' Defence of the case for continued habitual action. Such habits constitute a summation of past experience and provide an orientation to the future from their deposition in the present. In Peirce's own words, 'good habits are in much higher measure powers than they are limitations' (Colapietro, 1989:112). Certainly, American social psychologists heard the message that routinized action is preferable to 'rumination' (see *Journal for Personality and Social Psychology*, 1970 to date), and for a specimen title, take 'Thinking Too Much: Introspection Can Reduce the Quality of Preferences and Decisions' (Wilson and Schooler, 1991). This has not been the case in social theory.

Modern pragmatists have been much more concerned, not with the exorbitation of routine but, in their most emblematic book, with the *Creativity of Action* (Joas, 1996). Conversely, a number of modern Realists, brought up on the 'transformatory model of social action' (Bhaskar 1989) and some on the morphogenetic approach, today rank among the strong defenders of routine action, habits and *habitus*. In other words, both pragmatists and realists appear on the 'wrong sides' in the discussion of reflexivity – with pragmatists disposed to consider the contribution of reflexive deliberations to innovative action and some realists more concerned with our habitual dispositions. Ironically, this cross-over facilitates collaboration between them (see the contributions of Wiley [Ch. 2] and Vandenberghe [Ch. 4], on the one hand, and those of Sayer [Ch. 6] and Archer [Ch. 7], on the other).

Thus, for modern pragmatists, the stress upon creative or innovative action is a shift in emphasis upon a theme readily found within the original discussion of the reflexive internal conversation, or 'musement'. Because this shift has taken place in a time of rapid social change, it is less difficult to explain and, with it goes the renewed interest of some pragmatists in how reflexive deliberations design novel courses of action. In addition, there is no major strand of social theory in which 'routine action' now plays an axiological role, thus serving to deter this excursion into creativity. Moreover, 'traditionalism' has been forcefully consigned to an earlier era by Giddens, in particular, who presents it as standing in a zero-sum relationship with reflexivity in late modernity (1994). Finally, there are the radical, recent changes, generally grouped under the portmanteau term 'globalization', which have led interpreters to accentuate every variant upon the antinomies of routine action. In other words, there are indeed more 'problematic situations' confronting more people everywhere and fewer and fewer suitable, habitual responses. This makes the shift in emphasis and a renewal of interest in the dynamics of reflexivity (Wiley 1994) quite comprehensible and more readily understood than why certain realists have embraced habitual action, which had no equivalent strand in its original formulations.

This is something of a conundrum: why does 'the extended reflexivity thesis' encounter resistance from some realists? It is not that they have difficulties with the ontological status of subjectivity, its interiority or its causal powers (Archer, 2007). However, it seems no accident that such realists are also those who remain enduringly attached to Bourdieu's theorizing and his exorbitation of routine action. In this commitment, many realists are traditionalists in their urgency to identify the materially motivated carriers of transformatory potential.

Within Modernity, it is not the identification of a new vanguard group that preoccupies them but rather a lasting nostalgia for the traditional working class. Thus, resurgent interest in social class is augmented by certain realists swelling the ranks of its diverse defenders: sometimes by those feeling *ressentiment* towards the 'displacement' of class by gender and ethnicity; sometimes by disenchantment with the concepts of 'inclusion' and 'exclusion' usurping it; sometimes by the need to reinstate class in order to explore the 'intersectionality' of disadvantage and subordination in three dimensions; sometimes by dissatisfaction with the blood-less indices of socio-economic status on offer (NS-SeC 2000) and, perhaps most generally, by all those who believe that 'social class' endures despite transmutation. Class has not become Beck's 'zombie category', because it remains the powerful shaper of life-chances and life-courses.

To nearly all of those revindicating social class, Bourdieu's *class habitus* proves congenial. What they wish to retain is Bourdieu's central idea that the objective social order shapes/penetrates/conditions/influences/human subjectivity through the formation of internal dispositions to act (Archer Ch. 7). In other words, this is where again Mead's heirs and cultural Marxists can stand shoulder to shoulder. Both want to see social influences as internal to human agents rather than being confronted by them as external circumstances.

The self and its reflexivity: socially appropriated or emerging between humanity and the world

There are, indeed, some good reasons for this (convergent) accentuation of our internal sociality as intrinsic to mature human beings. Constituted as we neo-natal human beings are, we have to establish liveable relations with every order of natural reality – nature itself, the practical order of skills, and the discursive social order. These are real not analytical distinctions, although too many seem over-impressed by the fact that empirically they are, indeed, superimposed and have to be *disentangled analytically*. Logically, this empirical entanglement does not justify according complete hegemony to the social, because it does not mean that our encounters with the other two orders come to us sieved through society's discourse, thus making a 'linguistic turn' less than optional. Equally, since we do indeed need to establish a *modus vivendi* within the world if we are to survive and thrive, then our relationality must indisputably include social relations, making them part of us because we are ineluctably part of the social order. At the same time, this disposes of the implicit, critical and completely valid question from proponents of robust 'linguistic-mediation-and-internalization', namely: who is that Self to whom the social world is entirely external? The only answer is the monadic individual or Modernity's man, someone who is a complete alien to Realism.

Nevertheless, for Realists to assent to our inevitable sociality (and to agree that many of our most prized relational goods are quintessentially social in kind) does not exhaust our engagement with the world (see Maccarini and Prandini, Ch. 5). The world does not become flattened out into discursively mediated exchanges nor is our involvement in it impoverished to what can be squeezed into 'society's conversation' (Geras, 1995). Because neither is the case, realists retain the unique (emancipatory) possibility of declaring given social rules and institutions to be 'unnatural', on a stronger basis than those of social conventionalism or idealism. Equally, realism reserves the possibility of finding some social practices unacceptable because they are not practicable, by reference to our direct and unmediated knowledge of the practical order (such as housing old people in high rise blocks).

The possibility of our conversation on reflexivity rests on the fact that we can draw upon other strands in both pragmatist and realist thinking to explore 'just how an essentially social self can escape being a completely socialized self', in Colapietro's words (Ch. 3 p. 52). Even though the internal conversation makes (a distinctive) use of the linguistic code (Wiley, 2006; Archer, 2007: 65–86), we can build upon Peirce's invaluable insight that there are private purposes (imaginative, critical and transformatory) to which use of the public linguistic medium can be put. What this opens up is the distance required between ourselves and our circumstances, which is necessary for reflexivity (Mouzelis, 2009: 138). In brief, what private use of public language enables is for reflexivity to trump dispositions (personal and collective), precisely because it can assess them, find them wanting, and elaborate alternatives.

The empirical convergence described above has undoubtedly facilitated collaboration between pragmatists and realists, and helped to open up a richer vein of questioning about the social role of reflexivity, as demonstrated in this volume. Nevertheless, the meta-theoretical issues cannot simply be shelved because these always play a directive (not determinant) role in shaping explanatory frameworks and in the later advancement of substantive sociological analyses. Here, there are prospects – which will require considerable elaboration – for a more foundational, because ontological, reconciliation. Both pragmatism and realism take our human social relations with the utmost seriousness, since each approach to reflexivity is based upon them, despite profound differences over which relationships are respectively accentuated. However, what neither has fully taken on board is the relational order *qua talis*, which Vandenberghe hints at in his brief addition of a 'fourth World' of '*sociabilia*' to Popper's three-world plural ontology (Ch. 4, p. 58) and which is extended by Donati (Ch. 8) in terms of the 'relational order'. This depends upon human relationality *itself* being regarded *as the fons et origo* of our reflexive properties and powers, as, ironically, it is in both pragmatism (as our linguistically mediated relations with others) and in realism (as subjective relations with the objective). Yet, on both 'sides' there is a gap between this ready acceptance that 'relations' are something we humans ineluctably 'have' – like talking of 'having children' in the passive voice – and the tardy recognition that 'relationality' is alive and active and formative of who we are.

The move from talking about relations to embracing relationality is not a small semantic change but a gestalt-switch in theoretical orientation. Without really giving relationality – to which we all implicitly appeal – its real due, we would effectively be referring to encounters between monads and be complicit in treating inter-relations like those of Modernity's Man – unavoidable, instrumental, but impotent to make him other than the John Wayne loner. Conversely, if we think of our relationality panoramically – with nature, with artefacts, with others – as what constitutes us as persons, as the source of the best and the worst that anyone can experience, and as grounding our ultimate concerns and deepest aversions, we begin theorizing from new, open ground.

Certainly, doing so does not dissolve disputes over the sources of the self and its reflexive capacity – represented here by the divide between advocacy of 'the primacy of language' (pragmatist) and 'the primacy of practice' (realist) – but it dethrones them as ontological predicates and postpones the dispute by transferring it to the next order of research questions, rather than reducing conversations on reflexivity to the exchange of arms from embattled positions. With a huge amount of open-mindedness, what has been postponed could then furnish some more differentiated questions, whose generic formulation would be: What kind and quality of relationality generates or promotes what kinds of self and reflexivity? Does this imply an impossible if not oxymoronic 'open-mindedness', such that Mead, for example, has first to pull down on his own head the house built from 'significant symbols'? In fact it does not. This is because it only involves allowing what cannot be disallowed, namely that our relationships with the world are multi-faceted. When Mead began his discussion of shared symbols, he started from the gestures interpreted in common between fighting dogs, but he never claimed that was all there was to a dog's life.

The heterogeneity of reflexivity

Two theories have persistently dogged most contributions, 'reflexive modernization' and *habitus*. In every way but one, they are antithetical to each other. That antithesis is about the universal advent of 'reflexivity' in the former versus the durability of socialized habitual action in the latter. Such a difference precludes their combination, even at the empirical level, that is supposing differences in the conceptualization of individual and society were placed inside rather compendious brackets.

Their antinomy is too great. To stress the importance of reflexive deliberation is to allow that personal subjectivity filters how agents respond to the same objective circumstances. It thus enables us to explain the *universal absence of similar responses in situations that are objectively similar*. To accentuate habitual action is to emphasize regular differences between social groups in their responses to such situations. However, it is impossible to have the best of both worlds – reflexivity to account for inter-personal variations and routine action to explain inter-group regularities – because these contradictory characteristics would have been assigned to the same people, since groups are made up of individuals.

The one point of similarity is that, in both cases, every reference to reflexivity (or its absence) implies that the authors take reflexive practices to refer to a single and homogeneous phenomenon: either people are practitioners of reflexivity or they are not, either reflexivity has 'arrived' or it has not, either circumstances are propitious to it or they are not. The spell cast by this shared assumption is broken by the recognition that the practice of reflexivity not only can be but is, radically heterogeneous. This is what unites the sociological contributors here and enables them to explore a novel range of issues that are precluded by the homogeneity assumption. Porpora and Shumar (Ch. 11) take up my differentiation of four modes of practising reflexivity, associated with different social formations and varying within the same formation by differences in the particular social contexts that produce distinct personal biographies. They do so in order to ask whether or not we can conceive of 'full reflexivity' – by which they mean the use of all modes – versus 'partial reflexivity' – being confined to a single modality. In a similar vein, Flam (Ch. 10) explores subordinated groups for their repressed (silenced, short-circuited, inhibited) reflexivity. Although she avows that she comes from Bourdieu's stable, her fundamental question is about why all the dominated, humiliated and socially disdained do not manifest an identical form of undeveloped reflexivity. To ask why some can muster an internal 'voice', whose externalization transforms resentment into collective revindication, is to ask the unaskable within the confines of the homogeneity assumption.

If social transformations were analysed sociologically, then there would be an unusual unanimity about the irregularity of the progression of change, its differential impact upon component social groupings, and its variable reception by those differently situated. Why, then, should radical change be presumed to result in homogeneous consequences for the reflexivity of those affected – perhaps, at most, with time lags? By turning their backs on this assumption and directing their attention to the specific contextual changes impinging upon different collectivities, two contributors open up further, novel research questions. Mutch (Ch. 13) examines those whose employment in high-tech organizations places them at the forefront of the cyber-revolution. Again he argues that this is not conducive to the development of a standardized mode of reflexive practice, but varies with the precise contextualization of novel job descriptions reflecting the type of requirements imposed by the use of different forms of information technology.

In similar vein but with reference to exactly the opposite situation to the socio-cultural vanguard in the developed West, Mrozowicki (Ch. 9) examines the neglected post-Soviet workers in Poland – but not as an undifferentiated mass expected to display uniform courses of action stemming from a homogeneous reflexivity. Instead, he begins the other way around, with a sensitive analysis of the resources selectively available to some workers, the specific ethos carried over from the specificities of their past experiences, and the social networks accessible to them, to show how different courses of action are reflexively adopted by distinctive subgroups.

Finally, if the initial premise is that the modes through which reflexivity is practised are heterogeneous rather than homogeneous, then immediately a whole new research agenda opens up in relation to social institutions and institutionalized practices. On the basis of this simple but pregnant notion, Garcia-Ruiz and Rodriguez-Lluesma provide a copy-book exemplar of how to break new ground. Refusing the bromide characterization of late capitalism as a 'consumer society' and rejecting the simplicities of 'manipulated consumption', they ask what shoppers reflexively intend when they devise their lists (or not) and acquire their purchases. Not only do they reveal a diversity of consumption patterns, coincident with practising different modes of reflexivity, but they succeed in showing that unless we de-code the meaning of consumption from the role it plays in people's life-projects and give especial attention to the relational goods that they are seeking to promote *through* the consumer goods acquired, then consumption remains inexplicable if considered a homogeneous activity.

The crucial common denominator of all of the above contributions is that the agent is always active (or potentially so) rather than passive. They are people whose properties and powers, which is a dry way of referring to their pursuit of their ultimate relational concerns in a social context, always seek realization, even if – again reflexively – they are constrained to accept second or even third best. These agents are not rational maximizers but strong evaluators and, as such, they are emotionally involved, if emotions are taken as commentaries upon our concerns. Therefore, reflexive deliberations cannot be uniformly modelled on instrumental rationality. Structures exist, they impinge upon people by shaping their action contexts, but they do not work by pushes and pulls upon passive agents. The reception of such influences by active agents is therefore indispensable to understanding and explaining the eventual outcomes, which are mediated through their reflexivity. Minimally, this should encourage the incorporation of first-person accounts rather than substituting third-person imputations of motives by investigators. Maximally, attending to (heterogeneous modes of) reflexivity is an invitation to explore the interplay between social conditioning and agential responses, which cannot be theoretically disposed of by amalgamating them through central conflation. But this inter-space should not be pictured as an arena where two competing forces meet – lest we return to the dichotomization of 'individual and society' – but as the rich domain of relationality – lest we fail to appreciate that the 'goods' that figure as the ultimate concerns of singular persons and collectivities are incomprehensible without social relationality being both intrinsic *and* extrinsic to them.

References

Archer, Margaret S., (2003), *Structure, Agency and the Internal Conversation*, Cambridge University Press, Cambridge.

Archer, Margaret S., (2007), 'The ontological status of subjectivity: the missing link between structure and agency', in Lawson, Clive, Latsis, John, and Martins, Nuno, *Contributions to Social Ontology*, Routledge, London.

Beck, Ulrich, Giddens, Anthony and Lash, Scott, (1994), *Reflexive Modernization: Politics, Tradition and Aesthetics in the Modern Social Order*, Polity Press, Cambridge.

Bhaskar, Roy, (1989), *The Possibility of Naturalism*, Harvester Wheatsheaf, Hemel Hempstead.

Bourdieu, Pierre and Wacquant, Löic, (1992), *An Invitation to Reflexive Sociology*, Polity Press, Oxford.

Colapietro, Vincent, (1989), *Peirce's Approach to the Self: A Semiotic Perspective on Human Subjectivity*, State University of New York Press, Albany.

Comte, Auguste, (1975), *Cours de Philosophie Positive*, (Vol. I), Hermann, Paris.

Donati, Pierpaolo (2008), *Oltre il multiculturalismo: La ragione relazionale per un mondo comune*, Laterza, Rome-Bari.

Durkheim, Emile, (1964), *The Rules of the Sociological Method*, The Free Press, New York.

Geras, Norman, (1995), *Solidarity in the Conversation of Humankind*, Verso, London.

Giddens, Anthony, (1990), *The Consequences of Modernity*, Polity Press, Cambridge.

James, William, (1890), *The Principles of Psychology*, (Vol. 1), Macmillan, London.

Joas, Hans, (1996), *The Creativity of Action*, Polity Press, Cambridge.

Lyons, William, (1986), *The Disappearance of Introspection*, MIT Press, Cambridge, Mass.

Kant, Immanuel, (1983 [1804]), *What Real Progress has Metaphysics Made in Germany since the Time of Leibniz and Wolff ?*, Abaris Books, New York.

Mead, George Herbert, (1938), *The Philosophy of the Act*, University of Chicago Press, Chicago.

Mill, John Stuart, (1973 [1882]), *Auguste Comte and Positivism*, University of Michigan Press, Ann Arbor.

Mouzelis, Nicos, (2009), *Modern and Postmodern Social Theorising: Bridging the Divide*, Cambridge, Cambridge University Press.

National Statistics Socio-economic Classification (Ns-SeC) (2000), http://www.statistics.gov.uk/methods_quality/ns_sec/soc2000.asp

Plato, (1992), *Theaetetus* (Bernard Williams ed.), Hackett, Cambridge and Indianapolis.

Peirce, C. S, (1867–71), *Writings of Charles S Peirce: A Chronological Edition*, (Vol. 2), Bloomington Indiana Press, Bloomington.

Tomlinson, Brian, (2000), 'Talking to Yourself: the Role of the Inner Voice in Language Learning', *Applied Language Learning*, 11:1.

Vygotsky, L. S, (1964 [1934]), *Thought and Language*, MIT Press, Cambridge, Mass.

Wilson, Timothy D. and Schooler, Jonathan, (1991), 'Thinking Too Much: Introspection can Reduce the Quality of Preferences and Decisions', *Journal of Personality and Social Psychology*, 60:20.

Wiley, Norbert, (1994), *The Semiotic Self*, Polity Press, Oxford.

Wiley, Norbert, (2006), 'Inner Speech as a Language: A Saussurian Inquiry', *Journal for the Theory of Social Behaviour*, 36:3, 319–41.

Part I
Reflexivity and pragmatism

2 Inner speech and agency

Norbert Wiley

There is a well known argument that thought is exercised through inner speech. In this paper I am adding the claim that action too is exercised through inner speech. We talk our thoughts, at least a lot of the time. But we also talk our goals, options, deliberations, plans and moves. We talk our way through our actions.

In one sense, it is the whole self that decides and acts. But in a more localized or pin-pointed sense, action is the work of the dialogical self conversing with itself in the arena of inner speech. Of course, action is often also exercised or carried out through the body, as when we use our hands to dial a phone number or our legs to run. But inner speech is the controlling or directing factor in action.

Before getting to the main theme, I will sketch out, in Part 1, the inner speech theory I will be using. In Part 2 I will show why inner speech seems to be a necessary condition for agency. In Part 3 I will discuss the structure or stages of action and how inner speech is the control for each. In Part 4 I will discuss two specialized problems of agency: how the mental practice or performance of an act can perfect the motoric or 'doing' part of an act.

1. The pragmatist theory of inner speech

Let me explain how I am using the term, 'inner speech', also known as internal conversation, reflexivity, inner language, self talk, inner dialogue, etc. I use the pragmatists' version of this concept, i.e. that of William James, John Dewey and especially Charles Sanders Peirce and George Herbert Mead (Wiley, 2006a). The Russians, Vygotsky and Bakhtin, also have important versions of this concept (Vygotsky, 1987, Bakhtin, 1981), and their ideas can easily be integrated with those of the pragmatists (Wiley 2008). I will discuss the relation between the Russians and the pragmatists briefly at the end of this section.

For a long time in sociology Mead's 'I-me' dialogue was the only recognized form of inner speech (Mead, 1913, 1934). But this formulation was considered imprecise, opaque, and not readily available for empirical research. It did not help that Mead stayed quite abstract, giving no illustrations of the internal conversation. And, except for his making broadly descriptive comments, such as how we 'chide' and 'plume' ourselves (Mead, 1913, p. 142), he gave no concrete examples. In effect, inner speech was not a usable idea in sociological research.

But when Colapietro wrote his path-breaking book on *Peirce's Approach to the Self* (Colapietro, 1989), piecing together important ideas that were buried in Peirce's unpublished papers, Peirce's version of inner speech theory became, for the first time, easily available. Colapietro's book also had the indirect but important effect of bringing Mead's dialogical self to life. With this new window into Peirce, it was possible to see that his version of inner speech theory differed from but could still be combined with that of Mead. And the combination yielded a synthesis that was far superior to the work of either thinker taken alone.

This synthesis combines Mead's 'I–me' formulation with Peirce's, contrasting 'I-you' (or 'I-thou') insight. For Mead, the internal dialogue is between the 'I' or present self, on the one hand, and the 'me' or past self, on the other. The 'me' has several other important meanings in Mead, but for present purposes, it can be defined as the past self. For Peirce, in contrast, the internal dialogue is between the 'I' or present self talking to the 'you' or future self. Peirce defines the 'you' as 'that other self that is just coming into life in the flow of time' (5.421),[1] and he refers to the 'I-you' conversation as 'tuism' (Fish, 1982, p. xxix; see also Ratcliffe 2007 for an interesting extension of tuism).

When Mead and Peirce are combined, the dialogical self is the 'I' talking directly to the 'you' and indirectly or reflexively to the 'me'. Of course this proposition entails two versions of reflexivity: the well known backward one to the 'me' and the novel, forward one to the 'you'. Still, the internal conversation is an 'I-you-me' loop, a triadic reflexivity, encompassing a more comprehensive version of reflexivity than either of the two dyads can do by themselves.

When I use the personal pronouns 'I', 'me' and 'you', it may seem as though I am reifying abstractions. These three facets of the self are actually complex relationships and not, as may seem to be suggested by my usage, substances. My excuse is 'ease of utterance'. If I say 'I', 'me' and 'you', I can say a great deal in a few words, thereby saving tedious repetition. Given this disclaimer, I will continue with the present vocabulary, acknowledging that these are abbreviations for a more complex vocabulary.

To continue, the 'I-me' loop is into the past. It is a 180 degree, semi-circular view, (to shift to a visual metaphor). The 'I-you' loop is into the future. It is also a 180 degree view. But when you combine the two, as I think people actually do, both in their inner speech and in their thoughts, you have a 360 degree view, i.e. you can see your entire range of temporality. You can envision both the past and the future, along with the present, simultaneously. This omni-scopic vision allows one to go back and forth from past to future and also to see them together. If you can simultaneously see your settled habit system ('me') and your options for some new, i.e. non-habitual action ('you'), you can more easily integrate the two practical resources, structure and agency.

A diagram of the Peirce-Mead self is presented in Figure 2.1. The 'me', 'I' and 'you' are on the same line, the time line. I have listed five attributes of the 'me', approximately as Mead does. Peirce placed the 'critical self' in the 'you', but Mead placed this faculty in the generalized other of the 'me', so I will follow Mead. The generalized other is Mead's catch-all category, for it includes all socio-cultural

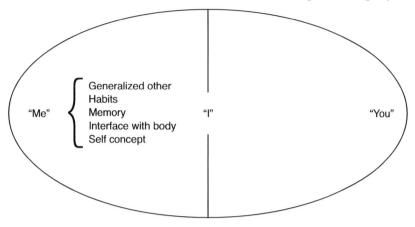

Figure 2.1 Peirce-Mead dialogical self.

standards, i.e. moral, cognitive-logical and aesthetic (Athens, 1994; Dodds, 1997). The generalized other also implies a personalized sense of society and culture, for an 'other' is a person. This suggests an affinity with Durkheim's collective consciousness. The habits are habits in the ordinary sense. Bourdieu's *habitus* is a more inclusive term, encompassing both ordinary habits and elements of the generalized other. Mead does not mention memory as part of the 'me', but it is implied. Memory is simply all of our experience, and it trails off into the unconscious, of both the Freudian and the cognitive studies varieties. The self does not include the body as such, but it does include a sense of, or interface with, the body. The traits of the body, including emotion, interpenetrate the self. Mead does not have a 'self concept', under that name, but, again, it is implied and it seems to belong in the 'me'. The self concept includes everything we think about ourselves, i.e. our self esteem and our traits. It is closely related, causally, to Cooley's 'looking glass self' (Wiley, forthcoming). The notion of 'self feeling', which James and Cooley thought was the defining feature of the self, could be understood as part of the self concept. Mead preferred the concept of reflexivity to self feeling, and he was cool towards this latter term, perhaps because he seems to have been threatened by and in competition with Cooley (Mead, 1930). So I will leave it out, although it could be a process leading into the self concept.

   This illustration of the self is not meant to be a definitive portrait. Others might view the Mead or the Mead-Peirce self differently. And I might well change my view at some point. Still, this picture seems reasonably usable to me at the present time, and I hope it provokes others to think further on this issue.

   Another advantage of combining Peirce and Mead in this triadic way is that it gives a sharper picture of how humans engage with temporality. We are three legged stools, standing simultaneously in the past, present and future. From the point of view of natural science, we are in the present existentially and in the past and future only imaginatively. But physical science has a limited view of how humans inhabit time.

For the human, time is primarily 'felt' rather than measured by the clock. In this sense – that of psychology rather than physics – we can be in the past and present existentially as well as imaginatively. The exact way in which we experience the three tenses depends on how we are at any given moment oriented towards the three temporal facets.

At one extreme we can include all of the future and all of the past into an all-encompassing present (Mead, 1932, pp. 23–4). But more often we have a present consisting of some meaningful or workable 'chunk' of time, i.e. William James's 'saddleback' present (broader than his 'knife-edge present), with futures and pasts that have the sizes we want them to have. The precise way in which we package the three facets of time depends on our purposes and in particular our projected and anticipated actions. The size of the felt present is in constant fluctuation.

In addition we are constantly in motion through time. The future of one instant is the present of the next – and the past of the one after that. The self, moving down the time line, is in the constant process of emergence. Our bodies grow old but our selves are ever new. We are always moving through what William James called the 'stream of consciousness,' although we are in a much larger swatch of that stream than he seems to have thought.

Another advantage of connecting Peirce with Mead is that we can now see both speaking poles of the conversation and how the dialogical self works. For Mead it was difficult to see the 'I-me' dialogue. He gave no examples, particularly of the 'me' talking to the 'I'. His 'me' was in the past and he confined the possibility of action to the present, so in terms of his own theory only the 'I' could talk. But the possibility of the 'me' responding was always implicit in Mead's notion of the specious present. If the felt present were enlarged enough to include the 'me', the 'me' could talk. In physical time the 'me' is in the past but in psychological time the 'me' could be in the (now enlarged) present. The 'me' could say 'No we've tried that'. 'We need something new.' Or even 'That's sleazy, don't even think about it.' Indeed the 'me', in its capacity as the generalized other, is constantly disagreeing with the 'I'.

It was Peirce's inclusion of the 'you' in the conversation which made it obvious that the 'I' is not the only speaker, for the 'you' talks in two senses. As just mentioned concerning the 'me', the 'you' can be in the felt present in such a way as it can stand on the speaker's platform and engage in speech. In addition, even in physical time, it is approaching the present, the status of 'I', and will soon be able to talk in that capacity. It was Peirce's addition of 'tuism' that disclosed the truly two-sided, dialogical character of inner speech. In fact, if all three facets of the self are together in the specious present, there is no reason why all three cannot take turns speaking, and for the dialogue to be between the 'me' and 'you', as well as between the 'me' and 'I' (or the 'you' and 'I').

This triadicity also makes the pragmatists more open to the Russians, Vygotsky and Bakhtin, who are much closer to the actual data of inner speech. The combining of Mead and Peirce facilitates the merger of them both with the somewhat different dyad of Vygotsky and Bakhtin. Mead and Peirce tend to be formal and proper, emphasizing the thinking and self-regulating functions of inner speech.

Vygotsky is much more detailed in treating the semantics and syntax of inner speech. And Bakhtin, particularly in his discussions of Dostoyevsky's tortured characterization of Raskolnikov, shows the closeness of inner speech to the life-defining existential emotions. A synthesis of the American and Russian approaches seems a useful idea

If thought is largely in the form of talk, as I think it is, the 'I-you-me' triad shows how the thought medium works. The triadic reflexivity can find and disclose more subtle connections within the self than a dyadic reflexivity can. The 'you' gives you access to the future, to problems that are coming down the road, and to opportunities for actions. The 'me' gives you your memory, the insights and practices of the culture, the habits and trajectories of the past and the results of previous actions. The 'you-me' arc is the pincers, which allows the 'I' to grasp anything in one's world. This linguistic device is your mind, surveilling the world, to cope with your problems and desires. Thoughts are abstractions designated by words, inner as well as outer. The key words are – in my opinion – 'I', 'me' and 'you', for they designate the structure of the self, which is a linguistic thinking 'machine'. The combination of Mead and Peirce seems to shed new light on how thought and the mind work.

Another result of the Peirce-Mead combination is that it gives a richer view of the structure of the self. Mead, as well as many others, defined the self as self-awareness or reflexivity. This is an intuitively attractive definition, for it is self awareness that seems to differentiate the self from all other entities. Everything that the self does, goes on in the arena of self awareness. But Mead's self awareness was attributed to the 'I-me' relationship, which ties it to the limitations of that dyad. If Peirce's 'I-you' is added to the definition of the self, we have a much bigger and more complex structure of which we are aware. The definition of the self is enlarged to include more features of the self. Just as reflexivity goes from a 180 to a 360 degree scope, self awareness goes from 180 to 360 degrees. Awareness of the 'me' is one thing, but awareness of the 'me' and the 'you', including the relation between those two spheres, is considerably more. The Mead-Peirce combination gives you a more comprehensive definition of the self.

Also, the relation between Mead's 'I' and 'me' is between subject and object. But the relation between Peirce's 'I' and 'you' is between two subjects. The 'I' is the subject now, and the 'you' will be the subject when it travels down the time line and reaches the present. Still, even when the 'you' is in the future, it is a subject in the grammatical sense (i.e. 'you' is in the nominative case). And when we think of the 'you' as in the specious or felt present, the 'you' is also a subject in a non-grammatical, that is, in an ontological sense.

Being two subjects the 'I' and 'you' can enjoy the intimacy only available to two subjects. Peirce's 'tuism' has two aspects: one's relationship to one's 'you' and one's relationship to any other person – what I have called a 'visitor' to one's inner speech – construed as a 'you'. Both 'tuisms' have the immediacy of two subjects. According to Albert Schutz the self, being a subject, can have a closer relationship to another person than it can have to itself (Schutz, 1962, pp. 172–5). He valorized the relationship between two 'I's. But this is only true if you define the self as an 'I-me' relationship, which is what Schutz did, following Mead. If instead you think in terms of Peirce's 'I-you' relationship, which Schutz did not do, you have the same interpersonal intimacy within the 'I-you' dyad of the self. When Husserl was giving an example of inner speech and said 'you must stop this' or when Fodor said to himself 'you can do it Jerry', they were talking as 'I' to 'you' or subject to subject, with all the intimacy that that relationship can carry.

The 'I-me-you' triad, as a definition of self awareness, has two features that make it more powerful than the usual, 'I-me' definition of the self. For one, the self is self aware of more features of itself, thereby making it a richer reflexive bundle. But in addition the self is also closer and more enmeshed, so to speak, with itself. 'I-me' is formal and somewhat distant, but 'I-you' is emotionally close and allows more intimate emotions in the intra-psychological sphere. Peirce's formula allows more easily of self acceptance and even self love, which is always an aspect of the self. In other words, Peirce's 'you' is the 'self' in a more intimate way than Mead's 'me' is the self. Therefore the 'I-me-you' circle allows of more internal closeness than was allowed in the 'I-me' formula.

Another nuance of the 'I-you' relationship is that, unlike the 'me', the 'you' is in the second person. The 'you' has considerably more 'otherness' than the 'me', which, like the 'I', is in the first person. So one internal dyad, Mead's 'I-me', is confined to the grammatical first person. But the other internal dyad, Peirce's 'I-you', has a less confined grammatical niche. This grammatical location reflects the greater ontological sweep of the 'I-you' relationship. The temporal zone between the 'I' and 'me' is inside the self, but the temporal zone between the 'I' and 'you' is, so to speak, outside the self. The past is in the self but the future is not. This is another sense in which the 'I-me-you' self has more reality or 'being' than Mead's 'I-me' self has.

I think both Peirce and Mead sensed that they wanted to poise the human dialogue as extending in both temporal directions, past and future. Mead's 'me' includes aspects of Peirce's 'you', and Peirce's 'you' includes features of Mead's 'me'. But neither was sufficiently explicit about this. You have to bend their concepts to bring this about. In the following text Mead shows he was trying to work in all three time periods – past, present and future – at once.

> Now it is by these ideational processes that we get hold of the conditions of future conduct as these are found in the organized responses which we have formed, and so construct our paths in anticipation of that future. The individual who can thus get hold of them can further organize them through the selection of the stimulations which call them out and can thus build up his plan of action. (Mead, 1932, p. 192, cited in Joas, 1985, p. 192).

But Mead is stretching words to make his point. It is easier to say, with a Peirce-Mead synthesis, that the person is simultaneously working with the present, past, and future in an 'I-me-you', triadic vision.

Finally, the 'I-me-you' relationship can be mapped onto concrete examples of inner speech. The idea that we speak directly to the 'you' and indirectly to the 'me' is a reasonable description of how we think and engage in self talk. Whatever we say to ourselves seems to be an attempt to interpret the past to the future.

2. The link between inner speech and agency

Turning to agency itself, this term is not standardized, and the various meanings that are used vary quite a bit. I will keep my definition simple, since I am primarily interested in the relation between agency and inner speech, not in all the intricacies of agency itself. Agency is the process of conscious and purposive human action, as opposed to automatic reaction. Habitual actions can be at the minimal pole of consciousness and purposefulness, but even in these cases we often make a conscious decision to engage the habit. I will however emphasize the less habitual, more deliberate acts, for here is where inner speech has its strongest effects. This process of agency involves: (1) the mental construction or design of a possible action, (2) the actual choosing of this or perhaps some other action from the options at hand, and (3) the behavioural carrying out of the action. So in agency we construct, choose and enact.

The kitchen sink is not draining properly, so I start mulling over the possible solutions. I consider trying to fix it myself, or asking my handy step-son to take a look at it, or phoning a plumber. I take a close, mental look at each of the three options. I then decide which path to take. I will ask my step-son, Dan. Then I phone him and ask if he has time to come over and look at the sink. At every step I am telling myself what to do and how to do it.

I need a new project so I consider writing a book on inner speech. I ask myself what it would look like, what issues I would consider, and how it would fit into social theory. I try summarizing some of the chapters. It seems to be a viable project, so I decide to start the actual research and writing. I begin churning out the chapters as conference papers and journal articles. The project is moving along, so I get a publisher, turn on the steam and finish it. Again I have talked myself through it, from start to finish.

In other words agency goes on during a series of processes, all of which usually entail inner speech. Action is not a single burst of energy, but a build-up or construction that proceeds through a series of sequential dialogical stages. It is parallel to speech itself in that it has meaning, proceeds chronologically as narrative and obeys rules of practical syntax.

Agency seems to be located primarily in inner speech and not in some other part or process of the self. One argument for this is that you can observe the agentic process by paying attention to your inner speech. We can watch or rather listen to how the dialogical self creates action. It does so in stages, not all at once, and this makes it easier to observe.

If you watch yourself making a minor decision, such as picking a movie or ordering at a restaurant, you can usually hear yourself discussing it with yourself. You may also be discussing it with others, but this does not disallow or supersede the discussion within yourself. The two discussions work together, with the inner one providing interpretation and direction for the outer one.

If it is an easy decision you will just get the approval, so to speak, of the partner in your inner conversation. Usually this inner partner is Peirce's 'you'. If the decision is a close one, say, between two good movies, you may stage a little debate with yourself. Is one of these movies leaving town soon? Which time of night is better? What am I in the mood for? And what does my wife want? This dialogue might be lengthy and systematic, short and perfunctory or so fast that it is more unconscious than conscious. Still there is a conversation, and you can usually observe how the drift of the conversation leads to the choice.

In the case of more weighty decisions, such as buying a house or changing jobs, the inner conversation is longer and more complicated. And, as mentioned, it will be interspersed within, and even during, conversations with other people concerning this decision. It will proceed over as many weeks as it takes to make the decision. If the external act has stages, say it begins with shopping around for options, you may search for a while and then retreat to inner speech and look at the big picture again, to see if you still want to go through with it. Do we really need a new house? There can be an indefinite number of false starts, retreats to thinking it all over again, and making still more starts. Yet, despite complexity, the process is there, you can easily observe it, and it seems to be the boss or master of the action. We assess, pick, and even sometimes re-make the act, and we do so by talking to ourselves about it.

At this point one cannot but remember the pragmatist idea that thought and inner speech are initially evoked by frustrations in one's flow of action. All four of the major pragmatists use this idea at times, but it is most explicit in Dewey (Dewey, 1910, pp. 11–12). You want something, you try to get it, your advance toward this goal is blocked by some circumstance, you pause and ask yourself what to do next, and you respond by describing the nature of the impasse and by searching for a way around it. Thought and inner dialogue can be a substitute for overt trial and error. The pragmatists were not always clear about whether the relation between frustration and inner dialogue was first encountered by the species (phylogenetic), by each individual early in life (ontogenetic) or by people throughout their lives. They merely asserted a functional relation between frustrated goal-seeking and inner dialogue. Regardless of whether this actually explains the origin of internal dialogue, it clearly fits the idea that agency is directed by inner speech.

Of course this does not mean that all inner speech is based on frustrated activity. Some is purposeless day-dreaming or reverie. It can amuse one and thereby be an end in itself. Some inner speech is an end in other ways, such as exploring imagery or an idea. And some inner speech is so quiet, involuntary and dimly conscious, such as the kind we engage in as we approach falling asleep, that the category of purpose does not apply at all. My point is rather that inner speech is often closely related to frustrations, even though many varieties are not.

There are also many cases of frustration and agency that are emotional rather than instrumental. We are sad and depressed but we are not sure why. It may be because of problems in our love life. We talk to ourselves about this sadness, trying to find the social cause, assuming there is one. A major component of this self talk will be the confusing emotions themselves. We will try to produce the emotion in our consciousness and take a good look at it. Naming an emotion can sometimes help us find its cause.

It is also possible to 'linguify' emotion, i.e. to find a syntactical way in which to place it in our sentences. The emotion can function as a part of speech, especially as a substantive or modifier. This 'sententializing' of emotion allows us to use the search function of inner speech to figure out the meaning of the emotion. If this self talk is done loosely enough it can come close to Freud's free association, hooking the power of this method to a different discipline from that Freud used.

Emotional problems often lead us to other-talk as well as to self talk. We can talk to friends, family, confidants, and the various kinds of counsellors. The power of the other can sometimes evoke emotions from us that we are not able to produce in self talk. This interpersonal talk will be combined with self talk.

My point in this aside about emotions, though, is to correct the perhaps over-analytical way I am looking at agency. The pragmatists emphasized the over-simplified problems of agency, such as fixing a car or curing an illness. But many problems of agency are emotional or semi-emotional, and they do not submit to analysis as easily as the more mechanical problems do. Still, to come back to my larger point, emotional problems respond, if anything, even more to inner speech than non-emotional problems do. So my argument for the connection between inner speech and agency seems well-founded.

A second argument for the agential role of inner speech is that people who have little or no ability to engage in inner speech also seem to have little foresight into the consequences of their actions. In other words, if inner speech is absent or impaired, people have a weakened power of agency. This applies to ADHD children (Barkley, 1997, pp. 278–82) as well as to most autistics (Whitehouse, 2006). Also, people with brain injuries that hinder inner speech seem to lack foresight. It is known through both physical and psychological tests that these latter groupings have little use of inner speech (Morin, 1993; Rohrer *et al.*, 2008.) And it is also known that these people frequently engage in actions that cause them frustration and difficulties. Since we already know, via self awareness, that self talk is a directing part of the deliberation process, and we can see that the absence of inner speech weakens agency, it seems reasonable to conclude that inner speech at least partially controls agency.

The former argument then, from self observation, indicates that where there is inner speech there can be planning and foresight. The latter argument indicates that where inner speech is absent, foresight is weakened. Together they permit a fairly firm conclusion that inner speech is a necessary and more or less sufficient condition for intelligent agency.

3. The stages of agency and inner speech

I will now look at the structural features of agency, the stages or parts, and how inner speech operates in these parts. The argument in the preceding section concerned the overall cause or relation between inner speech and agency, but the argument of this section, the examination of the stages of action, will show the more specific causal processes or pathways.

Defining

To define an action is to tell oneself what it is, or more specifically what it means. This includes characterizing the nature of the action, but more importantly examining the consequences of the act for oneself. In other words we take a close look at an action and we run it through our system of beliefs, values and desires. We inspect and we evaluate. We ask how the action articulates with ourselves. The whole time we are, so to speak, interrogating the option or 'talking' the definition.

This talk may even construct the reality to some extent. In other words the action we are talking about may become what we are saying it is. W. I. Thomas said, in a much quoted line, 'if men define situations as real, they are real in their consequences' (Thomas and Thomas, 1928, p. 572). Thomas's notion of definition may be an interpersonal process, based on what people say to each other, in which case it is 'social construction'. But it can also be an individual process, based on what we say to ourselves, in which case it is 'psychological construction'. Either way, Thomas's definition suggests that this process can entail two distinct relations to reality. We can both describe what it is and construct what we say it is. The line between these two processes is blurry and we often cannot know which component is the stronger. I think, at least in the short run, describing is usually the stronger statement and constructing is usually a modest addition. But there are several contemporary positions that credit construction as the stronger component. In any case, the Thomas theorem suggests that inner speech not only helps us define an action, it can also to some extent create the action.

Another way of looking at defining is to say that we are often searching for an act with a particular goal in view. We want a means to an end. For example, we are bored and we want something to alleviate the boredom. We may consider having a drink, calling a friend, listening to music, taking a walk or going to a movie. We list the possibilities to ourselves. And we may anticipate, mentally, the particular satisfaction each will give. This 'tasting' of an act can sometimes tell us if it is the one we want, i.e. the one that will most effectively relieve our boredom. We try out each act in our imagination and visualize its effect on our mood. This visualization, which can involve emotions and imagery as well as speech, may help us make the decision and find the act we want. But the searchlight itself is inner speech and related modes of dialogue.

Choosing

The process of choosing is much disputed in social theory, since it brings up the matter of free will. This is an issue that gets a divided response, since, as Samuel Johnson said, all theory is against (it); all experience for it. This is an 'essentially contested idea', by which I mean an idea that has one valid form of evidence arguing for it and another valid form of evidence arguing against it (modifying Gallie, 1956 a bit).

In particular it seems to be a necessary condition for society that the institutions presume non-determination or free will. In particular, rules pervade all societies and it is assumed that people have the capacity to obey or disobey the rules. If people were determined, or even thought to be determined, there would be no point in having rules. In democratic, industrial societies such specific rules as economic contract, law, and civil liberties also pervade the social fabric. So, one can think or theorize in a determined world, but it appears one cannot live a normal life except in a world that assumes free choice. And there is yet to appear a society that does not assume some freedom of choice.

It also seems unlikely that people would invest a lot of their inner resources thinking and planning to do things in a determined world if they then had to act in an indeterminate social world. Instead they 'think free will', even though this may be, in some technical ontological senses, a philosophical mistake. For, thinking in a determined world and then being unprepared to act in a seemingly undetermined social world would be a much bigger mistake.

The classical pragmatists themselves were of two minds about human freedom. On the one hand, they recognized the affinity between society and freedom. On the other, they saw that the epistemology of natural science requires a cause for every effect, a system of determinism and a complete absence of causal freedom. Peirce, James, Dewey and Mead all had commitments to free will but they also wobbled at times and tended toward the determinism of empirical science.

It is possible that there is an objective ontological split here, i.e. that there is both a deterministic physical world and a non-deterministic social world. We live in both worlds, moving back and forth from moment to moment. We check the weather (determinism) and we decide to take a drive in the country (non-determinism). We start the car (determinism) and we decide which music disk to pop into the player (non-determinism). We feel hunger pangs in our stomach (determinism) and we start looking for lunch (non-determinism).

I will now set aside the choosing we do in the determined world, since we seem merely to rubber stamp what nature requires of us anyway. As we say, we have no choice. Fighting against the determined world, for example jumping off a high cliff in hopes of defying the law of gravity, is something sane human beings rarely do. If we set aside the worlds of nature, then, this leaves the non-deterministic world, the part that has an intrinsically human component.

Speaking of mental illness though, there seem to be two reasons people are committed to mental hospitals, i.e. declared to be mentally ill. If one treats the deterministic world as though it were one where free will prevailed, for example if one started jumping off cliffs, etc. one would be declared out of touch with reality and perhaps too dangerous to self and others to live in the ordinary world. On the other hand, if you treated the social world as deterministic, by ignoring rules, refusing cooperation, obeying impulse and evading all issues of self control, this might also get you locked up – for again, you are not living in the real world. You are out of touch with reality.

The world of social institutions, then, is the one the Germans had in mind when they distinguished the human sciences from the physical sciences (Windelband, 1980). Max Weber called the former sciences the sphere of culture. And in contrast to the sphere of nature, he claimed that human beings 'make' this world. By this he meant that the social institutions are products or artefacts of human beings, somewhat in the same way that paintings, music and literature are the product of human beings. The institutions are less obviously so, since their origins are often buried in the past, and their authorship is much less that of single individuals than is the case with the fine arts. Still such social institutions as money, language and law are obviously not given to us in the natural world. They are not like the planets, oceans and continents. They are cultural forms and human products, however obscure their actual origins.

Decisions about the non-physical world, that is the human world, seem to have a voluntary or free component. But for any given act the volition or freedom may be extremely small. As Marx said, 'human beings make their own history, but not under circumstances of their own choosing' (Marx, 1983, p. 287.) He meant, given that history has its own structure and tendencies, humans cannot change it as they will. The free play or optional space may be very slight indeed. This is true of individuals in their lives too. Still, in principle there seems to be a modest amount of freedom in human affairs, sometimes more and sometimes less. The result, for present purposes, is that in the choosing moment of cultural actions, inner speech has a more important role than it does in actions confined to the deterministic, physical world because there is more to talk to oneself about.

In physical actions we merely tell or remind ourselves how to cooperate with the laws of nature: 'Put that there, hit that first, glue those two parts together', etc. But in voluntary actions we can both describe and persuade. The rules of society come into play, but one's own set of wants may also become engaged. Given the expanded options in a voluntary act, there are more 'moving parts'. There is also the whole cajoling or expressive vocabulary in play. 'You can do it'. 'Try harder'. 'Make your (wife? father? kids? friends?) proud of you', etc. In other words the inner speech for physical agency and cultural agency differs a lot. And most inner speech is for the voluntary side of life.

I would suggest that the dialogue in these cases is between our cognitive and volitional sides, our mind and our will. The mind says quite clearly that another drink at this cocktail party is a bad idea. It crosses the good health line and it may hurt your night's sleep. The will, itself fanned by the emotions, says it will taste good, it will keep the buzz buzzing, and it will make you smarter. The will might convince the mind to alter the picture a bit, to make the drink look less menacing and more delicious. If this happens the will is winning the argument. If, instead, the mind remembers something that toughens its stand, say, that you are near the legal limit for driving, the mind might start getting more insistent and the will might get less pushy. The argument can go back and forth for a while, but at some point one of the voices wins.

I am suggesting that this kind of dialogue is behind all free choice issues. We are trying to decide which is the best course: engaging in the action under consideration or not. These two pictures will be present in our overall definition of the situation. One picture will look best at the point of decision as a greater good, a lesser evil or possibly as an irresistible pleasure. I think the cognition, i.e. what you picture and how you picture it, will usually determine the choice. We will choose what looks best, and looking best is the product of our own cognitive definition.

Of course we did not make this definition out of nothing. We chose it, and the will or choice process had a lot to do with what the cognitive power elected to see. So the will determines the intellect and the intellect in turn determines the will. Both are boss, but in a circular fashion.

Before leaving this section, let me ask how the self's argument over the next drink fits into the 'I-you-me' scheme. The more cognitive, common sense spokesperson, which I called the mind or intellect, seems to be the 'I'. But this 'I' is drawing, reflexively, on the 'me' by invoking the driving laws and the science of what alcohol does to the body. This bank of rules and information is stored in the generalized other and the memory, which are aspects of the 'me'. The eager-beaver, pushing for another drink, seems to be the 'you'. For it is the 'you', i.e. the self just coming into the present, that will be the 'I' that actually makes the decision.

Enacting

Once a choice has been made the carrying out of this choice is often simple and unproblematic. But circumstances can cause trouble. For example, in the decision to commit suicide, to pick a sombre example, there is usually a time lag between the time of decision and the time when one can carry out the decision. This time lag will probably include plenty of internal dialogue concerning the action. For one thing one might be thinking about the more specific planning details, such as how or where to perform the act. But one might also vacillate in the decision, particularly as the moment approaches (Firestone, 1986).

The enactment can also entail several new choices. If you decide to sell your house there will still be new decisions about which one to buy. If you divorce your spouse there will still be decisions about what to do next. And, more trivially, if you decide to have a party there are still decisions about the guest list, the refreshments, etc. All this shows that the enactment itself probably has stages of its own. Just as, in the earlier stages of an act, this latter stage requires a lot of direction and the inner speech that guides that direction.

In law the enactment is more important than the decision. If you decide on, but do not act on, an illegal action, there is no crime. It runs the other way in some religious moralities. If you decide on a wrongful act, sinning in your heart, you may be as guilty as if you had carried out the act.

4. Establishing habits and skills via inner speech

To discuss habits and skills it will be necessary to stretch the notion of inner speech to include inner experiences that are slight variations from speech itself. In outer speech there are variations in such forms as body language and mispronunciations. These spheres of signification are continuous with speech, and normally they can be interpreted as forms of speech, but they are still structurally a bit different from formal speech itself.

In the case of inner speech there are also a variety of peripheral forms. Imagery, i.e. sensory, kinaesthetic and emotional, is an important area of inner experience. Yet images are not language as such, even though images can be incorporated into linguistic utterances. A special form of imagery is the mental practising of some skill, say artistic or athletic, which I will discuss in more detail later. Daydreams too consist largely of imagery, although they can include dialogue and narrative. Night dreams are characterized largely by images, including emotional imagery, although these dreams can also have dialogue.

In near-sleep states, to continue the list of peripherals, humans can have inner speech, often with lots of uncontrolled imagery. These near-sleep experiences sometimes seem to be happening to someone else, even though they are present in our consciousness. The sensation of falling through space is common in the near-sleep state. A variant of near sleep experiences are hypnagogic images, which are unusually sharp in their sensory features and which are often present in lucid dreams. Lucid dreams are dreams which we can control and which are known to be dreams, even as they are transpiring. Some people have lucid dreams and others do not. Another kind of peripheral is the uncontrolled fantasy, which, again, seems to be happening to someone else. In particular, paranoid fantasies, in which the person seems to be in some kind of danger, can take over consciousness as unwelcome guests. It can require considerable effort to dispel these daydreams from consciousness. Finally meditation, in which you concentrate, say, on your breathing and attain a state of deep relaxation, is related to inner speech. If you repeat a mantra or talk to your deity this experience is explicitly linguistic. In the case of inner silence, however, the near suppression of inner speech is what organizes the experience, and it is, in a way, a variant of inner speech.

These peripheral forms of inner speech can all be in the consciousness, and several of them, especially imagery, can be in your self talk. You can insert imagery in the sentences you use in your inner dialogue. Any non-linguistic image, e.g. visual, auditory, tactile, olfactory, gustatory, kinaesthetic or emotional can be inserted into some syntactical slot in an internal sentence. Notice you cannot do this in ordinary, person-to-person communication because the images are private to the speaker. You cannot send the odour of a cooking hamburger, linguistically, over to the person you are talking to, but you can shoot it from one part of your self to the other, i.e. from the 'I' to the 'you'. You and the other person do not share the hamburger image, but your 'I' and your 'you' do.

To take a comprehensive look at inner speech you have to take into account all of the peripheral forms, just as you have to do this for a comprehensive look at outer speech. Some of these non-linguistic modalities can be incorporated into inner speech by inserting them into sentences. But much of the time these forms are simply on their own in our stream of consciousness. Inner speech does not only have such formal functions as thinking and self-regulation. There are also less controlled activities such as passive daydreaming, dialogues with visitors, entertainment, browsing, just hanging out in one's mind and chit chatting with one's self. The peripheral forms of inner speech, perhaps better designated simply as inner experiences, tend to prevail in the less formal activities of inner speech.

Returning now to habit, William James has an incisive discussion of habits, including the way we might use determination and sentiments to make or break a habit (James, 1890, pp. 122–3). But Peirce went one better by suggesting that inner speech on its own can strengthen a habit, i.e. we can practise a habit mentally and covertly, getting some of the same strength we would get by practising a habit physically and overtly. His example was how his younger brother Herbert, probably in his mid-teens, acted when their mother's dress caught fire during a family dinner. Herbert immediately jumped up, grabbed a rug, wrapped it around his mother's body, rubbed her carefully and extinguished the flames. Later the amazed Charles asked Herbert how he knew what to do 'and he told me that since Mrs. Longfellow's death, it was that he had often run over in imagination all the details of what ought to be done in such an emergency' (Peirce, 1934, p. 487, note 4; p. 538, note 1).

Fannie Longfellow had died in a dress fire in 1861, when Herbert Peirce was about twelve. Her husband, Henry Wadsworth Longfellow, wrapped a rug around her all right, but the rug was too small, and Fannie died from her burns (Wagenknecht, 1956, p. 242; McFarland, 2004, pp. 243–4). Presumably, Herbert asked himself what he would have done. He must have located the right size rug and run through his mind how to use it to extinguish a dress fire. He said he went through this mental practise routine 'often'.

Peirce believed you could instill habits mentally, as his brother Herbert had done. Peirce was a century ahead of his time with this insight. But he gave no other instances of how to do this – none from his own life, for example. Peirce seems to have thought inner speech was more important for self regulation than it was even for thinking (Colapietro, 1989, pp. 99–118). And Peirce discussed self regulation brilliantly in an abstract, semiotic manner. But he did not do the obvious thing and give us extended examples. My guess is that he attempted to break bad habits and instill good ones in his personal life, but he was not as successful as he had hoped. Still, he is correct that working with habits is a major form of self regulation.

The idea of mentally practising a habit was not picked up by the other pragmatists, even though Dewey wrote a whole book on habits (1930). Peirce's comments were in his personal notes, however, and his unpublished papers did not become available until 1956. Dewey was using the notion of habit as the unit of culture, thereby opposing the racist idea that the sub-cultures of ethnic groups were instinctive and biologically determined. Peirce had not been using the notion of habit as the unit of culture, although he could have, since his notion of semiotics was almost the same as Boas's anthropological concept of culture (Wiley, 2006c). Instead he was using it as a way of explaining how self control works.

Peirce's idea lay fallow for a long time, but eventually it was used to see whether artistic and sports skills could be practised in the mind. Can you dance, play violin or paint better as a result of mental practising? Or can you improve your swimming, diving, kicking a football or shooting a basketball? In recent years a large number of surveys and experiments have been done in a variety of sports fields, which show that imaginative practice can improve sports skills (Holmes and Calmels, 2008). Mental practice bumps into the issue of whether mental imagery is pictorial or, in a highly technical sense, verbal (Tye, 1991; Kosslyn, 1994). This issue is too complicated for this paper, so I will touch on mental practice only lightly.

Repeating an act, e.g. swimming, overtly in the swimming pool, normally strengthens a habit. But repeating it covertly, in the mind, can also strengthen a habit. I have called this inner activity 'inner speech', since it can function as parts of sentences. But it is not just inner speech. It is also inner (or mental) swimming itself. And all forms of mental practice for any athletic or artistic skill are of the same nature. The mental use of injured muscles in the rehabilitation process, is still another form of mental practice (Holmes and Calmels, 2008). In all these cases inner speech does not just direct activity, it *is* the activity. To put it another way, what is going on here is not so much inner speech as inner agency.

Another way in which inner speech can be useful for directing habits is in the area of mental health. For several decades now cognitive therapy has used inner speech processes to intervene in mental health. This started with mood, especially depression, but now this therapy is used for psychopathologies of all kinds. For my example I will single out Donald Meichenbaum's way of confronting phobias with inner speech (Meichenbaum. 1977, pp. 201–14). Meichenbaum does not explain the inner speech aspect of his therapy in sufficient detail, so I will discuss his approach at some length.

In an ordinary phobic situation, for example fear of heights, the person starts getting anxiety symptoms when he or she is in the frightening situation. These symptoms typically include shortness of breath, rapid heartbeat, sweating, muscular tension and the feeling that you are no longer in control of your body. There is also a typical inner speech pattern. The theme of this frightened speech is a frozen passivity, and it is characterized by terror, surrender, the feeling of being dominated and the relinquishing of one's will. Your inner speech might be something like 'I can't', 'this is too much', 'others will see', or 'get me out of here'. Both the physical symptoms and the mode of inner speech will be inflexible, ritualized and in paralytic mode. The inner speech, in particular, will be simple, in a narrow range of meanings, and repetitive.

It might not be stretching it too much to say the power of inner speech is, for all practical purposes, non-existent in a terrified situation. People can lose their outer speech during intense fear, finding themselves reduced to a pathetic croaking sound. In nightmares too the power of speech can disappear, replaced by an animal grunting. So the status of inner speech in fear, even though it might seem to consist of a few words, can actually be paralyzed. When the voice freezes in terror, the job is to get talking started again. Any flowing inner speech at all is a victory when in fear. But of course the cognitive therapists want their clients to say particular things to themselves.

Meichenbaum thinks your inner dialogue is the crucial causal strand in these phobic situations. He encourages his clients to try to talk to themselves in some way that does not fit the terror. Instead of voicing despair, he asks them to say something that distances themselves from the physical symptoms. Unfortunately, he does not give concrete examples. But it is clear that he wants some kind of self-labelling that is incompatible with the fear reaction.

Staying with fear of heights, I will give a hypothetical example of what Meichenbaum seems to be getting at. If you have this fear, and you are, for example, driving over a high bridge, you may well find yourself with some of the fear symptoms described above. If the symptoms are severe, you are an unsafe driver, and you have to get across – or be driven across – one way or the other. But if the symptoms are not too severe, there are options for changing your inner speech.

Presumably you are saying things to your self about the frightening situation, i.e. the bridge, and also about your reaction to the bridge. What you are now saying about the bridge is that it is has overwhelming power over you and that you are unable to traverse the height in a normal, calm way. You are seeing and addressing the bridge as a unitary, undivided danger. What you need to do, Meichenbaum seems to be saying, is to start looking at features of the bridge other than its danger. This will not be easy, because fearful inner speech is tightly boundaried. It will be difficult to say anything that is not functionally related to the terror. But if the person, possibly with the help of a therapist, can use self talk that breaks out of the terrified mode, the cure can begin.

The frightened driver might take a second look at that bridge. Bridges are high so that ships can cross under them. But they do not have to be, and usually are not, uniformly high in their whole span. They can be low and then high, or they can have a low middle with higher beginnings and endings. In other words they can vary in how frightening they are. Since the driver is locked into a fear pattern, he or she may not notice that the fear stimulus is greater at some points than at others. The driver will be trapped into an unvarying fear pattern and inner speech response from beginning to end. But if the driver can say, 'this middle part is not quite as scary as the begInning and end', this is a clue for varying the inner speech pattern. The middle part can be gradually transformed into a 'time out'.

What Meichenbaum wants is for the client to alter the inner speech pattern so that it begins to be incompatible with extreme, uniform fear. If the fear can go up, down, and then up again, along with the rise and fall of the bridge, the driver may be able to begin altering his or her internal dialogue. If one can say, 'now I'm extremely frightened', and then 'now I'm a bit less frightened' and then 'now I'm very frightened again', the client will have adopted an inner speech pattern that is beginning to be incompatible with a uniformly terrified response.

If the therapy process goes as it is supposed to, the terror should be getting a bit less intense. The fear response should be moving to a less extreme level. And the symptoms themselves should be starting to change from dangerous to neutral – and eventually even to a positive, energizing state. Dividing up the stimulus, the bridge, into parts of differing danger is the beginning of constructing an inner speech pattern that is less overcome with fright. If you can say to yourself 'this part is less frightening' you have cracked open the ritualized clutch of fear.

Another way one might find what Meichenbaum is advocating, is to divide the span itself into 'going up', 'at the top', and 'going down' stages. If you can divide the stimulus into these three zones, you might be able to alter the nature of the fear reaction at each of the three moments. For example, you might say, 'going down is easier than going up … the height keeps decreasing and my fear can decrease with it'. Or maybe going up can be defined as less frightening than being at the top. The point is that dividing the span up in this way can again give you some cognitive flexibility, along with some control over the stimulus.

What Meichenbaum seems to be getting at is having the client create some 'cognitive dissonance' in the situation. This dissonance can serve as a lever for getting some purchase on one's inner speech and, as a result of that, on the symptoms themselves. Meichenbaum's method – learning to modify a frightened inner speech repertoire and thereby creating a cognitive structure incompatible with the phobic pattern – can be used for other psychopathologies. All of the phobias and compulsions might respond to this approach. An incessant hand washer can distinguish the wetting down, soaping up, rubbing around, watering down, etc, for example. And mood disorders such as depression have also been treated with inner speech modification. In all cases the therapist and the patient construct some kind of cognitive dissonance that raises the psychic costs of maintaining the symptom.

5. Durkheim and the solidarity of the self

Throughout this chapter I have been showing how the self uses inner speech to direct its action or agency. A procedure that underlies this process is the way the self uses inner speech to build up its own internal solidarity and empower itself for getting things done. In the classical social theory of Durkheim and Weber the person or self is regarded as the most sacred of entities, more so than even the cherished symbols of nations and religions. The sacredness of the self is especially characteristic of contemporary industrial societies.

This modern individualism is obviously important for human agency, for it gives the person dignity and social importance. If these resources are carefully husbanded they also give the person self-confidence, energy and a feeling of inner worth. The power of the contemporary individual clearly comes from social institutions, to a great extent. It is a result of the looking glass self, broadly speaking (Wiley, forthcoming). But this power also comes from within, as a result of how we look at and talk to ourselves. Humans are powerful because of things they do to and say about themselves in the theatres of their consciousness. It is largely inner speech that constructs the sacredness of the individual.

This process can be explained with the ideas of the French social theorist, Emile Durkheim. To use Durkheim to explain the sacred self, you have to begin with the sacredness of society, working your way step-wise down to the self. One of the most powerful ideas of Durkheim is that societies are held together by solidarity, and that this solidarity is engendered by social rituals.

Durkheim's explanation of how ritual works is also interesting. In the case of the

Australian Aborigines, the clan's rituals consisted of three actions. First the clan assembled in one place. Second the clan had to adopt a ritual mode, in the social psychological sense. This means they all had to focus their attention on the same thing, in this case the totemic symbols. The number of people in these annual assemblies varied between about twenty and forty. They also had to adopt a ritual state of mind, meaning they had to stop thinking of and attending to ordinary affairs and concentrate on the ritual itself. And, in modern terms, they had to engage in the 'willing suspension of disbelief' in the power of the ritual – which is what we do when we go to a movie or a play. The purpose of the ritual was to strengthen the clan, and the clan had to believe this would happen for it to come about. The third feature of a social ritual is the presentation of the key symbols and meanings. In Durkheim's example the meanings were derived from the clan's totem. These meanings promoted the health and welfare of the clan.

This Durkheimian tripartite scheme can be applied to any social ritual, ranging all the way from large religious or civic rituals down to family birthdays and thanksgivings. The three-element scheme works rather well for any ritual. Randall Collins has even argued, drawing on Erving Goffman, that face to face interaction has similar rituals (Goffman, 1967; Collins, 1982, pp. 130–2). Collins applies this scheme to the intimate relationship between two people in love. The close actions and gestures of these two people, including physical love-making, symbolize their love, much as Durkheim's clan's rituals symbolize their solidarity.

Returning to agency now, with Durkheim in hand, it seems clear that the self too is a kind of community which engages in internal rituals. Further, these rituals can supply the solidarity that gives meaning and worth to the self. When we ritualize our selves we engage in a form of self worship. And what we are worshipping, just as in Durkheim's clan, is our semiotic powers. We worship our ability to worship, i.e. our capacity to signify and represent.

How does this come about? People do not usually engage in explicit and formal self-worshipping or self-aggrandizing rituals. Instead these actions are done informally and often only half consciously. They are done when the self needs power, e.g. when we are in a weakened state, when we are called upon to perform well, when we are in a stage of transition, when we are trying something new, when we are in grave danger and when we have a chance to improve ourselves substantially. When the self is being called upon to 'step up to the plate' in baseball and be its best, we want to build up the solidarity of the self.

When I need to be my best I give myself a long, lingering smile. The philosopher, Jerry Fodor, speaks of saying 'you can do it Jerry' to himself. Athletes and other performers engage in encouraging self talk as they approach a competitive moment. And many people have lucky charms, mantras, pet names for themselves and other ways of inducing a ferverino. When we engage in these personal rituals we assemble the parts of the self, even if only for a moment. We enter a ritual, psychological mode, preparing to energize the self. And then we state the magic words, the 'you can do it' injunction, and get ready to act our best.

In terms of this paper, we engage in the three ritual moments. We assemble the community of the self: the 'I-you-me' reflexivity, earlier stages of the self, the key 'visitors' such as friends, family and perhaps deity, and all the things, symbols and people we identify with. Using this entire assembly we then reflect on and address our selves. And with our ritual words and symbols we increase the solidarity and power of the self. The strength of agency is to a great extent fuelled by the religious care of the self.

Conclusion

This has been an exploration of how inner speech intersects with agency. Inner speech is a fairly well defined idea, but agency is much more open ended. For this reason I had to pick and choose which of the many aspects of agency I would consider. Agency is a sea of meaning because self is also a sea of meaning. Self is one of our more or less limitless concepts, along with such notions as reality, meaning, truth, value and so on. We sample from these big ideas, and everyone's sample is a bit different.

A theme I tried to hit was that the self is an autonomous, *sui generis* entity. Whatever the self's ontology might be, its activity is largely controlled by its dialogical function. To quote Bakhtin, the self not only engages in dialogue, it is dialogue. Or as Peirce liked to say, the self is a sign.

But it is not an ordinary sign. For example, Robert Perinbanayagam characterizes the self as a maxisign (1991, pp. 9–11), meaning that it is an amalgam of all the varieties of signs. I like to think of the self as a generic sign. In Peirce's terms, the 'I' is the representamen, the 'me' is the object and the 'you' is the interpretant. When the 'I', 'you' and 'me' are in dialogue, they are also in the process of signification or sign-making. The self is a generic sign open to all species or varieties of signs. It is a significative network whose function is to carry dialogical communication.

Inner speech is the key self process. Dialogue steers the self, acting as our compass through life. My diagram of the self was meant to show, in some detail, how dialogue controls the self. For John Maynard Keynes, finance was the magneto of capitalism, and when the magneto failed, the whole system fell with it. Dialogue is the magneto of the self, the controlling process. The things being controlled are the structure and agency of the self, using these terms more or less as they were used in the debate between Anthony Giddens and Margaret Archer.

In the self the social structure is located primarily in the generalized other. Mead's term suggests that we encounter the social structure as part of the internal dialogue. This is why he gave it the personal name of 'other' rather than an impersonal name such as structure. For Mead the 'I-me' dialogue was largely between the 'I' and the generalized other, i.e. the internalized social structure conceived as a conversational other.

When you add Peirce to Mead the main strand of the internal conversation is between the 'I' and the 'you', although there is a simultaneous and indirect conversation between the 'I' and the 'me'. As I said earlier, Mead's conversation is now encompassed in a larger, more comprehensive conversation. And Peirce's conversation is similarly part of a larger conversation.

When we act we draw on all our resources, including both agency (our ability to design and complete an act) and structure (our access to the social rules and resources). Along with the generalized other, we also draw on the habits and memory. When, in the early part of this paper, I described the complex connections between the 'me' and the 'you', I was talking about the connections between structure and agency.

The interaction of structure and agency seems wide open and undetermined from either direction. We choose how dependent we will be on the structure, just as we choose how innovative we will be in action. Just how this balance works out will depend on the circumstances, the internal conversation, and the (slightly, in my opinion) free will of the agent.

The self is the crossroads of several ontological levels – culture, structure, person, physical body, etc. A variety of influences come together and influence the life of the self. But it is the dialogical process itself that produces these outcomes.

Note

1 I follow the convention of quoting Peirce with the notation 'CP (x.xxx)' referring to volume and paragraph in the *Collected Papers of Charles S. Peirce*, (1936–58).

References

Athens, Lonnie (1994), 'The Self as a Soliloquy', *The Sociological Quarterly*, 35, 521–32.

Austin, J. L. (1962), *How to do Things with Words*, Oxford, Clarendon Press.

Bakhtin, M. M. (1981, written in 1920s and 1930s), *The Dialogic Imagination*, Austin: University of Texas Press.

Barkley, Russel A. (1997), *ADHD and the Nature of Self-Control*, New York: The Guilford Press.

Colapietro, Vincent (1989), *Peirce's Approach to the Self*, Albany: SUNY Press.

Collins, Randall (1982), *Sociological Insight*, New York: Oxford University Press.

Dewey John (1991 [1910]), *How We Think*, Buffalo: Prometheus Books.

——. (1930), *Human Nature and Conduct*, Revised edition. New York: The Modern Library.

Dodds, Agnes E., Jeanette A. Lawrence and Jaan Valsiner (1997), 'The Personal and the Social. Mead's Theory of the "Generalized Other".' *Theory and Psychology*, 1997: 483–503.

Durkheim, Emile (1995 [1912c]), *The Elementary Forms of Religious Life*, translated and with an Introduction by Karen E. Fields. New York: The Free Press.

Emirbayer, Mustafa, and Ann Mische. (1998), 'What is Agency?' *American Journal of Sociology*. 103: 962–1023.

Firestone, Robert W. (1986), 'The 'Inner Voice' and Suicide', *Psychotherapy*, 23: 439–7.

Fish, Max H. (1982), 'Introduction' to *Writings of Charles S. Peirce*, Volume 1, Bloomington: Indiana University Press.

Gallie, W.B. (1956), 'Essentially Contested Concepts', *Proceedings of the Aristotelian Society*, 56: 167–98.

Goffman, Erving (1967), *Interaction Ritual*, Garden City: Doubleday.

Hardy, James (2006), 'Speaking Clearly: A Critical Review of the Self-Talk Literature', *Psychology of Sports and Exercise*, 7:81–97.

Holmes, Paul and Claire Calmels. (2008), 'A Neuroscientific Review of Imagery and Observation use in Sport', *Journal of Motor Behavior*, 40:433–45.

James, William ([1950] 1990), *The Principles of Psychology*, Volume 1, New York: Dover Publications Inc.

Marx Karl (1983), *The Portable Karl Marx*, New York. Penguin Books.

Kosslyn, Stephen M. (1994), *Imagery and Brain*, Cambridge: MIT Press.

Mead, George Herbert (1964 [1913]), 'The Social Self', pp. 142–9, in *George Herbert Mead. Selected Writings*. Indianapolis: Bobbs Merrill Company.

———. (1930), 'Cooley's Contribution to American Social Thought', *American Journal of Sociology*. 35:693–706.

———. (1932), *The Philosophy of the Present*, Chicago: University of Chicago Press.

———. (1934), *Mind, Self and Society*, Chicago, University of Chicago Press.

Meichenbaum, Donald (1977), *Cognitive-Behavior Modification*, New York: Plenum Press.

Morin, A. (1993), 'Self-talk and self-awareness: On the nature of the relation', *The Journal of Mind and Behavior*, 14:223–34.

Peirce, C.S. (1934), *Collected Papers of Charles Sanders Peirce: Pragmatism and Pragmaticism* (Vol. 5). Cambridge: Harvard University Press.

Perinbanayagam, Robert (1991), *Discursive Acts*, New York: Aldine de Gruyter.

Ratcliffe, Matthew (2008), 'The Second Person', pp. 152–253 in his *Rethinking Commonsense Psychology*, New York: Palgrave MacMillan.

Rohrer, Jonathan D. William D. Knight, Jane E. Warren, Nick C. Fox, Martin N. Rosser and Jason D. Warren (2008), 'Word-finding Difficulty: A Clinical Analysis of the Progressive Aphasias', *Brain*, 131:8–38.

Schutz, Alfred (1962), *Collected Papers*, Volume 1. The Hague: Martinus Nijhoff.

Thomas, W.I. and Dorothy Swaine Thomas, (1928), *The Child in America*, New York: Alfred A Knopf.

Tye, M. (1991), *The Imagery Debate*, Cambridge, Mass.: MIT Press.

Vygotsky, L.S. (1987, written in 1920s), *Thinking and Speech* in *The Collected Works of L.S. Vygotsky, Problems of General Psychology*, Volume 1, New York: Plenum Press.

Whitehouse, Andrew J.O., Murray T. Maybery, and Kevin Durkin (2006), 'Inner Speech Impairments in Autism', *Journal of Child Psychology and Psychiatry*, 47: 857–65.

Wiley, Norbert (1994), *The Semiotic Self*, Chicago: University of Chicago Press.

———. (2006a), 'Pragmatism and the Dialogical Self', *International Journal for the Dialogical Self*, 1:1.

———. (2006b), 'Inner Speech as a Language: A Saussurean Inquiry', *Journal for the Theory of Social Behavior*, 36: 3, 319–41.

———. (2006c), 'Peirce and the Founding of American Sociology', *Journal of Classical Sociology*. 6: 23–50.

———. (2008), 'Combining Mead and Peirce with Vygotsky and Bakhtin on Inner Speech', paper presented at California State University, Hayward,

———. Forthcoming. 'Bakhtin's Voices and Cooley's Looking-Glass Self', *Interdisciplinary Journal for German Linguistics and Semiotic Analysis*.

Windelband, W. (1980), 'History and Natural Science', *History and Theory*. 19:169–85.

3 Cartesian privacy and Peircean interiority

Vincent Colapietro

Introduction

Norbert Wiley and Margaret Archer are social theorists who have drawn deeply upon classical pragmatism in their exemplary work on human subjectivity, with a crucial emphasis on what might be called reflexive agency. Moreover, in their most compelling articulations of their respective positions, both have assembled a chorus of voices from this tradition, but have done so with a keen ear for hearing the uniquely inflected positions of Peirce, James, Dewey, and Mead. Finally, Wiley and Archer are drawing upon a philosophical tradition primarily for the purpose of advancing social theory, not entering philosophical debate.

The pragmatists upon whom Wiley and Archer draw, or against whom they react, are ones who have been the focal objects of philosophical criticism. This has nowhere been truer than in reference to the very topics and themes on which these two theorists concentrate. While they turn (for example) to Peirce's reflections on the self and related topics, praising in the highest terms his singular achievement in this specific regard, one of the most informed and sympathetic of philosophical expositors of American pragmatism has proffered a sharply contrasting judgement: despite providing many suggestive hints, 'there is', in Richard J. Bernstein's estimation, a serious incoherence in what Peirce does say about the self (1971, 196). The incoherence is allegedly so deep and thoroughgoing as to make a mockery out of Peirce's ideal of self-control. Focusing upon a quite different inadequacy in the Peircean approach to human subjectivity (at least, supposed inadequacy), Karen Hanson argues that Peirce, along with James, Dewey, and Mead (albeit in quite different ways), fails to do justice to the private self, that is, the private dimensions of our mental lives.

The irony is that what these two philosophers find lacking in the pragmatists is exactly what Wiley and Archer find *in* Peirce and (in Wiley's case) the other pragmatists to some extent. This includes, especially in Archer's case, a robust affirmation of human interiority (or 'privacy'). It might thus be illuminating to recall some of the main criticisms levelled against the pragmatic treatments of human subjectivity and, then, against the background of these criticisms, to consider how Archer and Wiley glimpse what a number of philosophers have failed to see – the invaluable resources in (above all) Peircean pragmatism for offering a compelling account of human subjectivity. This defines the twofold objective of my contribution to this volume. The issue ultimately at stake is, however, not who provides the fairer interpretation of the Peircean or, more generally, pragmatist position (the philosophical critics or the sociological innovators); it is not even who makes most creative *use* of these pragmatist authors. Rather this issue is how best to conceive finite human selves as social beings whose interior lives, whose emergent yet irreducible interiority, equip them with a reflexive form of genuine efficacy (or agency). In brief, the issue ultimately at stake here is one of self-understanding.

Is it the case that the pragmatists' aversion to subjectivism, their suspicions regarding privacy prompted them to ignore or distort important dimensions of human existence, including what might be called interiority or inwardness (Hanson 1994; cf. Colapietro 1989)? Or is it rather the case that one or another of them – or several in their complementary approaches – go a long distance toward doing justice to this dimension of our existence? In particular, does not Peirce or Mead – or the two in conjunction – show *how* the reflexive dialogue, so prominently yet variously evident in the actual lives of human beings (Archer 2003, Ch. 5), truly plays the role it appears to play, that of enabling human agents to alter a course of conduct or a disposition and in other ways to exercise a far from negligible degree of autonomous agency? Is it the case that, *despite appearances*, pragmatists such as Peirce and Mead do offer invaluable suggestions for how to explain the private lives of social selves (Archer; Wiley)?

As it actually took place, the pragmatic turn encompassed a semiotic turn. For the classical pragmatists, however, the semiotic turn itself encompassed more than a linguistic turn. Rather it involved a consideration of signs and symbols in their myriad forms and functions. Specifically with respect to humans (though almost certainly with respect other species of animals as well), the life of signs is not limited to those outward ones making possible interpersonal communication; it extends to inward signs making possible intrapersonal conversation. But the identity and autonomy of the 'I' in intrapersonal conversations, or reflexive communication, are matters calling for critical attention. If we make the participants in this conversation merely internalized representatives of the social groups out of which the 'I' and 'me' emerge and in which these facets of the self participate, we effectively strip the self of a unique identity and also genuine autonomy. These matters are ones to which Archer has given the most thoughtful consideration. She presses home the question, in reference to the inner conversation, 'who is talking to whom?' (2003, 72).

No less than the identity and autonomy of the 'I' and the 'me' in inner conversation, the emergent and temporal character of the self in conversation with itself calls for critical analysis. While Archer offers a nuanced account of the emergent properties characteristics of human subjectivity (distinguishing structural, cultural, and personal emergent properties), Wiley tends to make questions of temporality even more central to his account of the self. The temporally interwoven strands of a historically emergent self are, in his writings, foci of detailed and probing analysis. With both theorists, a rejection of certain forms of theoretical reductionism expresses itself in a carefully articulated conception of reflexive agency, defined largely in terms of the transformative possibilities generated by internal conversation. This conversation allows the self to distance itself from both itself and the structures indispensable for the emergence of this self. It also allows for the self to distance itself from those structures crucial for the *ongoing* social interactions of this reflexive agent. Whether or not such distance ought to be expressed in terms of separation (the capacity of the self to separate itself from its present form and also social structures) is not nearly as important as whether or not the self has the capacity to withdraw within itself, to make use of originally public media (or signs) in a private manner and for truly private purposes. If the inner conversation, as pragmatism conceives this, enables the self to establish and maintain such an inward domain (what Peirce calls an 'inner world'), it would seem pragmatism can acknowledge the 'solitary' or 'private' self.

But such conversation does not entail the reintroduction of Cartesian privacy (Kenny; Hanson 1994). It does however drive toward an affirmation of pragmatic interiority (or inwardness). A robust affirmation of human inwardness is, however, precisely what a number of critics contend pragmatism precludes or, at least, fails to offer (Hanson 1994, 2001). The creative appropriation of insights from classical pragmatism by Wiley and Archer can profitably be set against the background of philosophical criticism. In the next section of this paper, the criticisms on which I will focus are ones pertaining directly to the pragmatic portrait of human subjectivity. Then, in the following section, I will indicate in detail the way Archer and Wiley creatively appropriate what some philosophical interpreters have so severely criticized. In its overall structure, then, this paper is the site of an intersection between not only sociology and semiotics but also philosophical critique and sociological creativity. In one of its sections, moreover, it is the site of an intersection between two important contemporary social theorists who turn to the same tradition, though in different ways, for resources with which to sketch in detail a portrait of the self.

The deep reservations of an informed interpreter

In 'Pragmatism and the Secret Self', Karen Hanson addresses this question in an informed and thoughtful manner: 'Can the pragmatists account for the private aspect of the self?' She even wonders: 'Do they want to?' (28).The pragmatists on whom she focuses are Charles Sanders Peirce, William James, John Dewey, and George Herbert Mead. After sifting through the views of these pragmatists, she concludes: 'each of these philosophers – Peirce, James, Mead, and Dewey – through selective attention to the issues he feels most pressing, *overlooks* some problems and puzzles tied to our sense of privacy or *distorts* some aspect of the phenomena of our private experience' (44; emphasis added).

In at least two earlier essays, 'Affinity in Opposition: Peirce on Cartesian Doubt' (1988) and 'American Philosophy Continued: Peirce's Puzzles About the Self' (1993), Hanson has focused on Peirce's approach to the self, contending he at once is closer to Descartes and farther from the intractable phenomena of human experience (in particular, some of the most salient phenomena connected to our mental life) than he realizes. She seems to hold that any adequate account of human selfhood must accord a more prominent, a less qualified, place to the private facets of our individual lives than Peirce grants to these aspects of our selves. What we need here is nothing less than a robust acknowledgement of our irreducibly private experience. In her judgement, Peirce's commitment to the principle of continuity, however, works to minimize the import of our physical and moral separateness' (Hanson 2001, 44). On this construal, the secret or private self is the separate self. Peirce is emphatic in rejecting the notion of such a self, going so far as to link our adherence to such a conception with our wickedness (or fallenness) (cf. Peirce CP 7.571). Hanson is, however, equally adamant in her advocacy of the private self as a *separate* self. One question here is whether an adequate account of privacy entails a commitment to the concept of a separate or separable self. Another is whether Peirce's commitment to the principle of continuity precludes the possibility of the kind and degree of discreteness, of being cut off from others, seemingly exemplified in the various phenomena making up our private experience. However we may ultimately judge the force of her criticisms, the careful way in which Hanson has challenged pragmatist accounts of human selfhood, giving focal attention to a tangled cluster of thorny issues bearing upon private experience, greatly assists us in re-framing the most basic questions and also in returning to the most relevant texts.

The interior life of the social self: Margaret Archer and Norbert Wiley on reflexive agency

If we turn *from* Hanson's criticisms of Peirce's views *to* Archer's explication of those views, we discover (as already noted) something curious. Where Hanson finds Peirce either ignores or distorts some important facet of our private lives, Archer finds he offers a finely balanced account of both the social and 'secret' aspects of human existence. Whereas James offers in her judgement an 'under-socialized' model of human subjectivity and agency, and also whereas Mead defends an 'over-socialized' model, we find in Peirce's treatment of these topics a 'careful balancing act' (2003, 78). That is, Peirce's model is one in which socialization and external structures, on the one hand, and interiority and inner conversation, on the other, are given their due (2003, 78).

If we turn from Bernstein's criticisms of Peirce's views to Norbert Wiley's reconstruction of those views, we find something analogous. Whereas Bernstein judges the failure to work out a theory of the self is a failure not only in Peirce's philosophy but also in 'the entire pragmatic movement' (1971, 197), Wiley argues that the resources for articulating an adequate account of human selfhood constitute the most important contribution of this philosophical movement. By means of contrasting pragmatism with other positions (German idealism and, above all, faculty psychology), Wiley is led to identify 'six dimensions' characteristic of the pragmatic orientation, dimensions 'oriented toward the theory of the self' (18). These are the dialogical, social, horizontal, egalitarian, voluntarist, and cultural dimensions so prominent in the way pragmatists treat the self and other topics. Rather than being one of its most marked failures, then, he contends the theory of the self articulated along these lines 'is a major substantive achievement of pragmatism'.

Specifically in reference to Peirce, however, Wiley in effect concedes much to Bernstein. He does not hesitate to claim: A major problem with Peirce is that his theories do not always hang together very well. He is continuously brilliant and innovative, but in ways that do not always add up' (29). This is true of Peirce's treatment of the self: 'One of his most confusing arguments', Wiley stresses, 'is in his semiotics of the self'. The confusion arises because Peirce, on the one hand, asserts 'the human is only a sign of collection of words but, on the other hand, never maps the self [conceived as a process of semiosis] onto the "semiotic triad" of sign, object, and interpretant'. That is, he never explains what part of the self is a sign, what part is an interpretant, and what part an object. It seems clear that Wiley takes his own contribution to this discussion to include the execution of just this task, the mapping of the self onto the triad of sign, interpretant, and object. In any event, he is clear about what both Peirce and the movement derived from his thought failed to achieve: 'If pragmatism is America's greatest contribution to philosophy and Peirce is the greatest pragmatist – both of which I believe to be true – then the problem of Peirce's semiotics of the self is an important piece of unfinished business in America's cultural history' (29). Even in its unfinished form, however, the semiotic theory of human subjectivity to be gathered from the writings of the pragmatists is, in Wiley's judgement, 'a major substantive contribution'. It is hard to avoid inferring that, for him, it is *the* major contribution of the pragmatic movement. At least, it is hard for me to resist drawing this inference, especially when Wiley makes such claims as this about pragmatism: 'If the unity of this philosophy is sought in its logic, method or theory of knowledge, the movement is extremely loose, indistinct, and difficult to identify' (Hollinger, 1980). But if it is sought in the theory of the self, the unity is based on a more technical claim, specific enough to be testable and prescriptive enough to be politically usable' (18).

Both Margaret Archer and Norbert Wiley (as already noted) present their views of the self in critical dialogue with various intellectual traditions, including American pragmatism. As stressed above, they do so, however, without paying much attention to the philosophical criticisms of pragmatic approaches to human subjectivity. This is truer of Archer than Wiley, though even he does not so much engage with as allude to these criticisms. But each of these theorists does engage in a detailed, painstaking way with several pragmatists and, moreover, does so with explicit reference to historical figures and contemporary thinkers. Of far greater significance, both of these theorists are committed to making creative use out of the theoretical resources provided by the pragmatic tradition. In Archer's *Structure, Agency and the Internal Conversation* (2003) and Wiley's *The Semiotic Self* (1994), the books most relevant to our discussion, Charles Sanders Peirce and George Herbert Mead are the pragmatists with whom *both* theorists are critically engaged. While Archer moves to her reclamation of the internal conversation by way of tracing 'thematically the origins and the elaboration of the "internal conversation" through the work of James, Peirce, and Mead' (2003, 56), Wiley only touches upon James. While Wiley makes passing reference to Dewey, Archer does not mention this pragmatist at all.

In my judgement, Dewey is a neglected figure who is far more important to this investigation than Archer or Wiley appear to discern. His relevance becomes manifest in the recent work of the contemporary social theorist Hans Joas, who is also arguably the best expositor of Mead. In *The Genesis of Values* (2000), Joas stresses that for Dewey, 'the unification of the self' is unintelligible if we cut the self off from the world. Indeed, it is only possible for individuals to experience and indeed constitute themselves as unified 'if the world is introduced into the process of self-unification'. Thus, Joas rightly goes on to emphasize this point, by recalling Dewey's own words: 'The self is always directed toward something beyond itself and so its own unification depends upon the idea of the integration of the shifting scenes of the world into the imaginative totality we call the "Universe"' (2000, 115). But, in a dramatic manner, the self is directed *toward* the universe, what is beyond itself, *through* its ongoing engagement in deliberative imagination (the form of interiority Dewey is least hesitant to accredit or endorse). Deliberation 'penetrates into the inner core' of human needs, impulses, and desires: the character of these 'can itself be altered under the influence of such reflection' or deliberation (107). On the basis of these and other considerations, Joas is led to the conclusion that Dewey 'anchors the genesis of value commitments in experiences of self-transcendence and self-formation' (116). Such experiences are possible only because the self is envisioned by Dewey as a being who is, time and again, fatefully divided against itself (cf. Smith 1959), moreover, an agent striving to achieve the degree of unity and integration requisite for the maintenance or augmentation of its agency. Dewey, especially as interpreted by Joas, is thus a pragmatist who does not deserve to be assimilated (or allied) too quickly with Mead or to be distanced too far from Peirce. In other words, his distinctive voice needs to be amplified in the present discussion.

The triangulation of Archer, Wiley, and Joas on the topic of self-transcendence and self-formation (including the later phases of this always unfinished process, i.e. self-transformation), however, must wait for another occasion. At this time, the comparison of Archer and Wiley sets a task too large and complex to be completed within the limits of this paper. But, given its importance, it is a task worth commencing here. What makes this task so important is, as much as anything else, their use of pragmatism, the way they imaginatively put the pragmatists to work. To use Archer's expression in reference to Wiley as well as herself, both theorists are engaged in the project of reclaiming the internal conversation (see, e.g. Chapters 3 and 4 of Wiley's *The Semiotic Self* and Chapters 2 and 3 of Archer's *Structure, Agency and the Internal Conversation*) and, moreover, they are doing so through a critical engagement with pragmatic writings. Both are self-consciously trying to complete what, in their judgement, the pragmatists themselves left unfinished (Wiley 1994, 29; Archer 2003, 56–7). Both are deeply sceptical about eliminativist projects in which such basic concepts of 'folk psychology' as beliefs, desires, intentions, motives, agents, and even selves are eventually to be replaced by more adequate conceptions, ones almost certainly referring to impersonal mechanisms, structures, or processes (see, e.g. Wiley 1994, 210–11; Archer 38, 86, 107, and 157). Put positively, both are explicit and unabashed defenders of 'folk psychology', though reflective and informed defenders. Regarding psychoanalysis and thus the value of explanations in terms of the unconscious in the dynamic (or truly psychoanalytic) sense, however, they disagree: Archer appears to be no less sceptical of psychoanalytic approaches than eliminativist projects (see, e.g. 2003, 49), whereas Wiley is clearly more open than Archer to incorporating considerations of the unconscious in the strictly psychoanalytic sense into his account of the self.[1]

But Archer's antipathy toward psychoanalysis and Wiley's openness to incorporating the unconscious into his model of the self, ironically, derive from the same source. That is, their divergent assessments grow from the same root. While Archer appears to think psychoanalytic approaches to human subjectivity inevitably carry reductionist implications regarding our conscious agency, Wiley explicitly refuses to reduce mind to consciousness. In general, an animus against reductivism animates both Archer's and Wiley's efforts to reclaim pragmatic insights into human subjectivity, above all, ones pertaining to the essential link between the inner conversation and reflexive agency. Wiley helpfully summarizes his views regarding reductionism when he writes:

> The anti-reductions follow automatically from a well-theorized self. The pragmatists had a certain way of explaining autonomous human beings [a way inseparably connected to reflexive communication and the distinctive form of human agency made possible by such interior dialogue]. From this autonomy followed the clarification of the psychological level and its differentiation from [and irreducibility to] all other levels. (223)

So both theorists are led by their antipathy to reductionism to contrasting assessments of descriptions and explanations of our conduct and mentality couched in terms of the unconscious. For Archer, her antipathy toward reductionism encompasses an antipathy toward psychoanalysis; for Wiley, his rejection of reductionism underwrites his openness to the unconscious, though he makes only modest claims regarding the importance of this concept for his project.[2]

But what most deeply divides Archer and Wiley is their contrasting assessments not of the unconscious but of Mead. For her, Mead's account of the self effectively erases what Peirce's scattered remarks about human subjectivity allow us to sketch – a vivid portrait of reflexive agency. It is as though the Meadean hand of pragmatism takes away what the Peircean hand has given! For Wiley, in contrast, Mead complements, rather than erases, Peirce's contribution to the task at hand. Archer in a painstaking, illuminating reconstruction of a complex history shows how critiques of *introspection* have effectively eliminated the recognition of interiority. While we presume at every turn both the capacity to address ourselves in our radical, irreducible individuality (our ability *as individuals* to address our selves *as such*) and the efficacy of this capacity (our ability by this means to alter the course of our lives, our stance toward the world, and much else), the dominant theories today preclude systematic recognition of this definitive attribute of human agency. They also discourage empirical research on especially the *variable* ways in which human beings actually engage in internal conversation (or reflexive communication) (see, e.g. Archer 2003, 153–4). Finally, these theories can so distort the self-understanding of self-reflective beings as to undermine the confidence of these beings in their inner or individualized capacity. As a result of accepting these theories, individuals can come to believe that they lack the internal resources to transform their individual lives. While aiming at theoretical rigour as well as the degree and kind of impartiality attainable by a social theorist, then, Archer and Wiley are engaged in a discourse in which the political stakes of theoretical disputes are far from negligible. Social theory is required to come to *critical* terms with human autonomy, especially in the irrepressible yet fracturable forms of reflexive agency made possible by inner conversation. I suspect both would see such theory underwriting the elimination of autonomy and agency to be a sign not of sophistication but of bankruptcy.

For neither Archer nor Wiley do the critiques of introspection entail the eradication of interiority or inwardness. For both, we can reclaim the interior domain of human subjectivity by reclaiming more fully than contemporary theorists in philosophy, sociology, and other disciplines have done the inner conversation in its efficacious role in the engendering of subjectivity. For Archer, the reclamation of this conversation is aided by tracing in detail a narrative in which Jamesian, Peircean, and Meadean positions mark three successive (though not progressive) stages in an unfinished journey.

In the first stage, James in a halting yet suggestive manner 'initiated the movement move from "looking" to "listening" to ourselves as internal speakers'. On Archer's reading, however, the move from introspective awareness to internal conversation initiated by James takes us only a short distance to reflexive *dialogue*, for (in her words) he exhibits the self as listening, but fails to show the self as responding to what emanates from itself. That is, 'James conceptualizes thought as an inner monologue, but never as a dialogue' (2003, 63).

In the second stage, Peirce articulates a truly dialogical model of human thought. What enables him to do so is, as much as anything else, 'his non-reductionist treatment of the "outer" and "inner" worlds, coupled with his insistence upon their interplay (2003, 78). In brief, he grants interiority or inwardness its due. The internal conversation can be a transformatory process because in this ongoing dialogue what we have are 'different phases of the ego', of the 'I' as a more or less integrated cluster of densely sedimented habits *and* the 'I' as a more or less disruptive force on the present scene (to be sure, not at all a force like the Freudian 'id', a 'seething cauldron of primal urges' [2003, 73], but a force nonetheless). Though Peirce does not construe this dialogue in terms of an exchange between 'I' and 'me', Archer proposes we can do so to illuminating effect. Hence, she proposes to use 'me' to designate 'the historic phase of the ego' (72), and 'I' for the cutting edge of the ever newly emerging phase, incessantly appealing to the 'critical self' or historic phase. The 'I', as the present, agential self, is truly 'a source of creativity and innovation', whereas the 'me', as the historic phase of a temporally extended process reaching – at least in the case of adults – far into a personal past, is in the present a summation of that past (the bearing of a personal history on a dramatic present). Archer stresses the 'me' is an active participant in the internal conversation, for the 'me' is 'able to respond because it is alive in the present as a disposition [or set of dispositions] to act in particular ways' (73). This marks for her a fundamental divergence between Peirce and Mead: 'The Peircean "Me", as the personal conscience [in the form of consolidated habits] which is regularly consulted, is thus very different from Mead's "Me", as the generalized other', which furnishes society's guidelines to action'. Whereas Peirce allows for the 'me' to be 'a *personalized* sediment' (emphasis added), Mead allegedly makes of the 'me' nothing more than 'a socialized deposit' (73).

Archer acknowledges that 'we cannot evade an encounter with Mead as the most celebrated exponent of the "inner conversation" ' (79). But, on her account, Mead essentially robs the interior dialogue of its irreducible interiority (a point already anticipated). That is, she contends, 'Mead's internal conversation was not a conversation *with oneself*' (79; emphasis added). It is rather 'a conversation with society'. She attempts to make this case by subjecting to critical scrutiny the central Meadean concepts of 'I' and 'Me': First, she claims Mead's 'best-known "Me", which stands as the interlocutor of the "I", is no part of the first-person at all, but rather represents the second-person plural: the "Me" is really the "We" – what Mead called the "generalized other"'(79). Second, she insists: 'Mead's "I" does not speak for itself, but for another "We", that of a different community'. Accordingly, Archer concludes Mead's conception of the self signals 'a complete loss of all but formal interiority' (82). This is nowhere more evident than in Mead's treatment of the 'I' as the participant in the dialogue formally identified by him at certain points as a source of innovation and creativity. But, on Archer's narration at least, the 'I' as portrayed by Mead comes 'to play a diminishingly small part in my own mental life' (89). This bears directly on the mediating function of the internal conversation: in Mead's treatment of this exchange, it becomes 'not a medium through which *personal* causal powers are realized' (emphasis added), but a mechanism through which social structures are either re-inscribed or newly fashioned.

Archer contends, even though 'the exercise of dialogical reflexivity is essential to the normal functioning of human beings', we substantively 'know very little about the internal conversation' (2003, 153). The reasons for this are not hidden. 'The American pragmatists alone took a sustained interest in it and yet they were less than generous with examples of it'. The (presumed) universality of this dialogue has illicitly operated to underwrite the allegedly uniform or, at most, similar character of our inner musings.

From Archer's perspective, '"structure" and "agency" constitute two distinctive and irreducible properties' (14; cf. Giddens). It is, however, imperative to avoid allowing these properties to be juxtaposed to one another in such a way as to generate a dualism. One way to avoid this occurring is to identify mediating powers and processes by which structure and agency are dynamically and integrally conjoined.

For her, 'human reflexive deliberation plays a crucial role in mediating between' structure and agency (14). Thus, she insists: 'how people reflexively deliberate upon what they do in the light of their personal concerns has to form *a* part of a mediatory account' (15). She goes so far as to assert: 'human reflexivity is *central* to the process of mediation' (15).

Human reflexivity is manifest in the internal conversation in which the self addresses itself in its individuality. If the identity of the self in this conversation is not allowed to be anything more than an internalized placeholder for some social unit, then the 'internal' conversation falls far short of being truly internal (or private).

As the name for the powers and processes requisite to mediate between structure and agency, human reflexivity, as exemplified and indeed realized in internal conversations, must be: (1) genuinely interior, (2) ontologically subjective, and (3) causally efficacious (Archer 2003, 16). To compromise the interior character of the inner conversation (in particular, to qualify the identity of the participants in this dialogue so that they become formal placeholders for social forces rather than different guises of an individualized, personal, yet continuous *personal* force), or to fail to accord our mental life (or subjective being) its own irreducible ontological status, or finally to deny causal efficacy to the inner dialogue would, in Archer's judgement, destroy the inner conversation in the robust form she is committed to reclaiming.

Like Archer's, the work of Norbert Wiley is illuminating in a number of respects, not least of all for assisting us in thinking through the question of privacy or interiority. But, somewhat in contrast to hers, Wiley's serves in this way by bringing into sharp focus both relational and temporal considerations. In his efforts to do so, he strives to bring together what she works to rend asunder – Peirce and Mead. Wiley certainly does not ignore the discrepancies in Peirce and Mead's models of the internal conversation and, closely allied to these models, their distinctive semiotic approaches to human subjectivity. Whereas Archer primarily connects the different phases of the ego as distinctive roles in the (to be sure) temporal process of the internal conversation to considerations of the identity of the ego in both its temporal continuity and inevitable differentiations into temporal phases (more simply, whereas Archer principally connects these phases to considerations of the identity of the ego *as an individual,* a partly self-defined and self-directed agent), Wiley mainly connects the distinct interlocutors in the inner dialogue to temporal segments. Thus, he suggests: 'Mead's me-as-past connected the me, by way of temporality, to the I' (1994, 43). Wiley argues that Peirce presents an 'I-you' model of internal conversation, while Mead presents an 'I-me' model (see, e.g. 41). Wiley sees his achievement in this context as the result of merging or integrating the Peircean and Meadean models of internal conversation and also reflexive agency. As Wiley sees it, 'Mead's I-me scheme is not triadic in three ways: it lacks the future, it lacks the interpretant, and it lacks the "you" pole of the internal conversation' (221).[3] What Mead's model lacks, however, Peirce's includes, and what Peirce's lacks Mead's includes. Or so Wiley asserts: 'Peirce is non-triadic in lacking the Meadean elements: the past, the object, and the me' (221).

Wiley offers what might seem to some readers as an excessively complex model of human subjectivity, since it is a model involving a triad of triads. Humans are themselves 'a triad of triads', though one in which these distinguishable triads not only imply each other but also 'merge into one' (215). These are the *semiotic* triad of sign, object, and interpretant; the *temporal* triad of past, present, and future; and the *dialogical* triad of I, you, and me.[4] For Wiley, this means that 'the self is semiotically triadic in its structure as well as in its activities' (217). Moreover, the self is temporally triadic in its structure and its activities. For the self is an agent who 'can remember the past and anticipate the future'; s/he can also 'expand the present, in a psychological or "felt" manner, to include an indefinite amount of the past and the present'. The third of these abilities permits humans 'to go beyond time'. In addition, these 'time-binding abilities allow humans a great deal of control over temporality' (216). Finally, the self is dialogically triadic in its structure and its activities. If the self as a triad of triads is connected to the ongoing process of the internal conversation, we are forced to see that inner dialogue is an inherently complex and, to no slight degree, inevitably messy affair in which the identity of the participants in the dialogue calls for semiotic, temporal, and dialogical specification and indeed redescription.

While Archer's account of the internal conversation and the reflexive agency exhibited in this transformative process is more clearly and systematically articulated than Wiley's account (indeed, his portrait of the self is far more programmatic and sketchy than hers), Wiley's is arguably more suggestive. But what *both* Archer and Wiley help us to see is that the private lives of social selves constitute phenomena we should neither ignore nor distort to fit into our theories. One should add: the private lives of somatic selves, of embodied agents, also demand recognition in their own right. Contra Karen Hanson, it is however far from clear that Peirce has ignored or distorted matters. With its detailed consideration of the complex interplay among the distinguishable guises of the human self, especially when temporally inflected, Norbert Wiley's work helps us reclaim the inward dialogue so central to human existence. In one of its principal meanings, the *mental* signifies the self-addressed (the self in dialogue with itself).

In any adequate account of human subjectivity, the more or less integrated cluster of densely sedimented habits making up the 'I' in its historic phase (the 'critical self' is that to which the creative self is always appealing) cannot be overlooked. In addition, the determinacy of both integrated habits and identifiable objects cannot be gainsaid. There is, however, a far greater degree of indeterminacy here than most of us are likely to recognize. In any instance, the question, 'Who is addressing whom?' (cf. Archer 2000, 9), is always potentially pertinent. The self in some measure comes into being in the process of exchange. Despite the densely sedimented habits so central to the constitution of an integrated self, human selves are always in some measure precarious achievements. Part of the reason for this is the improvisational status of our present exertions (cf. Joas 2000) and, inseparably tied to this, the degree to which the self in the present makes itself up as it goes along. Unquestionably, the historical momentum of sedimented habits ordinarily secures the stability and solidity of the self, but the improvisational character of human agency ensures the individual self is always open to the most dramatic and unexpected transformations.

If Peirce is right, especially as read by Archer and Wiley, then human selfhood is itself also a personal achievement. The self is not so much given as wrought, not a datum but an accomplishment. If Wiley and Archer especially are correct in their emphases, then this accomplishment is a personal one having an irreducibly private dimension. We might think of the private selves as human beings insofar as they are cut off from others. In creative and destructive ways, the self is ineluctably cut off from others. Peirce's synechism was designed, in part, to explain, rather than explain away, this phenomenon. As a continuum, the self affords limitless possibilities for discrete phases of an open-ended history to insulate themselves from the onrushing course of a singular life. The singularity, the uniqueness, of this life is distinct from the separability of selves.

Archer prefaces her discussion of James, Peirce, and Mead by stressing, 'there is a domain of mental privacy within every conscious human being'. This domain is a busy place where the private life of the social agent is lived out (2003, 33). The main activity within this private domain is 'reflexive deliberation'. Such deliberation makes possible nothing less than 'strong evaluation' in Charles Taylor's sense. As we have seen, she concludes her discussion of these figures by summarizing why, on her reading, neither James nor Mead is able 'to conceptualise how we are capable of any form of internal conversation with *ourselves*' (2003, 90). Peirce is the hero of her narrative: 'Incomplete as Peirce's theorizing of the "internal conversation" undoubtedly was, and unusual as it may be to present him as the central thinker in this respect', he is nonetheless 'climacteric' (78). Whereas James's represents to her an 'under-socialized' model of agency, Mead's represents an 'over-socialized' model. Peirce rather than his successor Mead is the climax of this story because Peirce's model carefully balances 'our external lives in society and our internal life of the mind' (78; cf. 64). She judges this to be so, in large measure, because she is convinced – and, in my judgement, rightly convinced – that the 'private and innovative *use*' of public signs 'is just as significant as the fact that the public language is an indispensable tool for the emergence of the private inner world' (70). On Peirce's account, the 'I' who uses public signs in a truly private and innovative way is never merely the internalized representative of some social group. The acknowledgement of sociality is, accordingly, not allowed to so qualify the affirmations of creativity and privacy (or innovation and inwardness) as to empty these affirmations of the rich phenomenological content Archer insists upon.

In Wiley's account, the temporal structure of human subjectivity is stressed to an even greater extent than this structure is emphasized in Archer's treatment of subjectivity. In addition, his assessment of Mead's contribution differs markedly from Archer's evaluation. Whereas she takes Mead to rob the 'inner conversation' of any genuinely individualized actors, Wiley finds in this pragmatist a complementary model to that of Peirce's, a model enabling us to bring into sharp focus otherwise unseen (at least, inadequately discerned) facets of the self, as an ongoing temporal process.

The philosophical tradition of American pragmatism has been rendered an invaluable service by these two social theorists, in particular, by their creative appropriation of the largely unacknowledged insights of such pragmatists as Peirce and Mead into the nature of subjectivity. This paper is not the place in which to offer either a more detailed comparative analysis of Archer and Wiley's differences or a comparative evaluation of their models. Let it suffice here to say that my own inclination is to suppose Mead is better than Archer supposes, though appreciating that some of her trenchant criticisms of the Meadean position would force modifications of Wiley's appropriation of Mead. It would be very instructive to draw upon Hans Joas's interpretation of Mead as a way of exploring whether this pragmatist might contribute more to our understanding of the creativity of action and, in particular, the innovative, individualized agency of the 'I' in Mead's sense, than Archer grants.

This paper is, however, most of all the site of two intersections. On the one hand, it is the site of the intersection between a predominantly negative philosophical assessment of pragmatic approaches to the self and a truly creative sociological appropriation of these very same approaches; on the other hand, it opens the space for a more detailed comparative examination and critical assessment of Margaret Archer's and Norbert Wiley's notable achievements. Given the attention that both pay to the central role of signs in the inner conversation (indeed, to the varied role of signs in the life of human agents), also given their responsiveness to both the main currents of contemporary sociology and central figures in the history of their discipline, it is hard – at least for me – to imagine a better site for exploring the intersection between sociology *and* semiotics than the work of these theorists.

Conclusion

Is not the human organism a sufficiently substantial being to serve as an effective locus of autonomous activity? Indeed, is it not the proper *designatum* of the human subject, especially when the human organism considered in reference to both transformative processes of its ubiquitous acculturation and the self-transformative possibilities secured through inner conversation (Dewey, *LW* 14, 27; also 39)? Is not the human imagination, understood as an innate or instinctive capacity as well as a cultural and personally modified set of abilities, an indispensable resource for self-transformation? Is not the sense of interiority – the interior space or "inner world" so markedly characteristic of human life – the principal instrument by which a social being can effectively resist the ubiquitous pressures, promptings, and propulsions of the social world? Is not the Platonic conception of human thought as 'inner speech' one from which immense and still largely unrecognized consequences follow (Peirce, *W* 2: 172)?

Bernstein, Smith, Thompson, Hanson, and indeed other philosophers have done much to help us see how pragmatists such as Peirce, James, Dewey, and Mead failed to articulate a coherent, convincing account of the individual human self. In contrast, Norbert Wiley and Margaret Archer have done even more to assist us in seeing how failures in articulation should not be confused with failures of conceptualization. The account of the self that is derived by these theorists from the writings of the pragmatists, arguably, offers an accurate portrait of human subjectivity. In it, the highly detailed and prominent rendering of sociality is not allowed to efface privacy, in its most critical sense. The private self is never anything more than an irreducible dimension of the mental (or psychic) life of a social actor, but it is also nothing less than just this – an *irreducible* dimension of human existence. The solitary self is the singular achievement of a social actor whose innovative and (in no small measure) idiosyncratic appropriation and use of communal signs makes possible an 'inner world' of indefinite expanse. The solitary self is the social self in one or another of its reflexive engagements: it is the agent whose socially mastered use of 'I' enables – indeed, encourages and (in a sense) demands or determines – an irreducibly reflexive use of 'I'. Having acquired the capacity for social discourse, the human organism acquires in the same breath the capacity for the reflexive discourse of 'inner conversation' (Dewey, *LW* 1, 215). Inner dialogue is, quite frequently, far more than idle chatter or empty talk. Even though such dialogue might be far more often than either Archer or perhaps even Wiley acknowledge an unfocused reverie serving at once the diverse desires of a self who is never a completely resolute being, a fully composed individual (indeed, the exigencies underwriting deliberation underscore just these features of the self), it often decisively – and dramatically – assumes the function of a genuine deliberation. The consistent emphasis on the deliberative function of the internal conversation can, indeed, lead to an all too narrow conception of our private lives, lives in which undirected fancies and barely permissible self-disclosures (if these self-revelations are permitted at all even in the innermost recesses of our secret selves). Even so, the emphasis on this function is important, especially given the widespread denial of any legitimate function or genuine efficacy to our internal (or private) deliberations. And this point too needs to be stressed: in order for inner deliberation to be genuine, it must be efficacious. Such deliberation must make a difference, an individualizing difference; it must mark the effective intervention of a differential individuality in the individual's own life. It provides us with the resources by which we are able to talk back to whatever operates to negate or thwart or curtail our individuality. In sum, our individuality, as an expression of our interiority, is not only inexpugnable, but also efficacious.

A robust affirmation of human individuality, encompassing expansive depths of genuine inwardness, such as we encounter in the writings of Norbert Wiley and especially those of Margaret Archer, helps us to see, among other critical matters, just how an essentially social self can escape being a completely socialized self. The Platonic conception of the inner conversation, as taken up by Peirce and carried forward by Archer and Wiley, carries 'immense consequences' (including the one just noted), consequences even today 'quite unrecognized'. The exemplary work of these two social theorists, however, destroys any excuse for failing to recognize, at least, the most telling consequences of human inwardness.

Notes

1 Wiley claims: 'The classical pragmatists stuck pretty much to the conscious mind, and when Freud's ideas began to reach America, the pragmatists resisted serious confrontation with the notion of the unconscious (although Peirce occasionally used the term' (1994, 55). This is misleading since the pragmatists did *not* limit their attention to conscious mind, but took explicit account of unconscious mind. James, Dewey, and Mead did strenuously resist the Freudian conception of the unconscious, but they emphatically refused to identify mind with consciousness. I would go so far as to argue they put forth a genuinely pragmatic conception of the unconscious or, to use the term they preferred, subconscious (cf. Wilshire; Colapietro 2004, also 2008).
2 'I am not going attempt to fit', he informs his readers, 'the unconscious systematically into the model [of the self]. This would be premature. Lacan has concepts for doing this, e.g. his self vs ego distinction, but these depend on his dubious mirror theory [a theory Wiley does critically examine in The Semiotic Self]. … Instead, I can only assert that the unconscious belongs in the model and make preliminary attempts to find a position for this agency' (1994, 56) or, as I would prefer to say, this facet of our agency.
3 Archer's criticism of Mead's model is the mirror image of this: Mead lacks the 'I' pole of the internal conversation.
4 It is certainly curious – and noteworthy – that a social theorist of Wiley's critical sensibility should exclude here the third person (it, he, she, and they).

References

Archer, Margaret (2000). *Being human: the problem of agency*. Cambridge University Press.
——. (2003). *Structure, agency and the internal conversation*. Cambridge University Press.
Bernstein, Richard J. (1967) *John Dewey*. Washington Square Press.
——. (1971). *Praxis and action*. University of Pennsylvania Press.
Colapietro, Vincent (1989). *Peirce's approach to the self*. SUNY Press.
——. (2004). 'Pragmatism and psychoanalysis: C. S. Peirce as a mediating figure'. *Cognitio: revista de filosofia*, Volume 5, number 1, 189–205.
——. (2008). 'Toward a pragmatist acknowledgment of the Freudian unconscious'. *Cognitio: revista de filosofia*, Volume 9, number 2, 187–203. "
Dewey, John. (1981). *Experience and Nature, The later works of John Dewey*, Volume 1, edited by Jo Ann Boydston. SIU Press. Cited as *LW* 1.
——. (1991). *The later works of John Dewey*, Volume 14. Carbondale, Il: SIU Press. Cited as *LW* 14.
Giddens, Anthony. (1984). *The constitution of society*. Berkeley, CA: University of California Press.
Hanson, Karen. (1988). 'Affinity in opposition: Peirce on Cartesian doubt'. *Gedankenzeichen* (Tübingen: Stauffenburg Verlag).
——. (1994). 'Some Peircean puzzles about the self'. In *From time and chance to consciousness*, edited by Edward C. Moore and Richard S. Robin (Providence: Berg), 237–46.
——. (2001). 'Pragmatism and the secret self'. *Cognitio*, no. II, 28–45.
Hollinger, David A. (1980). 'The problem of pragmatism in American history'. *The Journal of American History*, 67, 88–107.
Joas, Hans. (2000). *The genesis of values*. University of Chicago Press.
Kenny, Anthony. (1989). *The metaphysics of mind*. Oxford University Press.
Peirce, C. S. (1958). *Collected papers of Charles Sanders Peirce*, ed. Arthur W. Burks,

Volumes 7 and 8 (bound in one). Cambridge, MA: Belknap Press of Harvard University Press. Cited as either CP 7 or CP 8.

——. (1984). *The writings of Charles S. Peirce: A chronological edition*. Bloomington: Indiana University Press. Cited as W 2.

Smith, John E. (1959). 'John Dewey: philosopher of experience'. In *John Dewey*, edited by Charles W. Hendel (NY: Liberal Arts Press), 93–119.

Thompson, Manley H. (1953). *The pragmatic philosophy of C. S. Peirce*. University of Chicago Press.

Wiley, Norbert. (1994). *The semiotic self*. University of Chicago Press.

Wilshire, Bruce. (1993). 'Body-mind and subconsciousness: Tragedy in Dewey's life and work'. In *Philosophy and the reconstruction of culture: pragmatic essays after Dewey*, edited by John J. Stuhr (Albany, NY: SUNY Press), 257–72.

4 Pragmatist and hermeneutic reflections on the internal conversations that we are

Frédéric Vandenberghe

I would like to defend the thesis that we do not merely have conversations with ourselves, but that we *are* these conversations. By changing the verb, I intend to bring back the conversation into language and conceive of the self as a hermeneutic and semiotic self – as a self-interpreting animal that is suspended in the conversational webs of language and who communicates with others within oneself. By foregrounding language and intersubjectivity, I not only aim to continue the great Socratic tradition of dialogue, but I also want to bring critical realism, pragmatism, hermeneutics and phenomenology into an ongoing conversation.

The mediation of meditation

Grafting pragmatism onto hermeneutics

All thinking is essentially dialogical. Even when we are writing texts, we are always thinking with and talking to others. Whether these others are our predecessors, contemporaries or successors, to use Schütz's typifications, whether they are past writers, future readers, or a bit of both, as is the case with the author who reads what he writes while he thinks, they are always somehow there as members of a virtual, potentially universal audience we are addressing in thought when we are writing. Consequently, our texts are not really texts, but contributions to an ongoing conversation that we inherit from our predecessors, address to our contemporaries and transmit to our successors.

'The conversation that we are is a never ending conversation' (Gadamer, 1995: 140). We are as much in the conversation as the conversation is in us. In his analysis of C.S. Peirce's semiotics of the self, Vincent Colapietro arrived at a similar conclusion. 'From the perspective of semiotics', he says, 'we are always already in the midst of others as well as of meanings; indeed, otherness and meaning are given together in our experiences of ourselves as beings embedded in a network of relations – more specifically, enmeshed in the "semiotic web"' (Colapietro, 1989: 27–28). This convergence and continuity between hermeneutics and pragmatism is, no doubt, an indication that we are on the right path. But with its firm insistence on human subjectivity, reflexivity and consciousness as a phase within action, pragmatism offers a welcome correction to the anti-humanism Gadamer inherited from Heidegger.[1] The existential analytics of *Dasein* is indeed conceived of as a *Fundamentalontologie*, and definitely not as a philosophical anthropology. Although the ontological primacy of the whole over the parts is well taken, one often has the impression that in philosophical hermeneutics it is language that is speaking in conversation rather than the subjects themselves. To foreclose the vanishing of the subject, I will therefore follow pragmatism's lead and think through not only how subjects use language to make sense of their world, their actions and their lives, but how they are also themselves 'processes and products of semiosis' who become who they are thanks to the internal conversations they have with others as well as with themselves.

Following the maxim of pragmatism – 'Consider what effects, that might conceivably have practical bearings, we can conceive the object of our conception to have' (Peirce, 1931–58: 5.2) – we will wade down the stream of consciousness from the antecedent conditions of thought (*terminus a quo*) to their consequences for action in the real world (*terminus ad quem*). To move from hermeneutics to pragmatics implies two movements: first, from the external conversations we have with others to the inner conversation we have with our selves and, then, back from the inner conversations we have *in foro interno* to the external conversations (communications) that take place in everyday life and in the public sphere. To explore the 'concomitant complementarities' between hermeneutics and pragmatism I will have to execute a delicate operation and 'graft' a pragmatic sociology of internal speech onto a phenomenological hermeneutics of language as the medium of conversation. With its focus on interiority, pragmatism extends the spirit of hermeneutics deep into subjectivity, into the self, into the soul. The natural flowing of the spirit of hermeneutics into the soul of pragmatism avoids the traps of solipsism and the quagmires of psychologism. Indeed, if the self is constituted by language in conversation with one's self and others, individual thinking cannot be the starting point for doubting the existence of the other. As Dewey had correctly understood: 'Failure to recognize that this world of inner experience is dependent upon an extension of language which is a social product and operation led to the subjectivistic, solipsistic, and egotistic strain in modern thought' (cited in Rochberg-Halton, 1986: 34).

While hermeneutics proposes language as *arché* and conversation as its medium, pragmatism conceives of the self as its product and the good society as its *telos*. The synthesis of hermeneutics and pragmatism I am proposing has various advantages: it avoids the Cartesianism of transcendental phenomenology; it solidly grounds pragmatism in holism and overcomes the individualism of W. James and H. Blumer; it corrects the political conservatism of German hermeneutics (Heidegger) with the progressivism of the American social reform movement (Dewey); and last but not least, it opens the way to a 'psychological sociology' (Durkheim) of intrasubjective social communication that would at the same time be an 'interspiritual psychology' (Tarde).

Following the lead of Peirce, Dewey, Mead and Cooley, prominent social theorists (Wiley, 1994, Archer, 2003, Collins, 2004) have finally opened the 'black box' of the mind and started to empirically investigate the internal dialogue people have with themselves – they discovered it is a 'chatterbox, full of voices!' In an ongoing dialogue with them, passing the theme through many and varied voices like in a polyphony, I will now move from philosophy to sociology and investigate what internal conversations can do for us.

Back to sociological theory

As sociologists, we are always concerned with the micro-/macro-issue. Whether or not this question has been imposed on us by chroniclers of the discipline (above all Giddens and Alexander), the fact is that, one way or another, we are all thinking about how we could satisfactorily link agency to structure (Giddens), the life-world to the system (Habermas) and the field to the habitus (Bourdieu). Well after the debate had degenerated into the tedium of high scholasticism, Margaret Archer (2003) introduced the theme of internal conversations in her challenge of the 'neo-orthodox consensus' (structuralism + language games).[2] Through a systematic integration of a few central concepts ('analytic dualism', the 'morphogenetic sequence', the ontological 'stratification of society') and theorists (Lockwood, Buckley, Bhaskar), she has convincingly shown (at least in my opinion) that structuration theory collapses structure (culture, structure and social systems) into agency – instead of linking agency to structure, it is busy 'sinking' the distinction (Archer, 1988: xii), as she puts it pithily. Owing to a double compression of agency and structure into practices, Giddens committed the 'fallacy of central conflation' and was, therefore, unable to conceive of either the emergence of a relatively autonomous cultural system from interactions (Archer, 1988) or the supervenience of social structure on the latter (Archer, 1995).

Dualism and reflexivity are connected, because it is only if the distinction between structure and agency is maintained that one can acknowledge that agents have the capability to reflexively examine their projects and their feasibility, given the objective circumstances in which they find themselves and which they have not freely chosen. Thus, agents can only reflect on the structural and cultural conditions of their action if they can distance themselves cognitively from them, be it to analyse them in a more theoretical manner or with the practical intent to change them. To question the rules and claim the resources presupposes reflexivity, not the immediacy that marks routine activity. Without 'paradigmatic dualism' (Mouzelis, 1991), *Verfremdung* (Brecht) or the reflexive estrangement of one's culture and society to analyse it or to change it 'with will and consciousness', cannot be properly theorized.

Now that reflexivity has been brought into the analysis, we can return to the theme of internal conversations. To expose what conversation analysis can do for us sociologists, I will move on to Pierre Bourdieu, whose brand of critical sociology is so well known by now that no introduction is needed. Whoever has seriously meditated on the intra-related concepts of field, habitus and capital, knows that the Achilles heel of the system is lodged in the short shrift it gives to reflexivity (Kögler, 1997; Lahire, 1998; Mouzelis, 2007). In Bourdieu, everything happens as if the subjects were somehow hypnotized into action. Actors are embodied agents rather than conscious 'subjects' (a word the French sociologist studiously avoids). In spite of the fact that habits are part and parcel of the pragmatist conceptual toolbox – for James, but also and above all for Dewey, who conceived of them as a 'dynamic force' (2002: 43)[3] – the habitus functions as the *malin génie* of frictionless reproduction of the social world. Indeed, in Bourdieu, the latter occurs in spite of the subject, thanks to his or her non-reflexivity. To break the circle of reproduction – in fact, it is a circus in which all display the tricks they have learned to play – it is enough to introduce the internal conversations people have with themselves in between the field and the habitus.[4] Through reflection and deliberation, agents ponder what they want to do not only in their life, but *with* their life, and the differential answers they give to these existential questions have implications for the reproduction and transformation of society.

Archer's central thesis – let's call it the 'thesis of the mediation of meditation' – can now be formulated: Reflexivity is exercised through people holding conversations with themselves in which they clarify, organize and systematize their 'ultimate concerns' (Tillich) in an existential and personal project to which they commit themselves. To find out who they are and what their 'mission' is in this life, people have to decide 'what they care about' (Frankfurt), and they do so through an inner dialogue with themselves and significant others.[5] It is this meditation of the actors on what really matters to them and what they are willing to forego or to invest in, in order to realize what they care about and have 'devoted' themselves to, that constitutes the mediatory mechanism which links the causal powers of structure to agency.

Social structures and cultural systems exercise their causal powers by structuring the situation of action through constraints and enablements *inter alia*, but to the extent that the activation of those causal powers depends on the existential projects that the actors forge *in foro interno* (no projects: no constraints or enablements), actors can be said to actively mediate their own social and cultural conditioning. Provided we transform Karl Popper's 'three-world theory' (Popper, 1979) into a 'four-world theory' that takes into account the emergence of social systems without reducing them to practices, it may be used to clarify the topology of the mediation of meditation. World 1 (*physicalia*, i.e. the physical realm of natural objects), World 3 (*intelligibilia*, i.e. the cultural realm of relations between ideas and theories) and World 4 (*sociabilia*, i.e the social realm of relations between positions and roles) are objectively given. They exist independently of 'World 2' (the psychological world of states of consciousness and objects of thought), but Nature, Culture and Society are only linked to each other via internal speech, which belongs to 'World 2'.

In accordance with the 'four-world theory', we can conceive of situations of action as concrete contexts in which actors try to realize their personal projects within the framework of natural, cultural and social circumstances that constitute both the means of achieving their aims and the constraints on that achievement. It is important to note that there is always an interrelation between the personal projects of the subjects and the culture of which they are part (World 3/World 2), as well as between the projects and the facts of both the physical (World 2/

World 1) and the social (World 2/World 4) context. It follows from this that neither the natural nor the cultural nor the social elements of the situation can directly determine the course of action; they can only do so mediately by constraining or enabling the projects. As courses of action are produced through the actor's reflexive deliberations about how they could possibly integrate their 'ultimate concerns' into sustainable life-projects that are feasible in the given circumstances, the constraints and enablements of the situation need to be activated by the actors themselves if they are to exercise their causal powers. Although Archer is conscious of the connection between Culture – which she refers to as the 'Universal Library of Mankind' – Society and internal conversations, I am afraid that in her valiant struggle against de/constructivism, she has significantly underemphasized the importance of language. Gently, I would therefore like to invite her to take the 'linguistic turn', which is, in fact, as we shall see, a turn to alterity and intersubjectivity.

Society, self and mind

Collective subjectivities

Like Peirce and Dewey, George Herbert Mead is a holist, a collectivist and a socialist of sorts. Influenced in his early youth by Hegel, he develops a dialectical social theory in which individual minds are interconnected with each other and brought into society thanks to and through a continuous conversation between the individual Mind and the collective Spirit. Like Dilthey, from whom he took a course when he studied in Berlin, he leaves no doubt about the ontological priority of language and society over the individual: 'The whole (society) is prior to the part (the individual), not the part to the whole; and the part is explained in terms of the whole' (MSS: 7).[6]

Mead's reflections on sociology and social psychology are dialectical exercises in merology (the science of parts and wholes). Societies are cooperative wholes, made up of interactions between elements which are not only parts, but which are wholes themselves. Like groups, individuals are associations of parts that are in interaction, conversation and communication with each other to coordinate their actions into a whole, but as parts of a whole they are themselves wholes, made up of various parts that are in interaction and communication with each other. The conclusion of these merological considerations on communication and conversation between and within parts of all kinds is that, as humans, we are only the end point of an evolution where the conversation becomes conscious of itself (the mind) and of its evolution (science). Speculative as ever, Mead affirms that the appearance of consciousness (of the first and second order) at the individual and collective levels is 'only the culmination of that sociality which is found throughout the universe' (PP: 86).

The movement from cosmology to sociology and social psychology is inwards – from the whole to the parts, from the external to the internal, from communication to imagination. Given the temporal and logical pre-existence of the social process to the self-conscious individual that arises in it, the analysis of the constitution of society has to precede the analysis of the constitution of the self. The constitution of the self is, after all, only a phase within the constitution of society. Consequently, the book that made Mead famous should really have been entitled *Society, Self and Mind* rather than the reverse.

All considered, symbolic interactionism is first and foremost a theory of linguistically mediated collective action. Its subject is society, understood as a 'collective subjectivity' that makes society.[7] Like all idealists, Mead neglects the systemic environments in which symbolically mediated interactions take place and tends to reduce society at large to an ongoing sequence of interactions of interactions, associations of associations or organizations of organizations. We might as well say that collective subjectivities do not only make society; they *are* society. Society is, ultimately, a subjective collectivity in the making that is becoming conscious of itself and that coincides, at the limit, with humanity as such.

Against this humanist background, one can better understand why Mead continuously insists on the necessity of adopting the perspective of the 'generalized other', which he identifies, in a first moment, with the 'whole community' and, in a second moment, with the 'universe of discourse'. By taking the perspective of the 'generalized other', the individual interprets his own action in relation to the actions of the other members of society and understands it as a contribution to collective action – a contribution that may well determine the direction of society.[8] The logic behind this social capability of the individuals to engage in concerted action and to interweave their action into a collective act is definitely organicist and functionalist – almost Durkheimian in its understanding of the division of labour as a form of social cooperation.[9] In the same way that the individual player of an organized game is able to collaborate with the other members of the team by understanding his own position in the total field of collective action, any member of a given community is, in principle, able not only to understand his function, but also to organize his own behaviour in the function of a larger whole of which he is part. As knowledge of the whole is 'distributed' over the agents in such a way that each member knows not only what the others know, but has also almost complete knowledge of what each member of the community knows, the agents use that collective knowledge to help solve a common problem of action or to realize a common plan.[10] The result of cooperation is a collective product that all have in mind and to which each has consciously contributed his part. 'It may be as different from the sum of what the individuals could have thought out in separation as a ship built by a hundred men is from a hundred boats each built by one man' (Cooley, 1983: 21).

For Mead, society is not a substance, but a verb that is conjugated in the first person plural. Each of the individuals is engaged in a complex series of organized acts that are moving toward a common end and that are continuously monitored in the process. The integration of all the individual acts into a common process is controlled in the movement, through continuous exchange of mutual perspectives, by the anticipation of the realization of the final cause.

Let us take a micro-example – a team of surgeons performing an operation *together*. A number of professionals are directly involved in the performance on and around the operation table. All attention is focused on a small part of the patient's body and each member of the working team is closely monitoring the acts of the surgeon and her assistants, while keeping an eye on the medical machinery. As a social object, the body means different things to all the persons involved, including the patient (and his family). An assistant hands the scalpel to the surgeon. She takes it without looking and nods, while another assistant prepares to remove the blood that will start to ooze in less than half a minute. Each anticipates the acts of the others and organizing their own response to the call of the other, their actions together constitute a single collective act that is moving towards a common end (which, for reasons of decency, I prefer not to call the 'final cause'). Let's now take another bloody example, but a macro one – war. However destructive the aim, it can only be brought off through the cooperation of all. As Kenneth Burke wrote: 'Millions of cooperative acts go into the preparation of one single act. Modern war characteristically requires a myriad of constructive acts for each destructive one; before each culminating blast there must be a vast network of interlocking operations, directed communally' (cited in Perinbanayagam, 2003: 76).

What holds for one community also holds for the next community. In pragmatism, society is conceived of as a multiplicity of interacting communities, each made up in turn of multiple primary and secondary groups (cities, neighbourhoods, gangs, families, etc.). Through identification and 'dis-identification' with the societies, communities, and sub-communities of which one is a member, collective subjectivities wax and wane. At any given moment, any denizen can join one of the multiple communities s/he belongs to in order to contribute to its functioning, making it stronger in the process, or defect from it, weakening it. By literally taking another role, I can change my social identity but, simultaneously, I can also join a group and cooperate towards the actualization of its potential. As I am writing this text in my office, some of my social identities (e.g. member of the Reflexivity Forum, hermeneutician and would-be pragmatist) are activated, while others (e.g. Belgian expat, amateur of fine chocolates) are de-activated. In any case, the possibility of simultaneous identifications that make and break collective subjectivities opens up a third way between nominalism and realism. Collectives are real to the extent that their potential is actualized; to the extent that it remains virtual they are nominal. But nothing precludes that a potential group, like the glorious Proletariat of yore, regains force as a world historical actor or that a powerful actor, like the bankers of Wall Street, becomes demoralized and weakened.

The standpoint of social behaviourism

I have often wondered about the reference to the 'standpoint of social behaviorism' that appears in the subtitle of *Mind, Self and Society*. I can only make sense of it in terms of the distinction between covert/internal/potential and overt/external/actual behaviour, which 'gears into the external world and alters it', as Schütz (1962: 20, 67, *passim*) would say. Whereas overt behaviour is observable, covert behaviour is not. Mead did not deny the existence of the mind, far from it, but he had serious doubts about the scientific use of the method of sympathetic introspection. To understand the meaning of human action, one does not need to enter into the mind of others to find out what they think. Instead of working from an elusive inside to an expressive outside, one should rather work from the visible (or audible) outside to the invisible (or inaudible) inside and consider the 'minding' as a phase within the organization of a publicly observable act. 'The act, then, and not the tract, is the fundamental datum in both social and individual psychology' (MSS: 8). It is not some psychic state that is the object of pragmatic inquiry, but the act in its totality and its sociality, as it is expressed in language. 'There's no private language', as Wittgensteinians are wont to repeat. Language is common and it is public. The meanings which are processed privately *in foro interno* are public meanings. Thinking is a moment of the organization of the collective act and should be understood as such. 'We want to approach language not from the standpoint of inner meanings to be expressed, but in its larger context of cooperation in the group taking place by means of signals and gestures. Meaning appears within that process' (MSS: 6) and, in good pragmatic fashion, it appears as its consequence.

The meaning is in the open, it is articulated within language as discourse. Instead of trying to get at deep meanings and inner states of the individual, one should understand inner conversations not only as internalizations of public communication, but also as public modes of description of inner thought that configure action as collective action (Cefaï, 1998: 246–61). In other words, the reasons and motives of actors that give meaning to their actions should be understood as 'vocabularies of motives' (Mills, 1940) or, as your local ethnomethologist would have it, as 'accounts' of action that are out there, not in the head of the actors. As Garfinkel (1990: 6) once said: 'There's nothing in the head of interest to us, but brains'.[11]

Interestingly, semiotics and hermeneutics converge once again. When we understand a text, or action as a 'quasi-text' (Ricoeur, 1986: 205–36), it is not a matter of penetrating into the spiritual activities of the author; it is simply a question of grasping the meaning or sense (*Sinn*) of the text. As Gadamer (1990: 297) says, with the force of conviction: 'The meaning of hermeneutical inquiry is to disclose the miracle of understanding texts or utterances and not the mysterious communication of souls. Understanding is participation in the common aim'. The question is, undoubtedly, an important one. In external as well as in internal communication, something comes into language. What we want to understand is not so much what is behind the text (the mind), but rather what is in front of it – the reference, what language talks about, the world.

To understand what someone says does not mean to transpose oneself in the mind of the other to re-live her experiences, but to understand what she meant. Although the meaning is intersubjective – it is what the conversation is about – it is also objective and in this sense, independent of the speakers. When the conversation is a successful one, the speakers come to a common understanding and a consensus on the issue. What matters is the thing (*die Sache*) one is thinking about in conversation – the thought not the thinker.[12] And in any case, to understand the thinker, whether it is oneself or another who's doing the thinking, one has to make a detour through signs (Peirce) and symbols (Gadamer). As Ricoeur (1986: 33) says – but one can find similar ideas in Peirce and Mead: 'There's no understanding of self that is not mediated by signs, symbols and texts'. In hermeneutics and semiotics, the way to the self is a long, winding and arduous one. Self-reflection is not direct, but mediated and broken by a triple detour through language, false consciousness and unconscious desires and, last but not least, the other (Ricoeur, 1969: 7–28).

This methodological position explains Mead's (1964) reticence with regard to Cooley's introspective sociology of the larger mind, which he otherwise admired. When Cooley proposed to write an 'autobiography of society', Mead thought the object was too hazy, not to say mystical, to be submitted to scientific investigation. Indeed, for Cooley, society is in the last instance an 'imagined community' of fellows that exists in our own mind: 'The human mind is social, society is mental [...] Society, then, in its immediate aspect, is a relation among personal ideas. In order to have society it is evidently necessary that persons should get together somewhere; and they get together only as personal ideas in the mind. Where else? Society exists in my mind. It exists in your mind as a similar group, and so in every mind. [...] Persons and society must, then, be studied primarily in the imagination [...] I conclude, therefore, that the imaginations people have of one another are the *solid facts* of society, and that to observe and interpret these must be a chief aim of sociology' (Cooley, 1964: 81, 119–21).

Although Mead was quite taken by Cooley's sentimental vision of a society of selves that are in continuous communication and conversation with each other, he objected that this conception was mental, not scientific: 'The locus of society is not in the mind, in the sense in which Cooley uses the term, and the approach to it is not by introspection, though what goes on in the inner forum of our experience is essential to meaningful communication' (Mead, 1964: xxxvi). Indeed, although we need to imagine society in thought if we are to coordinate our actions in the real world, society is extra-mental. It exists *extra nos et praeter nos*.

Intrasubjective intersubjectivity

The self and its other

By reading Mead backwards – from society to the self rather than the other way round – we have analysed the constitution of society as a 'collective subjectivity'. The time has now come to investigate the constitution of the self and the mind, which are at the very heart of his social psychology, *from within*. Mead's main thesis is well known: the mind and the self are social through and through. As personal properties, they emerge out of social life and are linguistically mediated. When it comes to the reflexive capacities of man, Mead is indeed a social constructivist – and so am I – but he also allows for the existence of non- and pre-reflexive spheres. As a pragmatist he does not deny that prior to an awareness of self and prior to the mind, there is 'the world that is there' (Miller, 1973: 88–102). Neither does he affirm that the world out there arises out of consciousness. It is rather the reverse: consciousness emerges out of, as well as in our engagement with the world that is there and it is constituted by social interaction and communication with others.

Although we are concerned with the self, we have to start with the mind, however, for the self presupposes thinking. To explain how the mind emerges, Mead has recourse to the gesture and starts his investigation of thinking with Wundt's 'conversation of gestures'. He opens the analysis with the legendary fight between two dogs, but quickly moves on to linguistically mediated communication between humans. The obvious aim of this move is to connect the mind to symbolism and self-consciousness to language. When 'significant symbols' are brought in, the conversation of gestures becomes a meaningful one. Taking the role of each other, each of the actors projects himself in the position of the other. Adopting his attitude, he does not only see himself as the other sees him, but he also hears himself as the other hears him. The crucial point is that thanks to the symbolization of gestures, each actor can arouse in himself the response he is calling out in the other. 'The importance, then, of the vocal stimulus lies in this fact that the individual can hear what he says and in hearing what he says is tending to respond as the other person responds' (MSS: 69–70). As the meaning is a shared one, the interlocutors can understand each other.

To understand each other, the actors have, however, to make the detour via the 'general other' and adopt the perspective of any ordinary language user. Through mutual adjustment of the expectations to one another, they can then, eventually, coordinate their actions. But before they act jointly, there is thinking, and according to Mead, who follows Cooley on this point, thinking is essentially an internalized, implicit and covert conversation the individual has with himself by means of symbols: 'Since higher thought involves language, it is always a kind of imaginary conversation' (Cooley, 1964: 92). 'The internalization of the external conversations of gestures which we carry on with other individuals in the social process is the essence of thinking' (MSS: 47). Thinking may be internal and take place in the individual's mind; it is nevertheless essentially a social phenomenon that finds its origin in communication. The individual is the locus of thought, but the contents of his thought are public. The meanings are not his, but they are common to all subjects who speak the language. Similarly, the symbols he uses are part of the process of communication and belong to a relational field, and it out of this field that mind arises. 'Out of language emerges the field of mind' (MSS: 47).

In the same way as the thought presupposes language, the self presupposes the other: 'We must be others if we are to be ourselves' (PP: 194).[13] There's no subjectivity without intersubjectivity and, we may add, no intersubjectivity without language. In vaguely Hegelian fashion, Mead defines the self (*ipse*) reflexively as a subject who experiences himself as an object. The self or *ipse* in Latin (*das Selbst* in German, *le soi* in French, or *si mesmo* in Portuguese) is a reflexive pronoun in the third person that has the particularity of being able to refer to all personal pronouns. Following Ricoeur (1990: 11–14, 137–66), I conceive of self-identity not in terms of formal or substantial sameness (*idem*), but as a reflexive, dialogical and narrative process of selfhood (*ipse*) that interweaves continuity and change through continuous, lifelong conversation between the self and the other, within or without oneself. Although I cannot develop the point here, I would like to defend a narrative conception of self identity. Narration is what 'emplots' and directs the internal conversation. To properly understand how personal identity is formed, one has to understand that the internal conversation takes the form of a narration, while the narration itself has to be understood as a conversation that is intrasubjectively intersubjective. Not only does one have conversations with 'oneself as another' (Ricoeur), but also with 'the other as oneself' (Mead). It is through an internal conversation with oneself that one communicates with the other. Even if one narrates one's self, the other remains present as an 'inner witness' of the personal identity to which I commit myself and for which I am morally accountable and ultimately responsible' (Vandenberghe, 2005: 233).

The subject who minds the other becomes an object to himself. He is both subject and object – or as Adam Smith (1976: 113) has it, both a spectator and an agent – and he knows that he is.[14] He becomes reflexive and conscious of himself as another, thanks to the other (and not owing to the other, as is the case in Sartre's existentialism, where the gaze of the other transforms the subject into an object that is under surveillance). By placing himself in the perspective of the other, he becomes an object to himself, but without, however, objectifying or reifying himself in such a way that his subjectivity gets lost (Kögler, 2009). The subject experiences himself as a self only through the mediation of others. To become a self, the subject has to see himself from the external standpoint of another self or, more generally, from any other self who has been fully socialized and can adopt the perspective of the 'participant observer' in the field of social action.

It is important to underscore that the subject does not have an immediate consciousness or unmediated awareness of himself. It is only by imagining what the other thinks of him, by anticipating the response he is going to evoke in the other, that he calls out in himself the response of the other. Through socialization, the subject is able to get outside of himself not just into the perspective of the concrete other (dad and mum, Peter and Paula), but of a 'general other', any other who knows not only the rules of the game (like an observer), but who also knows how to play it (like a participant). Language is crucial here, because it is largely through the mediation of language that the subject is socialized in such a way that he can enter into the perspective of the generalized other and understand himself as any other understands him. When the response of the general other is thus 'into' the subject – as the stimulus is 'into' the response, according to Dewey –, the subject becomes an object to himself and sees his self reflected in the mirror society holds up to him. 'Each to each a looking glass/reflects the other that doth pass' (Cooley, 1964: 184). Contrary to what edifying pragmatists may think, our essence is indeed a 'glassy one' (Rorty, 1979: 42–5). Our self reflects in the other like in a mirror (but beware of analogies: as the images continually change, so does the mirror itself). We become who we are, through reflection (as in a mirror) and conversation (as in speech). The point of *Bildung* (or edification) is not only to keep the conversation going, as Rorty has it, but also to find our own subjective truth. It is (partly) out of an image that society holds up to us that each develops a more or less coherent sense of self. To the extent that self is not a given, but a task, we can amend Freud's famous dictum: Where the Other was, I shall become.

The self, however, is not a unitary thing. Neither thing, nor unitary, it refers, in fact, to a duality within the subject. 'Two souls, alas, do dwell within his breast'. Insisting once more on the dynamic nature of everything, Mead conceives of the self as a process of alternation between two phases or poles, which he calls respectively the 'I' and the 'Me'.[15] The 'I' is linked to spontaneity and creativity, whereas the 'Me' is the organized set of attitudes of the community within the self. Like the impartial spectator, the 'Me' is the 'great inmate of the breast' (Smith, 1976: 130, 134, 262). If the 'Me' represents society as it appears in the mind's eye or, to switch from vision to voice, in the conversation one has with oneself, the 'I' stands for the spontaneous, impulsive reaction toward the collective. The 'I' is aware of the 'Me' and responds to it with varying degrees of creativity. When the 'I' is fully awake and potent, it brings novelty into the conversation. When it is completely knackered, it basically repeats the lines it knows. In reacting creatively to the community, the 'I' changes it, for the better or for the worst. 'The I appears in our experience in memory. It is only when we have spoken that we know what we have said' (MSS: 196). We all know from experience that however much we may rehearse an anticipated conversation in thought, the conversation we will actually have will be different from the one we imagined. It may even derail and go off track, leaving us astonished and the other flabbergasted by what we just said. 'Did I say that? Where did that come from?' is a common expression of surprise when one realizes that the 'I' 'acted out'. The 'I' speaks and the 'Me' listens. And then retrospectively, when 'I' can look back on myself, 'I' can see that by activating a train of memory in my mind, 'I' have made a new connection between ideas and brought some novelty into the world, which can then be stored and integrated in the 'Me' (my own personal one, but also, through communication, the collective one) as a fund on which I can draw next time when 'I' will resume the conversation and try out a new line.

Conversations on the great society

With the dialogical alternation between the 'I' and the 'Me', Mead has introduced a transformative dialectics of the self into his semiotic theory of self-reflexivity. In the conversation of the self, everything happens as if the American pragmatist had somehow transposed the dynamics between 'langue' and 'parole' of French semiology into the subject's self. If the 'I' has the capability to reflect on the stance of society and critically to respond to it, the demon of stable social reproduction within the self is silenced from the start. But, to become truly critical, innovative and creative, the dialogue has to become properly dialectical. This happens when the dialogue becomes conscious of itself – as in dialogue on dialogue, reflection on reflection, thinking about thinking, noêsis noesêos – and the self transcends its own society to project itself in the direction of an ideal society of free, autonomous and self-determining subjects. When dialogue shifts out into dialectics, the dialogue becomes transgressive and builds in the telos of universal communication into its own functionings. I like to think that this is what Mead had in mind when, in the final pages of the book, he drew moral and political conclusions and invoked 'the attainment of a universal human society' as 'the ultimate goal of human social progress' (MSS: 310).

From this utopian perspective of a fully reflexive self, formed by a continuous dialogue between a creative 'I' and a future 'Me', we can overcome the conventional conception of an 'oversocialized self' that has all the trappings not of a person, but of a personage who spends his or her life playing the role society has allocated to him or her. The fully reflexive self incorporates not so much the histrionic figure of the actor (the *prosopeion* of the Greeks and *persona* of the Romans, meaning the mask) who acts out society's script with a modicum of originality, as the one of the director who integrates the different phases of the self into a more or less coherent, harmonious personal project that is at once individual and social, singular and universal. The subject is not 'subjected' to society (the *hypokeimenon* as *subjectum*); s/he is a subject or a person in the emphatic sense of the term – someone who is at the same time fully human, fully social and fully herself – or himself. In Mead as in Dewey, the personal quest for the 'good life' is intrinsically connected to, and inseparable from, 'the search for the great community' (Dewey, 1954: 143–84). In a just and democratic society, the self-determination of the people and the self-realization of the person are two sides (external/internal) of the same coin. As in a virtuous circle, there is a continuous morphogenesis between the external and the internal dialectics. In a vibrant democracy, society becomes conscious of itself as a collective subject that determines itself, while its subjects are equally self-conscious as autonomous, yet interdependent subjects: 'There then arises a community in which everyone can be both subject and sovereign, sovereign in so far as he asserts his own rights and recognizes them in others, and subject in that he obeys the laws which he himself makes' (MSS: 287, note 17).

The self-identity of the fully reflexive person of the 'great community' is not conventional, but 'post-conventional' (in the sense that Kohlberg and Habermas have given to this concept). Rather than adopting the perspective of the existing society that judges acts through 'formal-rational' application of the law, s/he imagines an ideal and 'unlimited community of communication' of which s/he is a member and appeals to this higher court to contest the judgement of first instance. 'All intelligent political criticism is comparative' (Dewey, 1954: 110) – the critic sets up a larger community that transcends the specific order of which s/he is part and, taking the attitude of this ideal community, s/he anticipates its realization in thought and judges the existing society in the name of Reason (or, if one prefers, of one's own conscience).

Through the invocation of a higher and larger self, 'practical reason is both socialized and temporalized' (Habermas, 1988: 224) – socialized, because the projection of a hypothetical kingdom of ends has to be validated and recognized by one's contemporaries (potentially, by all; counterfactually, it even includes predecessors and successors) and temporalized, because the idealized form of communication is not only projected into a future, but presupposed as an existing moment of transcendence that grounds critique. Now, to the extent that this future society within one's breast has to be recognized by one's fellows as a legitimate one, individualism and universalism go hand in hand. Entering into the perspective of a larger community that coincides at the limit with the fulfilment of humanity as such, the individual projects and presents a future 'Me' that has to be recognized and validated by the others.[16] Given that this virtual identity is inevitably part of the individual's current identity; given, moreover, that the individual has to get out of himself to take on the perspective of a supposed 'impartial spectator' – 'this demigod within the breast' (Smith, 1976: 131); given, finally, that the individual has to adopt this perspective in the first person – 'never as a mere representative, but always in *propria persona*' (Habermas, 1988: 231) – the 'Me' is encouraged to remain him or herself, even when s/he adopts the perspective of society. As the spectator, thus, necessarily coincides with the actor, socialization is in no way opposed to individualization, but most emphatically includes it.

Conclusion

In the same way that socialization and individualization are complementary phases within a dynamic process, external communication and internal conversation have to be considered not in opposition to, but in continuity with each other. To show that the internal conversation continues external communication and is destined to return to it to strengthen it, let me refer to the debate between Jürgen Habermas and John Rawls. To maintain the drift of the argument I'll give a pragmatic spin to it and connect it to the theory of moral sentiments. A *Theory of Justice* by John Rawls (1972) is, without doubt, one of the most important books of the second half of the twentieth century. In spite of the fact that every page and footnote of the book has been submitted over and again to analysis and commentary, the book is mostly read as a liberal version of rational choice. Consequently, its connections with Adam Smith's theory of sympathy have been overlooked.[17] The guiding idea of the theory of justice is simple: a society would be just if it redistributed rights and duties in such a way that every one of its members would subscribe to the principle of fairness without reserve, because it would guarantee the rights and liberties of all, while accepting social inequalities only to the extent that it compensates the least advantaged.

The theory of justice is a strong theory of the social contract. The main device of this contract theory is the so-called 'original position' (Rawls, 1972: 1–53, esp. 17 ff.) in which each would be invited to adopt the perspective of a reasonable, yet sympathetic spectator before signing the contract that seals the alliance between the members. Thus, each would imagine him or herself in the position of the other and, when each would have adopted the perspective of all the others *seriatim*, s/he would hypothetically arrive at the principles of justice for the basic structure of well ordered society. Of course, this mechanism of serial identification of all with each and every one can only function on the condition that everyone abstracts from their own personal and social situation to retain only what is common to all human beings without distinction. In other words, in imagining oneself in the situation of the other to ascend to the superior and encompassing position of the impartial spectator, each is placed under a 'veil of ignorance'. As one would not know if the other is rich or poor, black or white, male or female, we can assume that the principles the members would hypothetically adopt to order their society would be just, not in spite of the anonymous character of the other, but rather because of it.

In Rawls, the justification and validation of the principles of the social contract are the result of the simulated internal conversations the impartial spectator has with his fellow citizens. The spectator sets up an 'inner forum' (Mead, MT: 375 and 401) in which he confers with himself. 'He asks and answers questions. He develops his ideas and arranges and organizes those ideas as he might do in a conversation with somebody else. [...] It has not yet become public. But it is part of an act which does become public. We will say that he is thinking out what he is going to say in an important situation, an argument which he is going to present in court, a speech in the legislature. That process which goes on inside of him is only the beginning of the process which is finally carried on in an assembly' (Mead, MT: 402).

In setting up this internal forum within himself everything happens as if the sympathetic spectator, comfortably seated on his couch after a long day of work, had called before his mind any person of his acquaintance and invited him or her into his internal conversation in the evening.[18] In his mind, he entreated his friends and acquaintances to sit next to him, discoursing with them about the principles that would be the object of the original agreement. Having left his dear friends, while enclosing them in the depths of his heart, he continued the imaginary conversation by inviting the friends of his friends to the dialogue. Eventually, through an eidetic variation of the friends of his friends, he arrived at a generic and faceless, but well informed, concerned and caring citizen who would 'look at the system from the standpoint of the least advantaged representative man' (Rawls, 1972, 151).

Through the clever device of representation of the original position, Rawls has thus created a public space in his innermost heart (*in foro interno*, as Kant would say). Habermas objected to the privacy of the internal conversations of his friend. Inviting his American colleague for a public debate, the German philosopher had gently convinced his colleague *in actu* of the necessity of continuing the internal conversation in an external exchange among equals that takes place in the public sphere.[19] It is by public communication, not just by internal conversation, that speakers progressively arrive at the common and impartial view of the 'Great Judge' (Smith, 1976: 262) or, more affectionately, the 'Great Companion' (James, 1950, I: 316). By inviting not only their friends who share their views, but also the neighbours who don't share them to *voice* their opinions in public, the citizens persuade one another, by means of the force of the better argument, of what is just or wrong.

According to Habermas, moral and political principles become objective and universal through the public use of speech and reason. Indeed, thanks to communication, the citizens can have mutual knowledge of the positions of the others and, thereby arrive, through overlap of the common content that is publicly communicated and commonly shared, at a consensus on the very principles that order a just society. By transforming the internal conversations that the sympathetic observer has with himself and all the others into a real communication among participants of an external conversation, we move at the same time from the private (Rawls) to the public (Habermas) use of speech. There is thus an ongoing dialectic – or a 'double morphogenesis', as Archer would say – between internal and external conversations. When the communication is over, the participants can continue the debate internally, and after mature reflection, they can then join the external conversation again. As the internal conversations are constitutive of who we are, individually and collectively, the reconstruction of society cannot be separated from the reconstruction of the human mind. To change society we have to change ourselves, and as the only thing we can change right now is ourselves, why not start social reconstruction with an internal revolution? After all, that is how mankind evolves to higher stages of development. 'Or in short, social reconstruction and self or personality reconstruction are the two sides of a single process – the process of human evolution' (MSS: 309).

Notes

1 What matters to Heidegger is not Man, but Being and what comes into being by Man. What Heidegger (1964) says about thinking in his *Letter on Humanism* also holds for language: 'Thinking is, in sum, the thinking of Being. The genitive has a double sense. The thinking is of Being in so far as thinking that partakes of Being belongs to Being. Thinking is at the same time the thinking of Beings in so far as it belongs and listens to Being (34). [...] Not Man but Being is essential (84) [...]. What matters is to put *humanitas* at the service of the truth of Being, but without the humanism in a metaphysical sense (138)'.

2 For a more extended presentation of Archer's morphogenetic social theory, I refer the reader to my review of the first four volumes of 'The Archers' (Vandenberghe, 2005). For a personal overview of the two decades taken to develop the morphogenetic approach, see Archer, 2007.

3 'Habit means a special sensitiveness or accessibility to certain classes of stimuli, standing predilections and aversions, rather than bare recurrence of specific acts. It means will' (Dewey, 2002: 42). In William James, habits are rather more sturdy. His philosophy of habits is, in the first instance, 'a chapter in physics' (James, 1950, I: 105). Approvingly, he quotes the Duke of Wellington: 'Habit a second nature! Habit is ten times nature' (Ibid., 120).

4 In my own take on Bourdieu (1999: 50), I had collocated Blumer's 'self-interaction' and Habermas's 'rational communication' in between the field and the habitus, but I concur that internal conversations are more elegant and powerful. To unhinge Bourdieu's system, one could also bring in a little existential crisis and see what that does to reproduction. I thank Gabriel Peters for this astute observation.

5 Although faith is, undoubtedly, the ultimate concern, it should be noticed that the internal conversations and the sequence that interlink concerns, projects and practices into a personal *modus vivendi* do not necessarily lead to heaven. 'There is nothing idealistic here, because "concerns" can be ignoble, "projects" illegal and "practices" illegitimate' (Archer, 2007b: 42). It would be interesting, though definitely not uplifting, to empirically track the internal conversations of youngsters from the *favelas* in Brazil who have been enrolled by the *narcotrafico* and transformed into 'soldiers' who attack to defend their turf and kill in order not to die.

6   All references to Mead's books are abbreviated as follows: PP (*The Philosophy of the Present*, 1932); MSS (*Mind, Self and Society*, 1934); MT (*Movements of Thought in the Nineteenth Century*, 1936) and PA (*The Philosophy of the Act*, 1938).

7   From a realist perspective, it is obvious that symbolic interactionism has difficulties in grasping the more structural and systemic aspects of society. Instead of granting to materialists and structuralists that collective subjectivities intervene in society, it identifies society with collective subjectivity, i.e. with a 'subjectivity of higher order', to speak like Husserl and Peirce. For an attempt to conceptualize societies and collective subjectivities in more realist terms, see Vandenberghe, 2007.

8   By conceiving of the mechanism of role taking as a moment in the coordination of action, Mead has given a cognitivist and pragmatic interpretation of sympathy and kindred moral sentiments, but without openly saying so. In the Scottish tradition of moral philosophy, role taking is linked to judgement: We see ourselves through the eyes of the other, observe ourselves in imagination as the other sees us and judge accordingly. As the moralist Adam Smith says: 'We either approve or disapprove of our own conduct, according as we feel that, when we place ourselves in the situation of another man, and view it, as it were, with his eyes and from his station. We endeavour to examine our own conduct as we imagine any other fair and impartial spectator would examine it' (Smith, 1976: 109–10). As can be gathered from this quotation, Mead's 'generalized other' is only an alias of Smith's 'impartial spectator'.

9   Mead's universal communitarianism chimes all too well with Durkheim's republican individualism. Both converge in a functionalist reinterpretation of Kant: 'The categorical imperative of moral conscience is taking the following form: prepare yourself to ultimately accomplish a determinate function' (Durkheim, 1986: 7).

10 For an outstanding presentation of 'distributed knowledge' (Norman, Hutchins, Kirsch, Conein) by one of the leading figures of the new French pragmatist sociology, see Quéré, 1997.

11 Inspired by Wittgenstein, Bakhtin, Volosinov or Vygotsky, the most interesting constructivist psychologists (like Rom Harré, Kenneth Gergen, John Shotter, Hubert Hermans), who focus on discourse and dialogue have arrived at similar conclusions. Namely, that one has to study cognition where it lives, in discourse. Wielding Ockham's razor, Rom Harré (1992: 6) goes too far, however when he decapitates the head and eliminates the mind: 'Not only is there no one thing that is thinking, in many cases there is clearly only the overt discursive activity. The myth of the mind has come perhaps from the observation that one soon learns to do privately (behind one's face, so to speak) what one first learned to do publicly'.

12 Personal experience confirms this conclusion. As I was thinking and writing intensively about internal conversations to write this chapter, I was out of myself – 'into the text', as I said to my friends to apologize for my being unavailable for external conversations. When I went to see my psychoanalyst to get my narratives straight, I had nothing personal to say, so we talked about the self in social psychology.

13 Unlike persons, who can exist by themselves (by the mere grace of God), selves are dialectical. The self presupposes, by definition, a non-self or other, either within or without oneself. Analytically speaking, the self cannot be a loner. As the relation between self and other is an internal one, the self presupposes the other as the other presupposes the self. Both are mutually constituted in and through the relation. The self, the other and the relation itself that constitutes them are one – three in one, one in three, like in the trinity.

14 What Mead analyses in a cognitive way, is described by Smith (1976: 113) in an affective and moral key: 'When I endeavour to examine my own conduct, I divide myself, as it were, in two persons. The first is the spectator, whose sentiments with regard to my own conduct I endeavour to enter into, by placing myself in his situation, and by considering how it would appear to me, when seen from that particular point of view. The second is the agent, the person whom I properly call myself, and of whose conduct,

72   F. Vandenberghe

under the character of a spectator, I was endeavouring to form some opinion. The first is the judge; the second the 'person judged of'.

15 Some commentators on Mead have interpreted the 'I' and the 'Me' as avatars of Freud's Id and Superego. More sophisticated readers have recognized the transcendental Ego of Kant in the 'I' and the Alter Ego of Freud in the 'Me'.

16 Drawing on the *Critique of Judgement*, Alessandro Ferrara (1998) has introduced the Kantian concept of 'reflexive judgement' into moral philosophy and developed an ambitious theory of reflexive authenticity that integrates the singularity of the self with the universal acclaim of its exemplarity. He not only advocates authenticity as a normative ideal, but also holds that authenticity, understood as 'exemplary congruency of an individual, collective or symbolic identity with itself', provides us with a new ideal of universal validity that shifts the emphasis away from the generalizable toward the exemplary and the authentic. Just like well-formed works of art, authentic identities inspire in us a sense of admiration.

17 As far as I can see, only feminist philosophers like Susan Moller Okin (1989) and Seyla Benhabib (1992: 148–77) have seen the connection between Rawls and Adam Smith, reason and feeling, justice and benevolence, fairness and care.

18 In a delightful passage, Cooley quotes Goethe's thought experiment, in which he speaks of himself in the third person: 'Accustomed to pass his time most pleasantly in society, he changed even solitary thought into social converse, and this in the following manner: He had the habit, when he was alone, of calling before his mind any person of his acquaintance. This person he entreated to sit down, walked up and down by him, remained standing before him and discoursed with him on the subject he had in mind' (Cooley, 1964: 91; see also Wiley, 1994: 54–5).

19 See the debate between two of the greatest political philosophers of the twentieth century in *Journal of Philosophy*, 1995, 93, 3.

References

Archer, M. (1988): *Culture and Agency. The Place of Culture in Social Theory*. Cambridge: Cambridge University Press.

Archer, M. (1995): *Realist Social Theory: The Morphogenetic Approach*. Cambridge University Press.

Archer, M. (2003): *Structure, Agency and the Internal Conversation*. Cambridge: Cambridge University Press.

Archer, M. (2007): 'The Trajectory of the Morphogenetic Approach. An account in the First-Person', *Sociologia. Problemas e práticas*, 54, 35–47.

Benhabib, S. (1992): *Situating the Self. Gender, Community and Postmodernism in Contemporary Ethics*. London: Routledge.

Cefaï, D. (1998): *Phénoménologie et sciences sociales. Alfred Schutz. Naissance d'une anthropologie philosophique*. Genève: Droz.

Colapietro, V. (1989): *Peirce's Approach to the Self. A semiotic Perspective on Human Subjectivity*. Albany: Suny.

Collins, R. (2004): *Interaction Ritual Chains*. Princeton: Princeton University Press.

Cooley, C. (1964): *Human Nature and the Social Order*. New York: Schocken Books.

Cooley, C. (1983): *Social Organization. A Study of the Larger Mind*. New Brunswick: Transaction Books.

Dewey, J. (2002): *Human Nature and Conduct*. New York: Dover.

Durkheim, E. (1986): *De la division du travail social*. Paris: P.U.F.

Ferrara, A. (1998): *Reflective Authenticity. Rethinking the Project of Modernity*. London: Routledge.

Gadamer, H. G. (1990): *Hermeneutik I*, in *Gesammelte Werke*, Band 1. Tübingen: Mohr.

Gadamer, H. G. (1995): *Hermeneutik im Rückblick*, in *Gesammelte Werke*, Band 10. Tübingen: Mohr.

Garfinkel, H. (1990): 'A Conception of, and Experiments with, "Trust" as a Condition of Stable, Concerted Actions', in Coulter, J. (ed.), *Ethnomethodological Sociology*. Aldershot: Ashgate Publishing.

Habermas, J. (1991): *Texte und Kontexte*. Frankfurt am Main: Suhrkamp.

Harré, R. (1992): "The Second Cognitive Revolution", *American Behavioral Scientist*, 36, 1, 5–7.

Heidegger, M. (1964): *Lettre sur l'humanisme/Über den Humanismus*. Paris: Aubier.

James, W. (1950): *The Principles of Psychology*, 2 vols. New York: Dover Publications.

Kögler, H. (1997): 'Alienation as Epistemological Source: Reflexivity and Social Background after Mannheim and Bourdieu', *Social Epistemology*, 11:2:141–64.

Lahire, B. (1998): *L'homme pluriel. Les ressorts de l' action*. Paris, Nathan.

Mead, G. H. (1932): *The Philosophy of the Present*. Chicago: Chicago University Press.

Mead, G.H. (1934): *Mind, Self and Society from the Standpoint of a Social Behaviorist*. Chicago: Chicago University Press.

Mead, G.H. (1936): *Movements of Thought in the Nineteenth Century*. Chicago: Chicago University Press.

Mead, G.H. (1938): *The Philosophy of the Act*. Chicago: Chicago University Press.

Mead, G. H. (1964): 'Foreword: Cooley's Contribution to American Social Thought' pp. xxi–xxxviii in Cooley, C.H.: *Human Nature and the Social Order*. New York: Schocken Books.

Miller, D. (1973): *George Herbert Mead. Self, Language and the World*. Chicago: Chicago University Press.

Mills, C. W. (1940): 'Situated Actions and Vocabularies of Motives', *American Sociological Review*, 5, pp. 904–13.

Moller Okin, S. (1989): 'Reason and Feeling in Thinking about Justice', *Ethics*, 99, 2, 229–49.

Mouzelis, N. (1991): *Back to Sociological Theory. The Construction of Social Orders*. London: Macmillan.

Mouzelis, N. (2007): 'Habitus and Reflexivity: Restructuring Bourdieu's Theory of Practice', *Sociological Theory Online*, 12, 6.

Peirce, C. S. (1931–58): *Collected Papers*, 8 vols. Cambridge, Mass.: Harvard University Press.

Perinbanayagam, R. (2003): 'Telic Reflections: Interactional Processes, as Such', *Symbolic Interaction*, 26, 1, 67–83.

Popper, K. R. (1979): *Objective Knowledge. An Evolutionary Approach*. Oxford: Clarendon Press.

Quéré, L. (1997): 'La situation toujours negligée?', *Réseaux*, 85, pp. 163–92.

Rawls, J. (1972): *A Theory of Justice*. Oxford: Oxford University Press.

Ricoeur, P. (1969): *Le conflit des interpretations. Essais d'herméneutique*. Paris: Seuil.

Ricoeur, P. (1986): *Du texte à l'action. Essais d'herméneutique II*. Paris: Seuil.

Rochberg-Halton, E. (1986): *Meaning and Modernity. Social Theory in the Pragmatic Attitude*. Chicago: Chicago University Press.

Rorty, R. (1979): *Philosophy and the Mirror of Nature*. Princeton: Princeton University Press.

Schütz, A. (1962): *Collected Papers I. The Problem of Social Reality*. The Hague: M. Nijhoff.

Smith, A. (1976): *The Theory of Moral Sentiments*. Indianapolis: Liberty Fund.

Vandenberghe, F. (1999): '"The real is relational". An Inquiry into Pierre Bourdieu's Constructivist Epistemology', *Sociological Theory*, 17, 1, 32–67.

Vandenberghe, F. (2005): 'The Archers. A Tale of Folk (Final episode?)', *European Journal of Social Theory*, 8, 2, 227–37.

Vandenberghe, F. (2007): 'Avatars of the Collective. A Realist Theory of Collective Subjectivities', *Sociological Theory*, 25: 4, 295–324.

Wiley, N. (1994): *The Semiotic Self*. Chicago: Chicago University Press.

Part II
Reflexivity and realism

5 Human reflexivity in social realism

Beyond the modern debate

Andrea M. Maccarini and
*Riccardo Prandini**

1. Realist sociology and the modern theory of reflexivity

One way to develop a theory is by marking its discontinuities with another tradition. The guiding purpose of this chapter is to point out the basic tenets of a realist sociological theory of reflexivity and discuss them in the light of the most advanced lines of thought emerging from the modern debate. In the contemporary sociological landscape, a major contribution to articulating a realist approach to this subject is found in the work of Margaret Archer (1988, 1995, 2000, 2003, 2007), which will be our reference point in this essay.

In its generic meaning, that is as a self-referential second-order observational activity, reflexivity has been widely regarded as a distinctive mark of modernization, particularly in its most recent wave (Bauman 2000, Beck, Giddens and Lash 1994; Luhmann 1998). And this is believed both to imply and to call for a *reflexive turn* in our entire conception of reality, whilst in the former phase of modernization the potential for such a revolution was completely dismissed or, at least, seriously underplayed by sticking to conceptions that are both empiricist and ontologically oriented.[1]

What does social realism have to do with this? Our major contention will be that modernity – particularly late modernity – has raised *and* betrayed reflexivity, as a theme for scholarly thought and as a human practice, and that realist social theory can contribute to a more thorough and consistent understanding of reflexivity.

To anticipate our core argument, the contribution of realism is held to hinge upon the following two points:

(i) Its non-empiricist, stratified, and relational *ontology* – whose key concept is that of *emergence*.

* This is a fully co-authored work. Andrea Maccarini wrote Sections 1 and 2, while Riccardo Prandini wrote Sections 3 and 4. The general framework was conceived and discussed together. The present version conveys opinions common to both.

(ii)   The *kind* of *engagement* with the (social and non-social) world which qualifies the relationship between human beings and the various orders of natural
reality.

In regard to the former, it means that a fully ontological conception of reflexivity
is not opposed to a fully realist view of reality. Indeed, it is only through the former
that a viable, non-conflationary version of the latter becomes possible.[2]

Concerning point (ii), Archer's conception of reflexivity as a process of engagement with the natural, practical, and social orders of natural reality is arguably a
vantage point that allows us to draw crucially important connections, which in
most other theories remain implicit and are confined to the role of preliminary
meta-theoretical statements. Our treatment of the modern debate on reflexivity
will try to strengthen the case for supporting these conclusions.

Within this broader context, the present chapter focuses upon reflexivity as
a property of human subjects. We do not want to tackle the much bigger issue
of a generalized conception of reflexivity that could possibly make it applicable
to social networks and systems as well as to human beings. Important as this
question may be, the bulk of a realist social theory consists of the idea that both
social and cultural forms, on one hand, and human beings, on the other, have
reality status in their own right. Therefore, reflexivity is a sort of a reality test
for humans being something more than merely the fusion of living matter with
social forces. It is the semantics of reflexivity as internal conversation that is the
object of the present chapter. Within the realist-morphogenetic framework, such
internal conversation is endowed with three main properties: genuine interiority,
ontological subjectivity, causal efficacy; and is itself defined as a personal emergent
property (PEP).[3]

The work of Norbert Wiley (1994) provides an instructive way of engaging
with the modern tradition in the theory of reflexivity. He takes stock of the pragmatist line of thought, particularly with reference to the seminal treatment of
inner speech by C. S. Peirce, which he seeks to blend with G. H. Mead's account
of human consciousness. Wiley identifies two forms of conflation in conceiving
of consciousness and the related 'interior' features that can be called human. We
will argue that both can be interpreted as deviations from a realist conception.
In Wiley's own terms, they are called 'upward' and 'downward' reduction (Wiley
1994: Chs. 7 and 8). 'Upward reduction' views the internal conversation as the
epiphenomenon of intra- and infra-human structures – e.g. on the neurological
level – thereby considering human beings only as behavioural and organic entities.
On the contrary, 'downward reduction' interprets consciousness as the internalized reflection of socio-cultural trends. In both cases, consciousness is regarded as
epiphenomenal and would therefore lack the three properties mentioned above.
We argue that these two types of reductionism represent the way modern social
thought first approached the theme of human reflexivity, and then deceived itself
about its nature.

Mead's 'I/Me' distinction, connecting the unsocialized part of the individual
(the 'I') to the socialized self (the 'Me'), can also be considered to reflect these

two forms of conflation. Within the landscape of modern sociological theory, it is indeed difficult to find any approach escaping, or overcoming this opposition.[4] The two sides of this distinction can be illustrated by two authors whose works we hold to be the most significant attempts to deal with the issue of reflexivity in contemporary, non-realist social theory: Niklas Luhmann and Jürgen Habermas. This statement should not be mistaken for the grossly oversimplified claim that Luhmann and Habermas respectively epitomize 'individualism' and 'holism' as general approaches to social theory and to human reflexivity. The fact that both authors ground their sociological enterprises on what they take to be a funda-mental turn away from the subject/object framework of thought to theories based on *intersubjectivity* and *communication* should suffice to dismiss such conceptual crudities.[5] What we mean is that Luhmann and Habermas may well start from a position nearer to Mead's 'I' or 'Me', but then put forward the most refined elabora-tions upon the 'I/Me' distinction, articulating complex relationships between its two elements, and thereby come virtually to exhaust the theoretical alternatives conceivable within that reference grid. In the process, both authors take modern sociological discourse beyond its limits, and formulate dilemmas that can be use-fully addressed from a realist-morphogenetic standpoint.

In the following sections we will provide an account of their ways of theorizing human reflexivity and compare it with the realist-morphogenetic approach. We do not claim to present a fully exhaustive reconstruction, but only a bridgehead to further study. We have not traced back all the nuances of their theoretical development, nor have we embarked on a full critical discussion in the light of all secondary literature. A satisfactory treatment of these authors and their relations to sociological realism is beyond the scope of this essay, which will necessarily reduce complex themes to a few paragraphs where a book-length treatment would be appropriate. What we intend to offer is a summary, in the form of a systematic analysis that highlights the major conceptual keystones in the relevant theories, and draws a comparison with the realist account of reflexive phenomenon.

We will thus outline similarities and differences, assuming that we can learn from both, and point to the added value that a realist-morphogenetic conception of human reflexivity can represent for sociological theory today.

2. Niklas Luhmann: functional counter-ontology and the self-despairing reflexives

2.1 Social theory 'in Meadean mood'

Since systems theory has traditionally been held to involve an oversocialized conception of man (Wrong 1961), it is likely that Niklas Luhmann would also be regarded as a downward conflationist. Although his profound difference from Parsons is widely recognized,[6] there has been virtually no attempt to draw out all the theoretical implications entailed by this difference.

This, we argue, may well be significant in explaining why Luhmann's Meadean connection has hardly been explored to date[7] and why no-one has used a realist approach to explore it. In doing this, we will see where Luhmann stands with respect to points (i) and (ii) above: that is, on ontology (Section 2.2) and on engagement with the world (Section 2.3). First, however, let us spell out the meaning and relevance of Luhmann's Meadean connection (Section 2.1).

The revival of pragmatism in the social sciences has mainly been welcomed because of its emphasis on indeterminacy.[8] This emphasis in turn has focused scholarly attention upon Mead's concept of the 'I', within the 'I/Me' distinction. In the Introduction to the 1952 edition of *Mind, Self and Society*, Charles W. Morris defined the 'I' as the principle of action and the impulse that changes social structure (Mead 1952: xxv). Beyond this deceptively simple statement, interpretations of the concept differ widely, ranging from a biological to an existentialist one. According to the former, the 'I' refers to unsocialized, animal impulses intruding into and disrupting what would otherwise be a stable social process. This notion emphasizes the endowment of the human being with a surplus of (non-deterministic) impulses having no principled limit, ones that social norms can only channel.[9] On the other hand, existentialist views take the 'I' as the purely undetermined instance of the personal self (Aboulafia 1986).[10] Despite their vast theoretical differences, what these interpretations have in common is that they both view the 'I' as 'remedial', that is as something that may counteract the socially constraining force of the 'Me'. Mead had already introduced the concept in his essay about the definition of the psychical (now in Mead 1964). The psychical consists in a moment of consciousness, which it is possible to regard as having cognitive value for that process. Thus it appears when critical reflection analyses our world (Mead 1964: 29–30).

The sharp difference between the level of consciousness and that of physical stimulation is underlined. Psychical states are not dependent upon physical excitation; it is always *activity* that determines in advance where attention will be directed and gives the psychical state its content (ibid.: 37). The psychical, therefore, is not any kind of object. It is neither the empirical 'Me' nor the transcendental self. Instead, the 'I' can be properly grasped as a *function*; but as soon as any particular content of subjectivity is delineated, it immediately becomes an object (a 'Me') (ibid.: 46–7). What function it has can be inferred from the characteristics of the specific phase of experience that Mead describes as a *problem*. When there is a problem, then old ideas are not useful. In this phase of subjectivity – the activity of giving attention to the solution of a problem – the individual has, and indeed *is* that function. 'It is the self of unnecessitated choice, of undreamt hypotheses, of inventions that change the whole face of nature' (Mead 1964: 54).[11]

Therefore, the self is 'that *phase of experience* within which we are immediately conscious of conflicting impulses which rob the object of its character as object-stimulus (…); but during which a new object-stimulus appears due to the reconstructive activity which is identified with the subject "I" as distinct from the object "Me"' (ibid.: 55, emphasis added). The subject intervenes to solve problems and make hypotheses about the new world, but at the same time Mead realizes that as soon as psychic content is produced, it becomes part of the object world. As a consequence, his main concern is to prevent the dissolution of the creative instance into the world of objects. 'The emergence of the new' thus comes to the fore as the bulk of Mead's actual and potential contribution to social theory (Joas 2001).

The problem lies in the very way such a process of emergence, and indeed the emergent itself, are conceived of. The process and properties of the 'I' simply remain unknown, since thinking otherwise would amount to shifting into the field of the 'Me'. The only path Mead can follow to avoid the pitfalls of objectification leads him to define the active self as a necessary convention, or as a merely functional 'point of immediacy', from which innovation springs suddenly into being. One may welcome indeterminacy, but when it becomes all that a self amounts to, it is difficult to escape the impression that such a self has a shaky ontological status. Consequently, the 'I' escapes oversocialization at the price of ontological emptiness. As Mead himself concedes, 'to treat the emergent as a permanently alien and irrational element is to leave it a sheer mystery' (Mead 1932: 16). The same fate applies to the self, under the heading of the Meadean 'I'. This might be one of the reasons why Mead admitted to having developed his whole idea of the psychical 'somewhat obscurely and ineffectively, I am afraid' (Mead 1964: 106).

The task of clarifying such obscurity, resolving ambivalence and developing the theory along a new radical path may well be attributed to Niklas Luhmann's approach to systems theory, with its autopoietic and self-referential turn. There are two, mutually related, points through which Luhmann's theoretical enterprise comes into contact with these Meadean premises:

(i) Luhmann rethinks *socialization theory* outside the constraints of a theory of social order;
(ii) Luhmann puts *self-produced indeterminacy* in the place once occupied by the ontologically substantive, non-material properties defining the human subject.

The first point is epitomized in the foundational statement according to which the belief that society is 'made of' human beings should be considered an 'epistemological obstacle' to sociological theorizing. As a result of this, he consistently chooses to drop any notion of *consensual* integration as constitutive of society. It is the ongoing process of communication alone that produces identities, references, eigenvalues and objects. Luhmann quotes Mead as the forerunner of this conceptual framework (Luhmann 1997: 24–30), which he maintains involves the theoretical decision to put human beings in the environment of society.

The consequences for socialization are profound: such a process is not meant to constitute the foundation of social order, but can only mean self-socialization (Luhmann 1995a; 2002). This is not a process based on internalization, which builds society and its culture into human personality, but a selective task performed by the psychic system. Through socialization man does not become a part of society, which in turn does not get into the psychic system. Society can offer meanings but cannot control the effects it has on psychic systems. This, Luhmann suggests, can correct the dominant socio-centric theoretical tradition and its positing of an 'original constraint' (*Urzwang*), which ensures the primacy of social penetration within consciousness (Gilgenmann 1986b: 72).

In this context, reflexivity appears as a 'self-observation' skill available to all meaning-based systems. However, the spontaneously operating system always escapes such self-observation. It can objectify itself only in the light of its past operations and observations (Gilgenmann 1991: 13). This difference corresponds to the Meadean distinction between the 'I' and the 'Me', and amounts to saying that the 'I' never appears in consciousness. It is beyond experience and remains behind the scenes. Uniting the spontaneously operating system and the objective unity of consciousness is a matter of reconstruction through second-order observation, that is, reflection.

This leads us to consider point (ii) above. Luhmann's conception of reflexivity is based upon the fundamental distinction between human beings and social systems, and is only made possible through his particular view of consciousness and the psychic system. Before turning to the core argument in Luhmann's theory of reflexivity, it is thus necessary to sketch an account of the view of individuality and subjectivity upon which he relies.

The theory of autopoietic social systems explicitly prompts an interest in the self-referential autopoiesis of psychic systems, together with the capacity displayed by psychic systems to articulate their own reproduction moment by moment (the 'flow' of their 'life of consciousness') in such a way that their closure is compatible with an environment made up of social systems (Luhmann 1995a: 415). The problem is how to distinguish between the two kinds of autopoiesis: that of social and that of psychic systems. Social systems rely upon communication. Psychic systems are also characterized by an operation of their own; they reproduce consciousness through consciousness. Consciousness is not any kind of *entity*, but is merely the way that psychic systems operate and, indeed, is itself an *operation*.[12]

This amounts to maintaining that the autopoietic system of consciousness consists of events – of elements that emerge and disappear instantly. Consciousness, therefore, exists as temporalized self-transformation (Luhmann 1995b: 57). Its basic elements are thoughts that are continuously produced and reproduced (*Ibid*: 60–1). The way this happens is called the system's operation. In an impressively Meadean mood, Luhmann goes on to say that there are no structures producing thoughts. Operations proceed within the distinction between thought and observation, the observation of a thought being called a representation. Consciousness thus proceeds reflexively, not 'proflexively', i.e. it works by looking back. It has no goals, but realizes what has happened to it (ibid.: 63). However, thoughts observe other thoughts on the grounds of a specific distinction: that of self-reference/ hetero-reference. This makes for the bi-stability of the system: it can use both sides of the distinction to proceed, which prevents consciousness from being a trivial operation. Consciousness – whether it wants to refer to itself or to an external referent – is dependent on its inner state, which makes its behaviour unpredictable. Since this also goes for itself, consciousness develops a means of self-interpretation that allows it to observe itself as an object of representation, i.e. in the form of hetero-reference. There is basic reproduction – from one representation to the other – and there is reflection, as a process occasionally activated, in which consciousness presupposes itself (Luhmann 1995a: 423).

Self-reference is all that individuality amounts to. Despite our helpless – and desperately amateurish – efforts to believe we are something more than that, Luhmann ironically concludes that the individuality of our consciousness is nothing but the closed circle of self-referential reproduction. To Luhmann, this conclusion results from systems theory and the reconsideration derived from it of the whole history of individuality (Luhmann 1986; 1995a: 415–20). Within his approach, to say self-reference means to assert that there is no self beyond sheer reference.

As a consequence, all boundaries that self-reference might run into while producing individuality are nothing more than provisional social constructions. Systems like consciousness are indeterminate. Each system has its own 'inner infinite', and none is observable, nor are the grounds of its choices observable. This goes for both social systems and human individuals (Luhmann 1995a: 414). They operate within the horizon of their *self-produced indeterminacy*.[13] The latter concept supersedes all non-material components in the traditional conceptions of man – e.g. soul, spirit, and self.

To sum up, this is the way Luhmann wants to defend the distinction between psychic and social systems. Individuality is not something subjects receive from any 'outside'; human beings constitute and do not internalize meanings and are not, strictly speaking, a 'part' of society.

It is a theory of free individuals that dismisses any form of downward conflation. The theory is also anti-reductionist with respect to the cognitive sciences and the neuro-physiological, organic aspects of human beings. Luhmann consistently points out that the psyche has its own operations, which cannot be reduced to any corresponding operations in the brain or the organism. Where these 'good intentions' lead him, as far as his theory of reflexivity goes, must now be spelled out in a more detailed way.

2.2. What is reflexivity? Complexity and the functional turn

Reflexivity has a pivotal role in Niklas Luhmann's theory of society and societal dynamics. Indeed, one could well say he makes a strong case for a 'reflexive imperative'[14] fuelling the morphogenesis of contemporary society. The German sociologist saw reflexivity as emerging in the context of the imperative to reduce complexity. Complexity and its necessary reduction appear as the keystone of Luhmann's treatment of reflexivity and this allows him to draw clear-cut conclusions about social change and the meaning of rationality. Our argument will be that he supplies a set of premises from which both similarities with and differences from the realist-morphogenetic approach to reflexivity are derived.

Luhmann starts by noting that rationalist Enlightenment, ontological metaphysics and the philosophy of consciousness have always dismissed complexity and the social dimension. Yet the Enlightenment can be regarded as representing a major attempt to make the contingency of the world meaningful to lived experience and action (Luhmann 1970: 85). Therefore, such enlightenment is not accomplished by enhancing reason as such, but by increasing the human potential to reduce complexity. This amounts to forming systems whose information processing takes place in a meaningful context, one that reinforces their selective capacity. The transcendental problem concerning the social contingency of the world turns into the problem of complexity, to be reduced by constructing systems. For these reasons, sociological enlightenment ends up with reflexivity, through which the reduction of complexity is achieved. The most profound meaning of enlightenment is believed to lie in this. Reflexivity is thus conceived of as a social mechanism, and not in terms of its functions for individual personality. The problem is that society, its ordering and its dynamics requires a comparative view of the reflexive mechanisms involved. The aim is ultimately to develop a (missing) generalized, comparative and unifying conception of the reflexive phenomenon (Luhmann 1970: 103–28).

Two theoretical tenets follow, which arguably constitute the core of the systems theory of reflexivity.

(i)   Reducing the complexity of the world entails producing and stabilizing a difference between the internal and the external, between system and environment.

(ii) Moreover, a mechanism[15] is called 'reflexive' when applied to itself (*ibid.*: 104). Mechanisms are reflexive when they take an identical mechanism as their object, i.e. when they refer to themselves in kind (*ibid.*: 343, note 6). By way of example, one could think of learning to learn, planning to plan, and so forth. From a specifically social perspective, reflexive mechanisms add up to a sequence of acts of communication: that is, a set of acts of the same kind to be referred to some given object.

These theoretical convictions are inherent in the whole Luhmannian view of reflexivity. This leads to the exploration of the meaning and function of reflexivity as a *form*, regardless of any particular mechanism that bends back on itself.[16] What is the point of applying some mechanism to itself, rather than to something else? What are the social presuppositions necessary for reflexive mechanisms to arise and become institutionalized?

To go back to the example of learning, its definition as a social mechanism refers to capabilities that any social system takes for granted in its ongoing processes; it means not only the capacity to produce knowledge but also the (constantly used) capacity to adapt one's expectations about lived experience. Its rationalization and differentiation involve detaching part of the learning capacity and devoting it to learning how to learn and to teach. Reflexive learning allows for a more objective style of discussion and enhances the potential for dealing with complex problems. To sum up, efficiency is increased and better control over complex conditions is made possible. Therefore, the answer to the first question above is simply that reflexivity is functionally and adaptively better.[17]

On the other hand, reflexivity comprises functions concerning order and evolution, and therefore keeps functional and evolutionary perspectives together.

Reflexivity grows with complexity and civilization, while simultaneously fostering social complexity. In this respect, reflexive mechanisms are considered to be *evolutionary universals*. There is a strict connection between mechanisms sequentially becoming reflexive one after the other and based upon each other and the level reached by social differentiation in the domain of action, norms, roles, systems of roles.

This ongoing process takes an evolutionary form – more complex entities become so because they are more reflexive and in turn require more reflexivity.

In this situation, traditional and non-reflexive attitudes, behaviours and ways of life are eliminated. This conclusion seems to dovetail with Archer's thesis concerning the demise of routine action (Archer 2007). Yet, it is precisely here that the considerable difference between the two approaches begins to emerge, with all its implications. Archer, too, highlights the growth of complexity and the rapidity of social change, concluding that an intensification of reflexivity accompanies them. However, Luhmann's functional turn moulds the argument in a totally different way. His anti-ontological view of reflexivity endows reflexive action with a particular meaning. This meaning becomes crystal clear when observed from the perspective of the function of enlightenment. The 'Illumination' of norms, roles, and institutions has turned into an exercise in discrediting and debunking. 'Being reflexive' has come to mean deconstructing social life and structures, discrediting officially held morality as well as personal values, and explaining the genesis of society through the repression of deviance. Luhmann criticizes this as evidence of an irresponsible theoretical and practical attitude: deconstruction is all very well, but is, in itself, insufficient to offer any alternative. How is complexity to be reduced anyway? Therefore, he advocates a more mature view of enlightenment. This, Luhmann argues, is exactly the gift of his emphasis on complexity. The easy emphasis on deconstruction and false consciousness is superseded by the consistent awareness that action is not optional and by the full-blooded understanding of complexity, with the result that alternatives are always *inevitably* implicit in *any* choice and action. Our actions and beliefs may be ill-founded, but after all the deconstructive work is done, we still have to act in this complex world!

We are now in a position to pull some of the strings together. Luhmann's reflexive imperative adds up to the imperative to reduce complexity, drawing and defending a distinction between system and environment. Indeed, *reflexivity is nothing but a function enhancing this capacity* for reduction. The resulting forms (choices, alternatives for action, identities, etc.) will then *all* appear to be deprived of any foundation. Worse than that, subjects become reflexively aware of their condition. The only advantage of this condition compared with 'irresponsible' deconstruction lies in the fact that the clarification of latent functions allows people to replace traditional orientations with rational decision-making techniques.

Non-reflexive ways of thinking, acting and living are wiped out in due course, leaving social systems and human beings in the bitterly ironic awareness that no 'purposive' or 'meaningful' conduct is ever possible because meaning can result from an ultimately arbitrary act of complexity reduction alone.

If we focus specifically upon psychic systems, whose operation is consciousness, we may now ask: what kind of identity can result from this type of reflexive process based upon complexity reduction? Although autopoiesis is the actual basis of the individuality of psychic systems and is external to all social systems, it is still possible to distinguish between the ongoing, basic autopoiesis and observations or descriptions produced by other systems or by themselves (Luhmann 1995: 424). Autopoiesis merely occurs or ceases. Self-description can be modified and is a process endowed with some specific semantics with which the system can consciously operate. Reflexivity, internal conversation and identity would fall within the latter. Within this framework, it is tempting to ask in what possible ways one could reflect upon oneself and conceive of oneself reflexively. In other words, what hopes does such self-observation extend to us?

Because complexity implies selectivity, individuals guide themselves through a continuous reflexive denial of other possibilities.[18] No directional – that is, purposive – movement is possible. Consciousness is constituted as selectivity from actual experience. Identity means that its self-referential constitution emerges from a huge number of actions and a vast experience (and its fragmentation). There is no autopoietic unity of all the autopoietic systems that compose the human being – and all unifying acts are merely conventional. For this reason, reflecting upon them is often destructive, as with the semantics of authenticity.

Luhmann illustrates this point by buttressing his theoretical argument with an excursus on the historical semantics of subjectivity, particularly those connected with the structurally induced individualism of modern society. He describes the subject as a symbol representing the unpredictability of the future, and the freedom of the human as being an absence of constraint, without any reference to his or her essential qualities (Luhmann 1986, 1997: Ch. 5). From this perspective, humans are seen as reflexive beings, that is, as *nothing but* second order self-observers. According to Luhmann, the idea of the subject has been built upon such foundations. Reflexivity, as the mere process of second-order observation, becomes the nickname for humanity. To put this more rigorously, subjectivity does not refer to any determinate human qualities as such, and the 'subject' amounts to a description of an ontologically empty, autopoietic and self-referential process. Here Mead's intuition about the 'I' being nothing but a function and a point of immediacy is given a sound and clear – if radical – theoretical underpinning. Of course, this does not mean that Luhmann would fall back on Mead's conceptual vocabulary; to him there is no dual or plural self, there is no 'I' versus the 'Me'. There is nothing to be recomposed or reintegrated. There is only a closed, self-referential, circular network of events.

Moreover, Luhmann adds that this was only a transitional semantics for an age which had no theory of society. Thus, society was conceptualized through appealing to the concept of human motivation. To cut a long story short, the discouse of subjectivity reveals a dramatic ignorance about both Man and society. For this reason, the appeal to the subject is explained away as an 'escape'.[19]

The question is what lies waiting at the end of such an escape? Modernity describes the human being as an individual, but can the individual describe himself as such? If this were the case, Luhmann maintains, the individual would use his own individuality as a matrix for his self-description and would only describe his ongoing reproduction as distinguishing himself from the environment. Yet, this description would add nothing to the observation of what is going on anyway, through the ongoing autopoiesis of consciousness – and only for as long as the latter lasts.

This situation triggers all the paradoxes and reaches all the dead ends that are typical of modern reflections upon the 'self'. From the point of view of his theory of autopoietic systems, Luhmann finds it easy to dismiss all attributions of meaning as being, in fact, meaningless solutions to the problem of our 'amateurish' will to be human (Luhmann 1986) and to make sense as such. The semantics of heroism, those of genius (naturally limited to the few), *l'homme universel* as a transitional phase, which is meant for all but only under certain cultural conditions, the provocative reactions of the *avant-garde*, revolution and deviation (a methodology of evil as a self-imposed critical attitude), and even the discourse on the loss of meaning (Luhmann 1995: 426); these are nothing but forms individuals invent when the differentiation between psychic and social systems is so accentuated that humans can use only their individuality to describe themselves (*Ibid*: 427). All these forms appear as necessarily paradoxical. To put it in slightly more formal terms: they cannot be used by individuals as forms of self-reflection without resulting in self-undermining arguments. Be that as it may, all individuals end up living as *hommes-copies*, precisely by copying the above models.[20]

When Luhmann wonders whether or not we should conclude that the rise of the individual has effectively been a decline, or that the idea of the individual describing himself as such only brings about meaningless solutions, he seems to envisage a different explanation for the paradoxes he has revealed. All these forms of self-reflection might be understood as a way social systems react to the impossibility of including the whole individual in any subsystem of society, i.e. as a way of adapting to the situation of man being radically 'out of' society. As a consequence of this, individuals are exposed to a variety of feelings if they cannot transform their claims into lived routine and they are induced to talk about themselves as different from anything else. Modern society is threatened by emotionality more than any other before (Luhmann 1995: 430). Individuals may react in various ways, amongst which is declaring that it is society, rather than themselves, which is sick. The resulting attitudes will range from anarchy to passive adaptation, from the claim to be able to act arbitrarily to the refusal to meet the claims of others of any kind. Such enlightened reflexivity produces a characteristically 'self-despairing subject', whose dynamism is 'achieved through self-desperation' (Luhmann 1986: 324). The self despairs of ever being able to find any foundation for his or her self-descriptions, inside or outside society.

Even if only half of this is true, the whole body of knowledge about consciousness, meaning, language, and internal speech must be reformulated, under the shadow of Luhmann's nocturnal warning:

> But beware: this is not a nice theory, neither a theory of perfection nor even of the perfectibility of the human race. It is not a theory of healthy states.

> Autopoietic systems reproduce themselves; they continue their reproduc-
> tion or not. This makes them individuals. And there is nothing more to say.
> (Ibid.: 325)

Here, Luhmann's argument comes full circle: the ontological emptiness of mere
complexity-reducing autopoiesis and the modern drift away from the tension
between solitude and society end up in sheer nonsense. So far we have dealt
with point (i) of our basic argument. Now, the reference to the increasing differentiation between psychic and social systems introduces a notion that deserves
treatment in its own right.

2.3. Engaging with the world: the constitution of self and the semantics of anxiety

The problem of engagement with the world emerges at the point where Luhmann's
view of self and reflexivity arrives at the conclusion that human subjects can find
no foundation for their identity either inside or outside society.[21]

An important insight is gained if we start from the assumption that it is a *particular and original relationship with the world* that qualifies us and our reflexivity as
being properly human. This assumption involves the acknowledgement that *our
very engagement with the world constitutes our being human.*

Anthony Giddens (1991: 48–55) produced a remarkable formulation of this
idea, when he established a strong relationship between existential questions and
forms of the self. The self is confronted with some basic questions challenging his
or her attempt to build a stable and consistent identity. They concern: (i) ontology and existence, (ii) time, human finitude and awareness of death, (iii) the
existence of other persons and, finally (iv) self-identity. Such questions raise a
fundamental anxiety about one's life, rooted in the perceived contingency of its
primordial conditions. Therefore, human *motives and plans are essentially born of
anxiety* (ibid.: 64).

Luhmann's thought can be considered to be fully consistent with this view.
When it comes to human beings, the dynamics of complexity-reduction are tightly
interwoven with a sense of existential anguish and anxiety, rooted in perceived
existential frailty and the ontological shakiness of the human condition. It is in
this context that Luhmann translates Weber's *wertrationalität* into the 'unavoidable presence of the meaning constitutive of living experience' (Habermas and
Luhmann 1971: 38), providing security and trust and helping to endure the
anxiety built into the necessity of living in this exceedingly complex world. Such
rationality as can emerge in social action is consistently reduced to an ever contingent task of stabilization.

Archer also defines human reflexivity as referring to our fundamental way of
engaging with the world and its complexity (2000, 2003, 2007). However, she
characterizes such engagement along the lines of a robust stratified ontology
based upon a consideration of the *way we are made and the world is made, and their
necessary relation*. The pivotal concept here is that of *concern*, which involves not

only fear and anxiety, but a semantics of *care* for and *commitment* to a given form of ourselves and of the world. Concern and anxiety are two considerably, though subtly, different ways of approaching the human condition. Depending upon the way we describe it, the world either appears as something tormenting us with its hopelessly obscure complexity or as attracting us as an object of our projects and commitment. It is this theme we now want to take up, in order to indicate its major import for the theory of reflexivity.

The relevance of the approach in question can be highlighted with regard to the related concepts of *purpose* and *denial*. The operation of reducing-and-maintaining the complexity of the world, Luhmann argues, is the way meaning emerges and, in turn, the way human subjects are constituted. Such an account of the form in which lived experience is elaborated involves a particular way of integrating actual living experience with other transcending possibilities. Because complexity entails compulsory selection, living experience implies an emphasis on denial. Consciousness is constituted through selection amongst actually experienced impressions. As a result of this, Luhmann conceives of the subject as guiding himself through excessive self-demands, ultimately grounded upon denial (Habermas and Luhmann 1971: 20–1). Through denial, various dimensions of living experience emerge: objective, social and temporal.[22] And it is through a complex web of denials that identities are built in these three dimensions of meaning (ibid.: 39). Because systems of meaning evolve through *reflexive denial*, the latter calls people's life-worlds into question.

In this context, it is clear that reflexivity consists in the 'thoughtful' denial of other possibilities. It is far less clear how this kind of reflexivity can result in motives, plans and actions, and ultimately in stable identities. In a nutshell: it is difficult to identify any kind of directional 'push' steering the selective imperative. The determinants of the selective function remain unknown.

Clarifying this question would imply a consideration of purposes and of the way they guide action. However, Luhmann's theory makes human needs and purposes invisible. The way it does this is by conceiving of the most complex 'chains of action' as leading from ultimate to proximate goals, the latter being immediately there to accomplish. With this, what other theories regard as the winning post becomes the starting gate, and is thereby hidden in the shadow of strategic inattention. The foundations of meaning amount to the ultimate reductions made, ones that are built on indeterminate ground and lie in the sheer absence of presuppositions.

As a consequence, identity only emerges in an empty space and to fill the inner void of the boring circularity of autopoiesis. Only his theory, Luhmann claims, can formulate the latent unity of the subject and its boredom, its *ennui*. There is only circularity, the autopoietic process reproducing thoughts out of thoughts. Motives, then, are to be thought of as filling the inner void, the empty circularity of pure autopoiesis, and boredom corresponds to the thinking of thinking (Luhmann 1986).

To Habermas (Habermas and Luhmann 1971: 95 ff.), Luhmann's theoretical *démarche* reveals him heir to the ambivalent heritage of Arnold Gehlen's *Weltoffenheit* anthropology and of Sartre's existentialist approach. The former is centred upon the necessity of confronting complexity and its overwhelming impact upon people's strategies of action, by developing institutions and prejudice structures to relieve subjects from such an unbearable weight. The latter involves the multiplication of possible alternatives for action with which to face the contingency of a risky world. In both cases, functionalism appears as a counter-ontology that creates latent structures and assumes the sheer survival of social, as well as psychic systems, as its ultimate source of meaning.

In regard to this specific point, we want to suggest that sociological realism exceeds both institutionalism and existentialism as forms of counter-ontology. The way it does so is to evoke the original and necessary relationship between humans and the world.

Following Archer, the reflexivity of human beings is generated within the *unavoidable relationship* they have with the various orders of natural reality: namely the natural, practical, and social. The key point is that these are the sources of basic *concerns* that the subjects cannot escape. Since they simultaneously participate in all three orders of natural reality, human individuals must accomplish a relatively successful dovetailing of their concerns and commitments in each of them, working out a *modus vivendi* that comes to represent the bulk of their identity. A human individual is essentially a being-with-this-constellation-of-concerns (Archer 2003). The key concept here is that of 'ultimate concern', expressing 'what we care about most' (Frankfurt 1988).

More broadly, the underlying morphogenetic model of agency can be summarized as follows:

(i)   an *original relation* between *human individuals* and the *world* – in its *natural, practical, and social dimensions* – triggering relevant *emotions* and *concerns*;

(ii) which generates *agency* as a process of *engagement* by human beings in each of these different environments;

(iii) this results in, and is sustained by *reflexivity*, whose medium is *internal conversation* and which continuously engages in three kinds of *activities: discernment, deliberation* and *dedication*;

(iv) a singular *modus vivendi* and a *full-blown* personal and social *identity* are the emergent effects of this morphogenetic cycle, which works both ontogenetically and analytically.

Note the stratified conception of agency that results: reflexivity is the way it operates, internal conversation its medium, but it comprises discernment, deliberation and dedication, prioritizing and evaluating, committing individuals to some ultimate concern, and doing this in relation to the various orders of reality from which particular kinds of concerns emerge.

Now this approach talks to our problem of engaging with the world by striking a particular chord: the concept of concern is multidimensional, comprising preoccupation as well as a distinctly purposive sense of care and commitment – it refers to what worries us, but also to what we want to accomplish because we care about it. Reflexivity consists of the inner activity through which we continuously observe, confirm or modify our *modus vivendi*, directing our action in the various spheres of life.

The result is a *unifying relationship* that reconstructs the unity of the subject by placing him or her in an oriented space: the subject can say *who* he is, and who he wants to be, observing *what* his ultimate concerns are, and *where* he is in relation to them. He can decide whether or not he is still willing to pay the costs required by his current *modus vivendi* or if he wants to switch to a new equilibrium. But any possible decision involves a dynamic placement: heading somewhere in an oriented space. The relevance of such a theoretical option is reinforced by its correspondence with Charles Taylor's famous thesis about human agency, according to which connection to 'inescapable frameworks' comprising some idea of the 'good' plays a crucial role in defining human agency and subjectivity. In his own words: 'the claim is that living within such strongly qualified horizons is constitutive of human agency, that stepping outside these limits would be tantamount to stepping outside what we would recognize as integral, that is, undamaged human personhood' (Taylor 1989: 27). Taylor goes on to claim that modern social sciences have suppressed or denied this connection, defining it away as the socially induced image of the self (ibid.: 33).

With Archer, sociology articulates a systematic theory that is clearly compatible with Taylor's conceptual framework, thereby simultaneously calling into question his judgement about social science. Insofar as that 'connection' can be held to rest on solid ground, one could maintain Archer is breaking a path that leads beyond the modern sociological tradition.

The decisive point is that the concept of concern entails our affective, cognitive and moral attachment to a given form of the world, and of ourselves in it, rather than our anxiety at having to confront a complex environment. In Harry Frankfurt's terms, Archer's theory evokes a human subject who is capable of rationality and love as the factors necessary in order to 'take ourselves seriously'.

In the last instance, Luhmann and Archer have conceived of two very different approaches to the human condition. The question is not which of the two can be regarded as 'better'; this is not an issue about preferences, not even morally qualified ones. The problem is about which viewpoint allows one to produce the more adequate description and analysis of reflexivity, as real people experience it in their real everyday lives, in the various regions, hot spots and remote backwaters of global society.

3. Escaping the dangerous self-misunderstanding of modernity's project

In this third section we consider the theoretical reconstruction of Mead's work undertaken by Jürgen Habermas. We take Habermas as an example of the theorists who downgrade the nature and functions of the 'self', transforming it into a sort of necessary 'place marker' for the imputation of responsibilities within the communicative processes. To him, society comes before the self, and personal identity represents solely an internalization of the different and diverse demands coming from (generalized) others: man is an animal who, thanks alone to his inclusion within a public network of social relationships, develops the skills that make him or her a person. Therefore, the human mind is constituted inter-subjectively. For Habermas we should conceive of subjectivity and self-consciousness as a glove turned inside out, whose stuff is made up of inter-subjective threads (Habermas 2008). The subjective mind – and its powers – receives its structure and content from participating in inter-subjective relationships among naturally socialized subjects. The pivotal importance assigned to social reality in the constitution of identity is a clear clue to its central conflationary nature, where the personal and the social are mutually constitutive. In the following pages we want to explain: (i) the ultimate reason why Habermas elaborates his theory of a post-conventional self; (ii) the relevance of G. H. Mead's thought in this theoretical reconstruction; (iii) the theoretical consequences of this theory for the concept of personal reflexivity.

3.1 The reason for conflation

From the very beginning of his work,[23] Habermas considered the idea of a society constituted by individualized and monadic selves not only as scientifically inadequate (actually a mere ideology), but also as a moral danger for society. Blending the idea of alienation, derived from Marx,[24] with the linguistic turn – especially taken from Heidegger (but also from Wittgenstein and part of the 'analytic' legacy) – he tried to answer 'his' fundamental question: why a man cannot be reduced to an observable thing – a mere object – among others? The answer, from the very beginning, and to date, has been: because man is a 'being' who possesses language, i.e. something that is intrinsically social. Alienation, therefore, is simply 'repressed dialogue', a misrecognition of the constitutive presence of others inside the self. The Cartesian image, currently taken up by certain cognitive sciences, of a conscious, recursively self-enclosed monad, is misleading. The self depends upon the internalization of the agencies that monitor his behaviour and, because of the historical diversity of these agencies, it is contingent.

For Habermas, the misrecognition of the pivotal relevance of the societal level of reality (compared with the natural, practical and psychological) for the creation of the self distorts the project of Modernity by leading towards a risky cultural self-description. Modernity represents itself as the land of 'institutionalized individualism'. This oxymoron, introduced by Parsons, splits itself in two contradictory, but simultaneously twin interpretations: as the exaggeration of a 'possessive individualism', unable to recognize the real presence of the 'Other', and as the enhancement of an autopoietic social system, which needs to attribute actions and experience to some 'thing', illusorily reducing the complexity of an anonymous matrix of recursive communications.[25] To Habermas, metaphysical thought develops in terms of a philosophy of consciousness based on the relationship of the knowing subject to himself. This *Ego Cogito* represents a 'spontaneous' source of cognition and action. It is a world-generating and autonomously-acting subject, originating from Fichte, who reduced the transcendental accomplishments of the knowing and practical ego to the common denominator of spontaneous activity. This Ego is radicalized in the picture of a primitive act of 'self-positing'. In positing itself as a self, and in reflecting on this 'self-position', something goes wrong: the self falls into the typical circle of every philosophy of consciousness: 'in consciously assuring itself to itself, the knowing subject unavoidably makes itself into an object, and it thereby falls short of himself as the antecedent source of all accomplishments of consciousness, a source that precedes all objectifications and is absolutely subjective. In its spontaneous activity the ego is supposed to make itself into an object' (Habermas 1992: 160). When this subjectivity faces other subjectivities – this is the decisive point – 'subjects can only be objects for one another, so that even in the reciprocally limiting influence they have on each other, their individuality does not reach beyond the objectivistic determinations of the strategic freedom of choice whose paradigm is the arbitrary will of privately autonomous legal subjects' (1992: 161). Modernity is therefore forced to dissolve the inter-subjective relationship into a subject-object relationship, i.e. into a mutual objectification. Here, Habermas finds the starting point of the 'possessive individualism' tradition that, in the nineteenth and twentieth centuries, became the most influential ideology concealing the 'reality' of the inter-subjective foundation of the self and of personal identity. It is on exactly these grounds that Habermas strongly criticizes Niklas Luhmann's thought. Luhmann paradoxically represents the ideological apex of this subjective philosophy. In the last pages of his famous book *The Philosophical Discourse of Modernity*, Habermas points out this drift dramatically.

First of all, he discloses the hidden connections between subjectivism and systemic thought, the 'secret' of systemic theory as disclosed in 'institutional individualism': 'the flow of official documents among administrative authorities and the monadically encapsulated consciousness of a Robinson Crusoe, provides the guiding images for the conceptual uncoupling of the social and psychic systems, according to which the one is supposedly based solely on communication and the other solely on consciousness' (1990: 378). Along with this abstract severing of psychic and social systems, we can witness the emergence of two contradictory phenomena: on the one hand, the cultural legitimation of a strategic actor who becomes worldless and who stands over and against the objective world, making decisions according to his 'idiotic' preferences alone; on the other hand, the emergence of a process of individualization that is systemically driven and does not leave room for an authentic emancipatory individuation qualified by an ethical self-understanding.

Second, Habermas censures the downgrading of language to a mere instrumental tool. This reduction is typical of every version of instrumental individualism: 'the solitary life of the soul, including discursive thought, is not formed by language from the very outset. Structuring by language only articulates the spontaneous flow of consciousness by pauses and lends it the capacity to form episodes (…) to the extent that language is involved in organizing series of representations and processes of thought, it by no means functions as an internalized derivative of speech' (1990, 380). Language is so underdetermined, as a medium of communication, that it is not designed to overcome the egocentrism of individual systemic perspectives through higher level, supra – or common – perspectives. The separation between the social and the substantial dimension is meant to exclude precisely the 'telos' of language: to ground the understanding of something through the possibility of reaching a consensus together. Language affords no real basis for a mutual consensus: 'My consent is a consent only in relation to your consent, but my consent is not your consent, and there is no sort of substantive argument or rational grounds that could in the end ensure the coincidence of the two'.

To sum up, Habermas sees Luhmann's theory as an ingenious continuation of a tradition that has left a strong imprint upon the self-understanding of early modernity in Europe and has been reflected, in turn, in the selective pattern of Western rationalistic development:

> the cognitive-instrumental one-sidedness of cultural and societal rationalization was also expressed in philosophical attempts to establish an objectivist self-understanding of human beings and their worlds – initially in mechanistic and later in materialistic and physicalistic worldviews, which reduced the mental to the physical by means of more or less complicated theory. (1990, 384)

At the end of the day, Habermas takes Luhmann's thought to be the paradoxical outcome of the subjectivistic-nominalistic-metaphysical turn in western civilization. This horizon simply represents cultural alienation, which seriously endangers the possibility of Modernity's utopia developing.

3.2. The importance of G. H. Mead for treading that dangerous path: recognizing the inter-subjective condition of humanity

To Habermas, the possessive individualistic tradition finds its discontents at the beginning of the eighteenth century. After the mediation of the language theory elaborated by von Humboldt and the refusal of the paradigm of self-observation, it is with G. H. Mead that we can find the downgrading of the absolute Ego into a 'Me', a Self that emerges inter-subjectively and is mediated by language. Habermas considers Mead as the first modern thinker who is able to escape the cognitive-alienating tradition of the 'knowing subject', shifting into the ethical self-reassurance of an accountable first-person who establishes herself according to a second person.[26] Within this new theoretical horizon, personal identity does not represent a cognitive description of oneself, but a guarantee which stands in need of confirmation by others. What is really at stake concerning identity formation (and its social representation), is not to 'have' it, but the necessity of an inter-subjective recognition, capable of giving fixity to a fragmentary life and supplying it with the required social warranty. We can appreciate the *tour de force* represented by Meadean thought through analysing the essential essay entitled *Individualization through Socialization: On George Herbert Mead's Theory of Subjectivity*.[27]

Habermas wants to underline that the process of individuation is not the self-realization of an acting and isolated subjectivity. In the process of socialization, the subject takes what the reference person expects of him and first makes it his own, abstracting between diverse expectations and integrating them in a coherent self. If this occurs, there arises 'an internal centre for self-steering of individually accountable conduct' (1992, 152). The realization/instantiation of a personal identity is not a problem of numerical identity or of an adequate cognitive self-description (always impossible), but of a qualitative identification through a unique biographical pattern. Its import is as a guarantee that is grasped by the person as soon as she knows that the other is vouching for her ability to be herself and when she consciously assumes responsibility for her life-history. Here, Habermas provides a resounding critique of the individualistic legacy:

> the self of an ethical self-understanding is not the absolutely inward possession of the individual. The impression that it is arises from the possessive individualism of a philosophy of consciousness that begins with the abstract self relation of the knowing subject, instead of conceiving the latter as a result. The self of an ethical self-understanding is dependent upon recognition by addressees because it generates itself as a response to the demands of another in the first place. Because others attribute accountability to me, I gradually make myself into the one I have become in living together with others. The ego, which seems to me to be given in my self-consciousness as what is purely my own, cannot be maintained by me solely through my own power, as it were for me alone – it does not belong to me. Rather, this ego always retains an intersubjective core because the process of individualization from which it emerges runs through the network of linguistically mediated interactions. (1992, 170)

The genesis of self-consciousness (that is, a result) is contingent upon the gaze of the Other. G. H. Mead was the first to have thought through this inter-subjective model of the socially produced ego. He breaks out of the circle of self-objectifying cognitive reflections, between a spontaneous 'I' and an objectified 'Me', through a transition to the paradigm of symbolically mediated interaction. Here the subject appears not in the role of an observer (so rejecting the idea of introspection and of cognitive self-observation), but in that of a speaker and from the social perspective of a hearer encountering him in a dialogue. From this position he learns to see and to understand himself as the Alter Ego of another Ego. In the first-person (of his performative attitude), the actor encounters himself as a second person, a 'You' with whom the 'I' seeks to reach an understanding, differentiating the 'something' about which he wants consent. In the 'I–You' relationship, the actor encounters himself as a 'social object', the self of self-consciousness. It is in this way that a 'Me' arises, as the memory of the spontaneous 'I' mediated by an Alter Ego.

At first, Mead finds this subjectivity in the breakdown of a familiar world or in its problematization. Something is not familiar, something is not as we have imagined, so that we are pushed into an internal landscape of personal fallibility. If something is not objective, then it must be subjective. Here we can find an interesting clue to what we can call 'the primacy of the natural or practical realm over the social', but Habermas does not proceed along this theoretical path. Instead he affirms that Mead himself has to abandon Dewey's model of an isolated actor instrumentally dealing with things and events. Mead expands this individualistic and behaviouristic approach with a social dimension, introducing the social double contingency. But he did it only in a pre-linguistic frame of communication, on the level of gestural communication. Habermas wants to translate this model into a linguistic one. With the 'vocal gesture' an organism learns to understand its own behaviour from the perspective of the other. It is only now that Mead can assume that the actor takes the perspective towards himself of another participant in interaction and becomes visible to himself as a 'social object'. Given this self-relation, the actor 'doubles himself in the instance of a "Me" which follows the performative "I" as a shadow because "I" as the author of a gesture am given to "Me" only in memory' (1992: 177). At the end of the day, the self of self-consciousness is not the spontaneous acting 'I', but instead this 'I' is given only in the refraction of the symbolically captured meaning it took on for its interaction partner in the role of the Alter Ego. In a nutshell, 'the consciousness that I centered, as it seems, in the ego is not something immediate or purely inward. Rather, self-consciousness forms itself on the path from without to within, through the symbolically mediated relationship to a partner in interaction. To this extent it possesses an inter-subjective core' (1992: 178).

It is precisely within the distinction between the epistemic self-relation of the knowing subject and the practical relation-to-self of the acting subject that Habermas shows how and why Mead is led to introduce the mechanism of 'taking the perspective of an Other' that is then extended into the mechanism of 'role-taking', where Ego takes over Alter's normative expectations. Now the 'Me' of the practical relation to self becomes an agency of self-control. This new 'Me' is the *Generalized Other*, i.e., the normative expectations of the social system that migrated into the person, from without to within. The practical relation-to-self is made possible by this 'Me' that places limits, from the inter-subjective perspective of a social 'We', on the arbitrariness of an impulsive and reluctant 'I'. It is here that we find the fundamental distinction, because 'in the practical relation to self the acting subject does not want to recognize itself; rather he wants to reassure itself about itself as the initiator of an action that is attributable solely to it, in short to become sure of itself as a free will' (1992, 181). For Habermas, it is only by internalizing these norms (the 'We') and social controls that we can constitute ourselves as accountably acting individuals. Yet, now we face another problem: if this 'We' is representative of a pre-modern society, it leads to only a conventional ego-identity. The 'Me', connected with this 'We' is a conservative force. Agency is not really reflexive, i.e. capable of creativity and innovations, and – even worse – identity is not a personal identity in the way we think of it today. The person is not able to recognize herself in her own identity. And society remains external, not really interiorized. What comes about here is the process of societal differentiation:

> it is in the ongoing process of civilization that the individual learns to become
> autonomous and to conduct his life consciously. Self-determination and

self-realization are waited for, in different ways relating to different forms of social differentiation. The more society becomes differentiated, the more the individual (the self) needs to reflect about his decisions and circumstances of decision'. (1992, 183)

The 'reflexive imperative' asks for new forms of personal identity, but these authentic/autonomous/independent selves are again socially constituted.

What is, then, the real difference between the traditional 'non-reflexive' selves and the modern 'reflexive' ones? The real difference does not concern the 'person', but only the 'form and content' of the relevant community that became a sort of larger society connected with a post-conventional morality: a forum of reasons, an idealized form of communication, a *locus* of 'ultimate opinion' in Peircean terms. For Habermas:

> the ego finds its way to itself only along a detour by way of others, by way of the counterfactually supposed universal discourse. Once again, the self of the practical relation-to-self can only assure itself if it is able to return to itself from the perspective of others as their Alter ego. But this time it does not return to itself as the Alter ego of some other Alter ego from among its own concrete group (as the 'Me'). It now comes upon itself as the Alter ego of all others in every community (...) Thus, the relationship between the 'I' and the 'Me' remains the key even for an analysis of the socially imputed postconventional ego-identity. (1992, 187)

Even in this post-conventional society the identities and biographies of people are 'theirs' only because the relevant culture requires it. Of course, 'I' – the citizen of western modernity – can regard my identity *as if* it were the product of decisions for which I am responsible. But this 'myself', which means to me my existence as a whole, is formed by the life contexts and formative processes that really shape identity. I am not a 'Person', but an 'Agent', becoming an 'Actor' only out of societal necessity. In this pluralistic society, with high structural and cultural differentiation, the Generalized Other expects the different 'I's to project themselves onto an ideal 'Me' that is not empirically present but nonetheless is culturally constraining. The moral and existential self-reflection of the individual is now 'socially' expected to be a normal skill, at least in certain spheres of actions. In a sense the relationship between the 'Me' and the 'I' is reversed, because the 'Me' expects the initiative of the 'I'.

Habermas concludes that 'in communicative action, the supposition of self-determination and self-realization retains a rigorously inter-subjective sense: whoever judges and acts morally must be capable of anticipating the agreement of an unlimited communication community and whoever realizes himself in a responsibly accepted life history must be capable of anticipating recognition from this unlimited community. Accordingly, an identity that always remains mine, namely, my self-understanding as an autonomously acting and individuated being, can stabilize itself only if I find recognition as a person, and as this person' (1992,

192). In a nutshell, individuation is only possible through socialization and is explained by the linguistic medium itself: 'the universal pragmatic presuppositions of communicative action constitute semantic resources from which historical societies create and articulate, each in its own way, representation of mind and soul, concept of the person and action, consciousness of morality, and so on' (1992, 191). What are real are solely the presuppositions of communications; what we can find through the cultural history of societies are contingent and relative 'concepts of the self', nothing less, nothing more.

3.3. Theoretical consequences of the idea of the person: losing the pre-social powers of the self and its capacity for personal self-reflection

The very consequences of this argument lead to a paradoxical situation: on the one hand, inter-subjectivity is fixed to 'save' individuals from the 'individualist' and 'reifying' drift of western thought; on the other hand, it is the person and her subjective properties and powers, specifically those emerging in her relationship with the natural and practical orders of reality, that are entirely lost. We can observe these losses in the famous work of Habermas dedicated to the *Future of Human Nature*. In that important book, Habermas states and underlines many times that subjectivity, individuation, personal identity and the 'person' are only possible within inter-subjective life forms. The following selection of quotations is illustrative: 'individuation is an outcome of socialization' (Habermas 2003a: 34); 'the logos of language embodies the power of the intersubjective which precedes and grounds the subjectivity of speakers' (2003a: 11); 'What makes our being-ourselves possible appears more as a trans-subjective power than an absolute one' (2003a: 11); 'Subjectivity, being what makes the human body a soul possessing receptacle of the spirit, is itself constituted through intersubjective relations to others. The individual self will only emerge through the course of social externalization and can only be stabilized within the network of undamaged relations of mutual recognition; 'Only within this network of legitimately regulated relations of mutual recognition can human beings develop and together with their physical integrity maintain a personal identity' (2003a: 34). Finally, Habermas exposes his thought clearly, when referring to the distinction between being a 'member of the species' and a 'fully fledged person':

> As a member of a species, as a specimen of a community of procreation, the genetically individuated child *in utero* is by no means a fully fledged person 'from the very beginning'. It takes entrance in the public sphere of a linguistic community for a natural creature to develop into both an individual and a person endowed with reason. In the symbolical network constituted by the relations of mutual recognition of communicatively acting persons, the neonate is identified as 'one of us'. He gradually learns to identify himself – simultaneously as a person in general, as a part or a member of his social community – and as an individual who is unmistakably unique and morally

non-exchangeable. This tripartite differentiation of self-reference mirrors the structure of linguistic communication.' (2003a: 35)

It is clear that for Habermas individuality, personal identity and the uniqueness of each personality, are all the 'gift' of the social community. The point is that the neonate begins to identify himself as a non-exchangeable person only if he lives in a contingent form of life that makes it possible. Even when he faces the most personal and individual of life's decisions, the ones concerning his idiosyncratic biography, his most secret and private resolutions and determinations, even when he selects his most personal ultimate concerns and self-commitments, he does it because he is talking with a post-conventional Generalized Other who, at the end of the day, constitutes him. The 'I' that talks with the 'You' on the basis of the past 'Me' is only a 'position' in the structure of linguistic conversation. But why is this structure so structured?

The latter question leads us to the 'last' Habermas, the one concerned with the problem of 'realism after the linguistic turn' (Habermas 2003b; 2007; 2008). The problem is always the same, and so are his answers. How is it possible to reconcile the 'naturalistic' and 'materialistic' images of man, as elaborated in our modern scientific systems, with the self-understanding of people as living persons? Is it possible to reconcile the agent's idea of free will – with its necessary corollary of *personal* self-reflection about himself in connection with reality – and the idea that we as individuals are determined by preconscious or unconscious physicochemical processes taking place in our brains? How can this epistemic dualism be reconciled with the ontological monism that describes mind as a part of the 'natural history' of evolution? How can this scientific self-objectivation be avoided, together with its corollary, that agents are led to understand themselves as natural 'puppets'? The answer is very intriguing and fully in line with our previous commentary, but it does not resolve the above problems. In a nutshell: we must reconcile Kant with Darwin. There are performative limits (again!) to naturalistic self-objectification. Individuals, i.e. natural beings, are embedded within a 'grammatical framework of the language game of responsible agency', itself embedded in a socializing context – namely, the life-world in which they grow up. Again, 'thoughts, intentions, and experiences can be attributed only to persons, who themselves can develop as persons only in contexts of social interaction' (2007, 24). What is important here is the distinction between individuality, subjectivity and personhood. The first two concepts indicate only a natural being, part of the world as it is; the person, instead, indicates individuals within the 'game of society', where they need to understand themselves as responsible agents. But, why do they need to describe themselves as persons? Here we find the most interesting answers. To Habermas, the world consists of everything to which we can refer in true propositions: 'this is why it is distinctive of ontological propositions that they cannot reflect anything but the grammatical form of the language in which they (along with the speaker's form of life) are expressed' (2007, 40). Everything else, as objects of possible referents, is merely an 'idea' and, after the linguistic turn, 'we are left with a realism without representation'. Thus, what are non-cognitive objects for us are also nothing but silent constraints to us. Habermas does not reject the possibility of a stratified ontology with strongly emergent properties characterizing each 'higher' level and with powers to influence 'lower' levels in a manner not susceptible of reduction. He simply observes that we lack the concepts to describe such interactions. Therefore, he proposes a radical 'detranscendentalization', based on natural history (Darwin), of our species-specific *a priori* knowledge (Kant), a sort of weak naturalism: 'the structures that form the intersubjective conditions of the possibility of acquiring knowledge turn out to be the result of less complex, natural learning processes' (2007, 41). The (naturally acquired) ability to take the perspective of the other and the mastery of a propositionally differentiated language mark a deep evolutionary break because, here, the reflexive self-relations of persons and a new socialized intelligence come to the fore. Naturalizing the mind means socializing it, if put in the 'right layer' of an inclusive natural history. Habermas believes that we need a synthetic theory of evolution whose key concepts are not based on 'physicalism'. Concluding this strange loop: 'the natural genealogy of the mind is a self-referential project: the human mind tries to capture itself in comprehending itself as a product of nature. If that enterprise is not to fall back into metaphysics, it must remain uncompromising in its orientation to empirical science; but empirical findings will contribute something to this project only if we interpret them at the same time in the historical context of how we came to learn about them' (2007, 42).

4. Personal emergence in the age of scientific disenchantment: a theoretical path away from the dis-solution and re-solution of the human being into something 'non-human'

The foregoing analysis brings home a strange, if partial, convergence between these two very different thinkers. This conclusion is meant to spell out some points that we regard as crucial features of such a comparison and simultaneously to indicate the path sociological realism should take to meet the major challenges that are highlighted here.

After this synthetic analysis it has become evident that Habermas and Luhmann leave no room for real self-consciousness and personal identity. Their sociological theories represent two cultural constellations in mutual conflict, with each surviving by and through its criticism of the other. Paradoxically, they are linked by a double theoretical move: first, a rejection of realism that leads them towards a sort of mutual and inescapable paranoia and, second, the treatment of society as an object of analysis that is inevitably severed from according a real ontological status to the 'internal conversation', as a personal emergent property. Very briefly, let us try to sum up their similarities and differences concerning the issue of personal identity and the internal conversation.

(i)   Habermas and Luhmann never directly refer to the *internal conversation* as interpreted here. Habermas' version of 'internal conversation' is a conversation with and on behalf of a post-conventional generalized other, one that leaves room for a complex identity emerging from conflicting role expectations and the rise of reflexive imperatives. These expectations (the gaze of others), are internalized by processes of socialization and supported by the everyday recognition of others. To Luhmann, 'internal conversation' represents a stream of psychic operations, without a real subject synthesizing it (no transcendental ego, no inter-subjectivity, and no consciousness in the meaning given to it by the metaphysical tradition). In themselves, these operations are 'blind', and second-order observations are needed to 'condense' them into illusory self-descriptions. In both cases, personal identity and internal conversation actually represent a 'socio-logical' necessity of attributing actions and experiences to someone, in order to address communications to them and thus regulate them.

(ii)   In both cases we face the priority given to the 'semantics' or discourses of the self and the subordination or omission of the 'sense of self'. What is considered to be important is the cultural representation of the self, and not the self as an individual ontological property. Neither Habermas nor Luhmann deny that 'organisms' or 'psychic systems' feel something (indeed they do, i.e. they discriminate!), but this does not lead to the emergence of real ontological properties and powers pertaining to the individual that indicate their locus and origin in human subjectivity.

(iii) Both theories constitute a kind of 'irrealism'. They give priority to epistemology (to how we can observe; to the forms of observation) over ontology (what is there?). In the case of Habermas, what is there is fully language-dependent. We cannot escape the epistemic priority of the linguistically articulated horizon of the life-world. The ontological priority of language-independent reality can make itself heard only through the constraints it imposes on our practices. This is what he calls 'weak naturalism', a kind of evolutionary link between Darwin and Kant, re-written in a non-positivistic mood. To Luhmann, ontology is only a particular form of observation. Cognition is the achievement of a secondary system tied to the primary one, namely the distinction between system and environment. Hence, reality is just a form by which a system elaborates and solves internal problems of consistency. Reality emerges where inconsistencies occur in the system's operations (Luhmann 1985). There is nothing outside the internal operations of distinguishing between internal and external states.

(iv)   These first three similarities lead the two scholars to mis-recognize, disempower and make the 'person' a matter of sociological contingency, instead of treating the 'person' as a real emergent and stratified being. Both: 1) rule out environmental and natural relations with the world through which the person can develop conceptions of herself as a subject; 2) overemphasize the other selves (though conceived of as '*personae fictitiae*') in the social environment, ones that logically antedate the consciousness of self; 3) certify the death of subjectivity, by denying ontological status to subjective; 4) deprive internal conversation of personal causal powers and 5) make the relationship between individuation and socialization asymmetrical. Habermas re-solves individuation into a socialization which needs to 'create' personal responsibilities; Luhmann dis-solves socialization into self-socialization, grounded upon a process of self-produced indeterminacy. To Habermas and Luhmann, society is an evolutionary emergent that gives rise to individuality and its semantics. It is worth noting that both thinkers are not representatives of reductionism! Both theorize and describe a multi-layered 'reality' (sic!) as a kind of material continuum, which comprises distinctive realms and boundaries. In Habermasian thought this is easy to see, even if the natural and the social in a certain sense collapse into one another. As he states: 'the linguistic socialization of consciousness and the intentional relation to the world are mutually constitutive in the circular sense that each presupposes the other conceptually' (2007). Mind depends on these emergent properties, which are simultaneously constitutive of socio-cultural forms of life. In the work of Luhmann this leads to the paradoxical dictum that 'systems really exist', even if this is only a (contingent) observation by some observer. For Luhmann too there is a material continuum, organizing itself in different ways and producing different systems (organic, psychic, social). These systems are, in certain cases, structurally coupled and give rise to new entities. A person is a structural coupling between the psychic and the social systems. In any case, both Habermas and Luhmann recognize *the lack of an elaborated theory of the relationship between these different strata of reality*.

At the end of the day, modernity – represented by these two great thinkers – fails to do justice to the person. On the one hand, the 'person' ends up as the Luhmannian fading and self-despairing subject, now tragically aware of the sheer contingency of all his attempts at self-foundation. On the other hand, the 'person' is postponed until the Habermasian dialogical utopia – one that can never be accomplished – in which personal subjectivity cannot but turn out to be a mere moralistic mirror of inter-subjectivity.

But a final question arises: why must the individuals in western and non-western societies alike build their identity as 'persons' with their own self-consciousness, duties and responsibilities? Why can they not simply and peacefully identify with blind evolutionary emergence?

The answers given by Habermas and Luhmann are not really satisfying: it is a necessity to individualize the flux of communications. But who actually needs this? 'Society', the evolutionary drift, cultural development, *l'esprit du temps* as new 'subjects' with their own needs? And what is the ontology that can support these new 'actors/*actants*'? Paradoxically, the will to erase the ontology of the human subject along with his internal conversation, calls for a truly extraordinary emergence of new subjectivities without any sound ontological foundations.

On the contrary, the realist alternative leads to the re-introduction of a stratified conception of human being (individual person, social agent and actor) and a corresponding ontology of society (yet to be fully developed).

To sum up, we provide three bullet points that we hold to be indicative of the value of sociological realism and the main lines of further research to which it usefully points in the near future:

(i) Endorsement of a stratified ontology which allows theorists and investigators to distinguish between social structures and personal agency, as well as natural and practical orders of reality, without losing their intimate and necessary, though still imperfectly understood, interrelations.

(ii) Following from the above, social realism can also offer an adequate and *sui generis* understanding of the purposive character of reflexive processes through the articulation of the concept of ultimate concern and the particular position it is given within the theoretical framework. This constitutes the first move towards a *sociology of engagement* with the world that would be a considerable contribution to reconstructing the theory of agency.

(iii) Sociological realism can also contribute to developing a new paradigm of socialization, which combines the internalization of values and symbols with the self-socializing dimension, i.e. the subjective elaboration of that input.

Notes

1 Note that these two tend to appear together in all 'radical reflexive' literature.

2 This statement clearly conflicts with most late modern and post-modern authors alike, and also with those 'dialogical' approaches which seek to transcend post-modernity, while still dismissing ontology. For a quite scholarly example of this see Sandywell, 1996.

3 Let us note that these alleged properties seem to coincide with some of the most 'powerful intuitions' about free will in contemporary philosophy (Habermas 2007: 14).

4 This conclusion is to be found in the quite thorough analysis of socialization theory conducted by D. Geulen, 2005. Anthony Giddens (1991: 52–3) criticizes the distinction in point, arguing that it should be interpreted as one internal to language, not one connecting socialized and unsocialized parts of the self. In his interpretation, the 'I' amounts to nothing but a linguistic shifter. It seems fair to say that it does not add any theoretical element that significantly exceeds the above conceptual coordinates.

5 See Habermas 1987: Ch. V; Luhmann 1997: 24–30. It is all too obvious to add that the two theorists then go on to conceive of 'inter-subjectivity' and 'communication' in very different, indeed, irreconcilable ways.

6 See the various articles by Vanderstraeten (2000a; 2000b; 2002; 2003). It is difficult to find any literature exceeding sheer narrative reconstruction on this subject. Arguably, socialization theory is a particularly underdeveloped domain within Luhmannian studies, perhaps with the sole exceptions of Klaus Gilgenmann and Tilmann Sutter. See below for some considerations on this point.

7 More generally, interest in comparing Mead's thought with functionalist theory has never been strong. In addition, the existing literature on this subject matter is focused much more on Parsons than on Luhmann. For one of the very few attempts at a systematic comparison between Mead and Luhmann (see Bender, 1989; Joas, 1996) develops a theory of action that tries to take on board both pragmatism and systems theory. See also Vanderstraeten (2006).

8 For this claim see Joas (2001: 89), where he approvingly quotes Alan Wolfe. From a different point of view, this is also the implication of Wiley (1994), whose aim is ultimately to use pragmatism's theory of the self to provide an adequate anthropological underpinning for American democracy. From this perspective see also the recent work of Lacey (2007).

9   This interpretation draws Mead close to Arnold Gehlen. See Joas (1985: 118).

10 We may note here that the swing of this pendulum – from Gehlen to Sartre – draws the exact profile of the presuppositions Habermas has held to constitute the philosophical background of Luhmann's theory of reflexivity.

11 This definition applies to what Archer calls non-routine action, that which requires the exercise of reflexivity as a personal emergent property.

12 Psychic systems, Luhmann argues, use consciousness only in their inner operations, while appealing to other levels of reality when it comes to external references (e.g. the nervous system) (Luhmann 1995a: 421). To say that the psyche *uses* consciousness raises the issue of whether or not psychic systems are anything other than consciousness itself, a question which would receive a thoroughly negative answer. Yet, who or what is *using* consciousness?

13 This assertion appears in many different texts. A very clear statement can be found in Luhmann (2002: 24–5).

14 I am using Margaret Archer's phrase here (Archer, forthcoming), to refer to the necessary intensification of reflexivity in the modern world – particularly in its present, nascent 'morphogenetic' stage of development (Archer 2007).

15 Luhmann's definition of mechanism is a performance that is specified in functional terms, one that can be repeated when needed, makes it the object for expectations and solves problems within a given system (Luhmann 1970: 103).

16 Luhmann 1970: 105. Note that this clause seems to point to *something else*, exceeding the very mechanism (and its entirely non-purposive nature), *which* bends it back on itself, an implication Luhmann would thoroughly reject. We speak of reflexivity here, without taking into account the Luhmannian distinction between reflexivity and reflection (1970: 114): the former refers to an act oriented to another act of the same kind, the latter to an act oriented to the system itself. This would distinguish the sense of self as a system in the world from our reflexive activity upon specific processes of consciousness (like thinking thought or willing to will). We hold such a distinction to be irrelevant for our argument, although it is certainly important for a general theory of reflexive processes.

17 It is useful to consider the difference between reflex and reflexivity. The former term is used by Luhmann to describe mere impulses, reactions to an interrupted flux of experience, which make the action bounce back to the actor. A typical case is that of disappointed expectations. Reflexivity, on the contrary, exceeds the function of eliminating turbulence and reconstructing the undisturbed stream of experience. Note the pragmatist undertone of this definition, which is held to be incomplete.

18 Luhmann has dealt with denial and its relevance in much of his work. See his seminal treatments in Luhmann (1968; 1971).

19 *Die Flucht ins Subjekt*; see Luhmann (1997: 1016–36).

20 This means Luhmann believes that modernity downplays the romantic subject. For the concept of *homme-copie* see Stendhal, *De L'Amour*, H. Martineau ed., Paris, 1972: 276.

21 The tendency to reconstruct a theory of agency and of its connection with social structure in terms of a sociology of engagement can be observed at least since Emirbayer and Mische (1998). We cannot trace the full profile of this emerging line of thought here, and will just outline a comparative reading of Luhmann and Archer from this viewpoint.

22 It is easy to see through these dimensions of meaning to Giddens's existential issues (i) to (iii), detailed above.

23 This commentary on Habermas' work does not elaborate his thought in an analytical and comprehensive way. We deal selectively with only a few essays, directly connected with our problem, in order to outline his position.

24 See also the critical re-elaboration of Habermas' theory by A. Honneth (1995; 2007).

25 See the critical review of Beck's work by Habermas (1992).
26 We do not have the necessary space to comment on the fundamental chapter V in the second volume of *The Theory of Communicative Action: Lifeworld and System: a Critique of Functionalist Reason*, dedicated to 'The Paradigm Shift in Mead and Durkheim: From Purposive Activity to Communicative Action' (1987) where, for the first time, Habermas attributes the shift from subjectivism to inter-subjectivity to Mead.
27 Habermas (1992, pp. 149–204).

References

Aboulafia, M. (1986) *The Mediating Self. Mead, Sartre, and Self-Determination*, New Haven and London, Yale University Press.

Aboulafia, M. (ed.), (1991) *Philosophy, Social Theory, and the Thought of George Herbert Mead*, Albany, SUNY Press.

Anderson, J. (2003) 'Autonomy and the Authority of Personal Commitments: From Internal Coherence to Social Normativity', *Philosophical Explorations*, 6, 3, pp. 90–108.

Anderson, J. (2007) 'Free Will, Neuroscience and Participant Perspective', *Philosophical Explorations*, 10, 1.

Archer, M. S. (1988) *Culture and Agency. The Place of Culture in Social Theory*, Cambridge University Press, Cambridge.

Archer, M. S. (1995) *Realist Social Theory: The Morphogenetic Approach*, Cambridge University Press, Cambridge.

Archer, M. S. (2000) *Being Human. The Problem of Agency*, Cambridge University Press, Cambridge.

Archer, M. S. (2003) *Structure, Agency and the Internal Conversation*, Cambridge University Press, Cambridge.

Archer, M. S. (2007) *Making Our Way through the World. Human Reflexivity and Social Mobility*, Cambridge University Press, Cambridge.

Archer, M. S. *The Reflexive Imperative*, forthcoming.

Bauman, Z. (2000) *Liquid Modernity*, Polity Press, Cambridge.

Beck, U., Giddens, A. and Lash, S. (1994) *Reflexive Modernization: Politics, Tradition and Aesthetics in the Modern Social Order*, Stanford University Press, Stanford.

Bender, C. (1989) *Identität und Selbstreflexion: Zur reflexiven Konstruktion der sozialen Wirklichkeit in der Systemtheorie von N. Luhmann und im symbolischen Interaktionismus*, Peter Lang, Bern.

Emirbayer, M. and Mische, A. (1998) 'What Is Agency?', *American Journal of Sociology*, 103, 4, pp. 962–1023.

Frankfurt, H. G. (1988) *The importance of what we care about. Philosophical essays*, Cambridge University Press, Cambridge.

Frankfurt, H. G. (2006) *Taking Ourselves Seriously and Getting it Right*, Stanford University Press, Stanford.

Geulen, D. (2005) *Subjektorientierte Sozialisationstheorie. Sozialisation als Epigenese des Subjekts in Interaktion mit der gesellschaftlichen Umwelt*, Juventa, Weinheim und Münich.

Giddens, A. (1991) *Modernity and Self-Identity. Self and Society in the Late Modern Age*, Stanford University Press, Stanford.

Gilgenmann, K. (1986) 'Sozialisation als Evolution psychischer Systeme. Ein Beitrag zur systemtheoretischen Rekonstruktion von Sozialisationstheorie', in H.J. Unverferth (Ed.), *System und Selbstproduktion: Zur Erschließung eines neuen Paradigmas in den Sozialwissenschaften*, Lang: Frankfurt, Bern, New York, pp. 91–165.

Gilgenmann, K. (1986) 'Autopoiesis und Selbstsozialisation. Zur systemtheoretischen Rekonstruktion von Sozialisationstheorie', *Zeitschrift für Sozialisationsforschung und Erziehungssoziologie*", 1, pp. 65–72.

Gilgenmann, K. (1991) 'Sozialisation, Individuation, Reflexion. Psychische Voraussetzungen der Verwirklichung pädagogischer Absichten',*Osnabrücker Sozialwissenschaftliche Manuskripte*, 7, pp. 27–46.

Habermas, J. (1987) *Theory of Communicative Action. Vol. 2. System and Lifeworld: A Critique of Functionalist Reason*, Beacon, Boston.

Habermas, J. (1990) *The Philosophical Discourse of Modernity. Twelve Lectures*, MIT Press, Cambridge.

Habermas, J. (1992) 'Individuation Through Socialization: On George Herbert Mead's Theory of Subjectivity', in his *Postmetaphysical Thinking. Philosophical Essays*, MIT Press, Cambridge.

Habermas, J. (2003a) *The Future of Human Nature*, The Polity Press, Cambridge.

Habermas, J. (2003b) 'Realism after the Linguistic Turn', in *Idem, Truth and Justification*, MIT Press, Cambridge.

Habermas, J. (2007) The Language Game of Responsible Agency and the Problem of Free Will: 'How can Epistemic Dualism be Reconciled with Ontological Monism?', *Philosophical Explorations*, 10, 1, pp. 13–50.

Habermas, J. (2008) *Between Naturalism and Religion. Philosophical Essays*, Polity Press, Cambridge.

Habermas, J. and Luhmann, N. (1971) *Theorie der Geselschaft oder Sozialtechnologie. Was leistet die Systemforschung?*, Suhrkamp, Frankfurt.

Honneth, A. (1995) *The Struggle for Recognition. The Moral Grammar of Social Conflicts*, Polity Press, Cambridge.

Honneth, A. (2007) *Disrespect. The Normative Foundations of Critical Theory*, Polity Press, Cambridge.

Joas, H. (1985) *G. H. Mead. A Contemporary Re-examination of His Thought*, MIT Press, Cambridge.

Joas, H. (1996) *The Creativity of Action*, University of Chicago Press, Chicago.

Joas, H. (2001) 'The Emergence of the New: Mead's Theory and Its Contemporary Potential', in G. Ritzer and B. Smart (eds), *Handbook of Social Theory*, Sage, London, pp. 89–99.

Lacey, M.J. (2007) 'Losing and Finding the Modern Self: Neglected Resources from the Golden Age of American Pragmatism', in W. M. McClay (ed.), *Figures in the Carpet. Finding the Human Person in the American Past*, William B. Eerdmans Publishing Company, Grand Rapids, Michigan and Cambridge U.K., pp. 33–67.

Lenzen, Dieter and Luhmann, Niklas (Eds), (1997) *Bildung und Weiterbildung im Erziehungssystem. Lebenslauf und Humanontogenese als Medium und Form*, Frankfurt a. M., Suhrkamp.

Leydesdorff, L. (2000) 'Luhmann, Habermas and the Theory of Communication', *Systems Research and Behavioral Science*, 17, pp. 273–88.

Luhmann, N. (1968) *Zweckbegriff und Systemrationalität: Über die Funktion von Zwecken in sozialen Systemen*, J. C. B. Mohr, Paul Siebeck, Tübingen, (reprinted for Suhrkamp, Frankfurt, 1973).

Luhmann, N. (1970) *Soziologische Aufklärung I. Aufsätze zur Theorie sozialer Systeme*, Westdeutscher Verlag, Köln-Opladen.

Luhmann, N. (1986) 'The Individuality of the Individual: Historical Meanings and Contemporary Problems', in T. C. Heller, M. Sosna and D. E. Wellbery (eds),

Reconstructing Individualism. Autonomy, Individuality, and the Self in Western Thought, Stanford University Press, Stanford, CA, pp. 313–25.

Luhmann, N. (1995) *Social Systems*, Stanford University Press, Stanford.

Luhmann, N. (1995) 'Soziologische Aufklärung' in *Die Soziologie und der Mensch*, Westdeutscher Verlag, Opladen.

Luhmann, N. (1995) 'Theory of a Different Order: A Conversation with Katherine Hayles and Niklas Luhmann', in *Cultural Critique*, pp. 5–36.

Luhmann, N. (1997) *Die Gesellschaft der Gesellschaft* (2 vols), Suhrkamp, Frankfurt.

Luhmann, N. (1998) *Observations on Modernity*, Stanford University Press, Stanford.

Luhmann, N. (2002) *Das Erziehungssystem der Gesellschaft*, Suhrkamp, Frankfurt.

Luhmann, N. and Schorr, K. E. (Eds), (1982) *Zwischen Technologie und Selbstreferenz. Fragen und die Pädagogik*, Suhrkamp, Frankfurt.

Mead, G. H. (1932) *The philosophy of the present*, Open Court, Chicago.

Mead, G. H. (1952 [1934]) *Mind, Self and Society. From the Standpoint of a Social Behaviorist*, University of Chicago Press, Chicago.

Mead, G. H. (1964) *Selected Writings*, edited and with an introduction by Andrew J. Reck, Bobbs-Merrill, Indianapolis, New York and Kansas City.

Sandywell, B. (1996) *Reflexivity and the Crisis of Western Reason. Logological Investigations Volume I*, Routledge, London and New York.

Taylor, C. (1989) *Sources of the Self. The Making of the Modern Identity*, Harvard University Press, Cambridge Mass.

Vanderstraeten, R. (2000a) 'Luhmann on Socialization and Education', *Educational Theory*, 50, 1, pp. 1–23.

Vanderstraeten, R. (2000b) 'Autopoiesis and socialization: on Luhmann's reconceptualization of communication and socialization', *British Journal of Sociology*, 51, 3, pp. 581–98.

Vanderstraeten, R. (2003) 'Education and the condicio socialis: double contingency in interaction', *Educational Theory*, 53, 1, pp. 19–35.

Vanderstraeten, R. (2006) 'How is education possible? Pragmatism, communication and the social organisation of education', *British Journal of Educational Studies*, 54, 2, pp. 160–74.

Varela, C. R. (2009) *Science for Humanism. The recovery of human agency*, Routledge, London and New York.

Wiley, N. (1994) *The Semiotic Self*, The University of Chicago Press, Chicago.

Wrong, D. H. (1961) 'The Oversocialized Conception of Man in Modern Sociology', *American Sociological Review*, 26, 2, pp. 183–93.

6   Reflexivity and the habitus

Andrew Sayer

Introduction

As an admirer of the writings of both Margaret Archer and Pierre Bourdieu, it troubles me that Archer rejects the latter's concept of habitus, while Bourdieu himself was dismissive of the everyday reflexivity that is the focus of Archer's recent work (Archer, 2003, 2007). I am struck by both the importance of the internal conversation and the power of the habitus in life. It is indeed extraordinary how little attention social science has paid to people's internal conversations, given their importance to us and given the fact that we hold one another responsible for so many of our actions, that is, capable of reflecting on what we should do. It is also indisputable that we do much 'on automatic'; we have many embodied inclinations, aversions, and skills. We could hardly be skilled actors if we needed to reflect and deliberate on everything before acting, and Archer's earlier discussions of practice in *Being Human* seem to acknowledge this (Archer, 2000). We have a feel for many familiar games, and in unfamiliar situations where we have no feel for the game, we may struggle, and feel uncertain, awkward and stupid. Bourdieu's concept of habitus helps us avoid what he termed the scholastic fallacy, in which academics unknowingly project their overwhelmingly contemplative and discursive relation to the world on to actors whose relation to the world is embodied and primarily practical.

In *Making Our Way Through the World*, Archer deploys two sets of arguments against Bourdieu's concept of habitus. One concerns the way in which the assumption of a perfect fit or complicity between habitus and habitat leaves no room for individual reflexivity to influence action; the dispositions of the habitus are already adjusted to circumstances and hence generate actions which are conformable with them. This is a general, transhistorical argument against the concept. Strangely, it is preceded by a quite different and historically-limited argument that the rate of change in modernity is such that there are now fewer opportunities for individuals to develop a habitus, for they do not remain sufficiently long in any particular position to develop dispositions that are attuned to it. This, of course, allows the concept of habitus at least a limited role in the past, if not in the contemporary world of 'reflexive modernity' where, supposedly, we have continually to decide how to act. I shall deal mainly with the general criticism, and only comment briefly on the historical argument.

My own perspective on these matters arises from two related interests: firstly in achieving a better understanding of the ethical dimension of everyday life, that is, how it is that people behave towards others, at least in part, in accord with ideas or feelings about what is good or right or conducive to well-being; and secondly, in understanding how class is lived, felt, evaluated and negotiated by people. The first requires us to consider how far ethical or unethical behaviour is a product of conscious reflection and how far a product of embodied ethical or unethical dispositions – or in older language, virtues and vices. The second reflects the beliefs that class is not merely a social location that is internalized in the embodied dispositions of the habitus, but something which people reflect on and try to negotiate, and sometimes contest, even if they often misrecognize it (Sayer, 2005).

Like Nicos Mouzelis, I feel we should be able to find a way of combining concepts of habitus and individual reflexivity, though some modifications to them are needed, particularly to the former (Mouzelis, 2008; Sayer, 2005). I shall first discuss these modifications, and go on to compare the two authors' treatment of emotions in relation to habitus and reflexivity. Next, I shall discuss ethical dispositions and decisions, comparing Archer's and Bourdieu's positions to those of Aristotle and more recent authors, particularly Iris Murdoch. Then I shall discuss some examples of the joint workings of the habitus and internal conversations, and conclude.

Approaching the habitus

> Class is something beneath your clothes, under your skin, in your reflexes, in your psyche, at the very core of your being. (Annette Kuhn, 1995)

At the centre of the concept of habitus is the idea of dispositions, inclinations, expectations and skills which are acquired, especially in early life, through repeated experience of the particular social relations, material circumstances and practices that prevail in the part of the social field in which the individual is located. Being adjusted or attuned to those circumstances, the structure of dispositions of the habitus reflects their structure, and gives the individual a 'feel for the game' in which they are located. Thus, other things being equal, children brought up in a high income, high status family are likely to gain a sense of security, ease and entitlement – a sense that cultural goods and positions of influence and standing are theirs for the taking. Continually interacting with adults already in such positions, they become practised in talking to professionals and managers and in making themselves acceptable to them (Lareau, 2004). Equally, children brought up in a low income, low status family, whose work primarily involves serving others, and who are not valued or listened to by members of the dominant classes, are likely to develop a habitus which is attuned to coping with such relations. When they enter the labour market, middle-class young people have a feel for the game in which the largely middle-class gatekeepers who control access to middle class jobs play. In addition to this class character, the habitus is also clearly gendered; thus, in our patriarchal society, most men lack a feel for the games of childcare and cooking (Skeggs, 1997).

To be sure, the habitus can change as we get used to new social environments, but this takes time and is often only partially accomplished; hence, the common phenomenon of upwardly mobile people of working class origin, who, despite evidence of their success, still don't quite believe they belong and feel that one day they will be 'found out'. Even though they know, *through their internal conversations*, that they have 'made it', the old dispositions or feelings haven't quite gone away. Their habitus has only partly changed.

The processes by which we develop a habitus range from a kind of osmosis or unconscious adaptation through to a more conscious process of learning how to do things so that we can come to do them without thinking. Bourdieu's accounts mostly suggest the former, yet his favourite example of the responses of the competent tennis player actually suggests the latter model. The player can do remarkably skilful things without thinking much about the details of what she is doing, through 'protension' rather than calculation; the player does not decide how to return the ball but is already moving to return it before she can think about it. No two games are the same so it requires attentiveness and responsiveness; even an automatic pilot is continually making adjustments. The player can also strategize and try out new tactics.

However, to get to this stage she must practise regularly and actively monitor what she is doing and correct faults; in other words, talk to herself about what she is doing. Bourdieu often responds to critics who find the concept of habitus too deterministic by reminding them of the creative nature of the habitus, but he consistently understates the role of reflection and reason, both in the acquisition of its constitutive dispositions and in their mobilization in particular contexts, and more generally in influencing action. This is not to say that there is not also likely to be some osmosis – a simple matter of getting used to playing tennis – for which, of course the enabling conditions for playing tennis must be present – but it requires a lot more than this. There are indeed many things that we can do on automatic (driving, from example), while thinking about nothing or something else, but we can also reflect on what we are doing and plan our actions. Reflection itself depends on many complex unconscious or semi-conscious processes (Lakoff and Johnson, 1999).

Bourdieu's claim about the relation between habitus and habitat is surprisingly strong. Archer notes Wacquant's summary of this:

> the relation between the social agent and the world is not that between a subject (or a consciousness) and an object, but a relation of 'ontological complicity' – or 'mutual possession' as Bourdieu recently put it – between habitus, as the socially constituted principle of perception and appreciation, and the world which determines it. (Bourdieu and Wacquant, 1992, p. 20)

As she notes, if we take this stark, unqualified claim at face value, then it leaves no room for individuals' reflexivity. If reflexivity – talking to ourselves about ourselves in relation to our situation – is possible, then that requires a distinction between subject and object. Archer categorizes Bourdieu as a 'central conflationist', that is, as a theorist who conflates subject and object, and hence leaves no space for reflexivity. I disagree on two grounds. First, particularly in *Pascalian Meditations*, Bourdieu attacks both subjectivism and objectivism and is at pains both to distinguish and interrelate the subjective and the objective in social practice (Bourdieu, 2000). Second, it has to be said that like many social theorists, Bourdieu frequently uses exaggeration to make his point; as he sometimes says, he feels it necessary to 'bend the stick the other way' to counteract the scholastic fallacy which presents action purely as a product of discursive reason. At times, particularly in his later work, he does acknowledge lay reflexivity, and his co-authored book, *The Weight of the World* is a collection of interviews with people relating their internal conversations (Bourdieu *et al.*, 1999). True, his later concessions were somewhat begrudging and often immediately neutralized by deflating the role of reflexivity. For example, 'It is, of course, never ruled out that the responses of the habitus may be accompanied by a strategic calculation tending to perform in a conscious mode the operation that the habitus performs quite differently ...' (Bourdieu, 1990, p. 53; see also Bourdieu, 2000). However, we don't have to be so begrudging.

I wish to argue that the concepts of habitus and protension or feel for the game, can be *strengthened* by *moderating* Bourdieu's exaggerated claim about ontological complicity between habitus and habitat. To do this we need to challenge the implicit assumptions of the perfectly malleable individual, and the unreflexive individual. To appreciate this, we need to attend both to the processes by which the dispositions of the habitus are acquired and the way in which they are activated once acquired.

Bourdieu's view of the alleged complicity of habitus and habitat seems to imply that whatever the nature of an individual's habitat in their early years, be it comfortable or wretched, a corresponding habitus that completely accommodates to and internalizes our relations to the rest of the social field automatically forms. Supposedly, dissonance can only arise either when we move to a different part of the social field with different influences that do not match those of our habitus, or else as a result of politicization – apparently 'from outside' – which enables us to think and act differently so that we do not merely reproduce the contexts in which we act. But even in early life, we are not indifferent to the processes which shape us, for we can only be shaped in consistent ways if we have certain physiological and psychological capacities which enable such shaping. This is why socialization does not work on plants or tables; they do not have the powers and susceptibilities to respond to it. Although we are susceptible to a vast variety of different kinds of socialization, there are some things we may never get used to, like abuse, and having to endure them produces various kinds of resistance and pathology. Like so much sociology, Bourdieu's work leans towards sociological reductionism because it lacks an examined notion of human nature, so that, by default, it produces an unexamined notion of human nature as infinitely malleable. Sociological reductionism is also a form of sociological imperialism for it expands the putative domain of the discipline at the expense of other disciplines' claims. On one of the rare occasions Bourdieu mentions biological nature he notes 'One of the tasks of sociology is to determine how the social world constitutes the biological libido, an undifferentiated impulse, as a specific libido' (Bourdieu, 1998, p. 78). A notion like this, of what makes us do anything is indeed required, but we need to avoid a sociological imperialism which imagines that the social world can 'constitute' – or better, shape – this libido, drive or neediness in just any way.

Yet, the mind-body already has particular aversions and inclinations, capacities for flourishing and suffering, and a sense of lack or neediness, before it gets habituated to a position within the social field: *indeed these are a necessary condition of the efficacy of socialisation: without them we would be indifferent to social pressures* (Dean, 2003). No-one is indifferent to what happens to them, and socialization works to the extent that it accommodates to and recruits our capacities and exploits our susceptibilities, harnessing our drives and satisfying at least some needs and wants. That socialization also generates new needs, capacities, susceptibilities, inclinations and aversions and modifies the innate ones is not in contradiction with this; rather, as Aristotle argued, 'new potentialities contingently develop out of innate ones, according to socialization'. Again, of all the things that come to us by nature we first acquire the potentiality and later exhibit the activity (this being plain in the case of the senses; for it was not by often seeing or hearing that we got these senses, but on the contrary that we had them before we used them, and did not come to have them by using them); but the virtues we get first by exercising them ..." (Aristotle, *Nicomachean Ethics*, II.i).

This 'default assumption' of complicity and compliance makes resistance hard to understand, and it is therefore not surprising that *Distinction* gives such an unrelentingly pessimistic view of the struggles of the social field, in which the dominated accept and rationalize their domination rather than challenge it. Ironically, it renders *The Weight of the World*, in which the interviewees complain and resist, unintelligible. Where Bourdieu does occasionally acknowledge resistance it is usually only to describe how it is doomed to failure, unless it is politically-informed.[1] Moreover, the assumptions of perfect malleability and complicity elide the difference between merely enduring and coping with a situation and *relishing, enjoying and feeling empowered* by it, for within the Bourdieuian framework all responses can only be construed as either dull compliance or practical mastery. Even though the latter presents the habitus as more active and skilled, it is apparently indifferent to whether the individual flourishes or suffers. Although he surely does not intend such an implication, his work treats people as capable, responsive beings but not as sentient and hence 'evaluative beings', as Archer puts it (Archer, 2000).

The other part of the problem is that, as Archer points out, Bourdieu leaves no room for individual reflexivity in mediating the effects of the social field and participation in social life on individuals. It would seem obvious that reflexivity, by mediating the influence of conditions upon us, is a source of resistance, though as Archer rightly points out, it plays a role in acquiescence to prevailing norms and pressures too; the 'communicative reflexives' in particular, choose to go with the flow and accept their existing circumstances (Archer, 2007 Ch. 4). However, I would want to argue that while reflexivity commonly plays such a role it is not necessary or always sufficient in making a difference. We often find ourselves resisting or embracing situations even before we reflect on our situation. As beings of only limited resilience, we often feel discomfort and pain where social and environmental conditions conflict with our innate and acquired dispositions and susceptibilities. Such embodied responses may quickly prompt reflection so that we decide how to reduce the problems, but our dispositions already incline us to do this. Reflection may alternatively lead us to suppress such responses, but this reminds us that there are initially unmotivated, embodied responses that need dealing with. We should acknowledge both our capacity for reflection on our circumstances, and the embodied dispositions of our habitus, remembering that the latter depend on prior needs and susceptibilities.

Just as we should moderate Bourdieu's claim regarding the complicity of habitus and habitat, we need to moderate Archer's basic claim about individuals' reflexivity in relation to social structures and events. To be sure, contrary to what she terms the 'hydraulic model' of social processes, individuals are not simply and passively moulded by constraints and affordances; rather, the effect or lack of effect of such contexts depends on the active mediation of individuals monitoring and deliberating on their situation. However, people's internal conversations do not mediate all such influences. It's an overstatement to say that 'the efficacy of any social property is at the mercy of the subjects' reflexive activity' (Archer, 2007; p. 12). We are not omniscient, omnipotent beings; some influences get beneath our radar, especially in early life, in our 'formative years', shaping our dispositions and responses without our even noticing them. Realists, of all theorists, have to acknowledge this.

Emotions, the habitus and reflexivity

This relation between subjects and their circumstances and concerns is one in which emotions play an important role. Here I want to comment on both Bourdieu's and Archer's treatments of emotions and the implications for their theories of action.

Given that Bourdieu places such emphasis on our embodied and partly subconscious practical orientation to the world, it is curious how little he wrote about emotional responses, especially given their influence on action and their connection to the habitus. Even though symbolic domination works partly by producing feelings of inferiority or superiority in people, and hence shame or pride and low or high self-esteem, and even though these are part of the experience of inequality and matter a great deal to people, affecting their psychological and physical health, this emotional dimension is left largely unexplored and for the reader to imagine (Sayer, 2005). Unless we take emotions seriously, we will produce alienated and alienating accounts of life and fail to understand why anything matters to people.

Emotions are clearly embodied, but they should not be reduced to mere feeling or 'affect', and counterposed to reason; rather, as Archer and others have argued, they are responses to and commentaries on our situations in relation to our concerns (Archer, 2000; Barbalet, 2001; Helm, 2001; Oakley, 1993). They are cognitive and evaluative, indeed essential elements of intelligence (Nussbaum,

2001, p. 3). They are strongly related to our nature as dependent and vulnerable beings. They are *about* something, particularly things which are important to our well-being and which we value and yet which are not fully within our control. Thus, the loss of a friend occasions a stronger emotional response than the loss of a pencil. Emotions are highly discriminating evaluative commentaries on our well-being or ill-being in the physical world (for example, pleasure in warmth), in our practical dealings with the world (for example, the frustration of failing to execute some task successfully) and in the social-psychological world (for example, self-esteem or shame) (Archer, 2000; Nussbaum, 2001). In virtue of these forms of intelligent response, we can speak of 'emotional reason'. Emotions also *motivate* us to act in certain ways. The coupling of cognitive and motivating properties implies that 'emotional reason' figures prominently in practical reason – in reasoning how to act. Life without emotions would be hard because without them we would lack a crucial indicator of our well-being and how the things that matter to us are faring. To be sure they are often quickly reflected upon – why do I feel so angry?; why do I feel ashamed? – and such reflections can modify our emotions, either calming or accentuating them, according to how we assess the import of the situation.

Emotional responses to events and circumstances and how people negotiate them are to be taken seriously, both because they matter to people, and because they generally reveal something about their situation, their concerns and their well-being; indeed, if the latter were not true the former would not be either (Sayer, 2005). At the extreme, emotions such as shame and pride may concern matters which people value more highly than their lives. While the rationalistic tendencies common in social science incline many to ignore emotions, to do so is extraordinarily irrational: 'simply, emotions matter because if we did not have them nothing else would matter. Creatures without emotion would have no reason for living, nor, for that matter, for committing suicide. Emotions are the stuff of life.' (Elster, quoted in Archer, 2000, p. 194.) Why would people bother to conform or resist, compete and struggle, as Bourdieu notes, if their success or failure made no emotional difference to them? As an opponent of rationalistic approaches to social science, it is surprising that Bourdieu paid emotions so little attention.

While Bourdieu's neglect of emotions is strange, given his concept of the habitus, Archer's dismissal of the concept of habitus is strange given her excellent analysis of emotions. The formation, reproduction and transformation of the habitus is mediated by emotional responses – for example, by the feeling of contentment at being valued and loved or the feeling of shame at being despised. Particular emotional responses tend to be influenced not only by current events but by the character of our habitus and personality; we may be optimistic and outgoing or pessimistic and reserved, confident or nervous, adaptable or inflexible.[2] Bereavement or prolonged unemployment may make someone depressed so that even when something good happens they are unable to enjoy it to the extent that others can. The depression can become deeply embodied so that even when circumstances improve, it takes not merely reflection on that fact but a slow process of adjustment and reduction of anxiety.

It is possible for actors not only to deliberate on their situation, but to strive to change their own habitus. This is illustrated by Farida, a French woman of Algerian parentage interviewed by Abdelmalek Sayad in *The Weight of the World*; she had struggled not only to escape her father's domination and oppression but to change and heal herself through considerable 'work on the self', which ranged from insomniac introspection to practising what other young women had learned to do throughout their youth (Bourdieu *et al.*, 1999, pp. 583–9).

> ... when I left, I realized the damage and destruction, as you say. I had to relearn everything ... No, I had to learn everything. To speak normally, to listen without trembling; to listen and think at the same time, something that I had never learned to do, I didn't know how to listen, to reflect on what someone's telling me since I wasn't listening. I learned to walk, to associate with people and not to run away; in a word, to live. Something still remains: I can't stand public spaces, I took a long time before going to the movies ...
> (p. 586)

Accounts like this are a testimony both to the power and inertia of habitus and the way in which it can be changed deliberately, at least in part, by repeated practice aimed at the embodiment of new dispositions.

(Un)ethical dispositions: virtues and vices

I now want to examine the relation between habitus, practice and internal conversations in more detail. I can best do this via the examples relating to ethical behaviour. One of the strange features of Bourdieu's work was his lack of interest in the way in which the dispositions of the habitus include ethical dispositions, or in philosophical terminology, virtues and vices – that is, broadly, dispositions to behave in ways which enable or prevent people to flourish. A 'good-natured' person is someone whose embodied dispositions incline them to be spontaneously generous, kind and friendly to others; such dispositions would normally be considered virtues. A 'spiteful' person has embodied dispositions to behave in jealous and vicious ways.

We acquire such dispositions through finding ourselves in certain relations and through repeating certain actions, and through the various kinds of encouragement or discouragement our actions prompt in others within those practices. If we are almost always treated with respect and get favourable or unfavourable responses from others according to whether we reciprocate, we will probably develop a respectful disposition. Again, people may act ethically or unethically on the basis of conscious deliberation as well as spontaneously, or sometimes semi-consciously, being just vaguely aware of what they're doing. We need to acknowledge the whole range. Ethical dispositions, once acquired, have some inertia, but their strength depends on the frequency with which they are activated, as well as on our reflexive monitoring of them. Change in such dispositions, so that individuals become more, less or differently ethical, tends to be gradual and again to require practice. For example, in the negative direction, people may find that engaging in minor immoral acts makes the transition to major ones less difficult, though they may realize, usually too late, that they have crossed a moral boundary (Glover, 2001, p. 35). This tendency is taken advantage of in military training: for example, novice soldiers are made to alter their ethical disposition towards violence through bayonet practice.

An Aristotelian approach offers us an understanding of the ethical dimension which embraces both habituation and reflection. People develop embodied dispositions and characters through acting within particular kinds of social relation and context, which then recursively influence their actions: 'by being habituated to despise things that are fearful and to stand our ground against them we become brave, and it is when we have become so that we shall be most able to stand our ground against them' (Nicomachean Ethics, II.3). Aristotle therefore recognized the importance of moral education – whether through teaching or experience, good or bad – in forming such dispositions. While Bourdieu's sociological account of practice and the development of the habitus has many Aristotelian echoes,[3] Aristotle left more room for reflexivity, responsibility and choice, for there can usually be different responses to any given context. Thus, there is nothing automatic about the development of virtues: people can act in a courageous or cowardly way in response to the same situation, 'for we are ourselves somehow part-causes of our states of character' (Nicomachean Ethics III.6).[4] Individuals still have some responsibility for how they respond to a given situation. On this view, virtue is therefore more than habit; although the courageous or generous person is one who has developed those dispositions through practice, they still choose to act courageously or generously where appropriate and know why it is appropriate (MacIntyre, 1998, p. 62).

Perhaps even Aristotle's account is a little too rationalistic, and underestimates the way in which we can *also* have 'unprincipled virtues', that is, a tendency to act in a reasonable, moral, way, without basing our actions on conscious, rational deliberation and hence without being able to articulate why they are reasonable or moral. Nomy Arpaly provides some interesting reflections on this phenomenon (Arpaly, 2003). One of her examples is from Mark Twain's novel *Huckleberry Finn*, in which Huckleberry gets to know Jim, an escaped slave. As a product of his time – a time when slavery was not seen as unethical – Huckleberry sincerely believes that the morally proper thing to do is turn Jim over to the authorities. But while he intends to do this, when the opportunity arises, he finds he just cannot do it, and afterwards he feels bad about his moral failings in not turning him in. It seems that in getting to know Jim, he had come to respect him, and to realize that he is a fully-fledged human being, so that at a semi-conscious level, returning him to slavery didn't seem right. Arpaly argues that this divergence between action and conscious reasons ('*akrasia*', as philosophers term it) is not necessarily irrational but a form of rational behaviour which the actor had not been able to articulate and justify at a discursive level. As Bourdieu himself put it:

> Agents may engage in reasonable forms of behaviour without being rational; they may engage in behaviors one can explain, as the classical philosophers

would say, with the hypothesis of rationality, without their behaviour having reason as its principle. (Bourdieu, 1994, p. 76)

Many of our actions are not based upon decisions resulting from systematic deliberation, such as working through a list of pros and cons for some action.[5] Sometimes we distractedly muse on a problem intermittently over a long period without clearly resolving it, indeed perhaps doing little more than acknowledging a bad feeling, and eventually 'find ourselves acting' in a way which decides the issue; for example, ending a relationship, or volunteering to take on an onerous job. Such actions are not purely accidental and arbitrary; the semi-conscious or distracted musings may have changed the balance of our embodied evaluations and priorities. Whether we later come to view them as rational or mistaken depends less on whether we arrived at them by a process of logical deliberation than on the appropriateness of the actions that followed. As Archer acknowledges, our internal conversations may vary from focused and coherent deliberation to fragmented and fleeting musings, but she seems unwilling to accept that the latter merge into the dispositions, learned responses and habits of thought of the habitus that enable us to cope with familiar situations.

Embodied habits of thought and action can remain important even where we change our minds through deliberating on some issue. Thus if people come to see that something they have believed is wrong, through encountering a convincing argument and decide that they should henceforth act differently, this in itself is unlikely to be sufficient to change their ways of thinking and acting completely. For example, even if a white racist comes to renounce her racism on the basis of argument, she may still find herself unintentionally making racist assumptions in everyday life – assuming that the new doctor will be white, that a black child cannot be academically gifted, and so on. Having become consciously and sincerely anti-racist she may feel ashamed about the persistence of these unreformed reflexes, but it can take many years of practice and reflection to re-shape these completely. The process involves not just acknowledging errors of thought and action, but becoming a different person with different embodied habits of thought. Although these examples seem to fit with Bourdieu's type of approach, they do involve at least some reflection and deliberation.

Iris Murdoch makes a convergent point, and one which again might incline us to modify, rather than reject Bourdieu's approach (Murdoch, 1970). She argues that modern philosophy has mistakenly equated normativity with free choice and the empty free will that steps back from, or out of the flow of practice, suspending emotions, abstracting from concrete matters, and deciding how to act purely on the basis of general principles (see also Filonowicz, 2008; Lakoff and Johnson, 1999). Rather, we should understand lay normativity as embedded in the flow of practice and concrete experience, in which we continually monitor and evaluate things, partly subconsciously through our emotional responses, and partly consciously through reflection, whether this involves ephemeral musings or focused deliberation. Although we do much on automatic, we do so with some degree of attentiveness, often noticing failures of things to work out as hoped, feeling good or bad about them in various ways, and it is through these repeated minor evaluations that we confirm or gradually shift our moral inclinations.

> If we ignore the prior work of attention and notice only the emptiness of the moment of choice we are likely to identify freedom with the outward movement [i.e. observable action] since there is nothing else to identify with. But if we consider what the work of attention is like, how continuously it goes on, and how imperceptibly it builds up structures of value round about us, we shall not be surprised that at crucial moments of choice most of the business of choosing is already over. This does not imply that we are not free, certainly not. But it implies that the exercise of our freedom is a small piecemeal business which goes on all the time and not a grandiose leaping about unimpeded at important moments. The moral life, on this view, is something that goes on continually, not something that is switched off in between the occurrence of explicit moral choices. What happens in between such choices is indeed what is crucial. (Murdoch, 1970, p. 36)

Hence:

> Moral change and moral achievements are slow; we are not free in the sense of being able suddenly to alter ourselves since we cannot suddenly alter what we can see and ergo what we desire and are compelled by. In a way, explicit choice seems now less important: less decisive (since much of 'decision' lies elsewhere) and less obviously something to be 'cultivated'. (Ibid., p. 38)

Here, ethical being is rooted in habits of thought reproduced and slowly changed through ongoing, often mundane practice, and the feel for how the game is going, including reflections on how we and the things we care about are faring. The work of attentiveness is done both by the habitus and through internal conversations, and there is a zone of overlap between the two. I suggest that this interpretation should be acceptable to followers of both Bourdieu and Archer.[6]

Habitus and internal conversations in practice

Having made some general arguments in favour of the compatibility of concepts of habitus and lay reflexivity, let us consider some examples in which both concepts are needed. The first two concern students applying to university, from recent research by Diane Reay *et al.* (Reay, 2005):

> I was put off Goldsmiths' [a College of the University of London], the interview there was really, really stressful. Oh, it was so stressful, it was two men and we'd done mock interviews here but it wasn't like that, this was kind of like what I'd imagined to be a conversation round a dinner table in a really upper class, middle class family and I was like 'Oh my God, I'm not ready for this. This is not for me'. It was awful. It was like they wanted me to have

really strong views about things and I'm more maybe this maybe that. But they wanted someone who knew for certain what their feelings were but I kind of found myself thinking should I say this or should I say that? It was terrifying. (Maggie, white English working-class Further Education student, quoted in Reay *et al.*, 2005, p. 102.)

Like many university applicants, Maggie has had a chance to rehearse her interviews, but lacking a middle class habitus, or at least the habitus of a child of the chattering classes, these were not sufficient to give her a feel for the game, and she felt out of place and fazed by the confidence and articulacy of her interviewers. Clearly, she is recounting her internal conversations on the subject, and no doubt she talked to herself a great deal about how she would tackle the interviews beforehand, but this did not compensate for the limitations of her habitus.

Compare this with another interviewee from the same research project:

I have kind of grown up with the idea that going to university is just what people do. Basically, my dad did music at university, as well, so I had always been encouraged to do music, when I started learning instruments, which was six or seven, and although, at some stage I always wanted to give them up, but I kept them up, because I was encouraged, I wasn't forced to, by my parents. And that sort of formed the basis and I really got a passion for music. And that sort of passion is really the reason why I wanted to study at university, to find out more and more than any other subject, so it was quite easy to decide, I knew well before I had to apply that I wanted to do music. So it was very easy. (Nick, white English middle class, university student, quoted in Reay *et al.*, 2005, pp. 101–2.)

Nick has clearly had plenty of internal conversations about his interests and skills, but his description also attests to his middle class habitus, with his sense of ease and entitlement, and distance from necessity, his embodied cultural capital, his ignorance of what life is like for others less fortunate than himself, and his feel for the games of the elite world that he is entering. It is easy for him to enter because he is already in that part of the social field, or moving towards it through 'protension'; just as the competent tennis player is already moving to return the ball without thinking about it. At the same time, he has not simply accepted all of his socialization without question, for he has sometimes considered giving up playing instruments. However, he seems unaware of his privileged class position in the social field and of the privilege of having a habitus which is already attuned to it. No doubt that very lack of self-consciousness helps him in the university environment; he is a fish in water. His reflexivity did not enable him to see that most people do not go to university; one might say that only a habitus developed in an elite part of the social field could generate the assumption that 'going to university is just what people do'. This is indeed an instance where reflexivity does little more than confirm what the habitus already disposes.

I generally find that working class students find it easier to grasp the concept of habitus than middle class students. This is not surprising: the latter, as fish in water, do not notice how well their dispositions fit with their context. Working class students, especially older ones who have been out of education for some time, find that their embodied dispositions do not prepare them for sitting around reading and discussing arcane topics for no immediate purpose. Even though, in their internal conversations, they have presumably rejected negative ideas and feelings about higher education as pointless – ideas that are understandable given the limited opportunities and pressing need to earn money in working class communities – it still *feels* strange. Their lack of feel for the game, stemming from the mismatch between their habitus and their new habitat, enables them to notice their habitus.

Insofar as Archer allows any role for the concept of habitus, it is in more stable societies than our own, and she argues that the progressive de-routinization of life produced by high modernity increasingly consigns it to history, by removing the contextual continuity required for its acquisition, so that, we can scarcely form, let alone rely on, the durable dispositions that make up a habitus. Yet most children still have enough continuity in their relations and experiences to adjust to them – the familiar home, the dull routine of school, the daily classed and gendered responses that they meet. While there probably is an increase in contextual discontinuity there is still plenty of stability, and they could hardly become competent social actors if they did not develop a feel for familiar games.

Further, the habitus continues to loom large even in the midst of contextual discontinuity. It might seem, for example, that the rise of marital break-up and serial 're-partnering' must signal the end of the habitus, but the online dating agencies that increasingly help people do this depend on their ability to get users to present themselves in their profiles in ways which enable others to estimate whether their habitus (and mode of reflexivity!) will be compatible with their own. Nor are mobility and habitus incompatible. The well-travelled middle-class student develops a habitus which is attuned to geographical mobility, and though he or she may confidently think that they 'can get on with anyone' and are beyond class, less-mobile working class students can easily identify their middle class habitus as different from their own. In the first chapter of *Making Our Way*, Archer gives examples of young people who, through the reflexive pursuit of their projects in their structural context, were all socially mobile in various ways, and concludes that 'These are not Bourdieu's people ...' (2007, p. 61). She also ends the book with other examples, designed to make the same point. Ideally, one would have to know more about these individuals, their biographies and trajectories through the social field, and preferably, meet them, to be able to assess this claim, but in the absence of such information, some of them seem to exhibit precisely the sense of security, enterprise and entitlement that marks the middle class habitus. To be sure, we need to pay more attention to individual reflexivity and the extent to which people do indeed make their way through the world, but I remain convinced as ever of the continuing influence of the habitus.

Conclusion

In our everyday lives we hold each other responsible for our actions, and assume that we have at least some room for choice. A student who blamed her habitus for her failure to do her essay would get short shrift, even from a tutor sympathetic to Bourdieu. This theory-practice contradiction, common not only in Bourdieu but in much other sociological writing, illustrates the absurdity of denying everyday lay reflexivity and the way it is presupposed in social interaction. However, we do not have to go to the other extreme of rejecting the concept of habitus, as Archer seeks to do. It is much easier for an academic to write an essay than for an adult who left school years ago because the former has, and the latter lacks, the embodied dispositions that it requires. Without a habitus, it is hard to imagine how we could ever be comfortable, competent actors, able to act partly without thinking what we are doing – or indeed able to act competently, even in a social situation, while having an internal conversation at the same time about something else. I agree with Archer that Bourdieu assumes too close a fit between habitus and habitat, as if we could simply adjust to any situation, however awful. We also need to acknowledge the embodied capacities, susceptibilities, needs and concerns, both innate and acquired, that make us beings capable of flourishing or suffering, and hence evaluative beings, and to incorporate these fundamental facts into our theory of the formation and transformation of the habitus. The dispositions of the habitus are related not merely to the dominant social context but also to embodied, sensuous experiences of flourishing and suffering therein. The semi-conscious responses that arise from the dispositions of our habitus merge into the conscious monitorings of our internal conversations. Our relation to the world is not merely one of practical engagement, or indeed contemplation, but of concern. Bourdieu was clearly deeply concerned about social suffering, but his model of human being gives us little idea of why people can suffer, hence why they are concerned about their position and the way they are treated. We need to combine analysis of both habitus and internal conversation to make sense of these relations.[7]

Notes

1 However, he does usefully distinguish the kind of resistance that changes the social field from 'competitive struggle' that merely accepts and plays within the existing rules of the game and social structures.
2 My thanks to Linda Woodhead for comments on general emotional stances or dispositions.
3 Bourdieu attributed the concept of habitus to Aristotle (Bourdieu and Wacquant, p. 128).
4 Actually I think Aristotle overestimated the extent to which people are likely to respond to the same situation in different ways, but he is surely right to refuse a wholly deterministic account.
5 As Arpaly notes, even where we do deliberate on something, such as where to go for our holidays, we don't necessarily decide to deliberate on it on the basis of some prior deliberation; it may just 'occur' to us to do so.
6 Bourdieu himself notes that the distinction between conscious and unconscious knowledge is overdrawn (Bourdieu *et al.*, 1999, p. 621n).

7 Abdelmayak Sayad's book *The Suffering of the Immigrant* (edited and completed by Bourdieu) does just this in a moving account of fractured reflexivity (Sayad, 2004, Ch. 7).

References

Archer, M. S. 2000, *Being Human*, Cambridge: Cambridge University Press.

Archer, M. S. 2003, *Structure, Agency and the Internal Conversation*, Cambridge: Cambridge University Press.

Archer, M. S. 2007, *Making Our Way Through the World*, Cambridge: Cambridge University Press.

Aristotle 1980 [1925], *The Nicomachean Ethics*, (J. L. Ackrill and J. O. Urmston revised ed.) Oxford: Oxford University Press.

Arpaly, N. 2003, *Unprincipled Virtue: An Inquiry Into Moral Agency*, Oxford: Oxford University Press.

Bourdieu, P. 1984, *Distinction: A Social Critique of the Judgement of Taste*, London: Routledge.

Bourdieu, P. 1990, *The Logic of Practice*, Cambridge: Polity.

Bourdieu, P. 1998, *Practical Reason*, Cambridge: Polity.

Bourdieu, P. 2000, *Pascalian Meditations*, Cambridge: Polity.

Bourdieu P. *et al.* 1999, *The Weight of the World*, Cambridge: Polity.

Dean, K. 2003, *Capitalism and Citizenship: the Impossible Partnership*, London: Routledge.

Filonowicz, J.D. 2008, *Fellow-Feeling and the Moral Life*, Cambridge: Cambridge University Press.

Helm, B.W. 2001, *Emotional Reason: Deliberation, Motivation and the Nature of Value*, Cambridge: Cambridge University Press.

Lakoff, G. and Johnson, M. 1999, *Philosophy in the Flesh: The Embodied Mind and its Challenge to Western Thought*, New York: Basic Books.

Mouzelis, N. 2008, *Modern and Postmodern Social Theorizing*, Cambridge: Cambridge University Press.

Murdoch, I. 1970, *The Sovereignty of Good*, London: Routledge.

Nussbaum, M. C. 2001, *Upheavals of Thought: The Intelligence of Emotions*, Cambridge: Cambridge University Press.

Oakley, J. 1993, *Morality and the Emotions*, London: Routledge.

Sayad, A. 2004, *The Suffering of the Immigrant*, Cambridge: Polity.

Sayer, A. 1999, 'Bourdieu, Smith and disinterested judgement', *The Sociological Review*, 47, (3), pp. 403–31.

Sayer. A. 2005, *The Moral Significance of Class*, Cambridge: Cambridge University Press.

Sayer, A. 2008, 'Understanding lay normativity', in S. Moog and R. Stones (eds) *Nature, Social Relations and Human Needs: Essays in Honour of Ted Benton*, Basingstoke: Palgrave Macmillan, pp. 128–145.

Skeggs, B. 2007, *Formations of Class and Gender*, London: Sage.

7 Can reflexivity and *habitus* work in tandem?

Margaret S. Archer

Introduction

There are four reasons why Critical Realists do not, in principle, have good cause to be strong defenders of 'routine action'.

First, social life in an open system is always at the mercy of contingencies so, by definition, people's responses cannot be entirely 'routinized'. Second, the co-existence and interplay of plural generative mechanisms often shapes the empirical situations encountered by subjects in unpredictable ways, thus requiring creative responses from them. Third, Realism's stratified social ontology includes a stratum of emergent personal properties and powers, which include the human capacity for innovative action.

Fourth, as a meta-philosophy of social science, there is nothing in Realism that accords axiomatic hegemony to structural and cultural properties over agential ones in determining particular outcomes.

It is thus unexpected to find Dave Elder-Vass (2007) Steve Fleetwood (2008) and Andrew Sayer (2009 and in this volume) each mounting independent defences of 'routine action' and seeking to accommodate reflexivity to it. All three articles tend to vaunt 'social conditioning' *over* subjects' degrees of freedom to produce non-determined, heterogeneous responses (not fully 'voluntaristic' ones, which no-one is defending) through their reflexive practices. Reflexivity was ventured to refine Realism's vague account of how the process of 'social conditioning' actually works (Archer 2003; 2007), by suggesting that people's reflexive deliberations constitute the *mediatory mechanism*. What is being counter-posed by the above authors is the equivalent importance of *an alternative process of mediation*, namely 'habituation' – hence their attraction to Bourdieu. But, because Critical Realists endorse a transformational or morphogenetic model of social action, involving change, innovation and creativity, their aim is to 'reconcile' *habitus* and reflexivity.

Thus, they also shun Bourdieu's most stringent French critic, Bernard Lahire (1998, 2002, 2003) and his attempt to replace the over-generalized attribution of *habitus* to a collectivity by a precise specification of the *determinants* of subjectivity at the level of the individual. As an explanatory programme in social psychology, this would deprive agency of all properties and powers other than malleability. Andrew Sayer rightly calls this 'demeaning reductionism' (2009, p. 115) and the other two authors endorse the compromise he advocates: 'Yes we do monitor and mediate many social influences, but much still gets in below our radar' (2009, p. 122). In other words, the social order is held partly to shape our subjectivity *internally*, rather than working as a wholly *external* feature encountered by people's independent *interiority* as, for example, in Rational Choice Theory.

However, the complete independence of personal subjectivity from social objectivity is not what divides us here. Sayer never attributes this presumption to me and Fleetwood (2008, p. 195) quotes a passage in which I explicitly deny it:

> Without nullifying the privacy of our inner lives, our sociality is there inside them because it is there inside us. Hence, the inner conversation cannot be portrayed as the fully independent activity of the isolated monad, who only takes cognisance of his external social context in the same way that he consults the weather. (Archer 2003, p. 117)

But, importantly, the passage reads on:

> Conversely, the internal conversation can too readily be colonized by the social, such that its causal powers are expropriated from the person and are reassigned to society'.

In other words, the role I have assigned to reflexivity aims to strike a balance between construing everything that human beings are as a gift of society (Harré 1983, p. 20)[1] and Modernity's monad, who is untouched by his social environment, as in the case of *homo economicus* and his kinfolk.

Only by striking the right balance between personal, structural and cultural emergent powers is it possible to explain precisely what people do, rather than falling back upon correlations between group membership and action patterns, which are necessarily lacking in explanatory power. To account for variability as well as regularity in the courses of action taken by those similarly situated means acknowledging our singularity as *persons*, without denying that our sociality is essential for us to be recognizable as *human* persons.

Three attempts to run *habitus* and reflexivity in double harness

Empirical combination

There is a considerable difference in the amount of *theoretical adjustment* that those advocating a *combination* of *habitus* and reflexivity deem necessary for the two concepts to work in tandem. At one extreme, Fleetwood (2008) and Sayer (2009) largely advocate an empirical combination involving quite modest theoretical concessions from Bourdieu's thinking and my own. On the one hand, both want me to be more generous in acknowledging the durable influences of socialization: that it imposes blinkers on the types of jobs that will be considered by those from lower class backgrounds and female gender (Fleetwood 2008); or that when novel occupational opportunities present themselves to the young adult – ones that did not exist in the parental generation – those from more privileged backgrounds exhibit 'precisely that sense of security, enterprise and entitlement that mark the middle class habitus' (Sayer 2009, p. 123). Thus, both maintain that family socialization continues much as it did throughout most of the twentieth century.

This is an empirical question, which may be answered differently for particular groups in given locales even within Europe. However, there is evidence (discussed later) that socialization cannot be treated as a constant and, that especially for those now reaching adulthood, this process bears little resemblance to the practices continuing throughout most of the last century. In other words, Bourdieu may have been substantially correct for the period to which the bulk of his work relates. What is empirically debatable, is whether the socialized *habitus* continues to generate a goodness of fit between dispositionality and positionality during the last two decades. On the contrary, it can be argued that the young of the new millennium are no longer Bourdieu's people because they no longer live in Bourdieu's world.

Both Sayer and Fleetwood assign a greater role to reflexivity than did Bourdieu because they accept that people make choices and must do so increasingly as the social order becomes more morphogenetic. Although the injection of reflexive deliberations would have the advantage of freeing Bourdieu's thought from charges of determinism (Alexander 1994), it is not clear that he would have accepted this olive branch. Despite his 'late concessions', he persisted in maintaining that such choices as we did make were orchestrated by the hidden hand of *habitus*: 'this is a crucial proviso, it is *habitus* itself that commands this option. We can always say that individuals make choices, as long as we do not forget that they do not choose the principals [sic] of these choices' (in Wacquant 1989 p. 45).

Fleetwood's and Sayer's empirical case for combining *habitus* and reflexivity rests upon the existence and protraction of large tracts of routine action, even as morphogenesis engages. Thus to Fleetwood:

> It does not follow that an open, morphogenetic system lacks routinized templates or established patterns, and/or moves too quickly for institutional rules to solidify and form habits with a degree of success … Some agents' intentions are non-deliberative, and the best explanation we have for such intentions is that they are rooted in habit. (2008, p. 198)

Similarly, Sayer maintains that 'habitus continues to loom large even in the midst of contextual discontinuity', to counteract my argument about the progressive de-routinization of life, which consigns *habitus* to more stable societies than our own, ones manifesting the 'contextual continuity' required for its acquisition. Thus he continues:

> Yet most children still have enough continuity in their relations and experiences to adjust to them – the familiar home, the dull routine of school, the daily reminders of their class and gender position. While there probably is an

increase in contextual discontinuity there is still plenty of stability, and they could hardly become competent social actors if they did not develop a feel for familiar games. (2009, p. 122)

Thus, both Fleetwood and Sayer settle for an empirical *patrim et patrim* formula, which accepts that there is sufficient change to make some reflexive deliberation inescapable, but enough continuity for the formation of routinized responses still to be realistic and reproduced in large tracts of life. Empirical claims can only be adjudicated empirically. One graduate, when confronted with data (Archer, forthcoming) about children reared by four to six 'caretakers' responded, 'Well, they're all middle class aren't they', which places a question mark over why similarity of class position is held automatically to trump differences in mother-tongue, country of origin, religion and politics in the process of socialization.

Hybridizing habitus and reflexivity

'Hybridization' (Adams 2006) entails more than the basic empirical assumption that in some situations *habitus* governs action 'quasi-unconsciously', whilst in others resort is made to self-conscious reflexivity. Specifically, it involves concept-stretching by advancing the notion of a 'reflexive habitus' in order to project Bourdieu's *dispositional* analysis forwards, despite contemporary *positional* transformations. In Sweetman's hybrid such societal changes are synonymous with those outlined in the theory of 'reflexive modernization' (Beck, Giddens and Lash 1994), and his aim is to link them to the extended practice of reflexivity – now itself characterized as a *habitus*:

> What is being suggested here is that, in conditions of late-, high-, or reflexive-modernity, endemic crises … lead to a more or less permanent disruption of social position, of a more or less constant disjunction between habitus and field. In this context reflexivity ceases to reflect a temporary lack of fit between habitus and field *but itself becomes habitual, and is thus incorporated into the habitus in the form of the flexible or reflexive habitus.*[2] (2003, p. 538)

The compromise concept of a 'reflexive habitus' elides two concepts which Bourdieu consistently distinguished: the semi-unconscious dispositions constituting *habitus*, and reflexivity as self-awareness of them. Moreover, what work does calling this a '*habitus*' do? Literally, it states that people now have a *disposition* to be reflexive about their circumstances and perhaps to be prepared for change rather than for stability. If so, 'preparedness' must be used transitively; one must be in a state of preparation for something determinate, otherwise this hybrid *habitus* cannot supply dispositional guidelines for action. Without these, the concept boils down to the statement that most people now *expect* to have to think about what to do in the novel situations they confront. True, but it is hard to see how calling this expectation a 'habitus' explains anything about either their deliberative processes or about what they do. In fact, given that for Bourdieu *habitus* underlined the preadaptation of people to circumstances and the 'semi-conscious', 'quasi-automatic' nature of its operations – all of which Sweetman accepts – it is difficult to think of any concept less apposite for characterizing conscious deliberations about novel choices.

Sweetman maintains that 'certain forms of habitus may be *inherently* reflexive, and that the flexible or *reflexive* habitus may be both increasingly common and increasingly significant due to various social and cultural shifts' (2003, p. 530). What does 'inherently' mean here, given that Bourdieu consistently held the formation of any *habitus* to be the result of socialization? What type of socialization can provide a preparation for the unpredictable and novel? This seems to be a contradiction in terms, unless it slides into vacuity – into something like the Boy Scouts' intransitive motto: 'Be Prepared!'

There are only two ways out of this impasse. One path is taken by Mouzelis who, consistent with Bourdieu, attempts to provide an answer in terms of a socialization that could result in the development of:

> a reflexive disposition acquired not via crisis situations, but via a socialization focussing on the importance of "the inner life" or the necessity to "create one's own goals". For instance, growing up in a religious community which stresses meditation and inner contemplation can result in members of a community acquiring a type of *reflexive habitus* that is unrelated to contradictions between dispositions and positions. (2009 p. 135)

Although such experiences may indeed promote 'meta-reflexivity' (reflecting upon one's reflections), the mode of life that fosters 'apophatic' as opposed to 'cataphatic' reflexivity (Mouzelis, forthcoming) does not seem to be widespread in either Eastern or Western religious communities, much less to constitute a model for contemporary secular socialization outside them.

The other path entails abandoning any claim that such a 'reflexive habitus' is acquired through socialization, but accepts that it is derived from the individual's own life experiences. The changes constituting 'reflexive modernization' are held to 'contribute towards a continual and pervasive reflexivity that itself becomes habitual, however paradoxical this notion may at first appear' (Sweetman 2003, p. 538). But what does calling reflexivity 'habitual' add to noting that it is 'continual and pervasive', given that it cannot be the motor of habitual action – as the author agrees? When the concept is voided of all connection with courses of action, paradox gives way to contradiction. For example, Ostrow writes that there 'is no clear path from dispositions to conduct. What does exist is a protensional field, or perspective, that contextualises all situations, setting the pre-objective framework for practice, without any express rules or codes that automatically and mechanically 'tell' us what to do' (2000). What perspective could possibly 'contextualise all situations', especially unpredictable and unintended ones? Fatalism alone fits the bill, but presents us with the 'passive actors' who have resigned any governance over their own lives, and is just as incompatible with Beck's notion of 'making a life of one's own', in a de-structured social order, as it is with my own version of 'making one's way through the world', amidst morphogenetic re-structuring.

Ontological and theoretical reconciliation

Although Elder-Vass contributes to the 'hybridizing' trend, the reconciliation he proposes entails a more radical theoretical revision in order to make *habitus* and reflexivity compatible. The following stages are involved: (i) that Bourdieu's con-ception of the social order in general and agential powers in particular should be detached from 'central conflationism' and be linked to an emergentist ontology; (ii) that the influence accorded to reflexivity should be limited by confining it to subjects' modifications of their *habitus*. Thus, Elder-Vass sees the main ontologi-cal 'adjustments' falling upon Bourdieu's work and the main theoretical ones on mine. If both are granted, he can then advance (iii); his key claim that most of our actions are co-determined by *both* our *habitus* and our reflexive deliberations' (2007, p. 335), on the basis of an 'emergentist theory of action'.

In response to (i), this is argued to be an unwarranted interpretation of Bourdieu's own thought; to (ii) it rests upon a widespread confusion between the kinds of knowledge required to play 'games' proficiently in the three orders of natural reality: the natural, the practical and the social; and to (iii) it does not succeed in justifying the proposed 'reconciliation'. Of course, the author may wish to adduce this 'reconciliation' as his own theory, to be assessed on its merits, rather than as the progeny of a shotgun marriage.

(i) Can habitus, emergence and reflexivity live together?

Elder-Vass seems correct in maintaining that if structure, culture and agency are regarded as being mutually constitutive, this is incompatible with reflexivity because reflexive deliberations depend upon a clear object-subject distinction. Reflexivity is precluded by 'central conflation', where the properties and powers respective to 'structures' and to 'agents' are elided. As Mouzelis argues:

> it is only when the objective-subjective distinction is maintained that it is possible to deal in a theoretically congruent manner with cases where situ-ated actors distance themselves from social structures relatively external to them in order to assess, more or less rationally, the degree of constraint and enablement these structures offer, the pros and cons, the chances of success or failure of different strategies, etc. (2009 p. 138)

Elder-Vass agrees and, as a well-established defender of emergent properties (2005), protests that Bourdieu's phrase 'the internalization of externality' leading to his description of 'structured structures predisposed to function as structuring structures' (1990a, p. 53), is an 'ontological error' in that 'it fails to distinguish between a social structure and the consequences that it has for our mental states' (2007, p. 334). Thus, it becomes crucial to distance Bourdieu and *habitus* from 'central conflation' if reflexivity is to be accommodated. The question is whether or not Bourdieu's thought can withstand 'adaptation' to an emergentist ontology. Specifically, can his theorizing in the *Logic of Practice* (1990a) be so adapted – a text in which reflexivity is scarcely mentioned – but upon which Elder-Vass relies most. Although he is right to say that Bourdieu did not seem exercised by ontological *debates*, this does not mean he had no ontological *commitments*.

Ontological commitments contain judgements about the constituents (and non-constituents) of social reality and thus govern what kind of concepts may properly be countenanced. Certain concepts are precluded from appearing in explanations, just as atheists cannot attribute their well-being to divine providence. No explanation is acceptable to a theorist if it contains terms whose referents misconstrue social reality as they see it (Archer 1998). Bourdieu's ontological commitments are so strong in the *Logic of Practice* that they shut the door on emergence because of their forceful elisionism – leaving the concept and practice of reflexivity outside.

The strongest of Bourdieu's ontological convictions is forcefully expressed in the first sentence of the book: 'Of all the oppositions that artificially divide social science, the most fundamental, and the most ruinous, is the one that is set up between subjectivism and objectivism' (1990a, p. 25). At one extreme, the subjectivist phenomenology of daily life cannot exceed a *description* of lived experience and excludes inquiry into the objective conditions of its possibility. In brief, it cannot penetrate the 'ontological complicity' (Bourdieu and Wacquant 1992, p. 20) between *habitus* and habitat and move from lay epistemology to the 'world which determines it'. At the other extreme, when academic social scientists pretend to 'objectivity', they occlude the necessarily *perspectival* nature of their epistemology, which places the inverted commas around their 'objective' accounts (Bourdieu 1990a, p. 28).

Because there is no 'view from nowhere' (Nagel 1986), the most that can be accomplished is akin to the Gadamerian 'fusion of horizons'. For academic observers: 'There is *only* a perspective seeing, *only* a perspective "knowing"; and the *more* eyes, different eyes, we use to observe one thing, the more complete will our "concept" of this thing, our "objectivity", be' (Bourdieu 1990a, p. 28). There is no such criterion as the Critical Realists' 'judgemental rationality' to modify our ineluctable 'epistemic relativity'. The same epistemic barrier prevents the lay subjects from being or becoming 'Pure Visitors', capable of receiving or reporting 'unvarnished news' about the objective social contexts they inhabit:

> The 'subject' born of the world of objects does not arise as a subjectivity facing an objectivity: the objective universe is made up of objects which are the products of objectifying operations structured according to the same structures that the *habitus* applies to them. (Bourdieu 1990a, pp. 76–7).

In consequence, ontology and epistemology are inextricably intertwined, for investigator and participant alike, thus rendering subjectivism and objectivism *inseparable* – the hallmark of central conflation (Archer 1995, Ch. 4), which is fundamentally hostile to the structural and cultural 'emergentism' to which Elder-Vass would 'reconcile' it.

Beyond insistence upon *inseparability* and its correlate, the aim to 'transcend' the objective/subjective divide, there is also the centrality of *practice* shared with Giddens: But when we do turn to practice, Bourdieu is equally inhospitable to construing lay subjects as acting for reasons, which are also causes of their actions.

For Bourdieu, the logic of practice 'flouts logical logic' because this 'fuzzy' logic 'understands only in order to act' (1990a, p. 91). This means responding to practical demands *in situ*, and such responses cannot be translated into the academic 'universes of discourse'. Thus, Elder-Vass appears to misinterpret Bourdieu's statement that: '[If] one fails to recognise any form of action other than rational action or mechanical reaction, it is impossible to understand the logic of all actions that are reasonable without being the product of a reasoned design, still less of rational calculation' (1990a, p. 50). This is interpreted as 'confirming ... that he [Bourdieu] accepts that *some* actions are indeed the product of reasoned design' (2007, p. 335). Not only does Bourdieu state the opposite above (the force of the word 'without'), but what is 'reasonable' is inscribed in *le sens pratique* and expressed in action, not in personal 'reasons' that can be articulated. Contextual embedding is all that *makes sense* to the subject of his/her actions: '[A]gents can adequately master the *modus operandi* that enables them to generate correctly formed ritual practices, only by making it work practically in a real situation, in relation to practical functions' (1990a, p. 90)'. Hence, *le sens pratique* is what Bourdieu opposes as 'reasonable' in contradistinction to personal designs (or instrumental rationality).

However, *le sens pratique* 'excludes attention to itself' (1990a, p. 92); the subject focuses upon 'knowing how', not 'knowing that' – or why. It follows that s/he is incapable of reflexivity: 'Simply because he is questioned, and questions himself, about the reasons and the *raison d'être* of his practice, he cannot communicate the essential point, which is that the very nature of practice is that it excludes this question' (p. 91). The answer is buried too deep in the historical and practical genesis of both practices and the logic of practice for the subject to disinter them. In consequence, and in the present, such subjects do 'not react to 'objective conditions' but to these conditions as apprehended through the socially constituted schemes that organize his perception' (p. 97). In many ways, Bourdieu never ceased to be an anthropologist, and *le sens pratique* is close cousin to the Azande (Evans Pritchard, 1937, p. 195), so enmeshed in the strands of their own coherent culture as to be unable to question their own thinking and incapable of acquiring the requisite distance for being reflexive about their own doings.

(ii) Are our actions co-determined by habitus and reflexivity?

When Elder-Vass moves over to consider *theoretical* 'reconciliation' of the two views on the relationship of human causal powers to human action, it is the turn of the morphogenetic approach to be accommodating. In fact, this is no more amenable to the proposed theoretical 'adjustments' than Bourdieu would have been to ontological revision. Although Elder-Vass agrees 'that we human individuals do, as Archer claims, have emergent powers of our own' (2007 p. 335), as far as reflexivity is concerned, this is reduced to half the story. The reconciling of the two perspectives rests on Elder-Vass's *own* theory that 'many and perhaps most of our actions are co-determined by *both* our habitus and our reflexive determinations' (2007 p. 335).

The reason for resisting 'co-determination' concerns the premise underlying Elder-Vass's 'theory of human action', that is, 'with the emergent roots of our power to *act*' (2007 p. 336). This key premise is that 'action' and 'social action' are homogeneous. Colin Campbell (1996) has documented how the two have indeed become elided in sociological texts and thus provided unwarranted support for social imperialism. The same premise is taken over directly from Bourdieu, to whom 'the feel for the game', embodied in *habitus*, is applied in an undifferentiated manner *across* the three orders of natural reality. However, this obliterates crucial ontological distinctions, discussed at length in *Being Human* (Archer 2000), as underpinning the different types of knowledge that human subjects can develop in each order. Bourdieu over-rode these, in typical Meadean fashion, by the 'colonizing' assertion that: 'Between the child and the world, the whole group intervenes' (1990a, p. 76). This automatically renders all action as social action and gives *habitus* epistemological hegemony in every order of reality. Conversely, it will be maintained that our different relations with the three orders give rise to distinct and heterogeneous forms of knowledge, which entail very different amounts of reflexivity.

In scrutinizing Elder-Vass's key claim that 'most of our actions are co-determined by habitus and reflexivity' this seems to beg the sociological question. Co-determination can mean the influence of two factors upon a given outcome varies between a 50/50 and a 99/1 contribution, by either. My argument is that the proportional contributions of *habitus* and reflexivity vary systematically with the order of reality in question and are least determinate for the social order. If correct, this renders the 'reconciliation' formally feasible but empty in practice.

The following simple figure represents Elder-Vass's defence of the role of *habitus* in 'co-determining' action. It also serves to show that *two* issues are involved.

First, are experiences the basis of human dispositions? This is crucial, because unless the move from (2) to (3) can be sustained, then the relevance of move (1) to (2) fails, and with it the purported influence of socialization falls. Second, can 'socialization' justifiably be regarded as a summary term governing the 'experiences' of groups, specifically social classes? This is an independent question from the first and will be examined in the next section.

1. SOCIALIZATION
↓
2. EXPERIENCES
↓
3. DISPOSITIONS = *habitus* = 'feel for the game'

Figure 7.1 A schema of Elder-Vass's argument.

Table 7.1 The three orders of natural reality and associated forms of knowledge

	Natural Order	Practical Order	Social Order
Relationship	Object/Object	Subject/Object	Subject/Subject
Knowledge Type	Embodied	Practical	Discursive
Emergent From	Co-ordination	Compliance	Commitment
Importance of Reflexivity	Minimal	Moderate	Maximal

My general argument is that the types of knowledge acquired through experience of the three orders of reality are not homogeneous in kind, are emergent from different relations between the subject and each order, which *sui generis* permit or require variable degrees of reflexivity from subjects. This makes 'co-determination' an equally variable matter in terms of the proportional contributions made by dispositions and reflexivity to actions based on the three types of knowledge. Whereas Bourdieu applied *habitus* indifferently to all orders, I will maintain that acquiring 'a feel for the game' is a metaphor that does not work equally well across the whole of natural reality.

The above table summarizes the argument advanced in *Being Human* (2000).

In nature, the relational requisite for 'experience → disposition' (say, to swim) is simply the co-ordination of a body with an environment (a watery one in the case of floating). This emergent skill (swimming) hinges upon the relationship between our physiological potentialities/liabilities and the positive/negative feedback received from the water. Generically, our reflexivity is irrelevant to our 'floatability', or babies could not be launched into swimming pools when a few months old. Of course, some might wish to argue that they already had an embodied *habitus*, after nine months of experiencing a watery amniotic environment.

So let us change the example. On two occasions, Elder-Vass uses the activity of walking to exemplify 'embodied knowledge', employed as second nature in mundane activities such as going to the kitchen. Certainly it is, but why do we need to introduce a *habitus* in relation to walking? I hazard that none of us were taught or explicitly thought to incline our body weight forward when going up hill and the reverse for down an incline; we just found it easier that way. In other words, reflexivity does not enter in to the acquisition of dispositions by trial and error learning, but neither does socialization. Moreover, it is impossible reflexively 'to forget' embodied knowledge, such as how to swim; all we can do is to refuse to practise it. Certainly, we get 'rusty', but that has more to do with losing muscle tone than having lost the skill, which is literally beyond us. As concerns 'co-determination', the generic abilities represented by 'embodied knowledge' are a hundred per cent owing to experience; reflexivity does not come into the picture in the natural order. Of course, this analytic statement is rarely manifested empirically – that is, where subjects are 'alone with nature' – but an instructor slowly deflating buoyancy aids doesn't actually teach anyone to float. Hence, the irony that where 'experience → dispositions' works best, this has nothing to do with socialization either!

In the Practical Order, tacit skills are emergent from the affordances and resistances presented by objects and the assimilation of and accommodation to them on the part of the subject. Activities such as competently playing tennis, a musical instrument, touch typing or driving all depend upon 'catching on' and, at more advanced levels (such as improvizing at jazz or manoeuvring an articulated lorry), upon acquiring a real 'feel for the game'. This is undoubtedly Bourdieu's territory, but the following statement shows him completely rejecting the 'co-determination' formula when discussing 'hexis' or bodily skills as permanent dispositions. 'The principles embodied in this way are placed beyond the grasp of consciousness, and hence cannot be touched by voluntary, deliberate transforma-tion' (1990a pp. 93–4). Where 'practical knowledge' is concerned, I fully support Elder-Vass, because to acquire *virtuosity* as a tennis or piano player requires com-mitment, precisely in order to bring about 'deliberate transformation', and thus entails personal concerns and reflexive deliberations about the priority to accord sport or music in the constellation of skills defining personal identity.

To maintain that people, at any level of competence, can choose to improve a given skill seems uncontentious. Thus, Andrew Sayer accepts that much of play-ing tennis is getting used to making returns of service, for example, whose speed is estimated to exceed that of decision-making. But he comments, 'To be sure, she can't do a review and plan each time she hits a backhand, but she can go away and work on it if she finds she's been over-hitting it' (2009, p. 121). Equally, Elder-Vass uses examples of 'hexis', frequently cited by Bourdieu: how we shape our mouths to speak or how we stand (in various situations) is generated by *habitus*, not by deliberation. Perhaps, but that does not preclude 'voluntary transformation'. Plenty of people (used) to take elocution lessons or (now) self-consciously change their accents, and 'deportment' featured on my school's curriculum.

Elder-Vass concludes that Bourdieu's *habitus* 'must be modified to show *how* we, as reflexive beings, are sometimes able to critically evaluate and thus modify our dispositions in the light of our experience, our reasoning capacities, and our value commitments' (2007 p. 345). In that case, he also sustains his argument for the 'co-determination of action' in the practical order. However, in the two orders of natural reality just touched upon, 'co-determination' did not maintain in the first, seemed appropriate in the second, and will be shown to vary dramatically *within* the social order. Hence, 'co-determination' does not even approximate to equal determination across the spectrum of natural reality.

(iii) Does Socialization generate shared experiences within social classes?

To acquire 'a feel for the game' was used literally in relation to the practical order but it becomes a metaphor when applied to the discursive social order. How appro-priate this trope is depends upon the historically changing state of the social world. However, it seems to me that Bourdieu almost elided 'a feel for the game' with a Wittgensteinian 'form of life', through the pervasiveness of his anthropological approach to later social configurations. After all, in the *Esquisse d'une théorie de la pratique* (1972), where the concept of *le sens pratique* was first formulated, this was intimately intertwined with detailed ethnologies of the Kabyle. The validity of projecting the metaphor forwards into modernity, onwards into high modernity and, perhaps, beyond that, is really what is at issue.

It is quite common for social theorists (Calhoun 1993, p. 82) to note that the workability of Bourdieu's *habitus* is dependent both upon social stability and high social integration, reproducing 'contextual continuity' over time. I will not repeat my own critique on these lines (Archer 2007, pp. 38–48) except to extract the precise connections that Bourdieu stipulates between 'class', 'experiences' and 'dispositions', all of which rely upon social stability and upon which Elder-Vass's argument also depends. First, 'class *habitus*' characterizes 'class practices' because all members of a class share '*indentical histories*':

> The practices of the members of the same group or, in a differentiated society, the same class, are always better harmonized than the agents know or wish … The habitus is precisely this immanent law, *lex insita*, inscribed in bodies by identical histories' (1990a, p. 59).

Second, such homogeneous class biographies are constituted by a communality of 'experiences', themselves constitutive of shared collective 'dispositions':

> The *habitus*, a product of history, produces individual and collective practices – more history – in accordance with the schemes generated by history. It ensures the active presence of past experiences, which deposited in each organism in the form of schemes of perception, thought and action, tend to guarantee the 'correctness' of practices and their constancy over time. This system of dispositions – a present past that tends to perpetuate itself into the future by reactivation in similarly structured practices … is the principle of the continuity and regularity which objectivism sees in social practices without being able to account for it' (1990a, p. 54).

Lastly, there is Bourdieu's own admission that this 'continuity and regularity' which was seen above as the outcome of *habitus* is also *the pre-condition of its operation*. This is because such reproductory practices work '*only to the extent that the structures within which they function are identical to or homologous with the objective structures of which they are the product*' (p. 61, italics added).

Now, Elder-Vass does not buy into a history of the Western world characterized by the smooth reproduction of 'contextual continuity'. On the contrary, he accepts historical variability and accentuates that the greater its magnitude, the more reflexivity comes into play: 'most obviously when the set of existing dispositions does not provide decisive guidance' (2007, p. 341) and this is also 'most obviously in situations which are not congruent with our previous experience. For example, when we adopt a new role, we may have to think carefully about *how* to perform it' (p. 342). He even maintains (a view shared by Lahire [2002]) that 'such situations are radically more frequent than Bourdieu seems to believe, and thus we are constantly presented with opportunities for reflexive review' (p. 341). That is precisely what allows a place for reflexivity. Nevertheless, for there *still* to be a place for *habitus*, Elder-Vass has to maintain (like Sayer and Fleetwood) that sufficient stability remains *despite* 'contextual discontinuity' for *habitus* to be of continuing relevance.

Indeed, these are the terms of his proposed 'reconciliation'. Once this continuing relevance is accepted, 'then Archer's account of the development of personal identity and social identity can be seen as *an argument about the extent to which we are able to modify our habitus*' (p. 344). Yet, this is not acceptable, precisely because it is premised on the durability of *habitus* today as a guide to action. Indeed, I have reservations about its blanket role in traditional societies, for was any ever so consistent in structure and coherent in culture that it could dispense with reflexivity when encountering unpredictable exigencies? The growth and impact of 'contextual discontinuity', as urbanization, political mobilization and industrialization engaged in Modernity, were argued to extend the scope and range of reflexivity. All the same, it was stressed that the slowness with which such processes developed allowed the newly urbanized, industrialized and, eventually, enfranchised working class to re-establish new forms of routine action based upon geo-local community (Archer 2007, pp. 48–52). What is resisted is the argument that *habitus* is of continuing relevance in the wholly novel situation of 'contextual incongruity' today, already manifesting itself because of the intensification of morphogenesis. Increasingly, natal background and socialization practices no longer provide guidelines to action for the young members of any class, let alone ones tantamount to assuring reproduction of social position.

The impact of 'contextual incongruity' upon socialization will be taken up in the final section but to round off the argument with Elder-Vass, let me cite the kind of argument that leads me to reject his proposed 'reconciliation': 'personal identity, which seems to be a co-requisite of reflexive deliberation "comes only at maturity and is not attained by all". Hence at any one time some people will not yet have become reflexive, and others will never do so – leaving them, it would seem in the grip of their habitus' (2007, p. 335). Leaving aside whether some will 'never do so', which I do claim in the absence of the necessary evidence, the one case of 'near non-reflexivity' presented in Archer (2003) was that of Jason. This 17 year old, who viewed himself more as a passive object than as an active subject, had been in the grip of both alcohol and drugs, whilst living on the streets since he was thirteen. But he was not in the grip of *habitus*. Kicked out of home by his parents, he had sought permission to live with either mother or father at their separate addresses but had been shunned. Far from having a *habitus* upon which to rely, he had tried to blot out his past in a haze of substance abuse. Four years later he had managed to get clean with huge determination and help from a programme for homeless young people. By means of his limited reflexivity, he sought an extremely routinized job in retail – perhaps wanting precisely that stability which had never been his. Does co-determination illuminate his human predicament by the reminder that, nevertheless, he could walk and talk?

Socialization isn't what it used to be

As early as 1934, Vygotsky (1964, p. 153) was calling for a 'history of reflexivity', recognizing that its nature and role did not remain constant in the face of social change. Equally, neither Sayer nor Elder-Vass deny that social transformation simultaneously transforms the relevance of reflexive deliberation compared with that of routine action. A very brief sketch of these changes, emphasizing the shifting contexts in which the young grew up and assumed occupational roles, is given in *Making our Way through the World* (Archer 2007, pp. 317–24). This accentuated the macroscopic historical shifts from 'contextual continuity', dominant in traditional societies, through the intensification of 'contextual discontinuity', gradually spreading with modernity itself, to the advent of 'contextual incongruity' in the last two decades of the twentieth century. This sequence was internally related to an increase in the scope and the range of reflexivity because of the growing number of novel situations encountered in the social order, where subjects could not rely upon routine action as guidelines to appropriate action. Correspondingly, and especially over the last quarter of a century, socialization has been decreasingly able to 'prepare' for occupational and lifestyle opportunities that had not existed for the parental generation: for social skills that could not become embodied (stock-market trading or computer programming), needed continuous upgrading, and readiness to re-locate, re-train and re-evaluate shifting *modi vivendi*. This new context surpasses the 'strictly limited generative capacity' of *habitus*, which is remote 'from the creation of unpredictable novelty' because it is restricted to 'the free production of all the thoughts, perceptions and actions *inherent in the particular conditions of its production – and only those*' (Bourdieu 1990a, p. 55).

Those conditions began to be superseded as the synergy between multi-national production and information technology resulted in unprecedented morphogenesis, whose generative mechanism is for variety to spawn more variety. With it, the *situational logic of opportunity* began to predominate at both corporate and individual levels for the first time in human history The prizes go to those who detect, manipulate and find applications for links between previously unrelated bits of knowledge; ones that have no necessary connection with one another but whose contingent compatibility can be exploited to advantage. The 'winners' become such by extruding and extending their skills to match the fast shifting array of opportunities or, even better, by making their own opportunities through their ability to innovate upon contingency. All of this introduces the 'reflexive imperative', because the old routine guidelines are no longer applicable and new ones cannot be forged because (even) nascent morphogenesis is inhospitable to any form of routinization.

Why, exactly, did this represent 'contextual incongruity' for the young? The major reason is that family background no longer constituted a corpus of *cultural capital* whose durable value could be transmitted to children, as distinct from cultural transmission *tout simple*. Parental culture is rapidly ceasing to be a capital good, negotiable on the job market and counting as a significant element in the patrimony of offspring. *Les Héritiers* are being impoverished by more than death duties. Culture is still their inheritance but is swiftly becoming an 'internal good' (MacIntyre, 1981; Sayer 2005, pp. 111–26) – valued at the estimate of its recipients, like the family silver – rather than an 'external good' with high value on the open market.

Consequently, strategies for ensuring the inter-generational transmission of cultural capital started to peter out, partly because it had been significantly devalued and partly because rapidly diminishing calculability made old forms of strategic action decreasingly applicable. Those middle class and higher class parents who stuck to past routines, which had served their own parents well, of 'buying advantage' through private schooling began to face offspring who felt they had had an albatross tied round their necks. Confronting the incongruity between their background and their foreground, an increasing number of Public School leavers began to blur their accents, abuse their past participles, make out they had never met Latin, refer to their school by its geographical location – all tokens of embarrassment reflecting their subjective recognition of the 'contextual incongruity' in which they were now placed.

Of course, it will be objected that such an education still gave privileged access to the oldest Universities, but some of the sharpest Public School leavers had no desire to go there. Equally, it will be protested that their graduates still have preferential access to careers in the Civil Service, in diplomacy, and in the traditional professions. However, that is quite compatible with the fact that by the end of the twentieth century some of those from privileged backgrounds began to discount these openings. The fast learners had got the message: the Stock Exchange wanted the 'barrow-boy' mentality on the floor. Effectively, their possession of old-style cultural 'capital' was a disadvantage *vis-à-vis* new openings and opportunities, although it retains lingering value for the more traditional occupational outlets.

In a very different way, working-class parents found themselves in much the same position of literally having nothing of market value to reproduce among their children. With the rapid decline of manufacturing and frequent joblessness, their previous ability to commend their high wages and to 'speak for' their sons also disappeared. With the computerization of secretarial, reception and much retail work, mothers found their daughters already more keyboard-proficient than they were themselves. With involuntary redundancies, makeshift jobs and frequent visits to the Job Centre, there are fewer and fewer remnants of working-class culture to be reproduced – especially the old attraction of a lasting group of convivial workmates – and decreasing incentives to reproduce employment practices among both parents and offspring. The latter, in any case, are now mostly 'at College', for varying amounts of time, but long enough for many to come to think that courses such as IT and Design present a blue yonder of opportunity. Meanwhile, many of their parents retreat into a non-directive goodwill towards their children's futures – usually expressed as: 'We'll support them whatever they want to do' – thus passing the burden of decision-making to the next generation.

The old homology between socialized dispositions to accept positions, which the young were then suited to occupy and predisposed to reproduce, is coming to an end. As the very notion of *transferable* cultural capital becomes more and more tenuous, simultaneously those intricate manoeuvres of substituting between different kinds of capital become outdated. Economic capital can decreasingly be cashed out in terms of cultural advantage. A gap-year, a well-used passport, graduating debt free; these are certainly financially advantageous, but they remain economic because what the offspring derive from them or do with them is at their reflexive discretion. *Social capital* is more enduring, but works through transmitting a confidence and a lack of trepidation (as Sayer noted – 2009, p. 120, 122) *in pursuing* the situational logic of opportunity. Nevertheless, *how* it is pursued is a task to be designed, followed up, and often revised or corrected by the young themselves, by means of their reflexive deliberations in relation to their personal concerns. Furthermore, the family unit of socialization increasingly fails *normatively* as a transmitter of values that underpin the concerns adopted and endorsed by their children. Today, more and more families transmit mixed messages,[3] which are themselves incongruous, and thus confront their children with the additional problem of normatively evaluating and arbitrating upon this mélange before they can crystallize their personal concerns.

Let us look briefly at one quite common example of parents actually intensifying the 'contextual incongruity' of their daughter. This was because their attempted socialization sought to reap the advantages of new opportunities by means of strategies belonging to the second millennium. As a South-East Asian student from a professional background who is taking her first degree in England, Han-Wing filters family socialization through her own personal concerns and what she herself finds congruent with them in her new Western context. Conversely, her parents seek to treat her as one of Bourdieu's *héritiers*, a recipient of their cultural and financial capital, used transactionally to secure their desired positional outcome – a daughter who will return home to practise as a qualified lawyer.

Han-Wing feels herself trapped between parental expectations and her own desire to explore her liberty: 'I come from a really conservative family … so they don't like me going out much. So when I came here, with the freedom, the new-found freedom, that sort of thing – but then I have this guilty conscience – I'd be like, oh they don't want me doing this, they don't want me to be doing that – but I still do it.' She can disobey when 7,000 miles away but, when visiting home finds it irksome to account for her movements and be back early. She can also lie from a distance but not at close quarters:

> My parents have an important influence in my life … but I don't agree on many of the things they say, like religion for one. They really want me to go to church and all, but I don't believe in religion, so that's one thing. My mum calls me up and she's like 'Have you gone to church today?' and I lie, which is really bad, but every time I go to church I feel suffocated because I don't believe in it.

The whole object of her studying in Britain was to become a lawyer, like her two brothers. Han-Wing has no idea yet what career she wishes to follow, but feels her parents only present her with a restricted list of options:

Because back in [X] we have this thing about comparing the children and 'oh, my son's a doctor', 'well my daughter's a lawyer' and all that. It's different here, you still get it but it's different ... Back there it's 'oh your daughter's a secretary' – not so good ... If I wanted to be a wedding planner they'd probably be like, 'What, we've spent so much for you to be a wedding planner!' They'd probably not be too happy. I feel I've disappointed them at home in so many things.

Yet, despite these interpersonal regrets, Han-Wing rejects a socialization that, to her, involves 'treating us like social objects'. Although not knowing what she wants to do, she feels that she must be free to respond to opportunities that are broader than 'doctor or lawyer' and that will entail getting away from home, probably to America. This attempt at social reproduction has actually generated 'contextual incongruity' for Han-Wing; parental efforts to 'embed' her have had exactly the opposite effect – and they might well have lost their daughter.

Conclusion: turning the tables

There is a paradox about old-style reproduction that can be called 'working at staying put'. Approximately a quarter of the general population interviewed and a sixth of the student interviewees, did embrace their natal context: dispositionally they were at one with it, and positionally they wished to remain in it or return to it. Yet, today, routine action is no longer the basis upon which such subjects can achieve the 'contextual continuity' that they seek. Instead, most have to exercise their reflexivity to produce this outcome, which is not a default setting or fall-back position. Their motivation derives from finding their natal contexts satisfying, their means for realizing 'contextual continuity' turns upon identifying a sustainable position within the bounds of their backgrounds – and the modality for bringing the two together is 'Communicative Reflexivity'. This is reflexive deliberation, exercised as 'thought and talk' with interlocutors, who are also 'similars and familiars' and trusted to complete and confirm the subject's inchoate internal conversations. It is only one of four modes of reflexivity regularly detected and it operates through a shared way of life to reinforce normative conventionalism amongst its practitioners (Archer 2003, Ch. 6).

'Communicative Reflexives' come from stable and geo-local backgrounds, where interpersonal relations are warm, convivial and lasting, with friendship networks including some of those with whom subjects grew up and went to school. Their natal context is unlike that of 'Autonomous' and 'Meta-Reflexives', whose family backgrounds are usually ones of 'contextual discontinuity' on a small scale, stemming from adoption, divorce, geographical mobility, boarding school, inter-personal disharmony etc. Such 'discontinuity' deprived them of continuous, trusted interlocutors, threw them back upon their own mental resources, and generally did little to recommend perpetuating the natal context, compared with the alternative opportunities they personally encountered.

Could or should these be termed 'dispositions'? On the one hand, the answer is affirmative as concerns these different orientations towards the social order: the protection and prolongation of 'contextual continuity' versus the acceptance of 'discontinuity' and pursuit of personal concerns that augment it. These very different forms of social orientation are, indeed, *interior to subjects* and pre-dispose them towards equally different social trajectories. On the other hand, the answer is negative if 'dispositions' refer to the courses of action that are assumed to lead to these ends pre-reflexively, because in neither case does routine action any longer suffice. In other words, whether or not the influence of natal contexts – their 'continuity', 'discontinuity' or 'incongruity' – are regarded as *dispositional* influences accounting for the mode of reflexivity practised by different proportions of the population at any given time and at different points in history – no modality can now work as a *habitus*.

Both points are nicely illustrated by reference to the 'Communicative Reflexives'. Here, Fleetwood misunderstands the point being made by and about a respondent called Angie (Archer 2003, pp. 170–6), who followed her mother, aunt and many family friends into secretarial employment. He argues that '[b]ecoming a welder never made it on to Angie's radar screen as a possible target for subsequent deliberation', because of the 'dead weight of (gendered) routines' (Fleetwood 2008, p. 199). This entails the shift from 'first-person' to 'third-person' authoritative interpretation, as was consistently Bourdieu's own procedure. But also, in pressing his conclusion about engendered routine action, he fails to note that neither did Angie settle down to a job in retail, reception or recruitment, to pick a few 'clean' and accessible alternatives. In order to maintain her 'contextual continuity' as closely as possible, she sought to do something much more demanding than the *reproduction* of her mother's social position, she wanted an exact *replication* of her occupational role and social circle. This is the extent of normative conventionalism induced by 'Communicative Reflexivity'.

Conversely, the next study (2007) showed how very non-routine was the maintenance of this 'continuity'. Job promotion, occupational re-location and even overtime were perceived as threats to an established and valued *modus vivendi*. By declining such advancement 'Communicative Reflexives' were active agents in monitoring and sustaining their own social *immobility* (Ch. 4), making objective sacrifices in order to protect their main concern, which was invariably family well-being.

However, three reasons make the maintenance of Communicative Reflexivity arduous and point to its likely diminution in the new millennium. First, the 'costs' become manifestly steeper if opportunities are turned down whilst many others 'get ahead' by taking advantage of them. Second, 'staying as we are' is diminishingly possible: new skills must be acquired if jobs are to be kept, new technology mastered if everyday life is to go on, and new experiences weathered because they cannot be avoided. Third, and most importantly, there will be a shrinking pool of 'similars and familiars' available as potential and durable interlocutors because many class-mates, work-mates, and neighbours will have embraced some element of their new opportunities or have had novelty thrust upon them. Communicative Reflexivity remains possible, but it has become considerably more 'costly' (in various currencies) and involves a great deal more effort to sustain. Above all, it has become a matter of active choice and personal ingenuity, bearing no resemblance to routine action.

If this diagnosis is correct, it also leads to a conclusion about Bourdieu's *habitus* and Elder-Vass's proposed 'reconciliation' between it and reflexivity. Bourdieu's *habitus*, entailing *both* social orientations (dispositions) *and* pre-reflexive templates for routine action (also dispositions) *effectively seems to presume* 'Communicative Reflexivity'. Because this mode entails 'talk' as well as 'thought', it is relatively easy to neglect the reflexive element. If this is the case, it places a date-stamp on Bourdieu's theorizing (despite his reference to '*transhistorical invariants* [Wacquant 1986, p. 36]) simply because times have changed. With them, so have natal backgrounds, socialization practices, and, ultimately, the social orientations of the majority and the deliberative nature of the courses of action they take. In other words, 'Communicative Reflexivity' flourishes most easily and appropriately when similarities are continuously distributed throughout the population – or stable classes within it – and similar situations are consistently encountered. This (Durkheimian) 'likeness', which is integral to 'contextual continuity', reconfirms the appositeness of conventional responses to them and, in turn, fosters social reproduction. The utility of the portmanteau term *habitus* peters out as the objective conditions for Communicative Reflexivity undergo radical transformation – as is now the case.

In relation to Elder-Vass's proposed 'reconciliation', this too aspires to be universalistic because of the *general* theory of action he advances. Later on, he indeed agrees that as change becomes more pronounced, so reflexivity becomes more extended. In that context, his current work on normativity (forthcoming), dealing with the scope and reach of 'norm circles', seems to be compatible with the modes of reflexivity I have advanced. In particular, the situation he describes where the 'proximate norm group' also coincides with subjects' 'imagined' and 'real' normative communities also seems to correspond to the heyday of 'Communicative Reflexivity'. The latter strongly tends to reinforce normative conventionalism (Archer 2007, pp. 270–9). In other words, it enmeshes the subject in local custom and practice, it drags flights of fancy down to earth, it valorizes the familiar over the novel, it privileges the public over the private, today over tomorrow and certainty over uncertainty. In sum, it encourages conventional, localized responses, in orientation as in action.

I also hazard that the domination of 'Autonomous Reflexivity' coincides, as Sayer argues in this volume, with the high tide of capitalist modernity and its intrinsic form of normativity – instrumental rationality. Practitioners of this modality appear to exaggerate the extensiveness of their 'imagined' normative community because they regard traditional adhesion to the conventions of community as outdated (*Gesellschaft* having replaced *Gemeinschaft*),[4] and have great difficulty in conceiving of moral action being rational at all. Lastly, it is ventured that those practising 'Meta-Reflexivity', who seek a better globalized society, in line with their value commitments, also set their gaze upon the whole of humanity as the one 'real' normative community.

This is an exciting prospect to explore, but one that can only be impeded by incorporating the residual *habitus* as part of the theoretical equipment.

Notes

1   A person is not a natural object, but a cultural artefact', Rom Harré (1983) p. 20.
2   This quotation continues: 'To the extent that Bourdieu's "non-reflexive" habitus depends upon relatively stable conditions and on "lasting experience of social position", his analysis may thus be said to apply more to simple – or organized – modernity, where the comparative stability of people's social identities allowed for a sustained, coherent, and relatively secure relationship between habitus and field.'
3   A term introduced to characterize theories where 'structure' and 'agency' are treated as inseparable because mutually constitutive. See Archer 1988 (Ch. 4) and 1995 (Ch. 4).
4   Taken from the in-depth interviews of young people analysed in *The Reflexive Imperative* (Archer, forthcoming).
5   Six examples of the development of 'community' from 'association' are provided by Pierpaolo Donati (forthcoming).

References

Alexander, Jeffrey, 1994, *Fin de Siècle Social Theory*, London, Verso.

Adams, Matthew, 2006, 'Hybridizing Habitus and Reflexivity: Towards an understanding of Contemporary Identity', *Sociology*, 40:3.

Archer, Margaret S., 1988, *Culture and Agency: The place of culture in social theory*, Cambridge, Cambridge University Press.

Archer, Margaret S., 1995, *Realist Social Theory: the Morphogenetic Approach*, Cambridge, Cambridge University Press.

Archer, Margaret S., 1998, 'Social Theory and the analysis of Society', in Tim May and Malcom Williams, *Knowing the Social World*, Buckingham, Open University Press.

Archer, Margaret S., 2000, *Being Human: The Problem of Agency*, Cambridge, Cambridge University Press.

Archer, Margaret S., 2003, *Structure, Agency and the Internal Conversation*, Cambridge, Cambridge University Press.

Archer, Margaret S., 2007, *Making our Way Through the World: Human Reflexivity and Social Mobility*, Cambridge, Cambridge University Press.

Archer, Margaret S., (forthcoming), *The Reflexive Imperative*.

Beck, Ulrich, Giddens Anthony and Lash Scott, 1994, *Reflexive Modernization: Politics, Tradition and Aesthetics in the Modern Social Order*, Cambridge, Polity Press.

Bourdieu, Pierre, [1980] 1990a, *The Logic of Practice*, Cambridge, Polity Press.

Bourdieu, Pierre, 1990b, 'The Intellectual Field: a World Apart', Ch. 9 in his *In Other Words: Essays Towards a Reflexive Sociology*, Oxford, Polity Press.

Bourdieu, Pierre and Wacquant, Löic, 1992, *An Invitation to Reflexive Sociology*, Oxford, Polity Press.

Bourdieu, Pierre, [1972] 1993, *Outline of a Theory of Practice*, Cambridge, Cambridge University Press.

Calhoun, Craig, 1993, 'Habitus, Field and Capital: the Question of Historical Specificity', in C. Calhoun *et al.* (eds), *Bourdieu: Critical Perspectives*, Cambridge, Polity Press.

Campbell, Colin, 1996, *The Myth of Social Action*, Cambridge University Press, Cambridge.

Donati, Pierpaolo, (forthcoming), 'Doing Sociology in the Age of Globalization', in his *Relational Sociology: A New Paradigm for the Social Sciences*.

Elder-Vass, Dave, 2005, 'Emergence and the Realist Account of Cause', *Journal of Critical Realism*, 4.

Elder-Vass, Dave, 2007, 'Reconciling Archer and Bourdieu', *Sociological Theory*, 25:4.

Elder-Vass, Dave, (forthcoming) 'From 'Society' to Intersecting Communities'.

Evans-Pritchard, E. E., 1937, *Witchcraft, Oracles and Magic among the Azande*, Oxford, Oxford University Press.

Fleetwood, Steve, 2008, 'Structure, institutions, agency, habit and reflexive deliberation', *Journal of Institutional Economics*, 4:2.

Harré, Rom, 1983, *Personal Being*, Oxford, Basil Blackwell, 1983.

Joas, Hans, 1996, *The Creativity of Action*, Chicago Il., University Of Chicago Press.

Lahire, Bernard, 1998, *L'homme pluriel: Les ressorts de l'action*, Paris, Nathan.

Lahire, Bernard, 2002, *Portraits Sociologiques. Dispositions et variations individuelles*, Paris, Nathan.

Lahire, Bernard, 2003, 'From the habitus to an individual heritage of dispositions. Towards a sociology at the level of the individual', *Poetics*, 31.

MacIntyre, A., 1981, *After Virtue*, London, Duckworth.

Mouzelis, Nicos, 2009, 'Habitus and Reflexivity', in his *Modern and Postmodern Social Theorizing: Bridging the Divide*, Cambridge, Cambridge University Press.

Mouzelis, Nicos, (forthcoming), 'Apophatic Reflexivity'.

Nagel, Thomas, 1986, *The View from Nowhere*, Oxford, Oxford University Press.

Ostrow, James, 2000, 'Culture as a Fundamental Dimension of Experience: A Discussion of Pierre Bourdieu's Theory of Human Habitus', in Derek Robbins (ed.), *Pierre Bourdieu*, (Vol. 1), Sage, London.

Sayer, Andrew, 2005, *The Moral Significance of Class*, Cambridge, Cambridge University Press.

Sayer, Andrew, 2009, 'Review of *Making our Way through the World*', *Journal of Critical Realism*, 8:1.

Sweetman, Paul, 2003, 'Twenty-first century dis-ease? Habitual reflexivity or the reflexive habitus', *The Sociological Review*, 51:4.

Vygotsky, L. S. [1934] 1964: *Thought and Language*, MIT Press. Cambridge, Mass.

Wacquant, Löic, 1989, 'Toward a Reflexive Sociology: a workshop with Pierre Bourdieu', *Sociological Theory*, 7:1.

Wiley, Norbert, 2006, 'Inner Speech as a Language: A Saussurean Inquiry', *Journal for the Theory of Social Behaviour*, 36:3, 319–41.

8   Reflexivity after modernity

From the viewpoint of relational sociology

Pierpaolo Donati

1. Introduction

1.1. In this paper, I am interested in comparing the theory of 'reflexive modernization', as put forward by Beck, Giddens and Lash, with my Relational Sociology,
which regards reflexivity as a complex operation, used in different ways by different
actors in different social spheres.

Reflexivity is not merely a need induced in individuals or groups by a risky environment. It is not only a reactive process, leading people from one condition of
uncertainty to another. It can also be a capability for reorientation and redirection,
helping to build up new social structures (or social formations) able to manage risks
and uncertainties according to new modes of reasoning. The practical interest is
to understand how reflexivity can be (or become) an operative *capability* creating
new social forms with self-steering competences.

1.2. 'Reflexive modernization' is a term devised by Ulrich Beck (1992, 1995) to
refer to the way in which advanced modernity 'becomes its own issue', in the sense
that questions about the development and employment of technologies (in nature,
society and the personality) are being eclipsed by questions concerning the political and economic 'management of the risks' of technologies currently in use.

Generically, the adjective 'reflexive' implies that modernity 'is becoming its
own theme' (Beck 1992: 19). However, to quote Beck, Bonns and Lau (2003: 3):
'"Reflexive" does *not* mean that people today lead a more conscious life'. On the
contrary, 'Reflexive' does not signify an 'increase in mastery and consciousness,
but a heightened awareness that mastery is impossible' (Latour, 2003). Simple
modernity becomes 'reflexive modernization' to the extent that it disenchants
and then dissolves its own taken-for-granted premises. This leaves the referent,
the purpose and the point of 'reflexivity' highly ambiguous.

Beck, Giddens and Lash conflate the different types of reflexivity; they do not
distinguish between the role of socio-cultural structures and the role of personal
and social reflexivity in producing system differentiation (in particular they do not
accord a proper role to social structures: Elder-Vass 2007a: 2007c). Furthermore,
they do not distinguish between the different semantics of reflexivity: they refer
only to the semantics of paradoxes and contradictions, while leaving aside those
semantics which conceive of reflexivity as a meaningful and consistent way for

an entity to refer to itself through/with/within the relationship to the other (for the human person it concerns emotions, cognitions, symbols, etc.; for social networks it concerns the forms of the relations within the network; for the system it concerns its rules as mechanisms). They ignore the semantics of reflexivity as an activity of what will be termed here 'relational reason' (Donati 2008b: 116–22).

In order to confront the shortcomings of the theory of 'reflexive modernization' (particularly in Beck's version), I propose to reformulate the notion of reflexivity according to Relational Sociology (Donati 1991), which defines reflexivity in wider and more comprehensive ways. This entails the following steps.

1 Reflexivity is defined as a social relation between Ego and Alter within a social context. *Alter* can be *Ego's* self, and in this case we refer to personal reflexivity or internal conversation (in Archer's sense). If *Alter* is another person or many persons, we observe social reflexivity (one of an interactive character). If *Ego* and *Alter* are parts of a system, we meet system reflectivity. In any case, reflexivity has nothing to do with the notion of *self-confrontation* as used by Beck (1992: 6), since the confrontation he speaks of is an undetermined backlash from another party that involves no bending back by the self upon the self (in this case at the level of the system).

2 The ambivalence of reflexivity is redefined as a differential property/ability possessed by actors, or networks, or systems with regard to their need for managing the outcomes of morphogenetic processes.

3 Paradoxicality pervades Beck's thinking about reflexivity. Whereas extended reflexivity should introduce more self-monitoring and self-control, in fact, it has the opposite results, since second wave modernity has no 'brakes or steering wheel' (Beck 1994b: 180) and undermines itself – 'modernization undercuts modernization …' (Beck 1994b: 177). This is redefined here as a need for connecting freedoms with regulations and controls (Donati 2000).

1.3. In order to develop a *relational theory of reflexivity* that is more adequate than the theory of 'reflexive modernity' for the analysis of globalizing society, I will build upon Margaret Archer's theory of reflexivity (2003, 2007) from a relational standpoint. On the basis of this framework, I will propose a sociological analysis of the ways in which the processes of globalization are differentiating the spheres of society, so to produce a newly emergent society. The concept of 'relational differentiation' will be ventured as a property inherent to the globalization process. It is one that also provides a basis for conceiving of an emergent 'civil society', quite different from that envisaged by the theory of 'reflexive modernization'. In conclusion, the theory of reflexive modernization is replaced by a theory of relational differentiation through reflexivity.

2. Reflexivity as viewed from relational sociology

The basic schema is presented in Figure 8.1 and is effectively that advanced in Archer's work to date. It describes reflexivity as an intervening variable between the forms of structural conditioning impinging upon individuals and the outcomes, the latter consisting in structural phenomena that emerge from the different types of reflexivity used by agents during interaction with one another in the intermediary phase of the morphogenetic process.

This schema puts forward the hypothesis that the social phenomena emerging in a globalized society are mediated by the different modes of reflexivity practised by individuals and social groups in their mutual interactions, under the constraints of structural conditioning. Reflexivity is synonymous with internal conversation, and therefore pertains to human persons and not to social networks and organizations. It can, however, be extended to social groups, in so far as they can express a collective mode of reflexivity.

Archer defines reflexivity as 'the regular exercise of the mental ability, shared by all normal people, to consider themselves in relation to their (social) contexts and vice versa' (Archer 2007: 4). She strongly and rightly criticizes Beck's notion of systemic reflexivity (Archer 2007: 30–2). Nevertheless, I think that her theory can be extended to include the distinction between *systemic* reflexivity and *social* reflexivity: the former refers to the socio-cultural structures and their interactive 'parts', with their powers and qualities, while the latter refers to (interpersonal) relationships among human persons.[1]

By suggesting this distinction, I wish to put forward a sociological theory which is able to recognize that there is a kind of reflexivity pertaining to socio-cultural structures themselves, which influences individuals and their interactions via the context in which they find themselves, and is bound to reappear in the outcomes (structural elaborations) of the morphogenetic process. This, of course, has nothing in common with Beck's notion of systemic reflexivity.

To be more precise, we should speak of *system reflectivity* instead of system reflexivity, in order to maintain the difference between the former, and, on the other hand, the subjective nature of personal reflexivity and the inter-subjective character of social reflexivity (as Archer rightly points out). In my vocabulary: *reflection* is a self-referential operation of an individual mind which bends back on itself within itself (e.g. the word 'reflection' is used in computer science to indicate the process by which a computer program can observe and modify its own structure and behaviour). *Reflectivity* is the same operation when performed by a system.

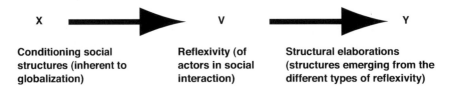

Figure 8.1 The basic schema for the social role of reflexivity in social change.

Conversely, *reflexivity* is a relational operation on the part of an individual mind in relation to an 'Other' who can be internal (the *Ego* as an Other) or external (Alter), but who also takes the social context into account. This generates a relationship which is an emergent effect from the terms related by it. When I use the expression 'system reflexivity' (according to widespread custom) I will always mean system *reflectivity*.

What such a sociological theory should be able to yield are answers to many questions which are still outstanding: specifically, does the systemic reflexivity of the conditioning structures change – in what ways and to what extent – during the morphogenetic process, between its start and its outcomes?

My relational approach lends itself to extending the first-order conceptual framework (Figure 8. 1) into a more complex model, in the following ways (summarized in Figure 8.2).

1 The conditioning structures are characterized in terms of social differentiation (see Donati 2008b: 77–90), as is also maintained by Archer. In particular, I am interested in exploring what we can learn by conceiving of structures as relational realities and by thinking of a new type of differentiation which I call 'relational differentiation', which goes beyond Durkheim's fissiparous notion of structural differentiation.
2 I propose extending the notion of reflexivity to social networks. Within the realm of social relations, we find kinds of reflexivity that are not personal mental activities (i.e. *personal reflexivity* = internal conversation), but a mixture of *social* and *system reflexivity*. In other words, social networks are not only a context where personal reflexivity takes place, but can have their own reflexivity of a distinctive kind in respect to personal (agential) reflexivity, provided that they have certain relational qualities (i.e. are not structures deprived of relationality).
3 Therefore, besides personal (internal conversation) and social (interactive) reflexivity, we can conceive of a reflexivity inherent to social structures (conceptualized as relational networks), which has its own dynamics that are operative throughout the morphogenetic process.

Figure 8.2 represents the extended schema that distinguishes the different ways in which reflexivity operates in the social world. 'System reflexivity', as conceived here, refers to the dynamics of socio-cultural structures, their powers and *mechanisms* (in Figure 8.2 it is indicated by the direct dotted arrow between X and Y); *social* reflexivity refers to the relationships of actors who have their own 'personal reflexivity' (in Figure 8.2 it follows the line from X to Y *via* V).

In Figure 8.2 it is assumed that the structural process (the direct line from X to Y), attributable to system reflexivity, is much weaker than the effects of social reflexivity (the indirect line from X to V to Y), because of the intervening factors constituted by personal and social (interactional) reflexivity. The latter presumption is necessitated by the very adoption of the morphogenetic framework to understand and explain the overall outcome.

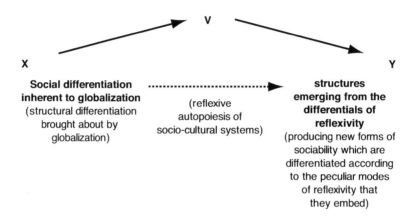

Personal Reflexivity (of persons) → Social Reflexivity
(emerging from interactions among individuals with their *personal*
reflexivity, in those social networks possessing relational emergent properties)

V

X

**Social differentiation
inherent to globalization**
(structural differentiation
brought about by
globalization)

(reflexive
autopoiesis of
socio-cultural systems)

Y

**structures
emerging from the
differentials of
reflexivity**
(producing new forms of
sociability which are
differentiated according
to the peculiar modes
of reflexivity that
they embed)

Figure 8.2 The basic schema extended according to the relational theory of society.

Empirical evidences of these routes of reflexivity can be found within 'shared informatics' (Berra, Meo 2001), and particularly in *co-production* and *peer-to-peer production* of cyber-commons (Bauwens 2009; see the documentation available at the website http://integralvisioning.org/article.php?story=p. 2ptheory1). For instance, conceived of as structural elaborations, such common intellectual goods are certainly intentional products of actors who want to create shared goods (as such, they are products of a social reflexivity connected to the personal reflexivity of each actor), but they are also the products of a (systemic) reflexivity that inheres in the social networks making up the internet. Individual actors are conditioned by these structures in which shared goods are created as opportunities that they can realize and manage (and, to a limited extent, guide).

This conceptual framework seeks to emphasize not only the search for different types of personal reflexivity, but, in addition, the differentials of reflexivity that are produced by social processes. These 'differentials' pertain to individuals as well as social networks (and therefore social groups) and characterize the emerging structures of the morphogenetic processes inherent to globalization.

The new kind of social differentiation suggested by the relational theory of society, i.e. *relational differentiation*, is only one of the possibilities opened up by the morphogenetic cycle under globalized conditions. *It emerges when structural differentiation introduces (what Archer calls) 'the reflexivity imperative' into social relations instead of sticking only to system reflexivity or relying upon personal reflexivity alone* or a mixture of the two.

In later sections I will try to clarify how the processes of globalization lead to new emergent forms of differentiation (Section 4) ones that, in turn, induce new needs for extended reflexivity (Section 5).

At this point, according to my extended schema, I shall have to show that the emergent effects (structural elaborations) are not produced directly by structural differentiation, but come in to existence through the intervening factor of social reflexivity, which depends on the personal reflexivity of the actors at the agential level of interactions between Ego and Alter (Section 6). These insights should help us to see how and why an emergent civil society can be envisaged as a product of specific reflexive processes. The concluding aim of this paper is to advance an alternative to the theory of reflexive modernization as put forward by Beck and colleagues.

3. Globalization and new forms of relational differentiation

'Reflexive modernity' can be understood either as a societal configuration derived from late modernity or simply as a stage of modernity *qua talis* coming about through processes of societal differentiation. Which forms of differentiation? Sociological theory usually distinguishes three paradigmatic types of societal differentiation: segmentary, stratified and functional (Luhmann 1982). Changes in the different spheres of society are social configurations which follow one another because they stem from the emerging modalities of societal differentiation.

From the perspective of Relational Sociology, the main phases of societal differentiation can be conceptualized schematically in four stages (Table 8.1), showing how each form of differentiation implies a prevailing mode of reflexivity (in accordance with Archer's theory). At the same time, the connection between a specific type of differentiation and a specific type of reflexivity implies a semantics or a principle (or symbolic code, in Luhmannian terms) of social identity and also allows for the emergence of certain social spheres as distinctive of a specific historical configuration of society.

1   At the beginning of human history, society is confined to the primitive tribe. The contemporary phenomenon of 'cultural tribes', as described by M. Maffesoli in 'post-modern' societies, also conforms to a very limited extent to this configuration, because it emerges in a societal context which is not only much more differentiated, but is fundamentally based upon differentiation as its constitutive principle. In any case, within this configuration, in which the individual identifies him/herself with belonging to a cultural tribe (for instance in the field of consumption), reflexivity assumes a character that depends on communication with significant others (it corresponds to the category of 'communicative reflexivity' as described by Archer 2003).

2   Within traditional (ancient and pre-modern) societies, societal differentiation is stratified into divisions of classes/strata (the market being residual). In the City State, these strata are configured as an organic and hierarchic body. Individuals are ascribed to a single social stratum and they can exercise their personal and social reflexivity within the limits of each social position (reflexivity works as a positional good).

3   Within modern society (characterized by the spread of the capitalist market, with its institutions, particularly the contract and political democracy), a

Table 8.1 Forms of societal differentiation and their related types of reflexivity, principles of identity, and associated empirical spheres in society

Historical forms of differentiation	Types of dominant reflexivity	Principle of identity (I = identity)	Related spheres of society
a. segmentary differentiation	Reflexivity is reproductive (tribal): it depends entirely on the communication with significant others = communicative reflexivity	I = collective conscience (personal I = collective I)	Tribe, primitive family forms
b. stratified differentiation	Reflexivity is stratified (i.e. it is exercised within the provinces of meanings corresponding to the strata of a hierarchical society) = autonomous reflexivity (within the borders of each stratum)	I = position in a social scale (I = belonging to a specific status or stratum as a limited province of action)	State, hierarchy, bureaucracy
c. functional differentiation	Reflexivity is functional in so far as it performs a specialized role within a social system which is an 'open society' based on acquisition/achievement = 'autonomous reflexivity'	I = system function as a specialized performance (I = not/not-I: the denial of what is not I)	Market
d. relational differentiation	Reflexivity is a relationship to the self through the other, or to the self as 'other' (within circuits or networks of reciprocity = 'meta-reflexivity')	I = a relationship between I and non-I (the other) (identity comes from the relationship with the other)	Third sector, social private spheres, new civil society

functional differentiation emerges. The dominant modality of reflexivity is homogeneous to the market, consequently the dominant type to emerge is acquisitive reflexivity which Archer calls 'autonomous reflexivity'.

4   What happens when societies encounter globalization? Luhmann holds that the form of differentiation inherent to globalization is still a functional one, although it becomes more complex. To him, societal differentiation cannot take an organic form any longer (as was supposed by Parsons, who followed Durkheim, in endorsing the part/whole paradigm). This becomes a more radical version of the self-referential reflexivity he terms 'autopoiesis'. I do not share this view. My argument is not that we should return to Parsons, since Luhmann is right when he claims that the functional differentiation of society cannot return to antecedent forms. On the contrary, I argue that a new form of societal differentiation is emerging, which I term *'relational differentiation'*. This is propelled by a specific – and to some degree new – *form of*

reflexivity centred on the social relation, meaning that it is a form of reflexivity *focused upon what social relationality offers, by its emergence, beyond the contributions of the single actors who trigger it.*

It is second-order reflexivity, in so far as it concerns the effect that social relationality, as an emergent phenomenon, has upon actors and their relationships within a social structure that has just differentiated itself on the basis of the same relation. Let us give an example. When functional differentiation between the family and the corporation has reached its limits, in the sense that co-ordinating measures are (or need to be) brought into play, such measures should reinforce the relationship between the family and the corporation in such a manner as to be a positive resource for both of them. What is at stake is precisely their relationship, which becomes a focus in itself and serves to guide what has to be done in both contexts – family life and the workplace – in order to make them reflexively positive towards each other (for instance: increasing, instead of depressing or consuming, their specific forms of 'social capital').

The mode of reflexivity that Archer terms 'meta-reflexivity' is particularly significant as a form of relational reflexivity. From the point of view of personal reflexivity, 'meta-reflexives' are those who are discontented with the relationship between themselves as well as being disappointed with the results of their courses of action. The 'meta-reflexive' examines the relationship before he/she evaluates the concrete goals or results of his/her action.

At the societal level, the macro-correlate of relational differentiation is the third sector and, more generally, a new post-bourgeois civil society composed of those social formations that are 'associational' in kind, being built up through networking. They do not pertain either to the market or to the state and they exceed family networks. These spheres are characterized by the fact that, within them, the circulation of goods proceeds on the basis of social rules and evaluative criteria that are based upon neither the profit motive nor legal commands, and go beyond motives of pure affection. Their *raison d'être* is to 'remain in this relationship', a social relation of a certain kind (quality), because only through it can one can enjoy particular fruits. Generally speaking these fruits are 'relational goods' (Donati 1991, 2003).

The 'fractured' ('impeded' and 'displaced') forms of reflexivity are found in every societal sphere as a modality that is pathological with respect to the form that should (in principle) be dominant in that domain (respectively: 'autonomous reflexivity' in the market, 'communicative reflexivity' in the family, and 'meta-reflexivity' in the third sector). In her empirical research, Archer does not touch upon the field of politics or the politicians. Is there something like a 'dominant form' of reflexivity in this latter domain? To my mind, this field may be characterized by a form of 'strategic-tactic reflexivity' which, particularly in post-modern societies, produces fractured people with typically paranoid behaviour because the strategic targets of politics are constantly undermined by the tactical moves made, and tactics continually undermine strategy.

Historically, we can say that society passes from one form of societal differentiation to another because groups of individuals leave the previous configuration by developing a morphogenetic process that produces a new configuration, characterized by a different form of societal differentiation, implying a different mode of reflexivity. In turn, new empirical social spheres are generated. Let us think of some crucial historical passages.

Stratified differentiation emerges when an aristocratic stratum (a class, status, power group) detaches itself from the 'common people' belonging to the primitive tribe and configures a political body constituting 'the state', for instance in the form of the Greek *Polis* or the ancient Roman Republic (remember the famous apologia by Menenius Agrippa). Functional differentiation first emerges from merchant groups overflowing from the medieval court (and called 'bourgeois', since they lived and flourished in the '*borgo*', the suburb outside the castle). Nowadays, the so called third sector (which I call 'the social private sphere') emerges from the capitalist market (functional society) thanks to social groups and movements that are searching for a different mode of social exchange and give priority to relational differentiation in place of the functional mode, which, when generalized, will constitute societal change.

In parallel, according to my critical-relational theory, reflexivity becomes more and more important as an operation necessary for generating 'identity'. This is because the historical process of societal differentiation requires an exercise of reflexivity that must be simultaneously more complex and more pertinent to each societal sphere.

With segmentary differentiation, reflexivity is basically reproductive. The differentiation of society is simply the replication of the same 'societal segment'. Society does not self-differentiate from inside itself. The identity of the individual coincides with the collective conscience of the tribe and is exercised automatically (as *habitus*), constantly inserting the collective 'I' into the personal 'I'. The dominant mode of reflexivity is therefore one that depends on communication. The other forms of reflexivity are either very scarce or absent.

Within stratified differentiation, reflexivity becomes a social activity which is formed through the distinction of different social strata. Social identity coincides with the social status to which one belongs, according to a predetermined scale of values. The social cleavages between strata are rigid and the constraints very strong. Reflexivity is distributed in such a way as to be freer and wider in the upper social strata, and more repetitive, constrained and narrower in the lower social strata.

With the advent of functional differentiation, identity is no longer formed through belonging to a social group (tribe or class or status), but derives from the position that the individual has in the functional division of labour in society, and is therefore a consequence of his/her functional performance. Social relations are thought of, and practised, as functional imperatives. Social identity assumes a strongly instrumental connotation. It becomes an aggregate of economic and political interests, leaving aside their 'cultural foundations'. Identity is now formed through a double negation: the Self is the negation of all that is not the Self, and develops in opposition to all that is a stranger to it, i.e. the Other (non-Self).

Identity is formed in an open market of autonomous subjects who potentially have no limits to their agency.

When this societal configuration reaches its limits (or, as some say: 'becomes mature'),[2] social identity suffers from commodification, to which it is subjected more and more. It is precisely at this point that social interactions (as exchanges) must redefine social identity taking into account the need for relating to the other in a non-functional way. This way may be called '*supra-functional*' since the relationship it implies is not a response to specific functional requirements: the functional imperative must cede to the 'reflexive imperative', as Archer calls it. It follows, of course, that the reflexive imperative must be more and more supra-functional. In my own words, the Self must now be formed through the relationship to the Other, and even to oneself as Other. When and how does this passage occur?

My answer is that this step becomes necessary when nation-states can no longer regulate the processes of globalization, i.e. when social systems cannot work satis-factorily within national boundaries, but are forced to act through a new form of relationality between the local and the global.

4. Globalization produces an 'emergent society'

Globalization is a societal process that radically changes the social division of labour and simultaneously modifies social differentiation. To begin with, let us see what happens in the field of work and economy, i.e. the field where the evalu-ation of functional performances is most prevalent. Globalization entails three great transformations of labour: these can be labelled as transfers, emergences and transcendences. Together they create an environment of an unprecedented kind for work activities (Therborn 2000).

1   First, globalization means intensified transfers (exchanges) and relations at the planetary level. Interchanges are internationalized. Not a single job can be immune from this new interactional enrrivonment. If every job becomes more and more interrelated with other jobs, then locality and globality come to be constituted in a reciprocal way.[3] Every job must exchange more and more with its environment.

2   Second, in quite an opposite – but at the same time complementary – direc-tion, globalization means increased interaction inside every work unit within the social system. This is due to the fact that every single dimension of work can exchange autonomously with the outer world. The whole effect is an emergent phenomenon, new jobs are created. Jobs become activities that are 'worlds in themselves', they include and exclude those elements and relations which do not fit the project of 'global experience', which is chosen as a *modus vivendi* and not merely as a standard of functional performance.

3   Third, as a consequence of the previous two features, globalization brings about new forms of transcendence of the distinctions that condition the units, systems and dimensions of work. In other words, work transcends itself by dissolving its own borders. Globalization is a process that leads the

boundaries between the inside and outside of jobs to dissolve. To my mind, in order to understand the social division of labour emerging under conditions of globalization, it is no longer enough to resort to contingency formulas: we need new *transcendence formulas* (Teubner 2008).[4]

Work contexts – as is the case for all other conditions of knowledge and practice – lose those space and time dimensions which were dominant in the previous configuration (in the industrial, Fordist economy). In the *surmodernité* they become *non-lieux* (Marc Augé 1992) and are de-temporalized. Yet, for precisely these reasons people need to reconnect them to a situated place and to a relational register of time.[5] Jobs must be projected at the 'global' level, but at the same time be 'local'. Both global and local become networks of exchanges and relations which were unknown in the previous stage of social differentiation. Work becomes a mobile node in a network of communicative networks. The world of objects and performances, which we used to refer to as working activities, becomes a world of signs: i.e., the symbolic meaning of work is accentuated. This does not mean more intentionality but, rather, an increased symbolic mediation, because this is needed for the transcendence formula. Work organizations become generalized systems of exchange along lines which imply a new vision of social exchange as the basis for new ways of doing work.

It is not surprising that this novel method of conceiving and of undertaking work activities brings with it new risks that are less visible than in the past. Instead of talking about its paradoxes, we can see here the emancipatory nature of the new configuration of labour, which transcends the previous exchange of equivalents. It is precisely in this that its potential for civilization lies. The new symbolic code conceives of work as a social relation, much more than a functional performance (Donati 2001). It is precisely this code which pushes forward new frontiers of social relationality such as 'corporate social responsibility', the 'reconciliation between work and family', new instruments to make work more relationally responsive to the surrounding community (in terms of 'social accountability', etc.), although to a limited extent and always within market boundaries (and still operating according to a competitive logic, instead of a meta-reflexive logic of opportunities, as Archer would put it). What is relevant here is the fact that a relational vision of work emerges as an activity which links not only the managers and workers (the actors in the workplace), but also the clients and all those people who have a stake in the working activity (*multi-stakeholders*). That is why, with many provisos, I suggest that grasping these new ways of conceiving of and undertaking work should be understood as processes that lead advanced societies to emergent forms of work differentiation that consist of social relations much more than of new material standards or functional performances. In the globalized societal configuration, work comes to be an emergent phenomenon of relationality (Donati 2001).

5. Reflexivity as a need induced by relational differentiation: structural and agential

5.1. The three keywords by which we can explain the current changes – which others refer to as 'reflexive modernization' – are: structural (relational) differentiation, reflexivity (in its different modes) and emergence. The connections between these three concepts can be illuminated by reference to the morphogenetic cycle (Archer 1997, 2003). Fig. 8.3 shows the place of reflexivity (in its various modalities) in this cycle, according to relational theory.

At time T^1, structural differentiation separates actors and social spheres which were formerly integrated in a certain way, so as to create new needs for a different kind of relationality among them.[6] As a consequence, at time T^2, the actors must interact in a new context. It is here, in the time span T^2–T^3, that *personal* reflexivity elaborates the interactions between Ego and Alter *in a network* (*social* reflexivity). The new structure emerging at time T^4([7]) depends on the kinds of reflexivity developing between T^2 and T^3.

The reflexivity that is activated in the interactional phase (time span T^2–T^3) is an expression of *agency*, which mediates the structures within which they operate. Where the structure is a market, then reflexivity will have certain features; if a public bureaucracy, another type will be favoured; if a third sector organization, another one; and so forth.

The passage from T^1 to T^2 is one of simple contingency (the behaviour of actors depends on how they relate to the socio-cultural structure as they individually perceive it). The interactions at time T^2–T^3 are, instead, of a double contingency (between Ego and Alter). As a matter of fact the passage from T^3 to T^4 must select and stabilize the double contingency between the actors. Therefore, the process can be regulated by a contingency formula or by a transcendence formula (as claimed above, relying upon Teubner 2008). If the former is adopted, we get 'reflexive modernity' as described by Beck and Giddens: i.e. a risk structure will be substituted by another risk structure (negative feedback loops cannot be avoided

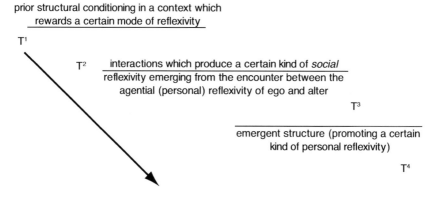

prior structural conditioning in a context which
rewards a certain mode of reflexivity

T^1

T^2 interactions which produce a certain kind of *social*
reflexivity emerging from the encounter between the
agential (personal) reflexivity of ego and alter

T^3

emergent structure (promoting a certain
kind of personal reflexivity)

T^4

Figure 8.3 The place of reflexivity in the morphogenetic cycle.

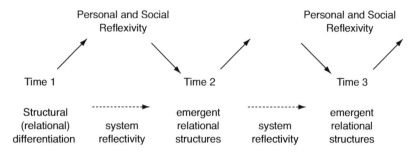

Figure 8.4 The temporal sequence of emergence of a social structure through personal, social and system reflexivity (better: system *reflectivity*).

and in fact are not avoided, so that one 'relational risk' is substituted for another 'relational risk' – and in all likelihood these are 'relational evils').

On the contrary, if a transcendence formula is adopted, then the emerging phenomena can influence social differentiation in the direction of a search for relational forms (relational goods) able to reduce risks and manage them so as to avoid relational undesirables. The adoption of meta-reflexivity is that option which is more adequate to control negative feedback and, thus, morphostasis and in particular the reproduction of risks. Relational differentiation is both an outcome of reflexive processes and the generator of new reflexive processes in a temporal sequence (as represented in Figure 8.4), operating at all levels: i.e. micro, meso and macro.

5.2. The new modalities for articulating socio-cultural identities in a reflexive manner are now producing an 'after-modern' society: I call it *after* (not post-) modern since it is generated by discontinuities which override the continuities.

What emerges are new practices of civil society, which are not defined by modern (bourgeois) distinctions, such as private *vs* public (or liberal *vs* socialist, or right *vs* left, etc.), but by distinctions which are ethical in kind. They refer basically to the human/non-human distinction.

This process modifies all the subsystems and institutional spheres of society.

1   It modifies the political system, since the symbolic code of a representative democracy does not have the support of a 'representative reflexivity' any more. This fact explains why the forms of representative democracy become weak and must give way to forms of deliberative democracy (which rely upon a different mode of reflexivity). Beck calls this change 'sub-politicization', but this term reveals a fundamental misunderstanding since the process facilitates 'other' forms of politics, and is not merely a slighter or diminished form of democracy.

2   It modifies the market, since the symbolic code (of 'money') can no longer remain utilitarian, in a context where accountability cannot be taken for granted. The utility of money is restricted to limited areas of the economy,

whilst it becomes useless to an increasing number of people who develop their projects, practices and *modus vivendi* outside those areas.

3　It modifies the family, because its symbolic code of 'love' is defied by the new communication media and the cultural environment they create, so that communicative reflexivity must change into forms that are of a new relational kind.

4　It modifies the third sector, or the associational world, since its symbolic code is no longer that of influence or persuasion (moral suasion), or charity (or non-profit as a residual means of action, when money and law have failed), but the search for other means of action, especially free giving and reciprocity within social circuits which defy the for-profit economy and representative democracy. *Reflexivity by reciprocity* is its latent, often unseen, *ethos.*[8]

What 'unifies' all these processes, as their common denominator, is precisely the change of the cultural system in such a way as to make reflexivity 'more relational'. At rock bottom, globalization generates a 'system' which acts as a context in which reflexivity is now necessarily in search of a different way to relate to the Self, to the Other, and to the whole world. *Relationality becomes an end in itself*, taking priority over the need for material or instrumental 'things' that have predominated to date.[9]

These are the new conditions that distinguish (difference!) a globalized 'after-modern' society. It is characterized by modes of reflexivity which abandon those forms that were dominant within modernity, i.e. the political and economic forms of reflexivity typical of industrial society with welfarist regimes. The *lib-lab* configurations of policies are restricted to limited areas of society, while the emerging forms of societal configuration must now make resort to the reflexivity of those social networks in which people can exercise a freer personal reflexivity.

Empirical evidence can be found in all the fields I have mentioned. Let me give a quick sketch. The mixing of public and private elements in social reflexivity is very clear when we observe phenomena such as the regulation of free giving (the gift of human organs, the gift of time in time banks, the gift of time to care for needy people, the gift on the internet, and so forth) (Donati 2003; Godbout 2007; Bauwens 2009); the regulation of intimate relationships (given the fact that Giddens' 'pure relationship' cannot be considered a form of reflexivity (Mouzelis 1999); the regulation of the *new economy* through reflexive networks, outside state control (Rullani 2001); the civil economy (Zamagni 2006), etc.

Bang (2004) has observed that a new connection between political authority and political community is taking shape outside the spheres of modern government and representative democracy. In a sense, he contends that some forms of deliberative democracy are emerging. Political authority is becoming increasingly both communicative and interactive in order for it to be able to meet complexity with complexity. It is employed for reforming institutions by opening them up towards culture and by tying them to the political attributes and capacities of self-reflexive individuals and to the transformation and self-transformation of their conduct. Bang calls this development *culture governance*. Culture governance is about how political authority must increasingly operate through capacities for *self-* and *co*-governance and therefore needs to act upon, reform, and utilize individual and collective conduct so that it may become amenable to its rule. Culture governance represents a new kind of top-down steering; it is neither hierarchical nor bureaucratic but *empowering* and *self*-disciplining. It manifests itself as various forms of joined-up government and network governance and proclaims itself to be genuinely democratic and dialogical. Bang has tried to give empirical evidence by a study of local Danish politics and policy in Copenhagen. Culture governance, he claims, constitutes a formidable challenge and threat to a political system which claims to be democratic, but in fact it always attempts to colonize the whole field of public reason, everyday political engagement, democratic deliberation, and so on, by its own logic of success, effectiveness or influence. The new processes seek to take charge of the working of the more spontaneous, less programmed and more grass roots politics of the ordinary in political communities, thus undermining the very idea of a non-strategic public reasoning as founding the practice of freedom. What is happening in the political realm may be also occurring in other fields, such as the revision of the welfare state and personal welfare services.

6. Conclusions: social differentiation through reflexivity

The 'reflexive modernity' to which many scholars refer, following Beck, Giddens and Lash, is usually understood as an unexpected (direct or indirect) effect of continuing to stress functional reflexivity which has dominated modernity so far, when the latter is forced to confront its consequences.

To emphasize (or 'radicalize') functional reflexivity means a further disembedding from structural, positional and situational constraints. Such a tendency, it is said, goes hand in hand with an increasing individualization of individuals' subjectivism and a parallel immunity against social relations configured according to 'other' modes of reflexivity, i.e. different from the functionalist code of modernity (Luhmann made this point very clear).

The supporters of this theory have no difficulty in recognizing the negative effects of these processes; (1) the expulsion of people from local communities and the creation of *non-lieux* that alienate their inhabitants; (2) the unceasing production of cultural diversities that are strangers to one another; (3) the creation of new inequalities between individuals, social groups and systems; (4) the diffusion of social deviance (juvenile crime, drop-outs, etc.), and many other social problems. The same scholars claim that these outcomes are not by-products, not unintended or perverse effects of modernity, but its very 'essence', its 'normal' way of being because modernity is precisely all the above, in the latter stages of its development.

In this paper, I have argued that this theory of reflexive modernization is lacking and defective in many ways. First of all, there is its generic, paradoxical and contradictory way of conceiving of reflexivity. The term 'reflexive modernization' seems to presume that individuals are acting in a reflexive manner, while the authors mean to deny that. Second, they fail in showing how the above mentioned outcomes are the products of different modes of reflexivity in individuals and in social groups or, indeed, their lack of reflexivity. In particular, they remain oblivious to the increase of social actors (individual and collective) whose reflexive agency is impeded, displaced, fractured, and, hence, self-defeating.

On this basis, I have argued that sociological research should start to take into account the direct and indirect outcomes of what is called 'reflexive modernization' from the point of view of human persons embedded in actual social relations, as they react to new types of social conditioning, and what kind of reflexivity they develop in response to their needs.

From this angle, one could possibly discover that the social differentiation we are witnessing today in advanced societies is generating new social forms which are problematic in many ways, but at the same time are able to find a certain stability and capacity for life, by differentiating themselves through particular forms of reflexivity.

What are these social forms? They may be conceived of as those civil social formations where caring about the relationship *per se* is pre-eminent. These spheres do possess a 'complex structure' (meaning that they are able to deal with complexity, understood in a systemic sense), which is concerned primarily with the social relations that it allows or inhibits. Relations are treated reflexively, which makes them flexible, meaning able to differentiate and integrate their internal as well as external components. To detect them requires an understanding of the differentiation of reflexivity as an operation of human persons, as well as of social groups and relational networks.

They respond to the void left by the lib-lab complex, i.e. by the instrumental rationality which speaks the language of means and ends and ignores the issues presented by rules and values. Modern functional rationality, and the forms of reflexivity supporting it, can maintain a certain primacy in limited spheres of society, but they lose ground in many other spheres. As a matter of fact, today we are witnessing the emergence of *supra-functional* forms of reflexivity, or at least forms of reflexivity which escape from the functional symbolic code (as theorized firstly by Parsons and subsequently by Luhmann), yet which are not post-modern (in Lash's terms, for instance), but '*after*-modern', in so far as their directive distinctions are discontinuous and no longer in continuity with modernity.

The birth of a new civil society takes place where new forms of reflexivity, both personal and social, come into existence outside the market and the state. Following Archer's findings, we can call them 'meta-reflexivity'. From my point of view, meta-reflexivity is that form of turning back on oneself by a subject who considers (internally as well as in interaction with others) the outcomes of his/her own deeds, both direct and indirect, and tries to relate them to a horizon of values that transcends what is already given. In a sense, these values constitute a utopian life-project, and the same goes for social organization as well. They are supposed to lead to a future where one's own concerns can be met by a 'relational reason', which can overcome the present contradictory, risky and paradoxical (personal and social) condition without escaping from the paradoxes. Meta-reflexivity is therefore a rational activity, not irrational, but of a kind wholly different from modern rationality (which is basically instrumental, in the trade-off between the economic and the political).

It is this kind of reflexivity that pushes forward what I call an 'after-modern' society. The process must rely upon a different kind of social differentiation, which I term 'relational'. Meta-reflexivity and relational differentiation go beyond what Beck and others call 'reflexive modernization', since they are discontinuous with regard to the kind of reflexivity (still modern!) which is inherent to the latter. From an empirical point of view, we can observe these phenomena in those forms of civil sociability which do not follow the modes of reflexivity that Archer calls 'communicative' and 'autonomous'. The new forms are relational, and surpass the requirements of functional integration, both in the realm of social interaction and in the domain of structural integration within the state bureaucracies and the market.

The actors who initiate these processes are those who can generate relational forms of reflexivity. They act not as a network of individuals, but as relational networks. In these networks personal and social reflexivity intermingle so to produce a system that incorporates meta-reflexivity as its way of managing the ever present 'contextual incongruity', which is always acknowledged by people who want to pursue an utopian project. That is why these people, and their context, incorporate reflexivity within their relations. Networks become relational to the extent that they can perform the task of making relations 'reflexive' in a transcendental way.

It is only in these networks that the dilemmas of the civil/uncivil and the human/inhuman, can be dealt with properly. A social network can be civil (or uncivil) depending on the type of reflexivity which is adopted at the meso-level, i.e. mediating between the micro level (interpersonal relations, individualization of individuals) and the macro level (globalization). The network society is bringing about and supports a relational reflexivity in which a high individual (agential) reflexivity must connect with the structural dynamics of intertwining networks. This process produces a new form of social differentiation, which I have labelled 'relational', lying beyond the forms already known (segmentary, stratified and functional).

Such relational differentiation is new since it operates by applying reflexivity to social relations, instead of being confined to individuals and to the social structures conditioning them. Therefore, what is fundamental in this historic change is the novel structural co-existence between new forms of reflexivity and their ways of producing social differentiation. Behind 'liquidity' there are phenomena of diversification and reticulation, where individuals are at the same time freer and more constrained than before, because of the relational character of the relational networks in which they live.

The so-called process of 'individualization of individuals' is, in fact, an expression of this new relational character of society. It is induced by structural changes, which influence social organizations and interactions, which, in their turn, influence the relational features of socio-cultural structures.

This whole societal process produces new *'differentials of reflexivity'*, which are spreading in our society. These differentials are unevenly distributed amongst individuals, depending on their positions within social networks. These positions, as the nodes of networks, can call upon unequal resources and have different goals, norms, and values. More and more these nodes become complex, since less people can live within one or a few networks, while an increasing number must live in a plurality of intersecting networks. Obviously, this means new inequalities and asymmetries – a fact that reinforces the need for a relational approach to social inequality, disadvantages, exclusions, and so forth. In my opinion, this is the meaning of the socio-cultural shift from a competitive logic to the logic of opportunity (Archer 2003).

Individuals must react to the new relational structures – in which competitive and non-competitive goods are relationally more or less available – by establishing new connections between their internal conversation and the objective positions they have in the networks to which they belong.

This is 'contextual globalism': individuals react to the globalization of their contexts by resorting to the kinds of reflexivity that are available in those situated contexts. The relative homogeneity of the societal change called 'globalization' has as its leitmotif the need to be contextualized in a way which must be more reflexive than in the past. The successful outcome of 'global contextualization' depends more and more upon our becoming 'relationally reflexive'.

Notes

1   In her new book Archer (*The Reflexive Imperative*, forthcoming, Ch. 1) writes: 'specific macro-level configurations of the social system will have been especially favourable to the emergence of a particular mode as the dominant one in the reflexivity of the general population'.

2   A functional configuration of society becomes 'mature', or better reaches its limits, when social issues or needs cannot be met by functional criteria any longer.

3   C. Ray (1999) has observed that Reflexive Modernity is bringing myriads of 'flexible spaces' into being in which socio-economic development can be animated and even defined. The act of territorial identity construction utilizes historical and cultural resources and thus represents an emerging form of local governance. The author examines how this focus on cultural–territorial identity feeds back to the psychological well-being of individuals, both within and outside the locality. The geographical focus is simultaneously global and local. Against this backdrop, actors engage with Reflexive Modernity through various forms of strategic intervention.

4   I am using the systemic language put forward by N. Luhmann. For instance, in the field of law, justice must be seen as a 'transcendence formula' and not only as a contingency formula (Teubner 2008). In Archerian language, we could say that, in the field of law, justice needs to work according to a meta-reflexive form of reflexivity.

5   In previous writings I have defined three registers of social time: interactive, relational and symbolic.

6   We can think, for instance, of the most recent mass media, and how they initially separated people and subsequently made them interact in new ways, so to produce a different set of relationships among them.

7   Obviously, temporalization is a central aspect of the whole process: cf. Adam (2003). Time marks dis/continuity or, as someone said, 'discontinuity arises from continuity'.

8   We must remember that the relation of reciprocity (instead of dependence between

Ego and Alter) is vital to the person and to society as well, since it contains a differ-ence (a 'differing' through the creation of dissimilar relations and/or entities = *differand* according to Lyotard 1988, or a gap = *différance* according to Derrida 1978). 'Vital' means generative of an emergent effect, and a relationship is vital only if it expresses a distinction which makes a difference (Luhmann 2006).

9 For example, in public art: '*it is the relationship itself, between artist and audience, that becomes the artwork*' (Demetrious 2003: 3, quotation from Lacy 1995: 20).

References

Adam B., (2003) 'Reflexive Modernization Temporalized', in *Theory, Culture &Society*, 20:2, pp. 59–78.

Archer M. S., (2003) *Structure, Agency and the Internal Conversation*, Cambridge University Press, Cambridge.

Archer M. S., (2007) *Making Our Way Through the World: Human Reflexivity and Social Mobility*, Cambridge University Press, Cambridge.

Augé M., (2007) *Non-lieux*, Seuil, Paris.

Bang H.P., (2004) 'Culture Governance: Governing Self-Reflexive Modernity', *Public Administration*, 82:1, pp. 157–90.

Bauman, Z., (1998) *Globalization: The Human Consequences*, Polity Press, Cambridge.

Bauwens M., (2009) 'Par cum pari. Notes on the horizontality of peer to peer relationships in the context of the verticality of a hierarchy of values', in M. S. Archer and P. Donati (eds), *Pursuing the Common Good: How Solidarity and Subsidiarity Can Work Together*, Proceedings of the XIV Plenary Session of the Pontifical Academy of Social Sciences (Vatican City, May 2–6, 2008), Vatican Press, Rome.

Beck, U., (1992) *Risk Society: Towards a New Modernity*, Sage Publications, London.

Beck, U., 'The Reinvention of Politics: Towards a Theory of Reflexive Modernization', in U. Beck, A. Giddens and S. Lash, 1994a, pp. 1–55.

Beck, U., 'Self-Dissolution and Self-Endangerment of Industrial Society: What Does This Mean?', in U. Beck, A. Giddens and S. Lash, 1994b, pp. 174–83.

Beck, U., *Ecological enlightenment: Essays on the Politics of the Risk Society*, Humanities Press, New Jersey 1995.

Beck U., Bonss W., Lau C., (2003) 'The Theory of Reflexive Modernization. Problematic, Hypotheses and Research Program', in *Theory, Culture & Society*, 20:2, pp. 1–33.

Beck U., Giddens A., Lash S., (1994) *Reflexive Modernization: Politics, Tradition and Aesthetics in the Modern Social Order*, Stanford University Press, Stanford (Italian translation *Modernizzazione riflessiva: politica, tradizione ed estetica nell'ordine sociale della modernità*, Asterios, Trieste, 1999).

Berra M., and Meo A. R., (2001) *Informatica solidale. Storia e prospettiva del software libero*, Bollati Boringhieri, Turin.

Boltanski L., (2005) 'Gli attuali cambiamenti del capitalismo e la cultura del progetto', in *Studi di Sociologia*, XLIII: 4, pp. 369–89.

Demetrious K., (2003) 'Reflexive Modernity and the Art of Public Communication' in *PRism*, 1:1.

Derrida J., (1978) *Writing and Difference*, Routledge, London-New York.

Donati P., (1991)*Teoria relazionale della società*, FrancoAngeli, Milan.

Donati P., (2000) 'Freedom vs. Control in Post-Modern Society: A Relational Approach' in E.K. Scheuch, D. Sciulli (eds), *Societies, Corporations and the Nation State*, Brill, Leiden, pp. 47–76.

Donati P., (2001) *Il lavoro che emerge. Prospettive del lavoro come relazione sociale in una economia dopo-moderna*, Bollati Boringhieri, Turin.

Donati P., (2003) 'Giving and Social Relations: The Culture of Free Giving and its Differentiation Today', *International Review of Sociology*, 13: 2, pp. 243–72.

Donati P., (2008) 'La teoria del realismo sociologico è una Ragione sociologica che fa esperienza della realtà: come? e di quale "realtà"?', in A. Maccarini, E. Morandi and R. Prandini (eds), *Realismo sociologico. La realtà non ama nascondersi*, Marietti 1820, Genoa-Milan, pp. 163–82.

Donati P., (2008) *Oltre il multiculturalismo. La ragione relazionale per un mondo comune*, Laterza, Roea-Bari.

Elder-Vass D., (2007a) 'Searching for realism, structure, and agency in Actor Network Theory', Paper presented to BSA Realism Study Group, London, 18 January 2007.

Elder-Vass D., (2007b)'Luhmann and Emergentism. Competing Paradigms for Social Systems Theory?', *Philosophy of the Social Sciences*, 37:4, pp. 408–32.

Elder-Vass D., (2007c) 'For Emergence: Refining Archer's Account of Social Structure', *Journal for the Theory of Social Behaviour*, 37:1, pp. 25–44.

Elder-Vass D., (2007d) 'Social Structures and Social Relations', *Journal for the Theory of Social Behaviour*, 37:4, pp. 463–77.

Giddens A., (1994) 'Living in a Post-Traditional Society', in U. Beck, A. Giddens and S. Lash (eds) *Reflexive Modernization*, pp. 56–109.

——. *Risk, trust, reflexivity*, in U. Beck, A. Giddens and S. Lash, pp. 184–97.

Godbout J., (2007) 'Ce qui circule entre nous. Donner, recevoir, rendre', Seuil, Paris. In 'T Veld R.J. *et al.* (eds) (1991), *Autopoiesis and Configuration Theory: New Approaches to Societal Steering*, Kluwer Academic Publishers, Dordrecht-Boston-London.

Kerr A. and Cunningham-Burley S., (2000) 'On Ambivalence and Risk: Reflexive Modernity and the New Human Genetics', *Sociology*, 34:2, pp. 283–304.

Lacy S., (1995) 'Cultural Pilgrimages and Metaphoric Journeys', in his (ed.), *Mapping the Terrain: New Genre Public Art*, Bay Press, Seattle, pp. 19–47.

Lash S., (1994a) 'Reflexivity and its Doubles: Structure, Aesthetics, Community', in U. Beck, A. Giddens and S. Lash, pp. 110–73.

Lash S., (1994b) 'Expert-systems or Situated Interpretation? Culture and Institutions in Disorganized Capitalism', in U. Beck, A. Giddens and S. Lash, pp. 198–215.

Lash S., (2003) 'Reflexivity as Non-Linearity', *Theory, Culture & Society*, 20:2, pp. 49–57.

Latour B., (2003) 'Is Re-modernization Occurring – And If So, How to Prove It?', *Theory, Culture & Society*, 20:2, pp. 35–48.

Luhmann N., (1982) *The Differentiation of Society*, Columbia University Press, New York.

——. (1992) *Beobachtungen der Moderne*, Westdeutscher Verlag, Opladen.

——. (1997) 'Limits of Steering', *Theory, Culture and Society*, 14:1, pp. 41–57.

——. (2006 [1991]) 'System as Difference' *Organization*, 13:1, pp. 37–57.

Lyotard J., (1988) *The Differend*, University of Minnesota Press, Minneapolis.

Mouzelis N., (1999) *Exploring Post-Traditional Orders. Individual Reflexivity, 'Pure Relations' and Duality of Structure*, in M. O'Brien *et al.* (eds), *Theorising Modernity*, London, Longman.

Ray C., (1999) 'Endogenous Development in the Era of Reflexive Modernity', *Journal of Rural Studies*, 15:3, pp. 257–67.

Rullani E., New economy e regolazione: il capitalismo delle reti alla ricerca di nuove istituzioni, in *Foedus*, n. 2, 2001, pp. 35–50.

Teubner G., (2008) *La giustizia autosovversiva: formula di contingenza o di trascendenza del diritto?*, Edizioni La Città del Sole, Naples (Italian translation of the paper *Self-subversive*

Justice: Contingency or Transcendence Formula of Law presented at the annual meeting of The Law and Society Association, TBA, Berlin, Germany, 24 July 2007).

Therborn G., (ed.), (2000) 'Globalizations Are Plural', *International Sociology*, 15:2.

Zamagni S., (2006) 'L'economia come se la persona contasse. Verso una teoria economica relazionale', in P.L. Sacco and S. Zamagni (eds), *Teoria economica e relazioni interpersonali*, il Mulino, Bologna, pp. 17–51.

Part III
Modes of reflexivity

9 The agency of the weak

Ethos, reflexivity and life strategies of Polish workers after the end of state socialism

Adam Mrozowicki[1]

The problem of the agency of workers is almost as old as academic sociology. In the social thought of Marx, blue collar workers were considered the privileged agents of revolutionary social change. However, at the beginning of the twenty-first century, this grand narrative can only veil the actual diversity of workers' actions. In Western capitalist countries, blue-collar workers were largely included into the political order. In Eastern Europe, the narrative of working-class agency first became a smokescreen for attempts to subordinate workers to communist parties, and then the foundation for anti-communist movements. The failure of the state-socialist project and the triumph of liberal capitalism coincided with the expansion of ideas that identified the notion of 'agency' with the construction of social identities unconstrained by the structural locations of social agents (Beck 1992; Giddens 1995). Yet, does this discourse really fit into the experiences of the socially disadvantaged members of 'new' capitalist societies?

Developing the notion of the 'agency of the weak', this chapter explores the life strategies of Polish manual workers after the end of state socialism. Workers were certainly not the primary beneficiaries of the post-socialist transformation. Their positions were challenged by the emergence of a deregulated economy, the decomposition of old industrial milieus in the course of economic restructuring and the weakness of trade unions, in particular in the new private sector (Ost 2005). Meardi (2000: 154) captures their situation well: 'industrial workers, the former pillars of the nation and the victors over communism, were suddenly deprived of their standard of living but above all, of their role within politics, within the economy, and within the plants'. Given the scope of structural constraints, it is legitimate to ask if, how and under what conditions workers are still able to be active agents, capable of developing life strategies that provide them with some control over their lives and their social environment?

This chapter addresses this problem by examining the processes of monitoring, adapting to, and resisting structural changes in working-class milieus in one of the industrial regions of Poland (Silesia). It makes use of the concept of life strategy, understood as the individual's way of achieving his/her desired 'modus vivendi' (Archer 2007: 88), developed reflexively and taking into account the structural and cultural contexts that people confront, and have contended with throughout their life and work histories.[2] The life strategies of workers, which represent the 'agency of the weak', have been approached and theorized in three different ways. First, the sociology of post-socialism presents workers as the passive victims of systemic change and, very rarely, as reflexive social actors. Second, culturalist working-class studies, concentrate on the extent to which the reflexivity of workers is precluded by their limited resources and class habitus (Savage 2001). Third, there are general sociological theories, which address the relationship between the structured dimension of action represented by the theory of Bourdieu (2002), and its reflexive dimension, elaborated within a critical realist framework by Archer (2003; 2007).

Between cultural and structural determinism: research on post-socialist workers

Despite notable exceptions (Dunn 2004; Latoszek 1994; Stenning 2005), sociologists have rarely considered the working-class experiences of post-socialist transformation as an interesting subject for investigation. As noted by Ost (2005: 17), 'for most social scientists the only way workers seemed to "matter" was as a potential obstacle to democratization'. Workers were considered to be a hindrance both in terms of mental traits attributed to them, such as collectivism and fatalism, and because of their very presence in industrial branches which had to be restructured (Faliszek *et al.* 2001). Even those who did not see labourers as a barrier tended to describe their actions as largely determined by structural and cultural factors. At the one extreme, structuralist researchers claimed that the new capitalist system made workers the losers in this systemic change (Słomczyński *et al.* 2006). At the other extreme, those taking a culturalist studies approach explored the weakness of trade unionism in Poland and suggested that the ethos of the anti-communist struggle and reorientation to capitalist beliefs have made employees support market changes against their own welfare (Ost 2005).

While both of these accounts correctly describes some aspects of the post-socialist reality, it is crucial to note that they lack a theoretical approach which would enable us to explore how individuals who differ from each other in their past experiences and objective possession of resources also deal reflexively with their changing social circumstances in different ways. Consequently, they make it difficult to account fully for the internal diversity of responses and fail to supply a causal mechanism governing the bottom-up transformations of working-class milieus. The focus on workers' resistance against restructuring, as correctly noted by Ost (2005), neglects the central role played by the active support, given by employees and their trade unions, to the organizational changes and privatization of state-owned firms. The thesis asserting the enduring weakness of Polish labour is challenged, in turn, by the recent processes of trade union revitalization in the private sector (Meardi 2007). Comparably, the emphasis on workers' fatalism and disempowerment overlooks active efforts to cope with changes at the individual level, such as family entrepreneurship or mass migration abroad after the enlargement of the European Union.

In this context, accounts documenting the 'negotiated' agency and social consciousness of workers seem to be more convincing. Gardawski (1997) argued that industrial workers in Poland accepted the discourse of marketization and democratization, but adapted its meanings to the context of their living conditions. In her study on Polish steelworkers, Stenning (2005: 993) identified 'alongside the real experiences of loss, new, renewed and persistent forms of working-class politics, values, cultures and communities'. In a similar vein, Latoszek (1994: 111) suggested that workers' life strategies reflect 'the dialectic of adaptation to modernising change and the preservation of [their] identities'. All such accounts implicitly assume that the agency of workers emerges at the intersection of socio-structural conditions, accumulated beliefs and resources, and reflexive life-projects. However, attempts to understand workers' life strategies in theoretical terms are limited. If Polish labourers indeed 'negotiated' their ways of life after the systemic change, their reflexivity needs more theoretical attention than it has been given in the mainstream sociology of post-socialism.

Class experiences and workers' life-projects: culturalist working-class studies

While workers' reflexivity is rendered marginal in the sociologies of post-socialist transformation, it appears in a much more explicit manner in some of the recent debates in the field of culturalist working-class studies (Devine and Savage 2005). One of the topics connecting this body of research with the questions asked by the sociology of post-socialism is the tension between the legacy of class cultures and individualization. This tension is not new. Classical studies on 'affluent workers' (Goldthorpe *et al.* 1969) explored the privatization of working-class consciousness, as manifested in the increasing importance of lifestyles centred on family life. Renewed interest in working-class studies emerged in the 1990s in the course of the discussion about the radical individualization of social identities in late capitalist societies. According to Giddens (1995) and Beck (1992), 'reflexive modernisation' involves agential disembedding from taken-for-granted class communities. As a result, a person's biography is said to be 'placed in his or her own hand, open and dependent on decisions' (Beck 1992: 128). New working-class studies challenge this view from two theoretical angles. On one hand, they follow post-structuralism and explore the constitution of working-class subjects through the relations of power and the variety of discourses (Skeggs 1997). On the other hand, they lean on Bourdieu's (2002) analysis of habitus as unconscious 'schemes of perception, thought and action', reflecting the subtle effects of class background.

New working-class studies radically 'socialise' human abilities to enter into reflexive relations with the social environment and the self. In post-structuralist formulations, exemplified by the analysis of Skeggs (1997: 163): 'the project of self is a Western bourgeois project', which 'legitimates powerful groups and renders other groups unworthy of the designation "individual"'. From a different perspective, Bourdieu's analysis also entails denying the reflexivity of those belonging to the lower classes. For Bourdieu (2002: 372–6), working-class habitus is based on the pre-reflexive mechanism of 'a resignation to the inevitable', resulting from a durable deprivation of both economic capital and cultural competences. In this vein, Charlesworth (2000: 7–8), following Bourdieu, describes 'a relation to being, contained in working class people's economic and social conditions, that forecloses and make almost impossible autonomous ways of becoming a self-developing subject' in a de-industrialized town in the North of England. Comparably, Savage (2001: 84–5) claims that 'the reflexive individual is less a product of global restructuring and more the product of a particular class habitus, associated with the academic and intellectual middle class'.

Both post-structuralist studies of the working-class and those following Bourdieu combine a renewed emphasis on the subjective side of working-class lives with a tendency to question the abilities of workers to reflexively transform their social identities and the surrounding social environment. Contrary to such a view, Lamont (2000: 2) has demonstrated the central importance of positive life-projects among American and French working-class men, underpinned by their abilities to 'self-discipline themselves and conduct responsible yet caring lives'. Lamont (2000: 243) emphasises that workers' agency 'is bounded by differentially structured context in which people live'. This raises a more general issue. Instead of theoretically precluding the agency of lower classes, it is appropriate to ask under what conditions workers' reflexive relations with their social environment assume 'disempowered' forms, versus those assuming a 'self-transformative' character?

Ethos, resources and reflexivity: the potential of conceptual bricolage

The sociology of post-socialism and culturalist working-class studies documents, in different ways, the tension between the 'structured' and 'reflexive' aspects of workers' life strategies in a changing socio-economic reality. At the general theoretical level, a similar tension is exemplified by the theory of habitus and its various forms of capital, advanced by Bourdieu (2002), and the realist theory of agency developed by Archer (2003, 2007). In a nutshell, the former suggests that the conditions for acquiring dispositions, which enable an individual to develop reflexive life-projects, are defined by 'the possession of economic and cultural capital required in order to seize the "potential opportunities" theoretically available to all' (Bourdieu, 1990: 64). In contrast, Archer considers human reflexivity a universal generative mechanism, whose emergence is related to a continuous sense of self and embodied practices in the world that are held to be 'prior to, and primitive to, our sociality' (Archer, 2000: 7). Leaving aside ontological differences between the two theories, which are difficult, if not impossible to bridge (Elder-Vass, 2007: 332), it is suggested that both can offer relevant theoretical insights into workers' life strategies. This conceptual 'bricolage' is possible if the autonomous role of reflexivity in mediating structural and cultural conditioning, which is central for the realist ontology developed by Archer, is maintained.

Bourdieu's notion of habitus can be useful for understanding the co-shaping of the life strategies of workers through the cultural legacies of the state-socialist past and of class cultures developed under it. Yet, some reformulation is required to allow more space for reflexivity. Fundamentally, such a radical systemic change demands a revision of taken-for-granted dispositions. However, according to a range of critics (Archer 2007; Mouzelis 1995), Bourdieu's theory is incapable of accounting for a reflexive elaboration of habitus and, more generally, underplays the role of conscious deliberations of human actors in shaping their actions. Tackling this criticism, I propose to adopt the concept of ethos, which is inspired by a non-deterministic reading of habitus (Elder-Vass 2007; Sayer 2005: Ch. 2). The study of different forms of ethos has a long tradition reaching back to Aristotle's discussion of an ethical form of life acquired through habits, through Weber's analyses of the Calvinist ethos, into much more local Polish debates, including the discussion on the 'ethos of Solidarność' (Szawiel 1991). Like the understanding of habitus proposed by Elder-Vass (2007: 334), ethos is not reducible to the interiorization of 'social structure' by individuals. Instead, it refers to practical and moral beliefs, which are influenced by individual experiences of social structures and cultural contexts, but is not 'the internalisation of externality'.

Ethos is only one potential mechanism affecting life strategies. Arguably, another important mechanism is connected with resources. The role of resources is emphasized both by Bourdieu (1986) and Archer (2003: 131). According to Bourdieu (2002: 112), various forms of 'capital' allow actors to gain advantages within fields constituted by social relations among individuals devoted to particular kinds of activities. Simplifying Bourdieu's (1986) classification, economic resources, social resources (potentially useful social networks), and cultural resources (formal education and practical skills) can be considered important means towards shaping life strategies. Linking the effects of class location to individual destinations, Bourdieu suggests that 'to a given volume of inherited capital there corresponds a band of more or less equally probable trajectories leading to more or less equivalent positions' (Bourdieu 2002: 110). However, to what extent does such a straightforward relationship hold in a society marked by the rapid devaluation and revaluation of resources?

While both Bourdieu and Archer acknowledge the role of resources in co-shaping life strategies, the strong link between resources and the formation of habitus makes Bourdieu's theory incapable of explaining why social agents, who share comparable class experiences, do not always respond in the same way to changing social conditions. Arguably, Archer's theory (2003, 2007) offers more suitable theoretical tools to address this problem. It suggests that in order to account for what different people do within structurally shaped situations, their modes of their reflexivity, understood as the ways of conducting 'internal conversations' about oneself in relation to society, need to be taken into account. Breaking with the homogeneous view on reflexivity, Archer (2003: 344) suggests that the sources of the different modes of reflexivity 'are found at the nexus between contexts and concerns'. Those experiencing the continuity of social contexts tend to develop a 'communicative reflexivity', one that requires familiar others to confirm their life-projects before resulting in a course of action. Others, who experience discontinuous action contexts, are likely to develop an 'autonomous reflexivity' (self-contained internal conversation directly leading to action) or a 'meta-reflexivity' (critical reflection about one's own mode of reflexivity and courses of action) (Archer 2007: 93). Finally, the powers of reflexivity 'may be suspended' by 'the intervention of other mechanisms or by contingency' (Archer 2003: 298), resulting in 'fractured reflexives' whose internal conversations do not lead to any purposeful action.

Archer's theory gives us important conceptual tools to study representatives of the underprivileged social strata as potentially active agents. However, it also leaves some open questions. On the basis of her research in the UK, Archer (2007) relates the development of all modes of reflexivity (apart from the 'fractured') with the intentional choices of individuals, striving either for continuity or discontinuity of their action contexts. It can be asked, however, to what extent does such a 'high modern' scenario hold in the case of workers in post-socialist Poland? A comparable question can be directed at the relationship between reflexivity and ethos. Although post-socialist transformation resembles a situation of massive 'contextual discontinuity', there is a large potential for persistence in terms of the social positions occupied by some fractions of workers' milieus. Consequently, the mutual reinforcement of social positions and ethos cannot be excluded. While Archer criticizes Bourdieu for assuming 'an exaggerated continuity in the socialisation of personal identities' (Archer 2007: 48), she acknowledges the role of dispositions by asserting that 'dispositionality and reflexivity (...) emerge contemporaneously and interact with one another'. This creates a theoretical space for examining the relationship between ethos and reflexivity. The need for this kind of analysis emerges both from general theoretical debates (Adams 2006; Elder-Vass 2007; Sayer 2005) and from the discussion about the 'negotiated agency' of Polish workers.

The hypothesis of this study is that the properties of both ethos and the modes of reflexivity are mediated by the experiences of contextual continuity and contextual discontinuity. If the situation of post-socialism generates systemically induced discontinuity, it also creates the potential for a reflexive elaboration of an ethos. However, the equation of a systemic change with a radical biographical discontinuity does not need to be universally valid. First, the experiences of continuity and discontinuity can themselves be mitigated (and affected) by the resources possessed. Second, in order to protect the continuity of action contexts, to transform them, or to search for more suitable social environments in which to pursue life strategies, people can engage in reflexive work on their resources. In some cases, their reflexive projects can be fractured by the properties of action contexts. In other cases, 'conditional influences may be agentially evaded, endorsed, repudiated or contravened' (Archer 2003: 131). This raises the empirical question: which of the above scenarios holds for the life strategies of workers who differ from each other in terms of their resources and biographical experiences that have shaped their ethos and modes of reflexivity?

Back to the people: biographical research on Polish workers

The empirical research was designed as a combination of the biographical approach and grounded theory methodology (Glaser and Strauss 1967). The main method of data collection was through biographical narrative interviews (Schütze, 1983). Each interview began with a question about 'the whole story of the narrator's life, from childhood up to the present moment'. The questions asked in the second part clarified biographical events that were obscure in the first part. In the last part of the interview, questions were focused on areas that were meaningfully related to workers' life strategies, including *inter alia*, occupational and educational careers, family life, and patterns of sociability. The informants were full-time employees performing manual and semi-manual tasks in manufacturing, construction and retail services. In order to grasp a diversity of workers' life strategies, the region of Silesia (Lower Silesia, Upper Silesia and Opole Silesia) was chosen as a research site. Research in Silesia, consisting of old industrial areas (Upper Silesia) and territories marked by high socio-economic development after the systemic change, made it possible to examine the effects of old and new cleavages within working-class milieus on working-class life strategies.

The data collection was carried out in three stages during 2002–4, each followed by analysis of the interviews undertaken. The process of joint data collection and data analysis underlay the theoretical sampling strategy (Glaser and Strauss 1967: 45). The sampling was driven by the principle of the maximization and minimization of differences between comparison groups, representing distinctive configurations of categories describing life strategies. In sum, 166 interviews were collected and transcribed. Informants were diversified in terms of (1) their age, (2) gender, (3) work-related resources (craftsmen and foremen versus workers performing low-skilled jobs), (4) work organizations (old industrial companies, i.e. former socialist 'core' versus newly established private firms), (5) trade union experiences (union activists versus passive members and non-unionized workers).

Data analysis relied on a twofold coding procedure developed in the original Grounded Theory Methodology (GTM) (Glaser and Strauss 1967; Glaser 1978).[3] An overall form of biography ('modus narrandi'), assumed by a narrator presenting his or her life story (Schütze 2005: 319), was considered as representing a good approximation to a dominant life strategy aimed at achieving the 'modus vivendi' desired. The ultimate goal of data coding was to connect categories generated in the course of research and to account for patterns of behaviours which were 'relevant and problematic for those involved' (Glaser 1978: 93). The result of the latter procedures was the development of a typology of life strategies, which is presented in the remaining part of this chapter.

Life strategies of workers after the system change: a typology

Data coding made it possible to identify four basic types of life strategies, documenting distinctive configurations of the main biographical concerns of informants: 'embedding', 'integrating', 'getting by' and 'constructing'. Reducing the complexity of analysis, the typology was based on the crossing of two continua of properties (Figure 9.1). The first continuum refers to the dominant mode of reflexivity. Community-centred reflexivity is manifested in the dense interconnections between an individual life story and the collective history of milieus exceeding family confines, e.g. craft communities and local communities. The main concern of practitioners of this mode of reflexivity, focuses on the preservation and/or the transformation of collectively shared action contexts, in which their internal conversations are embedded. By contrast, private-centred reflexivity denotes the ways of reflecting upon one's life which are largely detached from the framework of communitarian experiences. Individual concerns are placed first and foremost, within family life and in terms of individualized aspirations, leading either to 'bricolage-like' life-projects (the 'constructing' type) or to a 'fragmented' life perspective (the 'getting by' type).

The second continuum describes the modes of structuring individual life-projects, i.e. the interrelations between the properties of life strategies and of action contexts. It was assumed, in accordance with Archer (2007: 12), that 'only if there is a relationship of congruence or incongruence between the social property and the project of the person(s) will the latter activate the former'. Structuring agency depicts the situation in which the properties of action context and individual resources are mobilized as different forms of capital in the active pursuit of life-projects. By contrast, structured dependency denotes conditions in which these properties predominantly play the role of constraints, which limit the biographical autonomy of action.

In constructing the typology, the analysis focused on the dominant logics of

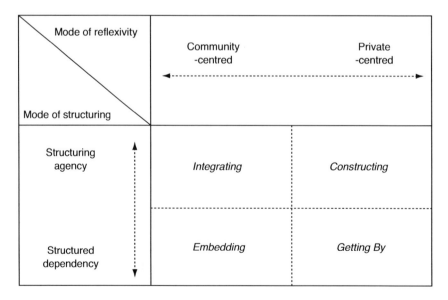

Figure 9.1 The typology of life strategies: the modes of reflexivity and the modes of structuring.

action as they were represented in the life stories collected. While sequential and simultaneous engagement in different life strategies is possible, not all sequences and configurations were equally present. Even though the numbers of workers within each type cannot be estimated, due to the lack of a representative sample, some tendencies are worth noting. First, the patterns of 'structured dependency' were more common (107 out of 166 cases),[4] thus documenting the disempowerment of workers after the systemic change (Meardi 2000). Second, and qualitatively, reorientation towards the privatized types was dominant.[5] The privatizing tendencies were subjectively interpreted either as being structurally driven (those making the transition into 'getting by') or as intentionally shaped (those making the transition into 'constructing'). Third, in their attempts to cope with the consequences of systemic change, the great majority of informants developed hybridized life strategies, which combined some properties of the privatized types and communitarian types.

Embedding

The pattern of 'embedding' involves the interplay of community-centred reflexivity and the endorsement of structural constraints affecting an individual life. The central biographical concern accentuates the preservation of broad social bonds, which have both an autotelic value and an instrumental relevance. Those people within the 'embedding' type share many characteristics with the 'communicative reflexives' discussed by Archer (2003: Ch. 6). Their decisions about what to do 'are held open to the dialogical influences of those with whom they share their concerns' (Archer 2003: 167). Like the 'communicative reflexives', their activities are predominantly defensive. Confronted by structural obstacles, they restrain their aspirations, withdraw into dense communitarian networks, and rarely attempt to influence their collective situation by concerted actions aimed at transforming the relevant action context. 'Embedding' was more typical of older workers, the long term employees in large companies, who represented local industrial traditions reaching back to socialist times and earlier periods. For them, a crucial asset in coping with new economic uncertainty is social capital, in the form of useful social connections and recognition in the workplace and local community. Cyryl provides a very typical narrative:

CYRYL: This year, I've got a jubilee: 25 years of work in the same post, in this department (…) And I don't complain that I stayed, because I work here, we live here. But now, just like in other countries, I feel an anxiety, the fear of job loss, I mean, that this plant will be closed. (…) This is a casting shop, 200 to 250 years old … The only reason why are we still here, the credit for that goes to the mentality of the Silesian land, is its thrift, frugality, and hard work. […] To sum up these forty years of my life, I'm glad of them. Everybody has some dreams, everybody has some ambitions, but for me it's enough, as I said, to be healthy, to have a job and a family, and I've got them. [W-93] (M, 40, a steelworker, large company in the public sector.)[6]

The dominant life strategy of Cyryl, a steelworker in a small city in Opole Silesia, is based on his lasting attachment to a large family (living in the same neighbourhood), local community and the community of craftsmen. The logic of embedding is determined by the mode of reflecting upon the social world which, due to the continuity of the action context, is closely interconnected with the dispositions of the moral ethos ('thrift, frugality and hard work') acquired through collectively shared experiences. The ethos of self-limited aspirations, resembling the working-class habitus described by Bourdieu (2002), is not, however, unconsciously taken for granted. Instead, it is a subject of reflexive elaboration and conscious attempts to maintain 'contextual continuity', in which both ethos and mode of reflexivity are anchored.

Systemic change influenced the 'embedded' type in two critical ways. First, the disintegration of milieus that had been created around large factories under state socialism means that the preservation of 'embedding' as a core life strategy ceases to be an 'obvious' aim. Among those possessing weaker resources, including women and those performing low-skilled jobs, the erosion of 'embedding' is likely to lead to the privatized 'getting by' pattern. By contrast, informants who in the past accumulated more diversified forms of capital, tend to recombine the 'embedded' pattern with active, family-centred economic strategies ('constructing'). Second, the decomposition of the trade union movement and, in particular, of Solidarność, underscored biographical transition from 'integrating' into 'embedding'. A good example is Janina:

JANINA: In the 1980s, during the Martial Law, I also participated in a strike committee. Well … my mum helped me a lot, because … I devoted a lot of time to it. Anyway, during these three famous days … I stayed in this Factory, together with its staff. And … my children … er – they were practically left on their own with my husband. They were left to their own fate, weren't they? I … tried to explain them that this was for all of us. And now my children reproach me for having done this. They ask: 'Why were we alone? It's so hard, we don't have a job?' (…) [Janina cries] And, you see, now … We sit here, they destroy our Factory, and we're piteous, aren't we? [W-7] (F, 52, a domestic appliances assembler in a large privatized plant.)

Janina, who joined Solidarność in 1980, has remained involved in union activity until now, but lost her belief in collective action. Her feeling of collective agency is replaced by a deep-seated feeling of guilt, both with regard to her own children and in the context of her work milieu, which suffers the negative consequences of restructuring. As revealed in other parts of the interview and in similar biographies, the sense of disempowerment is deepened if uncontrollable processes at the collective level are combined with unfavourable events in the subject's private life, e.g. in Janina's case, separation from her husband.

If practitioners of 'community-centred' reflexivity are threatened by uncontrollable changes in their collectively shared action contexts, the 'ritualization of ethos' is likely to emerge. This 'ritualization of ethos' denotes the structurally conditioned form of hybridization of life strategies. As collective resources undergo rapid devaluation, community-centred reflexivity leads the individuals affected to fortify themselves in beliefs which they ascribe to a more cognitively coherent past. The outcomes are different forms of re-traditionalization, such as a renewed emphasis on craft solidarity, ethnic identities, broad family bonds and traditional gender roles. Since collective resistance against macro-structural changes appears to be futile or inefficient, contextual continuity has to be reaffirmed by individual practices of adaptation. As a result of the combination of collective ritualism and individual survival strategies, hybridized coping patterns emerge.

Integrating

Workers who pursue the 'integrating' strategy share the community-centred mode of reflexivity with those classified as 'embedded'. Simultaneously, however, they differ from the latter category in their attempts to co-determine and transform action contexts, which give meaning to their internal conversations. As such, they have some characteristics of both 'communicative reflexives' and 'meta-reflexives', sharing with the latter a strong commitment to co-operative organization, voluntary association, and community service (Archer 2003: 360). In the sample, the most common variant of this 'integrating' type was supported by the continuity of occupational and local experiences combined with engagement in organizations representing collective interests at work (trade unions) and/or in civic local organizations. The 'integrating' strategy leads to the acquisition of 'delegated' social capital based on the representation of group interests (Bourdieu 1986: 251). In turn, the amplification of social networks supports biographical stability, in which community-centred reflexivity is founded. The 'integrating' pattern was most typical of long-standing union activists, employed in positions as craftsmen in large firms. An example is Krystian:

KRYSTIAN: Today, as you see, I am a unionist (…). My earliest memories include exactly this firm (…) My father already worked here (…) When I came to [the mill] (…) I tried to be active in a youth organization – called The Union of Socialist Youth – to do something, but in the sense of doing something for people. (…) When it was possible to create unions, which were independent of the employer, the state, the government, and so forth, we began to change something. For sure, today it's not that which was [planned] (…) But what we managed to do is that finally it's normal (…) Today there is economy, everything must be calculated […] Lower wages allowed us to survive, but because of that we need to do something extra for the people [W-60] (M, 45, a steelworker in a large company in the public sector.)

Krystian, a Solidarność leader in a steelworks in Upper Silesia, constructs his biography as a story of becoming a social activist, emphasizing an ethos of 'working for people'. Strong craft resources, stable occupational careers and long-term embeddedness in the same locality make for an ethos and community-centred reflexivity that are strongly interconnected. The ethos provides cultural motives to justify concerted actions aimed at preserving contextual continuity in which internal conversations are founded. In this and similar cases of long-standing union activists, these preservation strategies included the acceptance of the reduction of economic benefits for the sake of the company's survival in the new capitalist reality.

The decline of old industrial communities in Silesia and the low efficiency and legitimacy of trade unions' actions are the main foundations underlying the erosion of workers' collective commitments. Yet, this is not an irreversible tendency. Having faced changes in their social environment that were unmanageable by individual means, some workers have reflexively modified their concerns. Sharing limited experiences of collective involvement in socialist times, they joined or established unions in previously non-unionized companies or became engaged in civic activism at a local level. Their pathways to social activism involved discontinuous occupational careers, which underlay the initial development of private-centred reflexivity. Their point of departure was pragmatic; they attempted to solve concrete problems in their companies and local communities. In the praxis of their actions, their reflexivity acquired some properties of the community-centred type. An example is Marcelina, a lone mother, who co-established Solidarność in a large hypermarket in Upper Silesia:

MARCELINA: When I started to work here, there were no unions. It was very different work. At the moment when unions appeared, they started to really respect us (…) I felt like somebody important, and I liked it. My family doesn't like it, though, because it is brought back home. There is no day off, no holidays, no sick leave. I was once on a sick leave but I still acted as a union leader … Easter was coming … I had pestered the director for 3 weeks, because I knew there was money for people […] I'm a lone mother with three kids, but this doesn't hamper me […] [My kids] got used to it, because they see that it brings me satisfaction. [W-166] (F, 45, a check-out assistant in a private hypermarket.)

Marcelina defines her union activism both in terms of selfless engagement in collective goals and of individual empowerment. On the one hand, the ethos side of collective involvement is manifested in the emphasis on the respect due to an employee, rooted in the traditions of Solidarność, Catholic culture and working-class culture (Meardi 2000: 268). On the other hand, this communitarian ethos is reflexively refitted to changing conditions and combined with an individual project of empowerment, marked by the attempts to overcome constraints set by the employment situation and gender-related family roles.

The 'reinvention of ethos' is a mechanism, which accompanies collective attempts to re-establish more stable and secure frameworks for individual experiences under conditions marked by radical, systematically driven contextual discontinuity. It indicates an intentional hybridization of life strategies, in which established communitarian ideas – such as social embeddedness, solidarity and the defence of human dignity – are actively used to justify attempts to regain control over individual life-projects by means of concerted action. Although the dominant biographical transitions indicate a centrifugal dynamics from 'integrating' to other life strategies, the 'reinvention of ethos' suggests the possibility of a reverse tendency. When contextual discontinuity is overcome by collective means, reflexive work on ethos motivates collective strategies whose cumulative effects are institutional innovations.

Getting by

In contrast to the strategies of 'embedding' and 'integrating', the pattern of 'getting by' is founded on the combination of private-centred reflexivity and the progressively limited autonomy of action. Disbelief in any possibility of changing the subject's situation, a retreat into family life and enforced pragmatism, understood as personal efforts to protect life stability against the threat of economic degradation, are the most important characteristics of 'getting by'. Those affected by this pattern resemble 'fractured reflexives'. Their internal conversations provide them with no instrumental guidance about what to do in practice (Archer 2003: 299). The fragmentation of life-projects usually emerges when a previous continuity of biographical experience is broken by structural changes and contingent life events. Within the sample interviewed, the 'getting by' pattern was typical of workers employed in 'peripheral' positions in new private firms, whose occupational experiences involved lay-offs, demotions, involuntary job mobility and dead-end careers. It is also the most 'feminized' pattern, demonstrating the interplay of gender and class constraints (Pollert, 2003). Its properties are illustrated by Halina's case:

HALINA: I remember times, when it was cool in this factory, a lot of people, and, in general, there was work and very good atmosphere (…) [Afterwards] management insisted on decreasing wages, we earned too much. And it came to the point that we went on strike in this factory, with Solidarność. And it came to a sticky end for us, because we were accused of being [subversive] elements (…) So many people gave up their jobs at this time that they made only one shift (…) From January till March we've worked practically every Saturday, overtime (…) I had no time even for my son, not to say for … for my husband or anybody else (…) When I was on maternity leave, I did some training, in operating a PC and … what else … a cash register. But so far there has been no opportunity to change this job, because you know how difficult it is after vocational school. [W-43] (F, 29, a seamstress in a large privatised textile company.)

Halina's story demonstrates a negative interplay of life-projects, action contexts and resources in the emergence of the 'getting by' pattern. They include organizational changes in her firm leading to intensified work and very low wages (in 2003 she earned about €150 per month), unsuccessful experiences of collective resistance, the limited effects of re-training and, finally, the impossibility of mobilizing family resources because of the long-term illness of her husband. Similar to the 'embedding' type, the susceptibility to disempowerment increases if insufficient occupational resources, including low-valued and devalued skills and education, are combined with unhappy 'micro events', such as health and family problems.

Falling into the 'getting by' pattern highlights the discrepancy between 'life then', which is sometimes identified with socialism, and 'life now'. This discrepancy indicates the fragmented ethos, manifested in oppositional categories, such as economic security versus economic insecurity; social embeddedness versus social disintegration; meaningful work experiences versus meaningless work. The dissolution of collective life-worlds as the stable social foundations of ethos is particularly visible in the narratives of young workers, who share the experiences of patchwork-like occupational careers. An example is Kuba:

KUBA: I was working in a construction firm for nine months, the ... dope didn't want to extend my contract, eh? (...) He didn't do it and I showed him 'up yours' (laughing) And I went to the army (...) I got out and ... for half a year (...) I was on the dole, eh? I got angry. My mate fixed me up with a job in S-city where I've been working till now. (...) I work 8 to 12, even 13 hours, I had a few shifts of 24 hours, I'm ... flexible in that firm because I have to be. It's not that I want it, but that's the reality of that frigging life. Life is hard, you have to slog, that's it [...] [Do you want to achieve more than your parents?] I don't care about it. What I care about is to live a dignified life, to have well paid – I mean, to be paid for my labour. [Question to clarify migration plans] I would go anywhere, if there is work, nothing keeps me here." [W-32] (M, 24, a construction worker in a small private firm.)

The biography of Kuba demonstrates a significantly different relationship between ethos and life-projects than would be expected from a mechanism of 'making virtue out of necessity' (Bourdieu 2002: 372). On the one hand, there is a feeling of an overwhelming powerlessness, reducing his influence on an action context to symbolic gestures as a defence mechanism in constraining situations. On the other hand, instead of the passive acceptance of a particular situation, there is a constant longing for its betterment, which is motivated by an ethos-driven desire to live a 'dignified life'.

The fragmentation of ethos indicates the growing incoherence of its components, which reflects the structurally conditioned form of hybridization of life strategies. The notion of social embeddedness is openly disavowed as inapplicable in a ruthless, Hobbesian reality. Simultaneously, a strong emphasis on personal dignity persists, and motivates chaotic attempts to avoid further exclusion by any available means. If a chance to break out of the vicious circle of 'getting by' appears – through migration and work in the informal economy – it is seized upon, leading to the transition between 'getting by' and 'constructing'. In other cases, atomized resistance might be transformed into collective actions. Yet, while the fragmentation of ethos opens up a space to experiment with ways of life, enacting reflexively defined life-projects requires resources. As long as life strategies are not accompanied by the accumulation of more reliable social networks, material assets and/or skills, they remain volatile and uncertain.

Constructing

The last type, 'constructing', reflects the development of future-oriented life strategies aimed at improving the subjects' position and, more often, the family situation, especially in economic terms. Supportive factors are the possession of generally stronger and more diversified capitals, including the social capital of recognition at work, multi-faceted occupational skills and/or relatively high formal education. Biographical paths to the 'constructing' type involve relatively discontinuous biographical experiences in the work sphere and outside work. What matters most, subjectively, is the logic of bricolage (Levi-Strauss, 1967), referred to by workers as resourcefulness – meaning marshalling whatever resources are available for pursuing their life-projects. In terms of Archer's (2003: Ch. 7) modalities, workers pursuing the strategy of 'constructing' resemble 'autonomous reflexives'. Instead of attempting to transform their social environment, they try to transform their identities and resources and/or search for more suitable action contexts in order to advance their private strategies. The logic of 'constructing' is never fully specified in its goals, but involves a constant refusal to accept limitations. 'Constructing' pervades life stories either as a durable logic of action, encountered mainly in the life stories of middle-aged craftsmen, or as a new strategy prompted by new opportunities after the systemic change. A good example of seizing upon newly emergent educational opportunities is Adam's narrative:

ADAM: It is somehow grouped in my life, you know? (…) [First], at primary school, something happened and I passed to this vocational school. It taught me something. (…) My experiences from the apprenticeship and the observations of what's going on around contributed to a greater commitment in the technical college (…) I left this college, I got into the Car Factory, and I began university studies (…) And, meanwhile, in the last days, it happened that I was offered work in an office (…) It's not a kind of a brilliant career like the one of TV stars some years ago, but, I would say, a one up to my personality, up to my possibilities, isn't it?" [question about his evaluation of systemic change] (…) I've achieved more than I could have achieved, let's say, in this real socialism. Communism would lull me to sleep, you know? In the sense, that I'd finish vocational school, I'd get a job somewhere in a factory or else … you know? What else would I need? [W-2] (M, 25, a car assembler in the automotive industry in a large private plant.)

For Adam, like other young workers following weekend university studies, biography becomes the reflexively elaborated plan of 'educational' self-construction. Growing up in a broken family of an engineer and a surgeon's assistant, he first follows the standard trajectory of vocational education. Having experienced harsh working conditions during his apprenticeship, he decides to continue his schooling within the framework of weekend university studies. The expectations of upward mobility reinforce the symbolic divisions within the workers' milieus and distance him from the socialist past. In other parts of the interview, Adam describes his older co-workers as 'living in unconsciousness' and trade unions as 'a storehouse of blockheads'.

Private-centred reflexivity combined with the successful accumulation of resources fosters the reinterpretation of the subject's situation in terms that resemble the discourse of market individualism, including risk-taking, individual flexibility, self-reliance and orientation towards the future. Yet, behind the façade of radical individualism, some ways of thinking and acting that are bonded with the collective ethos persist. They range from the reinterpreted ethos of self-limitation, exemplified by Adam's idea of a career 'up to his possibilities', into autotelic roles in the family and craftmanship. An example of a hybridized strategy, which combines 'embedding' and 'constructing', is the narrative of Bożena:

BOŻENA: There was a period in our factory, when everything started somehow … these lay-offs of the people (…) I went with my director by my side outside the gate. We were laid off. Afterwards we opened up, together with my husband, our own business, in which I had flowers, fruits, vegetables, and foodstuffs (…) It was very good job for me, perhaps because I just like to work with people (…) And, finally, I got ill afterwards … I lost my ability to speak, and we decided, together with my husband, to sell [the shop], because, you know, it was needed. … We sold that kiosk, and what to do next? I can't live without work. First, I pondered what to do. I began to regain this … this power of speech. And … Well, I got a job, I worked in a school as a janitor […] And afterwards I came back to P-district, to the factory […] If you know me and my husband, you can be sure that we won't stay without a job for a long time. We're such characters that we won't sit and start to cry. [W-9] (F, 42, a cutting machine operator in a small private firm).

If structural constraints and/or unfortunate biographical events, e.g. illness, discourage a primary life project, the 'constructing' logic leads people to 'actively use their reflexivity to devise 'second' or 'third' best projects for themselves' (Archer 2007: 19). Instead of 'accepting the unavoidable', Bożena recombines all available resources to find an exit from a constraining situation. Yet, she also remains embedded in broad social networks – her family, local community and work milieu. Social embeddedness helps her not only to start and run her small shop, but also to return to work in a factory when this initial project fails.

The logic of 'constructing' indicates a form of agency, which is not 'removed from given [social] determinations' (Beck 1992: 177), but presumes reflexive attempts to combat objective structural constraints. In interviews representing the 'constructing' type, the effect of this reflexive adaptation was the recombination of the collective ethos with market-oriented strategies. As workers moved among different fields and milieus in order to advance their private strategies, they tended to preserve some of their communitarian beliefs and resources. They did so not only to minimize the uncertainty associated with their life-projects, but also because the reduction of life to its market-utilitarian dimension contradicted their ethos. The recombination of a communitarian ethos with market pragmatism reflects the intentional hybridization of life strategies, which is not only more achievable, but also more desirable to Polish workers than the ideal of infinitely flexible, mobile and uprooted (post)modern individualism.

Conclusions

This chapter has addressed the problem of the agency of the socially disadvantaged in the context of radical social change. The research on Polish workers led to two main conclusions. On the one hand, the distance between the patterns of 'structuring agency' and 'structured dependency' is structurally mediated. It reflects the joint effects of the configurational logics of constraints and of contingent life events, the negative consequences of which are greatest for those possessing weak or rapidly devalued resources, who found themselves in the peripheral segments of employment. On the other hand, there are some traces of resistance, whose emergence within these disadvantaged factions cannot be fully explained by their structural locations. Reflexivity is the foundation of the agency of the 'weak'. If the workers with whom I talked were not reflexive, it would be difficult to understand their attempts to overcome socially imposed limitations. These attempts were often ambivalent and hybridized. Yet, their incoherence, regardless of how disturbing it sounds to social scientists, cannot be ignored for the sake of analytical purity. It is the main feature which confirms that a grand narrative about the working class – as a victim or agent of social change – cannot do justice to the variety of workers' efforts to pursue their life-projects in actually existing class societies.

The typology of life strategies advanced here improves our understanding of negotiated agency implicitly proposed by some earlier research on post-socialist workers (Gardawski 1997; Latoszek 1994; Stenning 2005). The practices of coping with social change and socio-structural constraints lead to the hybridization of communitarian and privatized life strategies. Intentional hybridization relies on mobilizing all available resources in order to circumvent or transform structural constraints. If interlinked with private-centred reflexivity, it is manifested in the 'recombination' of a communitarian ethos with market-oriented, individual and family strategies. In regard to community-centred reflexivity, it takes the form of reinterpreting beliefs from the ethos beliefs in order to justify concerted actions, which combine the goals of individual and collective empowerment. The opposite, 'conditioned' pole of hybridization reflects broken and blocked life strategies. In combination with community-centred reflexivity and the devaluation of resources, it involves the ritualization of ethos and a retreat to more traditional ways of coping, such as reliance on extended social bonds and craft solidarity. Alternatively, conditioned hybridization is indicated by a growing distance from both market beliefs and communitarian ethos, resulting in the development of chaotic survival strategies.

The hypothesis of hybridization also offers new insights into the field of culturalist working-class studies. Contrary to Bourdieu's conviction (1990: 64), limited educational and cultural capital did not preclude reflexivity amongst the workers. Conversely, like the labourers studied by Lamont (2000: 11), they did not resemble 'post-modern men who recreate themselves anew every morning' either. As noted earlier by Archer (2007), the reduction of the concept of reflexivity to a single homogeneous form is an oversimplification. There is more than one modality of reflexive relationship with the social environment. Private-centred reflexivity assumes the development of internal conversations within a framework of individual and family projects. Practitioners of this mode of reflexivity resemble either of two types elaborated by Archer (2003): 'autonomous reflexives' or 'fractured reflexives'. Yet, despite the dominant privatizing trends, community-centred reflexivity persists, too. It is centred on the preservation or transformation of collectively shared action contexts. Polish workers, who resembled 'communicative reflexives' (Archer, 2003), did not just passively experience the continuity of their action contexts. They also attempted to co-determine and secure this continuity through innovative individual and collective courses of action. Notably, some salient characteristics of 'meta-reflexives', such as critical commitment to social values and civic engagement, were also present in interviews with workers, especially within the 'integrating' type. Yet, they were mixed with very practical, community-centred and private-centred concerns. This might indicate a specific variety of meta-reflexivity which coexists with rather limited educational resources.

At the most general theoretical level, the analysis of the biographical transitions between life strategies can contribute to debates about the hybridization of ethos and reflexivity (Adams, 2006; Elder-Vass, 2007). Under conditions of 'contextual continuity' – which is less and less 'given' and requires an active adaptation of resources – community-centred reflexivity and ethos are densely interconnected.[7] Contrastingly, the discontinuity of action contexts makes the explanations of actions in terms of an ethos more problematic and fosters the development of the private-centred modes of reflexivity. If the breakdown of possibilities to act autonomously is combined with weak and devalued resources, the incongruity between ethos and action contexts comes to the fore. In such conditions, people tend to develop volatile survival strategies that are weakly guided by collective shared beliefs. Alternatively, they can be immobilized in collective inaction. Another scenario emerges when discontinuity and biographical changes are intentionally sought by social agents who attempt to overcome structural constraints. In such cases, action is motivated to experiment by using the existing stock of practical knowledge in quest of the best ways to cope with contextual and biographical discontinuities. The recombination and reinvention of beliefs associated with ethos becomes a driving force of social change, either through the aggregate effects of individual actions or through the innovative forms of corporate agency. While the hypothesis of hybridization of ethos and reflexivity requires further elaboration, various scenarios discussed in this chapter might be a useful starting point for future research.

Notes

1 This chapter is based on my doctoral thesis, defended in 2009 at the Centre for Sociological Research, at the Catholic University of Leuven (Belgium).
2 Reflexivity is understood here, following Archer (2007: 4), as the 'regular exercise of the mental ability, shared by all normal people, to consider themselves in relation to their (social) contexts and vice versa'.
3 At the first stage, open coding procedure was applied, aimed at assigning data to categories through a line-by-line analysis of interview transcripts. Next, about half of the interviews were selected for selective coding on the basis of their relevance for the theoretical saturation of the contrastive configurations of life strategies.
4 'Embedding' was the dominant logic of story-telling in 50 cases and 'getting by' in 57 narratives, as compared with 28 cases representing the 'integrating' type and 31 cases – the 'constructing' type.
5 Even within 'embedding' and 'integrating' there was a tendency to define the 'privatisation' of social relations as the main consequence of systemic change. A similar proportion of cases representing 'community-centred' (78) and 'private-centred' (88) types seemed to reflect the statistical over-representation of workers employed in traditionally communitarian industries, such as mining and metallurgy.
6 Labels contain a code number, age, sex, occupation, and the type of company in which employed. All names have been changed.
7 It can be noted that according to Archer (Ch. 7 in this book), normative conventionalism as presupposed by the notion of habitus is most typical of communicative reflexivity and reflects the experience of contextual continuity. The 'embedding' type is the strongest reflexive manifestation of such conventionalism.

References

Adams, M. (2006) 'Hybridizing habitus and reflexivity: towards an understanding of contemporary identity?', *Sociology*, 40(3): 511–28.
Archer, M. (2000) *Being human: the problem of agency*, Cambridge: Cambridge University Press.
Archer, M. (2003) *Structure, agency and the internal conversation*, Cambridge: Cambridge University Press.
Archer, M. (2007) *Making our way through the world: human reflexivity and social mobility*, Cambridge: Cambridge University Press.
Archer, M. 'Can reflexivity and *habitus* work in Tandem?', in this volume.
Beck, U. (1992) [1986] *Risk society: towards a new modernity*, London: Sage.
Bourdieu, P. (1986) 'The forms of capital', in J. Richardson (ed), *Handbook of theory and research for the sociology of education*, New York: Greenwood Pres, pp. 241–58.
Bourdieu, P. (1990) *In other words. Essays towards a reflexive sociology*, Cambridge: Polity Press.
Bourdieu, P. (2002) [1984] *Distinction. A social critique of the judgement of taste*, Cambridge, MA: Harvard University Press.
Charlesworth, S. J. (2000) *A phenomenology of working class experience*, Cambridge: Cambridge University Press.
Devine, F. and Savage, M. (2005) 'The cultural turn, sociology and class analysis', in F. Devine, M. Savage, J. Scott, and R. Crompton (eds) *Rethinking class: Culture, identities and lifestyle*. Houndmills: Palgrave Macmillan, pp. 1–23.
Dunn, E. (2004) *Privatizing Poland: Baby Food, Big Business, and the Remaking of Labor*, Ithaca, NY: Cornell University Press.

Elder-Vass, D. (2007) 'Reconciling Archer and Bourdieu in an emergentist theory of action. *Sociological Theory*, 25(4): 325–347.
Faliszek, K., Łęcki, K. and Wódz, K. (2001) *Górnicy. Zbiorowości górnicze u progu zmian*, Katowice: Wydawnictwo 'Śląsk'.
Gardawski, J. (1997) *Przyzwolenie ograniczone. Robotnicy wobec rynku i demokracji*, Warszawa: Wydawnictwo Naukowe PWN.
Giddens, A. (1995) [1991] *Modernity and self-identity: Self and society in the late modern age*, Cambridge: Polity Press.
Glaser, B 1978, *Theoretical sensitivity. Advances in the methodology of grounded theory*, Sociology Press, Mill Valley.
Glaser, B. and Strauss, A. (1967) *The Discovery of Grounded Theory. Strategies for Qualitative Research*, Chicago: Aldine Publishing Company.
Goldthorpe, J. H., Lockwood D., Bechhofer F. and Platt, J. (1969) *The Affluent Worker in the Class Structure*, Cambridge: Cambridge University Press.
Lamont, M. (2000) *The dignity of working men. Morality and the boundaries of race, class, and immigration*, New York and London: Russell Sage Foundation and Harvard University Press.
Latoszek, M. (1994) 'Drogi życiowe i tożsamość robotników', *Studia socjologiczne* (1): 107–24.
Lévi-Strauss, C. (1968) [1962] *The savage mind*, Chicago: University of Chicago Press.
Meardi, G. (2000) *Trade union activists, East and West. Comparison in multinational companies*, Aldershot–Hampshire: Gower.
Meardi, G. (2007) 'More voice after more exit? Unstable industrial relations in Central and Eastern Europe', *Industrial Relations Journal*, 38(6): 503–23.
Mouzelis, N. (1995) *Sociological Theory. What went wrong? Diagnosis and Remedies*, London: Routledge.
Ost, D. (2005) *The defeat of Solidarity. Anger and politics in postcommunist Europe*, Ithaca and London: Cornell University Press.
Pollert, A. (2003) 'Women, work and equal opportunities in post-communist transition', *Work Employment and Society*, 17(2): 331–57.
Savage, M. (2001) 'Class identity in contemporary Britain: the demise of collectivism', in G. Van Gyes, H. de Witte and P. Pasture (eds), *Can class still unite? The differentiated work force, class solidarity and trade unions*, Ashgate: Brulington, pp. 79–100.
Sayer, A. (2005) *The moral significance of class*, Cambridge: Cambridge University Press.
Schütze, F. (1983) 'Biographieforschung und narratives Interview', *Neue Praxis*, (3): 283–93.
Schütze, F. (2005) [1984] 'Cognitive figures of autobiographical extempore narration', in R. Miller (ed.), *Biographical research methods*, London: Sage, pp. 289–338.
Skeggs, B. (1997) *Formations of class and gender*, London: Sage.
Słomczyński, K. M., Janicka, K., Shabad, G., and Tomescu-Dubrow, I. (2007) 'Changes in Class Structure in Poland, 1988–2003: Crystallization of the Winners/Losers' Divide', *Polish Sociological Review*, 157(1): 45–64.
Stenning, A. (2005) 'Where is the post-socialist working class? Working-class lives in the spaces of (post-)socialism', *Sociology*, 39(5): 983–99.
Szawiel, T. (1991) 'Etos i szansa', *Kultura i Społeczeństwo*, 35(2): 111–22.

10 Emotion, and the silenced and short-circuited self

Helena Flam

Introduction

In the 1970s quite a few social scientists invested considerable intellectual effort in investigating the learning, decision-making and planning capacities of the industrial welfare states (Mayntz and Scharpf 1975). In the 1980s some instead, theorized about how institutions think (Douglas 1986). By the 1990s focus shifted to how societies/modern systems reflect, while some scientists posited, but did not directly explore, human reflexivity (Beck, Giddens and Lash 1996; for a critique see Archer 2007: 41–58). Finally, in organizational studies and research on social movements, everyday reflexivity as expressed in narratives or (internal) conversation has become a legitimate object of sociological inquiry (Wiley 1994; Archer 2000, 2003, 2007 and forthcoming); Czerniawska 1997; Collins 2004; Orbuch 1997; Miethe and Roth, 2005). This text is concerned with obstacles to developing inner conversation.

For analytical purposes it is necessary to position the self not only in a moral or social context (Wiley 1994; Archer 2000, 2007),[1] but also in the power matrix of society. Neither the depth of our moral commitment to, nor the extent of our integration into society, is people's only problem. Relations of domination keep specific social categories from developing a self-confident 'voice'. Faced with the contempt of the powerful, many members of the dominated groups come to feel deep humiliation and suppressed anger (Scott 1990; Flam 2004). These emotions silence their 'voice', and their individual capacity to imagine, to wish and to choose. To develop my argument about the silenced self I will focus on a negative form of integration, via subordination. I will then draw attention to the anxious or over-confident 'short-circuited' self, one which is unable to organize a constructive internal conversation but, rather, engages in self-blame, obsessions, self-deceptions, or scapegoating. Since emotions play a paramount role in both (i) silencing and (ii) short-circuiting reflexive processes, I argue that (iii) it makes sense to switch from Mead to Cooley's feeling-self in theorizing about the self. In these ways it is hoped to contribute to research on everyday reflexivity.

The eloquent versus the silenced self

As research directly concerned with class, 'race' and gender shows, it is crucial to include these three types of relations of domination in theorizing about the self, because these relations largely determine its very constitution. Class, 'race', and gender – as types of domination – are reinforced by specific discriminatory beliefs/discourses, practices, experiences and emotions. Pierre Bourdieu (see for example 1987[1979]: 639–642, 647–57, 670, 255–61) as well as the antiracist and feminist literature, detailed how relations of domination generate emotions that 'silence the voice' of dominated groups. I will present and link these three kinds of theory to Kemper's ideas on the emotional implications of unequal status and power relations.

Bourdieu's well known idea is that the dominant groups can reproduce their positions in society because they possess not only much economic, but also social, cultural and symbolic power. In his early texts he supplies the missing 'emotional link' between power and self-sense. Bourdieu proposes that the dominant classes – in possession of self-assured and eloquent voices – keep the dominated groups locked in a state of collective 'humiliation'. He stresses 'the role of shame, that self-defeating emotion which arises when the dominated come to perceive themselves through the eyes of the dominant, that is, are made to experience their own ways of thinking, feeling and behaving as degraded and degrading' (Wacquant, 2005: 393–4; Schultheis, 2007).[2] It is when they internalize the outsider's view of themselves that the dominated become silenced, *even when* their sense of self-pride or indignity at what is happening to them does not disappear. Their self-feelings remain – at best – ambivalent, moving between shame, humiliation and anger.

Albert Memmi's (1992: 48–9, 86–7, 69, 100–1) classic text on racism explicitly addresses the emotions sustaining racist relations of domination, which entail contempt for and the humiliation of the 'Other'. When biological differences can no longer be made believable as the grounds for racist relations of domination, the mentality, culture or customs of the 'Other' become a target of contempt. The voice of the dominant group can be heard as it attributes blame to, slanders, imposes its law upon or gives vent to its aggression against the 'Other' (Memmi, 1992: 86–7, 119). The 'Other' is negated symbolically, his humanity denied. The victims, feeling their powerlessness, or worse, having internalized racist valuations (Memmi, 1992: 62), sentence their own selves to silence.

Finally, feminist research discusses very similar processes: women learn early on that they, their thoughts and feelings are worthless. They unlearn speaking and trusting their own cognitive and moral judgement, their own emotions. Their voices become silenced, their selves 'defective or diminished. The fear of demeaning treatment [can] be seen in the cringing before an Other from whom such treatment [can be] anticipated: shame [can] be read even in the physical constriction of their bodies' (Bartky in Luke, 1994: 216, 211).

In sum: members of the dominated class, 'race' or gender (and 'unfit' members of the elite) are more likely to become objects of monitoring, ridicule, condescension, intimidation, cruelty and violence (Griffiths 1995: 121, 115–19; Gilligan

1982). The difficulties attending their self-articulation stem from the shame they feel about their 'unwelcome' characteristics, the painful effort at self-denial, and the constant fear of rejection. Humiliation, disappointment and saddness kill their self-esteem, making voice unlikely.[3] Constant and disdainful treatment produces traumatic and chronic shame that stamps – often in an indistinct, pre-reflexive, and unremarked manner – the way in which they see and respond to the world (Woodward 2009: 94–5). This kind of non-verbalized. deep and debilitating shame works as an action predisposition, as part of one's habitus. It is profoundly disempowering, very hard to verbalize, and harder to overcome (but see Flam 2005: 22, 26 and Woodward 2009: 79–108 for transformative shame-anger or shame-pride sequences).

These ideas are broadly compatible with Kemper's (1978, 1981) theory of 'real emotions' which states that losses of status and power, as experienced in interactions with others, produce (i) shame and frustration, when one blames oneself for these losses, and (ii) (suppressed) anger, when one sees the other as the cause of these same losses. Being a member of the lower classes and/or women or minority groups raises the likelihood of repeatedly experiencing such downgrading and, given societal discourses contemptible of the lower classes, women and 'other races', blaming themselves for them. It thus increases the likelihood of developing a sense of constant, deep, de-mobilizing, debilitating shame and humiliation, perhaps – as feminists and Bourdieu argue – accompanied by suppressed anger over being forced to feel so about oneself. While the constant self-directed shame and a sense of humiliation unsettle and discourage, they also destroy and silence the 'I' – the inner voice of the self.

It is the constant experience of being invisible, silenced and/or being made to feel 'inferior', 'inadequate' and/or being corrected – verbally or in practice – that makes one internalize this negative, undesired, and inadequate 'you'. The outsider's 'you' that 'I' become.

Mirroring eyes and signifying voices

Let me now step back for a moment to compare two major accounts of internalization that are essential to discussing the silencing of the self. In the first account *looking, seeing* and *mirrors* are the words that are used to explain the processes of internalization. In the second account, *speaking, hearing,* and *voice* play an identical role. Both of these ways of evoking the self are part of our everyday language. We see, are seen or are made invisible. We hear, and are heard or are unheard/silenced. In scientific texts these semantics are often mixed, yet we are dealing with two distinct modes of comprehension. The first goes back to Greek philosophy and its concern with the question of whether human senses, especially the eyes, suffice adequately to mirror/perceive the world as it is (Cavarero 2005: 26–7, 35–6, 50–1). It equates an idea/a thought with truth, with the mind's eye seeing a true image of an object. The second has Hebrew roots and, in contrast to the Greek philosophy that looked for the generic envisioned form, is concerned with the question of creativity, uniqueness and interpretation.

Cooley's (1970) concept of the 'looking glass self' can be better understood, I think, if we interpret it in reversed 'Greek' terms. His question then becomes how do we know who we are – that what we see in ourselves is true. His answer is that we find a reply to this question in part by looking into the *constituting mirroring eyes* of the other that both show and affect our self-image. Cooley had a rather democratic idea of the self, regarding its development as a tense compromise between how the 'I' sees itself, and how others see/mirror it. To the seeing/mirroring eye of the other, he attributed considerable but not decisive definitional powers. The mirroring eye can push the mirrored self to feel ugly or beautiful, loved and appreciated, hated and despised, but the actual outcome depends in part on the ideals and aspirations of the 'I'. These, taken together with the mirroring eye, determine the self-image.

In contrast to Cooley, Sartre (1994) and Foucault (1975) posited the gaze/eye of the other as an instrument of domination, control and discipline – capable of constituting or destroying the 'I'. To these authors the gaze of the Other is the 'to be or not to be' of the 'I'. Also Bourdieu, antiracists or feminists argue that, even if we start out with joyous self-pride in our qualities, as posited by Cooley, we end up seeing ourselves as shamefully inferior when we are constantly mirrored as such. This hierarchical conception of the self has only two parts: the onlooker and the looked upon.

The other account of the internalization of inferiority draws attention to the Other who has a power over us because of her/his *constitutive, signifying voice* (Cavarero 2005: 34). In a top-down or tyrannical version, this voice is *ein Befehl*, an order that subordinates. Alternatively, it is naming, making us ugly/unworthy/inferior/uncertain. When one's 'I' is defined by the eloquent Other as wild/inadequate/illiterate/illogical/substandard, it recoils, its voice is silenced. In submitting to such external negative judgements, we lose not only 'voice', but also the capacity to understand what is going on. The burning feeling of deep shame about our deficits, our senses of humiliation at rejection and of inferiority, make us numb or keep us from exploding in anger at the indignity we suffer when exposed to significations that negate us, to judgements that deny our selves.

In a democratic version of the self and its development, two voices rather than one are heard (Cavarero 2005: 30, 176–7). Talking and hearing stand for a true process of communication between two unique voices, which seek and grant one another mutual social recognition. The voice, speaking and listening – the elements of communication – imply creative powers, but also reciprocity, proximity and relationship. They posit a speaker not as an isolated individual who sees or is seen, but as a participant in a process of communication involved in the mutual give and take of a dialogue. This democratic version implies a self that is not only communicating with others, but is also capable of having its own inner conversations. In contrast to the eye/the gaze, in this version the voice stands for uniqueness and for relationships – both of which seem to be presupposed by and form the basis of internal conversations.

Whether formulated in terms of *mirroring eyes* or *signifying voices*, the idea is that what others see and how they think of and feel about us does matter. As the main elements in any interaction/communicative action, their thoughts and emotions about us co-constitute us. The 'other' influences whether or not we can develop as autonomous, thriving human beings with a positive self-image, with a capacity to hold inner conversations, and to assert ourselves in relation to others. Our selves are 'produced and reproduced by way of communicative action ... our emotional habitus is the result of a shared history ... [E]motional responses, as they [become] manifest in communicative situations, draw upon [this] habitus ...' (Crossley 1998: 33).

Self-seeing-self and inner voice

It could be maintained that the argument so far is not nuanced enough: in fact, not all middle class people develop the eloquent voice and there are some lower class people or minority group members who do speak up. Indeed, some middle class members lose their voice when repeatedly defeated in competition with their peers. The educational system claims its toll, strengthening and cultivating the voice of its best students while silencing the others. Competition and hierarchies in enterprises also do their part in this. The difference is that women, minorities or migrants are subjected to much more encompassing forms of domination that are likely to silence their voices. But, of course, in these categories we also find exceptions – especially if the families or social milieus of these individuals work as a shield (see Jaggar 1997: 396; Griffiths 1995: 88; Lutz and Davis 2005). These exceptions explain the rebellious *self-seeing-self* or *inner voice*, to which I will now turn.

What is missing in the accounts of the self that I have touched upon so far is the explicit idea that we also have an *inner voice* and/or a *self-seeing-self*. Colloquial expressions, such as 'She could not look herself in the eyes' or, as part of an inner conversation, 'Yes, but will you be able to face yourself when you do this?' or '... will you be able to look in the mirror next morning?', all refer to one's own capacity to see oneself – in a censoring, moralizing, laudatory or, at any rate, a split, way. European myths and paintings, when de-gendered, also suggest that one's mirror-sessions can be understood not only as acts of censorship or self-doubt, of putting oneself before the high judge/court/jury of one's own 'better judgement' or 'better self', but also as a sign of vain self-love or simple approval – the last gesture of checking-over and self-approbation before submerging oneself into the world of action (Meyers 2002: 99–147). Art, as well as everyday language, thus suggests that one's own seeing eyes, directed at one's self, are the other determinant of one's self-image. The equivalent of one's own seeing eyes is the *inner voice* that is mostly dormant, but in critical situations comments – in whispers or in screams – upon one's conduct. The inner voice can be congratulatory and reassuring or full of self-doubt and hatred but, whatever emotions and judgements it carries, it remains private, to be heard out loud perhaps only in the most intimate relationships. It is the inner voice and the self-seeing-self, I suggest, that need to be understood as 'how you see yourself' in Cooley's looking glass self, which then acquires the following components: (i) the *mirroring eyes* of the other/how others see you; (ii) how you see yourself, that is, your *self-seeing-self/inner voice*; (iii) these two, possibly in uneasy tension, amount to one's *self-image*. Now if the significant others (who may be real or fictional) of the individuals who belong to categories suffering from discrimination, effectively shield them from its worst consequences and help them to develop a positive self-seeing-self/inner voice, these individuals have a good chance of not succumbing completely, even if the mirroring eye/signifying voice of the other is contemptuous or hateful. Such people can be expected to transcend shame and to feel pride and/or anger.

The naïve and the sophisticated subject

Let me historicize my argument. The silenced self that Bourdieu, antiracists or feminists addressed can be characterized as the 'naïve' subject because both its oppressors and this self take the existing relations of domination for granted. However, historically speaking, in the (post-)colonial and Western World counter-discourses about the relations of domination emerged, starting in the 1960s and producing new, *challenged* relations of domination. These counter-discourses have generated a new constellation of voices: the (no longer) self-assured, sovereign voice of the dominating groups, and the chorus of challenging, empowered and empowering voices, raised by the Marxists, feminists, anti-colonial/antiracists, lesbians and gays, environmentalists, the handicapped and other social movements and critics.

For example, key feminists have proposed that emotion and reflection work in tandem to break the silence of the silenced, to help them gain voice. Alison Jaggar (1997: 396) argued that the status quo is supported by our emotional socialization and that the prescribed emotions that accompany our roles 'limit our capacity for outrage … and blind us to the possibility of alternative ways of living'. But she also stressed that this emotional socialization is imperfect and the 'hegemony that our society exercises over people's emotional constitution is not total' (p. 396). In specific situations, and also more generally, individuals who belong to groups that 'pay a disproportionately high price for maintaining the status quo' come to feel negative 'outlaw emotions', such as humiliation, sadness, indignation, anger or fury instead of rather pleasant but complacent prescribed emotions: these individuals experience the 'outlaw' emotions at first as inexplicable, inappropriate, unconventional, unexpected and unacceptable. If they are isolated, they may feel confused by these emotions, find themselves 'unable to name their experience' (Jaggar, 1997: 396, but see also MacKinnon, 1989: 85–95 and Griffiths, 1995: 88), but when their emotions become

> shared and validated by others … the basis exists for forming a subculture defined by perceptions, norms and values that systematically oppose the prevailing perceptions, norms and values. By constituting the basis for such a subculture, outlaw emotions may be politically (because epistemologically) subversive (Jaggar, 1997: 396).

Creating a counter-discourse to describe and account for one's experience amounts to finding one's voice, learning to speak for oneself. Also Griffiths (1995: 88–90, 122–3, 142–148, 169, 176–9) more recently argued that one can learn by reflecting upon the emotions destroying one's self-esteem: feeding on one's own anger and taking note of these emotions prompts one to try to understand and to change society 'by [c]oining a new word', 'reclaiming the language'. In this manner she echoed American feminists who in the 1970s and 1980s 'conceived anger … as an emotion that is not only basis for a group but can also politicize a group, as an emotion furthermore that is *created* in a group, one that is enabling of action and not inhibiting of it' (Woodward 2009: 46; italics in original).

Although pinpointing crucial external and some internal conditions that lead some to develop or adopt a critical self and/or 'outlaw emotions', the feminist explanations leave unanswered the question about where within the self this critical reflection and these 'outlaw emotions' are lodged. In particular, they explain neither where anger comes from nor how debilitating shame develops into mobilizing anger (see also Flam 2005).

Bourdieu's and Jaggar's insight that the 'I' is experienced as ambivalent when rendered 'inferior' – both degraded and angry/indignant about this degradation – is worth holding onto (see also Gould 2002; Kleres 2005). The very ambivalence is crucial because it promises to answer the question of where the critical – cognitive and emotional – impulses come from. It is from the suppressed anger at the humiliation and indignity experienced that the exemplars of emancipation, be they social movements or therapists, tap into in order to reverse what we feel about ourselves. As Flam (2005), drawing on accumulated research on social movements shows, this is indeed what has happened in the last half century: women's, gay-lesbian, handicapped and other social movements have worked on their members' deep sense of shame, humiliation and anger, often succeeding in mobilizing anger and pride. In turn, this mobilization helped to put pressure on politicians, lawmakers and public opinion in general to bring about legal and institutional changes, making it easier for these social categories to strive for social recognition and be put on an equal footing with the rest of society. As helpful as these ideas are, they fall short of telling us why the 'inferiorised' 'I' can have the capacity to feel ambivalence, that is *both shame and anger*.

Introducing the concept of inner voice/self-seeing-self helps to answer this question: it explains where anger and reflection come from in the self. It is the self-seeing-self/inner voice that is the locus of critical reflection as well as of anger and indignity. As against earlier models with only two parts to a self – the degraded and the angry-indignant, living in an uneasy tension with each other – I propose an expanded Cooley model consisting of: (i) the mirroring eyes/signifying-outer voice as the carriers of hatred and contempt, (ii) the self-seeing-self/inner voice as the locus of anger and indignation at one's degradation by the other, and, finally, (iii) a self-image which is an uneasy tension between these two: containing both deep shame and anger. If habitual and debilitating shame did not completely destroy (ii) the self-seeing-self/inner voice, anger and indignation dominate and are felt/ expressed when alone or with like-minded peers; shame and a sense of degradation dominate in the presence of contemptuous others. Supportive (real or fictional) others, social movements, or therapists can affect one's self image by shifting the balance away from the mirroring eyes/signifying-outer voice to the self-seeing-self/ inner voice that tells one that one is lovable after all (for words of warning against emotion-constructing experts, see Crossley [1998: 35]).

However, and here I briefly address a blind spot in the feminist and social movement literature, only when these supportive others encourage self-reflexivity and social criticism, rather than recommending pacifying medication or violence, will anger have a chance to have an emancipatory rather than a destructive effect. Anger does not guarantee 'clarity of vision' (Woodward 2009: 49–50). Contrary to many feminists' arguments, anger in and of itself is neither moral nor liberating. It can be as easily directed at a scapegoat as at the true oppressor (see below). Moreover, for those whose self-seeing-self/inner voice was completely destroyed, who do not feel any anger, this anger, far from waiting to be released, needs first to be constructed and mobilized (Woodward 2009: 50; Flam 2005). In any case, both collective reflection and self-reflection pre-date the emergence of the constructed, emancipatory anger.

From this perspective we can better understand the role played by the emancipatory counter-discourses developed by social movements. These helped many previously silenced but potentially critical individuals to 'find' – or to develop – their inner and their public voice. At the very least, they converted them into 'sophisticated subjects' fairly well aware of their dominated position.

In turn, these challenging counter-discourses created new silenced voices – among yet unheard/suppressed minorities but also among representatives of the dominating groups who now became less certain of their own positions and the right to speak-up (in whose name?) (Luke, 1994; Woodward 2009: 54–6). As the acceptance of critical voices and social movements grew in the public sphere, it also turned out that it is easier to sign an open letter or participate in a large demonstration than to confront one's family, friends or work colleagues about their machismo, national chauvinism or racism (Flam 2007). Many have succumbed to tiredness and cynicism, whilst watching how easy it is for the old relations of domination, although challenged, to reproduce themselves. It is hard for an isolated, yet critical self to raise a dissenting voice (Hercus 1999). Frustration, exhaustion or cynicism keep this critical self from speaking up, breaking the silence, and taking on too many everyday battles. In the case of such a sophisticated subject, the inner voice is present and critical, but it does not translate into a public voice.

The short-circuited self

Although Wiley occasionally refers to contrary examples, he is primarily interested in 'mentally healthy', 'fully socialized' individuals (Wiley 1994: 114, 119–121, 124, 126). Archer, even though she devotes a chapter to 'fractured reflexives' in her *Structure, Agency and the Internal Conversation* (2004: 298–361), and later also occasionally refers to this mode of reflexivity to capture how the distressed 'go round in circles' as characteristic of the 'passive agent' (Archer 2008: 3 and

2007: 93, 96), devotes most of her attention to the reflexive aspects of striving for and achieving personal integrity, living a 'dedicated life' – her work up to date[4] is mostly about individuals who actually manage to set priorities (Archer 2004: 231, 243; Pizzorno 1986).

Many people, however, rely not on self-critical rationality but instead on rationalizations. Pizzorno's (1986) 'identifiers' are unable to criticize either themselves or the ideas and collectivities to which they have become devoted. Many individuals shy away from 'healthy' self- or other-criticism. Instead, they become obsessed, self-deluded or find a scapegoat (see Memmi 1992; Douglas 1995). Yet others over-indulge in dead end self-blame.

Practising psychologists point out that in a typical inner conversation the attribution of *self-blame*, expressing itself as (constant or very frequent!) 'negative self talk', is very widespread. In 'negative self talk', the 'I' expresses regrets, formulates self-accusations, puts itself down and so forth. Therapy involves teaching the 'patients' how to transform their negative, discouraging, depressing 'inner voice' to produce positive, energizing, forward-looking rather than de-mobilizing thoughts (Braiker 1989).

If we take *obsessions*, which produce a circular routine while blocking reflexive thinking, it turns out that up to three per cent of the American population suffers from obsessions, this proportion being much higher for young people. *Self-deception, self-delusion and self-denial, in brief S-DDD*, is also very widespread. In small quantities these are necessary as strategies for coping with the normal anxieties accompanying our lives (Lawley and Tompkins 2004). When it is first advanced, S-DDD is counterproductive, taking the form of denied addictions, compulsions, physically or psychologically abusive relationships, weight problems, self-harm, etc. It makes seemingly normal people handle money in the most erratic and irresponsible manner (Lane 1992). Underlying emotions range from extreme personal insecurity to hope of improvement in the current state of affairs.

Scapegoating is yet another way of 'coping', not only in society at large, but – as it turns out – also in families and organizations (Namka 2003; Douglas 1995). It is outward directed blame which displaces self-blame and introspection. Research on scapegoating discloses that family members treated as scapegoats are also easily pushed into this role in the organizations for which they work. Research on racism and anti-Semitism pinpoints that *scapegoating* constitutes their key element, *scapegoating* being a favourite elite *and* mass pastime. It is not just a thing of the past, because today it is widespread, being typical of groups, organizations and public affairs (Douglas 1995).

Low self-esteem, insecurity, anxieties, lack of confidence, but also over-confidence – very widespread emotions – are said to be at the root of the type of 'short-circuited thinking' (my term) which is associated with self-blame, obsessions, S-DDD and scapegoating. Self-blame, obsessions and some forms of S-DDD lead to inaction or cyclical action.

Lest it is argued that I am addressing here only marginal and pathological forms of thought, let me first stress that considered in aggregate terms they would probably turn out 'normal' rather than 'deviant'. Indeed, some of these forms of thinking are quite typical of organization members. In *Exit, Voice and Loyalty* Hirschman (1970: 92–98, 113–19) deals at length with opportunists who delude themselves that they have to stay in the organization, executive board or advisory body of which they have become highly critical by telling themselves that without them, it and its decisions would become much worse. This is a very widespread form of self-deception, yet few observers would classify it as pathological. It reveals fear of losing power, privileges and/or life chances as a source of motivation. Moreover, recent research on organizations and professions shows that the institutional blinders, self-censoring, conspiracies of silence, strategic deception, numerous forms of denial, scapegoating (also known as 'blame time'; see Jackall, 1988), myth-making, face work or rituals belong to their standard action repertoire (Meyer and Rowan, 1977; Jackall, 1988; Machado, 2008; Zerubavel 2006: 20–45; Cohen 2005: 38, 41, 47–50, 59–68).

This amounts to saying that work organizations, instead of fostering critical rationality rely on a variety of self- and other-deceptions to cultivate the belief that they are rational and that the people working for them are in fact competent professionals (Tacke 2006; Machado 2008). Organisations turn into hypocrites because they have to deal with multiple and often contradictory demands of

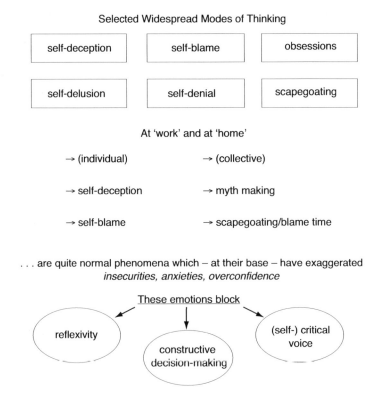

Figure 10.1 The short-circuited self.

stockholders, clients, trade unions or environmental groups (Brunsson 1993 [1989]). They cannot afford to tolerate open criticism or a process of discovery. Instead, they demand (faked) enthusiasm, commitment and devotion. Moreover, it is very hard for the individuals who find their working conditions intolerable to admit to themselves that they hate their jobs, despise their bosses, or oppose the organizations for which they work. Should they do this, they would have to act on their emotions and quit, for such is the logic of emotions in our culture (Rosenberg 1990: 7; Flam 1993, 1998). And such a decision would imply financial losses and reduced life-chances, feelings of failure or other undesired consequences and emotions. Many people find self-blame, self-deception, obsessions or scapegoating preferable to the intolerable feelings that quitting would bring forth. Individuals working for organizations react by tolerating, compromising, circumventing, spiting and manipulating them, anything but using their voice or quitting (Oliver 1991).

We should not forget that, as Hochschild (1983) tells us, hypocrisy has become an inherent part of employed labour, especially in the service sector. Modern employers fight for market share by demanding that their personnel put on a display of positive emotions in relationship to desired clients, while treating debtors or undesired clients to a display of negative emotions. Arguably, people working for such organizations lose touch with their own emotions. Although Hochschild's critics stress the playfulness and autonomy of the employees much more than she does, they do not deny that modern working conditions promote emotional insincerity. Bogner and Wouters (1990) in particular point out that putting on a display of positive emotions that are not necessarily genuine, goes back – as Norbert Elias tells us in *The Civilizing Process* – to the time of the absolutist royal courts. Emotions are constructed and therefore should not be treated as 'authentic' – that is, as the key parts of our moral compass or as trustworthy 'commentaries' that tell us which values or commitments to choose (Taylor 1995, 1989; Archer 2003; Flam 2009). This applies not only to organizational but also to domestic life.

Turning to couples, Hochschild (1990) and Beck-Gernsheim (1992) pinpoint how self-deception keeps emancipated women from taking the exit option when exit (divorce) implies economic and possibly even social risk. Rather than keeping up an open conflict about a fair division of childcare and household labour or divorcing, most women fall back upon the illusion that the work is shared fifty-fifty, even though in fact the husband takes care of the hobby room or garage and his wife the remaining three floors. Economically insecure but traditional couples stage a performance that helps them believe that her babysitting at home is not work and he is just being gallant when he helps her with 'unmanly' household cores. Hochschild's book is a goldmine of such family myths, self- and other-deceptions. These keep the economy of gratitude and a (more or less tired) love relationship going. Her argument is that these self-deceptions and collective myths are the result of gender ideologies and emotions underpinning them, which the partners (and their relatives and peers) are unwilling or incapable of renouncing. The continued economic dependence of women on men reinforces these self-deceptions and myths. It is worth stressing that Hochschild's research focuses on a fairly benign pole of the sociology of family. At the other pole we find routine self-deception, conspiracies of silence, and the denials that are crucial in sustaining long-term alcoholism, incest, sexual abuse, rape and domestic violence (Zerubavel 2006; Cohen 2005: 120–4).

Thus, it seems that obsessions, self-blame or self-deception, like insincerity or myth-making, have deep emotional, organizational and societal roots. These prevent comfortable and sophisticated conversations about the past, present and future within the semiotic self. Although both symbolically and morally laden, for many people, conversations become 'wired' in very specific ways, preventing them from thinking ahead or reflecting upon their selves as these 'really' are, could or should be.

Conclusion

In this text I have argued for the expansion of research devoted to every(wo)men's reflexivity by pointing to (i) the hierarchy-bred, humiliated, possibly angered, yet 'voiceless' selves, and (ii) also drawing attention to 'short-circuited' selves. I stressed that relations of domination are conveyed by and produce emotions that are crucial to the process of losing one's voice. These emotions co-determine the constitution of our selves: whether or not we develop a strong or a silenced voice, a truly reflexive, or a short-circuited way of handling key issues.

The material reviewed here suggests that human reflexivity is not necessarily straightforward or perfect. Instead, it seems that very many human beings cope with complex, contradictory, and shifting judgements about their selves – often asking themselves which self-image, which self-feeling to trust. There are tensions and conflicts within each person, just as in collective life. Distorted or blocked reflexivity is our everyday bread – providing social movements and therapists with plenty of work.

I also pointed out that when emotions follow conventional rules governing feelings, they work to support the status quo, reproducing the established structures of domination. However, when they turn subversive they stand a chance of becoming a motor of social change but only if validated by (successful) social milieus or protest movements. Last but not least, emotions can block constructive thinking, leading instead to short-circuited reflexivity.

This amounts to saying that emotions cannot and should not be treated as our moral guides, as, for example, Charles Taylor (1995) or some feminists (see Held 1995) argue – certainly not without first being checked against a list of human rights to ensure that they do not dictate seemingly moral courses of action which in fact degrade others (Jaggar 1997; Flam 2009).

If, as I have argued in this text, emotions are indeed so important as to decide whether or not we develop a self-confident voice and/or short-circuited reflexivity, it would seem to make more sense to take Cooley's instead of Mead's ideas as a point of departure for theorizing about the self.[5] In contrast to Mead, Cooley (1970) theorized emotions. He (i) defined self as self-feeling and thus emotions as an intrinsic part of the self, (ii) attributed these emotions to the 'I', (iii) cast the 'I' as an unevenly socialized self-centred emotional part of the self that, via its emotions, (iv) becomes *connected* – positively or negatively – to the others among whom it (v) seeks social recognition (vi) by routine *comparisons*. For all these reasons Cooley's 'looking-glass self' lends itself much better to the task of proposing different types of selves (for an earlier version, see Flam 2008).

(I) When social recognition is not forthcoming, the 'I' – which sees itself negatively reflected in the *mirroring eyes* of the others – becomes endangered and shrivels. This 'I' – conceptualized as *self-seeing-self* or *inner voice* – starts negating parts or the whole of its self. It loses its capacity to feel healthy self-pride, to retain any positive *self-image* or to produce *voice*. Its ability to engage in an inner or public conversation on its own terms disappears. Such a silenced type of 'I' offers only diffuse images and sensations in decision-making situations. It has no or few words for what it feels, offers no or unfinished or contradictory sounds, words or sentences. Its emotions are *confused* (Woodward 2009: 52, 53, 92, 95–7; MacKinnon 1989: 85–95) and cannot assist with decisions. It may not even be able to conceive of asking 'What do I want?' Perhaps it is anxious, engaged in self-blame, or absorbed by a myriad of obsessions and self-deceptions. At any rate it is often unaware of/ denies the sensed frustration, depression, shame and humiliation experienced in unequal relations (Scheff 1994, Bourdieu 1984; Archer 2003: 307, 311, 314, 324) and can provide little clear guidance to thought or action. Indeed, the 'voiceless' self is literally squashed under the weight of disregard and the negative emotions that press it down. This 'I', 'as a result of long years of oppression, ha[s] been so completely drained of self-respect and a sense of "somebodiness"' that it fears and resents but remains complacent (King 1991: 77).[6] Therapeutic, protest group, organizational and societal discourses may hinder or help the naming and framing processes that would assist this self in developing a positive inner and public voice (Patrick Clair 1998: 73–122; MacKinnon 1989: 91–105). The silenced 'I', however, constitutes only one possibility.

The second possibility is that the 'I' feels ambivalent, pulling the inner conversation in different, even contradictory, directions. Its self-seeing-self and/or inner voice is split or short-circuited. It cannot provide any guidance for engaging in action. What is feels has to be disentangled, interpreted, de-constructed. The 'ambivalent' self oscillates between possible cognitive frames and emotions corresponding to these frames: when it blames itself for the disregard in which it lives, it feels shame and despair, but if it blames the oppressor, it feels resentment and glowing hatred. Caught in the relations of domination, it moves between despair, patience, love, fear and resentment, and bitter, glowing hatred (King 1991: 73, 77), unable to decide which frame and which emotions are adequate. In fact, its emotions often come in *contradictory pairs* (love and hate, or shame and anger) or *sequences* (hate-love-hate; shame, frustration, anger, shame) (Simmel 1999; Nedelmann 1988; Freud in Woodward 2009: 44) or *mixtures* of the 'really felt' – moving between the prescribed and the proscribed (Hochschild 1979; Illouz 1997: 187–247; Archer 2003: 310–313, 323–4; Flam 2009), so that the answer to the question 'What do I *really* feel?' has to be answered, prior to or as part of any inner conversation about the future. This is the 'I' on which social movements and therapists work with a great likelihood of success, when they tap into the emotional ambivalence felt by the 'I'.

Possibly the silenced and ambivalent 'I' corresponds to Archer's 'fractured reflexives' whose 'inner dialogue does not work as a guide to action' and whose 'self-talk ... is primarily expressive. Its effect is to intensify affect. It leads the subject to feel an ever more poignant emotional distress about her condition ... [t]heir internal conversations simply do not work for them – by enabling subjects to propose courses of action to themselves. Instead, their inner dialogues go round in inconclusive circles, which increase the subjects' disorientation' (Archer 2003: 303).

Both the silent and the ambivalent 'I' immobilize. The existing relations of domination leave little or no room for the assertive self-expression of the 'I'. However, three qualifiers are called for. First, the same 'I's that are silenced or ambivalent in one area of life, do not necessarily remain passive, distressed or disoriented in others. Arguably a silenced wife can still make a very competent employee (Hochschild 1989; Archer 2004). And, silenced or ambivalent 'I's should not be mistaken for the category of silent, introverted individuals. Possibly they engage in *scapegoating and/or abusive, hate speech* – a reverse of self-blaming – making others responsible for their unsatisfactory situation. Finally, not everybody's 'I' stays silenced or ambivalent – some will develop 'subversive' emotions. These I will address soon.

The third type of 'I' contrasts with the first two. This self has a voice, is capable of sophisticated internal conversations in which emotions are verbalized. Socialization and experience taught it to name an entire array of emotions as well as the 'feeling rules' pertaining to these emotions (Hochschild 1979). This makes it possible for the 'I' to connect to others and/or express its quest for self-assertion, autonomy and social recognition in words, arguments, and action. I believe that this is the 'I' on which Wiley and also Archer focus. To the extent that this 'I' moves within the framework of predominant action and feeling rules, it reproduces the established hierarchies and moral conventions, pursuing self-assertion and social recognition on their terms.

However, domination is never perfect so that the 'I', confronted with shaming and disrespect by the other and/or paying too high a price for social acceptance, may develop 'subversive' emotions and frames, given (real or fictional) significant others who help to develop positive self-seeing-self/inner voice. The 'subversive emotions' and frames do not fit into the realm of the socially approved or expected, yet are at the base of any process of transvaluation (Kemper 1978, 1981; Merton 1967; Flam 2005). When these 'subversive emotions' receive group validation, when they become constructed as appropriate and desirable by a movement, they have a chance of also acquiring legal and political backing and becoming a motor of societal change. This entire process may start with what is perceived by a large majority as an exaggerated and irrational disruption of a comfortable private and public life.

For, as Diana Tietjens Meyers (1997: 2) argues, 'several emotional attitudes that are ordinarily considered to be epistemic vices can be ... epistemic virtues'. Given a choice between an angered woman who is labelled and dismissed as insecure, nasty, charmless, humourless, snotty, prudish, furious, bitchy or simply crazy and another woman who is compassionate or bears her fate with dignity, we should always go for the 'crazy' one, simply because this one is more likely to detect and address the real issues in society. What others dismiss as amoral or irrational 'hypersensitivity, paranoia, anger, and bitterness – can be seen to faciliate moral insight into culturally and institutionally entrenched practices of domination and subordination'. This is also a more realistic expectation than, for example, Martha Nussbaum's feelings of friendship or compassion which so many other feminists also define as a source of heightened moral perception and response (Meyers 1997: 2–3; Held 1995; Woodward 2009: 113–25). Not compassion, but rather angered emotional engagement is more likely to sharpen moral perception, mobilize others to action and effect necessary social change.

Notes

1 Both Wiley and Archer write from within the integrationist discourse, excluding the issue of power. Wiley's self is over-socialized, since in his model both the 'you' and the 'me' are intensely moral, leaving it unclear how the 'I' could possibly be amoral. Archer argues that it is the role of the discussion between the 'I' and the 'you' to decide just how much they care for community rules while sorting out their long-term concerns/ commitments. They do so in a three-step decision-making process in which they rely mostly on 'emotional commentaries' about their past, present and future. In Archer's later texts (2003: 298–341, 2004: 298–361, 2007a, 2008), the self becomes more socially embedded. For all the disclaimers, the focus is on self-confident reflexivity.

2 Andrew Sayer develops similar ideas about the British class system (2005: 153, 154, 157–8). He distinguishes three types of shame – aesthetic, performative and moral, all of which he sees as 'common in the context of class inequalities' (Sayer 2005: 153). To Sayer, shame is 'a product of internalisation of others' [unwarranted] contempt for one's [class] identity' (Sayer 2005: 153–154). The low-level shame experiences lead to withdrawal and 'inarticulacy in terms of a feeling of lack of authority to speak, and hence lack of practice in articulating one's situation, at least in the presence of class others … The poorest are thus not only materially deprived but linguistically dispropriated and hence disempowered subjects' (Sayer 2005: 157–8). The upwardly mobile continue to feel 'that they are not good enough, and that one day they will be 'found out' (Sayer 2005: 158).

3 See Frey Steffen 2006: 31, 50–1, 62–5, 81–2; Luke 1994: 211; Hercus (1999) on the association of voice with control and power in the feminist literature.

4 The 'fractured' type is explored at length in *Structure, Agency and the Internal Conversation*. It is bracketed in *Making our Way through the World*, although in the sample, this mode of reflexivity is no less frequent than the other three (Archer 2004: 298–361, 2007a: 96). In her forthcoming book, Archer devotes more attention to this mode.

5 As Mead's unpublished essays become increasingly available, his 'theorizing away' of emotions may turn out to be yet another myth about the origins of sociology, but at present Mead's theories are not very helpful in situating emotions.

6 '… when you are humiliated day in and day out by nagging signs reading "white" and "colored"; when your first name becomes "nigger" and your middle name becomes "boy" (however old you are) …, and when your wife and mother are never given the respected title "Mrs"; when you are harried by day and haunted by night by the fact

that you are a Negro, living constantly at tip-toe stance never quite knowing what to expect next, and plagued with inner fears and outer resentments; when you are forever fighting a degenerating sense of "nobodiness"; then you will understand ...' (King 1991: 72–73)

References

Archer, M. (2000) *Being Human: the Problem of Agency*. Cambridge: Cambridge University Press.

Archer, M. (2003) *Structure, Agency and the Internal Conversation*. Cambridge: Cambridge University Press.

Archer, M. (2004) 'Il realismo e il problema dell'agency', *Sociologia e Politiche Sociali*, 7(3): 31–49.

Archer, M. (2007) *Making our Way through the World: Human Reflexivity and Social Mobility*. Cambridge: Cambridge University Press.

Archer, M. (2008) 'Continuing the Internal Conversation'. *Theory. The Newsletter of the Research Committee on Sociological Theory*, ISA, pp. 2–3.

Beck, U., Giddens, A. and Lash, S. (1996) *Reflexive Modernisierung. Eine Kontroverse*. Frankfurt a.M.: Edition Suhrkamp.

Beck-Gernsheim, E. (1992) Arbeitsteilung, Selbstbild und Lebensentwurf. Neue Konfliktlagen in der Familie' *Kölner Zeitschrift für Soziologie und Sozialpsychologie* 2: 273–91.

Bogner, A. and Wouters, C. (1990) 'Kolonialisierung der Herzen? Zu Arlie Hochschilds Grundlegung der Emotionssoziologie', *Leviathan* 18(2): 255–79.

Bourdieu, P. (1987[1979]) *Die feinen Unterschiede*. Frankfurt a.M.: Suhrkamp.

Bourdieu, P., Boltanski, L. (1981) ,Titel und Stelle. Zum Verhältnis von Bildung und Beschäftigung' in P. Bourdieu, L. Boltanski und M. de Saint Martin (Hg.) *Titel und Stelle. Über die Reproduktion sozialer Macht*, S. 89–114. Frankfurt a.M.: Europäische Verlagsanstalt.

Braiker, H. (1989) 'The Power of Self-Talk', *Psychology Today*, December, 23–7.

Brunsson, N. (1993 [1989]). *The Organization of Hypocrisy: Talk, decisions and actions in organizations*. New York: John Wiley & Sons.

Cavarero, A. (2005) *For More than One Voice: Toward a Philosophy of Vocal Expression*. Stanford, CA: Stanford University Press.

Cohen, S. (2005) [2001]. *States of Denial: Knowing About Atrocities and Suffering*. Cambridge. Polity Press and Blackwell Publishers.

Collins, R. (2004) *Interaction Ritual Chains*. Princeton, NJ: Princeton University Press.

Cooley C. H. (1970) *Human nature and the social order*. New York: Schocken Books.

Crossley, N. (1998) 'Emotion and communicative action: Habermas, linguistic philosophy and existentialism' in G. Bendelow and S.J. Williams (eds) *Emotions in Social Life*, pp. 16–38. London: Routledge.

Czarniawska, B. (1997) *Narrating the Organization: Dramas of Institutional Identity*. Chicago: The University of Chicago Press.

Douglas, M. (1986) *How Institutions Think*. Syracuse, N.Y.: Syracuse University Press.

Douglas, T. (1995) *Scapegoats: Transferring Blame*. London: Routledge.

Flam, H. (1993) 'Fear, Loyalty and Greedy Organizations' in S. Fineman (ed) *Emotion in Organizations*, pp. 59–75. London: Sage.

Flam, H. (1998) *Mosaic of Fear: Poland and East Germany before 1989*. Boulder, Co: East European Monographs, distributed by Columbia University Press.

Flam, H. (2004) 'Anger in Repressive Regimes: A Footnote to Domination and the Arts of Resistance by James Scott'. Special Issue on Anger in Political Life. Guest editor Mary Holmes. *European Journal of Social Theory* 7, 2: 171–88

Flam, H. (2005) 'Emotions' map: a research agenda' in H. Flam and D. King (eds) *Emotions and Social Movements*. London: Routledge.

Flam, H. (2007) 'Protest – Schweigen – Emotion. Über die risikoreiche und risikolose Empörung' in Agnes Neumayr (Hg.) Kritik der Gefühle: Feministische Positionen, S. 216–35.Wien: Milena Verlag.

Flam, H. (2008) 'The sentient "I": Emotions and Inner Conversation'. Theory, The Newsletter of the Research Committee on Sociological Theory, International Sociological Association, Spring/Summer 2008, 4–7.

Flam, H. (2009) 'Authentic Emotions as Ethical Guides? A Case for Scepticism' in Mikko Salmela and Verena Mayer (eds) Amsterdam: John Benjamins Publishing (with the press).

Foucault, M. (1975) *Surveiller et punir*. Paris: Gallimard.

Gilligan, C. (1982) *In a Different Voice*. Cambridge: Harvard University Press.

Glazer, M. P. and Glazer, P.M. (1989) *The Whistleblowers: Exposing Corruption in Government and Industry*. New York: Basic Books.

Godbout J. (2007) *Ce qui circule entre nous. Donner, recevoir, rendre*. Paris: Seuil.

Gould, D. (2002) 'Emotions and the Development of ACT UP' *Mobilization* 7(2): 177–200.

Griffiths, M. (1995) *Feminisms and the Self: The Web of Identity*. London: Routledge.

Held, V. (ed). (1995) *Justice and care. Essential readings in feminist ethics*. Boulder, CO: Westview Press.

Hercus C. (1999) 'Identity, emotion and feminist collective action'. *Gender & Society* 13(1): 34–55.

Hirschman, A. O. (1970) *Exit, Voice and Loyalty*. Cambridge, Mass.: Harvard University Press.

Hirschman, A. O. (1992) 'Abwanderung, Widerspruch und das Schicksal der Deutschen Demokratischen Republik'. *Leviathan* 20: 330–58.

Hochschild, A. R. (1983) *The Managed Heart: Commercialisations of Human Feeling*. Berkeley: University of California Press.

Hochschild, A. R. (1989) *The Second Shift*. New York: Avon Books.

Hochschild, A. R. (1993) 'The Economy of Gratitude' in D. Franks and E. Doyle McCarthy (eds). *The Sociology of Emotions*, pp. 95–113. Greenwich, Conn: JAI Press.

Illouz, E. (1997) *Consuming the Romantic Utopia*. Berkeley. University of California Press

Jackall, R. (1988) *Moral Mazes: The World of Corporate Managers*. New York: Oxford University Press.

Jaggar, A. M. (1997) 'Love and Knowledge: Emotion Feminist Epistemology' in Diana T. Meyers (ed.) *Feminist Social Thought: A Reader*, pp. 385–405. London: Routledge.

Jasper, J. M. (1997) *The Art of Moral Protest*. Chicago: The University of Chicago Press.

Kemper, T. D. (1978) 'Toward a Sociology of Emotions: Some Problems and Some Solutions'. *The American Sociologist* 13: 30–41.

Kemper, T. D. (1981) 'Social Constructionist and Positivist Approaches to the Sociology of Emotions'. *American Journal of Sociology* 87(2): 336–61.

King, Martin Luther Jr. (1995)[1963]. 'Letter from Birmingham City Jail' in H. A. Bedau (ed.) *Civil Disobedience in focus*, pp. 68–84. London: Routledge

Kleres, J. (2005) 'The entanglements of shame: an emotion perspective on social movement demobilization', in H. Flam and D. King (eds) *Emotions and Social Movements*, pp. 170–88. London: Routledge.

Lacy, S. (1995) 'Cultural Pilgrimages and Metaphoric Journeys', in Lacy, S. (ed.), *Mapping the Terrain: New Genre Public Art*. Seattle: Bay Press, pp. 19–47.

Lane, R. E. (1992) 'Money Symbolism and Economic Rationality' in M. Zey (ed.) *Decision Making: Alternatives to Rational Choice Models*, pp. 233–54. London: Sage.

Lawley, J. and Tompkins, P. (2004) *Self-Deception, Self-Delusion and Self-Denial: And How to Act from What You Know to be True*. http://www.cleanlanguage.co.uk/Self-DDD-1.html

Luke, C. (1994) 'Women in the academy'. *British Journal of Sociology of Education* 15(2): 211–30.

Lutz, H. and Davis, K. (2005) 'Geschlechterforschung und Biographieforschung: Intersektionalität als biographische Ressource am Beispiel einer außergewöhnlichen Frau' in B. Völter et. al. (Hg) *Biographieforschung im Diskurs*, S. 228–47. Wiesbaden: VS. Verlag für Sozialwissenschaften.

Machado, N. (2008) 'The Stabilization of Social Order: Social Cognitive Dissonance Theory Applied to Hospitals and Clinics' in H. Flam and M. Carson (eds) *Rule Systems Theory: Applications and Explorations*, pp. 131–50. Berlin: Peter Lang.

MacKinnon, C.A. (1989) *Toward a Feminist Theory of the State*. Cambridge, Mass.: Harvard University Press.

Mayntz, R. and Scharpf, F. (1975) *Policy-making in the German Federal bureaucracy*. Amsterdam: Elsevier.

Mead, G. H. (1956) *On Social Psychology*. Chicago: The University of Chicago Press.

Mead, G. H. (1967 [1934]) *Mind, Self, and Society*. Edited and with an Introduction by Charles W. Morris. Chicago: The University of Chicago Press.

Memmi, A. (1992 [1982]) *Rassismus*. Frankfurt a.M.: Hain Verlag.

Merton, R. (1967) 'Social Structure and Anomie' in his *Social Theory and Social Structure*, pp. 131–60. New York: The Free Press.

Meyer, J.W. and Rowan, B. (1977) 'Institutionalized Organizations: Formal Structures as Myth and Ceremony'. *American Journal of Sociology* 83(2): 340–63.

Meyers, D. T. (1997) 'Emotion and Heterodox Moral Perception: An Essay in Moral Social Psychology' in Diana T. Meyers (ed.) *Feminists Rethink the Self*, pp. 1–14. Boulder, CO: Westview Press.

Miethe, I. and Roth, S. (2005) 'Zum Verhältnis von Biographie – und Bewegungsforschung' in B. Völter et.al. (Hg.) *Biographieforschung im Diskurs*, S. 103–19. Wiesbaden: VS. Verlag für Sozialwissenschaften.

Mouzelis, N. (1999) 'Exploring Post-Traditional Orders: Individual Reflexivity, "Pure Relations" and Duality of Structure', in O'Brien, M., Penna, S. and Hay, C. (eds.) *Theorizing Modernity: Reflexivity, Environment and Reflexivity in Giddens' Social Theory*. London: Longman.

Namka, L. (2003) 'Scapegoating – An Insidious Family Pattern of Blame and Shame on One Family Member'. http://www.angriesout.com/grown19.htm

Nedelmann, B. (1988) '"Psychologismus" oder Soziologie der Emotionen? Max Webers Kritik an der Soziologie Georg Simmels' in B. Nedelmann (ed) *Simmel und die frühen Soziologen*. S. 11–35. Frankfurt a.M.: Suhrkamp.

Oliver, C. (1991) 'Strategic Responses to Institutional Processes', *Academy of Management Review*, 16(1): 145–79.

Orbuch, T. L. (1997) 'People's Accounts Count: The Sociology of Accounts'. *Annual Review of Sociology* 23: 455–78.

Pizzorno, A. (1986) 'Some Other Kinds of Otherness: A Critique of "Rational Choice" Theories' in A. Foxley, M.S. McPherson and G. O'Donnell (eds) *Development, Democracy, and the Art of Trespassing: Essays in Honour of Albert O. Hirschman.* Notre Dame, Indiana: University of Notre Dame Press.

Rosenberg, M. (1990) 'Reflexivity and Emotions' *Social Psychology Quarterly* 53(1): 3–12.

Sartre, J. P. (1994) *Der Blick: Ein Kapitel aus das Sein und das Nichts.* Walter van Rossum (Hg.) Mainz: Dieterichsche Verlagsbuchhandlung.

Sayer, A. (2005) *The Moral Significance of Class.* Cambridge: Cambridge University Press.

Scheff, T. (1994) *Microsociology: Discourse, emotion, and social structure.* Chicago: University of Chicago Press.

Schultheis, F. (2007) *Bourdieus Wege in die Soziologie.* Konstanz: UVK.

Scott, J. C. (1990) *Domination in the Arts of Resistance: Hidden Transcripts.* New Haven, CT: Yale University Press.

Simmel, G. (1999) *Soziologie. Untersuchungen über die Formen der Vergesellschaftung.* Gesamtausgabe Band II. Hrsg. von O. Rammstedt. Frankfurt a.M.: Suhrkamp.

Steffen, T. F. (2006) *Gender.* Leipzig: Reclam.

Tacke, V. (2006) 'Rationalität im Neo-Institutionalismus. Vom exakten Kalkül zum Mythos' in K. Senge und K. Hellmann (eds.) *Einführung in den Neo-Institutionalismus.* Wiesbaden: VS für Sozialwissenschaften.

Taylor, C. (1995 [1985]) 'Self-interpreting animals' in his *Human Agency and Language, Philosophical Papers 1*, pp. 45–76. Cambridge: Cambridge University Press.

Taylor, C. (1989). *Sources of the self: The making of the modern identity.* Cambridge, Mass.: Harvard University.

Völter, B., Dausien, B., Lutz, H. and Rosenthal, G. (2005) *Biographieforschung im Diskurs.* Wiesbaden: VS Verlag für Sozialwissenschaften.

Wacquant, L. (2004) *'Following Pierre Bourdieu into the field'.* www.sagepublications.com Vol. 5,(4): 387–414. London, Thousand Oaks, CA: SAGE Publications. http://sociology.berkeley.edu/faculty/wacquant/wacquant_pdf/FOLLOWBOURDIEUINFIELDpub.pdf

Wiley, N. (1994) *The Semiotic Self.* Cambridge: Polity Press.

Wiley, N. (2006) 'Pragmatism and the Dialogical Self', *International Journal for Dialogical Science* 1(1): 5–21.

Woodward, K. (2009) *Statistical Panic.* Durham: Duke University Press.

Zerubavel, E. (2006) *The Elephant in the Room: Silence and Denial in Everyday Life.* Oxford: Oxford University Press.

11 Self talk and self reflection
A view from the US

Douglas V. Porpora and
Wesley Shumar

As Robert Darnton (1984) observes, it is continually surprising how different people are from each other – and especially from ourselves. With the post-modern influence on the social sciences, 'difference' has come to be a key theoretical category (Derrida 1978, Deleuze and Guattari 1987, Fabian 1983, Rosaldo 1989, Appadurai 1996). Yet, even for social scientists, ever on the watch against ethnocentrism, it is often difficult to realize how deep our differences go.

In particular, qualities of our own that we may consider generically human may turn out on inspection to be socially specific. So it may be with forms of self-reflection or reflexivity. In the absence of empirical investigation, it is natural for everyone to assume that everyone self-reflects in the same way as he or she does. Intellectuals and academics in particular are likely to engage in much internal self talk and to assume that everyone else does so as well. This assumption may well be mistaken and part of what Bourdieu (1997) has called 'the scholastic fallacy'.

It has in fact been an unquestioned assumption of social theory that all human beings reflect on themselves and reflect on themselves in the same generic way, i.e. through internal conversation. In the existentialist tradition, for example, Sartre (1956) cited reflexivity as the basis of human self-transcendence, the distinct human ability to make oneself an object of one's own observation. Such self-reflective capacity, Sartre believed, makes humans uniquely capable of free will and moral responsibility.

In sociology, Sartre's sensibility was shared by the symbolic interactionists. The whole point, for example, of Mead's (1964) 'I-Me' distinction is that, qua 'I', each of us is always something more than the product of social forces and past experiences (the 'Me') that we have become at any moment. Because the 'I' always reflects on the 'Me', each of us is always able to become something new, something not rigidly determined by outside forces.

This Meadean position has been maintained and deepened by the symbolic interactionist and pragmatist traditions (namely, James 1890; Peirce 1958). More recently, Wiley (1994) formulates self-reflection as a dialectical interchange among an 'I', a 'Me', and a 'You'.

Within the tradition of Anglo-American philosophy, self-reflection has been considered constitutive of selfhood (Margolis 1978, 1987; Porpora 1997, 2001; Taylor 1982, 1989). Whereas at least all higher animals may be considered conscious, humans alone are said to be self-conscious, precisely because of their distinct ability to regard their own selves as an object. It is this very capacity for self-consciousness moreover, that makes humans into selves in the first place (Margolis 1978, 1987; Porpora 1997, 2001). We are selves, in other words because we can and do treat ourselves as selves. Indeed, contrary to post-modernists who would dissolve the self (Butler 1990; Foucault 1972, 1977), there cannot be any concept of self-consciousness without a self that is simultaneously the subject and object of that consciousness (Margolis 1978, 1987; Porpora 1997, 2001). Self-consciousness and selfhood thus go together.

Among other places in sociology (such as the entire structure–agency debate), the connection between selfhood and self-consciousness is recognized by the literature on identity (see, for example, Stets and Biga 2003). According to the standard model in this literature (Burke 2003; Burke and Cast 1997; Tsushima and Burke 1999), actors internally compare their beliefs, choices, and actions against their own self-conceptions or identities, thus generating feelings of self-verification – or its lack.

Are humans the only animals to exhibit self-reflection? The question is compli-cated. Leary and Buttermore (2003) identify five different kinds of self-consciousness that humans exhibit, which, they argue, did not all evolve simultaneously. The first form of self-consciousness, shared by most animals, is 'ecological consciousness'. It is the somatic consciousness animals possess of their own bodies in relation to their environment and other actors (e.g. predators or prey).

At a higher level is 'extended self-consciousness', the ability to conceptualize oneself as the same self from one time to the next. This is the kind of self-consciousness that allows one to act in the present so as to secure future outcomes for oneself. Leary and Buttermore (2003) make a good case that certain non-human animals such as chimpanzees share an extended self-consciousness. In animals other than humans, however, this form of consciousness is both limited temporally and fragile.

'Public consciousness' and 'private consciousness', two other forms of con-sciousness identified by Leary and Buttermore are, likewise, the two dimensions of consciousness distinguished by the 'self-consciousness scale' developed by Fenigstein *et al.* (1975). Like ecological consciousness, public consciousness is an awareness of one's environment. In this case, however, it is specifically the social environment that is referenced. Public consciousness is thus the consciousness one has of the interactions one is having within a social order. Among humans, this consciousness certainly entails some at least tacit awareness of the kinds of behaviours explored by Goffman (e.g. 1971). Yet, as is suggested by Goffman's debt to ethology, other social – and even some non-social – animals share this kind of consciousness.

Public consciousness too is the kind of consciousness detected by the so-called 'mirror test', the ability to recognize oneself as oneself in a mirror. Children become able to do this at approximately age two (Leary and Buttermore 2003; Morin 2002). Chimpanzees and some other higher animals also pass the mirror test (Leary and Buttermore 2003; Morin 2002).

Private consciousness is the consciousness of one's own mental states. This capacity is needed not only to know why one feels, believes, and acts as one does but also to exercise empathy. One empathizes with others after all by identifying what is shared with oneself (Leary and Buttermore 2003).

The final kind of consciousness identified by Leary and Buttermore is 'conceptual consciousness'. Leary and Buttermore describe it as the abstract self-consciousness associated with symbol use and language and they argue (2003) that, in the archaeological record, conceptual consciousness coincides with what has been called the 'big bang' of culture – the time when we find a sudden explosion of cultural artefacts.

The five kinds of consciousness are not completely independent. Indeed, it is one of the properties of conceptual consciousness that it enhances and deepens all the others. The ability to talk to oneself, for example, widely expands extended self-consciousness, enabling one to imagine oneself much further into the future.

The importance to self-reflection of inner conversation was recognized early on by the symbolic interactionist and pragmatist traditions. Meade (1964) spoke of the advantages to self-reflection afforded by symbols over gestures, and Peirce (1958) went on to develop an entire semiotics.

With the so-called 'linguistic turn' in both philosophy and the social and behavioural sciences, the connection between language and selfhood has moved to centre stage. Language is now understood to be not only a means of communicating thoughts we already have independently but also a necessity for us to have many complex thoughts in the first place. Post-modernist thought goes too far, literally dissolving the self in language (e.g. Butler 1990; Foucault 1972, 1977; Derrida 1976), but it cannot be denied that we become the human subjects we are only through language and social discourse. As Durkheim (1951) put it long ago, human persons are social emergents.

Reflexivity, likewise, has been an important theme of post-modernist thought in particular and contemporary social theory generally. For the most part, however, attention to reflexivity has been at the cultural level. Giddens (1991) for example, has written on the proliferation of self-help books and Bellah et al. (1985) of the rise of therapeutic consciousness. Similarly, in anthropology, the turn to questions of representation and interpretation has led the field to question how much of the world view of others we can understand (Stewart 1996, Geertz 1995, Clifford 1988).

Still, Archer (2003) rightly describes the internal conversation as a topic that sociology has neglected after the early work of Meade, James and Peirce. After reviewing what those theorists wrote about the internal conversation, Archer did something new. She collected a small sample of people and examined empirically how they converse with themselves.

What Archer (2003, 2007) unexpectedly found is that people do not all self-reflect in the same way. In fact, Archer identified the following four categories of people: (1) 'communicative reflexives', who, however much they engage in internal conversation, must also talk to another person before making important decisions in their lives; (2) 'autonomous reflexives', who seem to already have their lives mapped out for themselves and can make important decisions in their lives based entirely on internal conversation with themselves but who focus primarily on instrumental matters; (3) 'meta-reflexives' who, like autonomous reflexives, can comfortably rely exclusively on self talk to make important decisions in their lives but who care not so much about instrumental matters but rather inhabit a moral universe and reflect deeply on ethical matters; and (4) 'fractured reflexives', who at least at the moment have difficulty self-reflecting at all, either through self talk or with others.

Archer (2003) conceptualizes meta-reflexives as having what Porpora (2001) referred to as moral purpose. The concept of moral purpose in turn can be understood in terms of Charles Taylor's (1989) notion of a 'hypergood'. A hypergood is a good, the pursuit of which subordinates all other goods pursued. It is much like what Tillich (1957) referred to as an 'ultimate concern'. Our ultimate concern is what concerns us ultimately. It is that to which we are ultimately committed and from the pursuit of which we derive ultimate meaning. Those with larger ultimate concerns, Porpora (1996, 2001) found, are also more likely to have what Weber (1976) referred to as a sense of 'calling'. Similarly, they are more likely to have personal heroes and a more articulated sense of the meaning of life. As indicated, Archer's in-depth interviews suggested that people who tend to engage in an internal conversation about their character and emotions also tend to be people who have a larger sense of moral purpose.

Archer's work has been compared with the work of Basil Bernstein and Pierre Bourdieu as they also have developed systems for thinking about the ways in which people engage in forms of reflection (Archer, forthcoming; Elder-Vass 2007, Fleetwood 2008, Sayer 2009). Bernstein's early work on elaborated and restricted codes draws attention to the relationship between social class background, linguistic patterns and cognitive styles. One of the things Bernstein discovered was that ways of interacting and talking learned at the university and then used by the individual in their profession (Bernstein calls this elaborated code) tended to be communicated to children, and gave those children an advantage in school.

Archer (2003) indicates in her work that styles of reflection seem not to be related to class. The data she uses to support this argument is that while the majority of communicative reflexives are working class in origin, a percentage of individuals who are working class in origin end up being autonomous reflexives. Thinking about the relationship between restricted and elaborated code and communicative/autonomous reflexives is an important issue. We tend to agree with Archer that her analysis of the modes of reflexivity is different from Bernstein's interactional codes.[1] But we are not as convinced that there is not some relationship between them and social class background. While we certainly would not see the relationship as deterministic, there may be tendencies for structural conditions to influence choices individuals make.

One way to interpret Archer's findings is that she may be explaining an aspect of intergenerational class mobility. Individuals who, for whatever reason, gain the skills to engage in a more internalized style of self-reflection may be in a better

210   D.V. Porpora and W. Shumar

place to do well in the educational system and become upwardly mobile. So we may be looking at a feature of consciousness that is complementary to Bourdieu's notion of habitus and explains why habitus is only a tendency toward certain actions and choices – as Bourdieu himself would admit – and not a determinant of choices. Bourdieu's sociology is probabilistic in that his notion of habitus is an effort to explain the kinds of choices people make as a result of the internalized cognitive dimensions of rountinized practices that are themselves the product of the structures that shape human behaviour (Bourdieu 1998). The details of that habitus though are often not articulated. In the styles of self-reflection, and the social contexts that reinforce them, we may be able to see one area where structural context and habitual practice produce differential effects. Someone who is more oriented toward autonomous reflexivity may in fact engage in taste choices in different ways than one who is a communicative reflexive. And this fact may explain why the social classes do reproduce but there is always a 'counter-trajectory' of individuals who may engage in more social mobility than most of their peers.

Recent developments in cognitive sociology and anthropology have also drawn attention to the way that culture, social structure and the individual inter-relate. Culture is no longer thought of as a uniform and universal force operating equally among all members of a social group. Rather, it is a set of patterns that are unequally distributed in a population. And these patterns tend to, again through habitual practice, produce 'schemas' or mental representations about the world that are shared by individuals who engage in the same set of practices in like structural contexts (Strauss and Quinn 1997). This means that culture and practice, while patterned, are more heterogeneous in a population.

Getting back to Archer, the fact that not all working class people use one style of reflection does not necessarily negate a relationship between class and reflection style. It does suggest that modes of reflection may be significant for class mobility and individuals who are able to learn to be autonomous or critical reflexives will be in better positions to engage in upward mobility. In his later work, Bernstein (1996) suggests that the way that educational institutions work to reproduce inequality is by differentially acting upon consciousness. What is suggested here is that forms of power and control shape the way people communicate with one another and hence how they think and act. One possible avenue for this operation of control is through the ways people learn to reflect on themselves and others. It is a great advantage in such a system to plan and strategize internally to the self as well as to engage in auto-critique. These ideas could in fact be a model for why we might be seeing a 'Communicative Meta Reflexive' in the United States. Perhaps the different ways these forms of power and control operate are encouraging different forms of agency on the part of people.

Our study

Stimulated by Archer's (2003, 2007) findings, we wanted to know whether we too could find different styles of self-reflection in the United States. We, accordingly, designed an exploratory study based on a survey instrument to be administered to

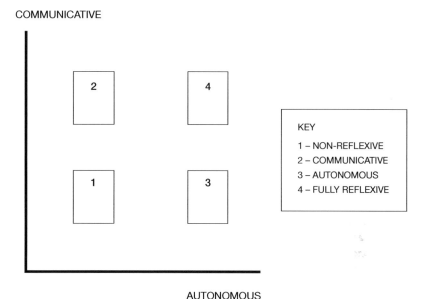

COMMUNICATIVE

AUTONOMOUS

Figure 11.1 Scale conceptualization.

students in our university. In contrast with Archer, we were not in a position at this point to follow up our survey data with more in-depth interviews, although that would be the natural next step in our research.

In the way we operationalized reflexive styles, we departed some from Archer's approach. Archer conceptualized autonomous and communicative reflexivity along a single continuum so that as one becomes more autonomous, one becomes less communicative, and vice versa (see Figure 11.1).

If one thinks in terms of how one ultimately decides important matters – with or without final consultation with others, then autonomous versus communicative reflexivity are certainly opposites. We, however, wanted to track in more quantitative terms how frequently respondents rely for their self-reflection on internal conversation and how frequently they rely on conversation with others. Allowing autonomous and communicative practices to vary independently of each other, we arrived at the alternative conceptualization depicted in Figure 11.1. Thus, drawing on five of the ten mental activities Archer employed, we formulated our questions in such a way that they did not force a choice between autonomous and communicative forms of reflexivity. Thus, in our study, it was theoretically possible for one to be high or low simultaneously in both autonomous and communicative reflexivity. This format results in four possible categories:

- Total reflexives (high on both autonomous and communicative reflexivity)
- Autonomous reflexives (high on autonomous reflexivity but low on communicative reflexivity)

- Communicative reflexives (high on communicative reflexivity but low on autonomous reflexivity)
- Non-reflexives (low on both autonomous and communicative reflexivity)

Essentially, the questionnaire we developed contains questions comprising three scales: a scale coding for autonomous reflexivity; a scale coding for communicative reflexivity; and a scale coding for the kinds of affective and ethical reflection that Archer associates with the category she calls meta-reflexives.

In relation to meta-reflexives, we again departed some from Archer's conceptualization. Archer considers autonomous and meta reflexives to be two distinct types with different background contexts and different concerns. On the other hand, in Archer's formulation, autonomous and meta reflexives tend to conduct their self-reflection in the same way, that is, with ultimate reliance on their own internal conversation.

In contrast, we wanted to separate further the manner of self-reflection from the content of self-reflection. Thus, we sought to construct our study in such a way for it to be theoretically possible that those who self-reflect in a communicative style can also self-reflect on many of the same affective matters as Archer's meta-reflexives. To allow for this possibility, in our study design, we asked a module of questions on ideal and affective matters separate from the questions comprising the scales associated with autonomous and communicative reflexivity.

The scales for autonomous and communicative reflexivity were both constructed by adding together responses to two, respective sets of five questions drawn from Archer's list of ten mental activities, each formulated in Likert format with the following responses: (1) Never (2) Rarely (3) Occasionally (4) Often and (5) All the time. Together, 10 questions asked respondents how often, first in their own minds and second, in talk with family or friends, they did each of the following:

- plan their own future;
- rehearse what they would say in an important conversation;
- imagine the best and worst consequences of a major decision;
- review a conversation that ended badly;
- clarify thoughts about some issue, person, or problem.

Theoretically, each of the two scales – for autonomous and communicative reflexivity – could vary between scores of 5 and 25, with a midpoint of 15. With those parameters, we were able to determine tendencies toward autonomous and communicative reflexivity in absolute terms. Scores of 15 and below were judged to be low in each kind of reflexivity and scores above 15 were judged to be higher. We also created a scale of comparative autonomous and comparative reflexivity by dividing low and high at the empirically observed medians in our data, which was higher – 19 – for autonomous reflexivity but actually the same – 15 – for communicative reflexivity.

Once scales for absolute and comparative reflexive tendencies were constructed, two further scales were constructed for absolute and comparative style overall. These scales identified absolutely and comparatively, respectively, to which of the four reflexive styles identified above the research subjects seemed to conform: i.e. total reflexivity; autonomous reflexivity; communicative reflexivity; non-reflexivity.

Finally, there were two sets of two questions asking whether or not people thought through in their own minds or with family and friends (i) what matters most to them; and (ii) why they feel the way they do. These formed the basis of two further scales, one for autonomous meta-reflexivity and one for communicative meta-reflexivity.

Results

In absolute terms, the subjects were almost evenly split between low (48 per cent) and high (52 per cent) communicative reflexivity. That result was hardly duplicated for autonomous reflexivity. Instead, only 13 subjects, just 7 per cent of the total, were absolutely low on autonomous reflexivity (i.e. <= 15).

The overwhelming tendency in our sample toward higher autonomous reflexivity is interesting. Possibly, it reflects a sample comprised exclusively of college students, who as such are already functioning somewhat separately from their home communities. They might be expected, therefore, to tend toward autonomous reflection.

Alternatively, the result may indicate something more ontologically fundamental. Human language may be social in origin and with it also the dialogical self that makes the human person, as Durkheim (1951) thought, something socially emergent. Private human self-reflection too may be just internalized conversation and as such, something derivative of external communicative interaction. Still, it may be that once humans acquire language and thereby become persons, their private use of it for self-reflection assumes a kind of ontological priority so that, contrary to post-modern or post-structuralist thought (see Levi-Strauss 1966; Barthes 1974; Derrida 1976, 1978), humans are not just passive sites through which discourse passes but active subjects autonomously using discourse for their own purposes.

Table 11.1 Absolute and comparative reflexive style

	Absolute reflexive style % (N)	Comparative reflexive style % (N)
Unreflexive	–	26% (47)
Exclusively communicative reflexive	1% (2)	22% (39)
Exclusively autonomous reflexive	43% (71)	20% (35)
Fully reflexive	56% (94)	32% (57)
Total	100% (167)	100% (178)

Table 11.1 shows how our sample was distributed in reflexive style, both absolutely and comparatively. As can be seen in absolute terms, no one in our sample was unreflective and only a negligible percentage (2.4 per cent) represented communicative reflexives only. In absolute terms, 44.4 per cent of the sample was exclusively autonomously reflexive and 53 per cent reflexive both autonomously and communicatively or, as we call it, fully reflexive.

Table 11.1 also presents a more comparative distribution of reflexive styles, that is, one in which autonomous reflexivity in particular was adjusted so that 48 per cent of our sample was considered low in autonomous reflexivity and 52 per cent high. The result, as can be seen, is that now 28 per cent of our sample was considered comparatively unreflective (low on both autonomous and communicative reflexivity) and 20 per cent communicatively reflexive only. This time, only 19 per cent are exclusively autonomously reflexive and only 33 per cent fully reflexive.

Table 11.2 presents the relation between gender and reflexive style. The results are as might have been expected. Whether we look in absolute terms (Table 11.2a) or comparatively (Table 11.2b), women tend much more strongly than men to include communicativity within their reflexive style. In absolute terms, men are more likely to exhibit only autonomous reflexivity, whereas women are more likely to exhibit both absolute and communicative reflexivity.

When we look comparatively (Table 11.2b), the picture becomes more complex

Table 11.2 Gender and reflexive style

Table 11.2a. Absolute reflexive style

| Gender | Reflexive Style | | | | |
	Unreflective % (N)	Communicative % (N)	Autonomous % (N)	Fully % (N)	TOTAL % (N)
Male	–	–	50% (44)	50% (44)	100% (88)
Female	–	3% (2)	35% (27)	62% (49)	100% (78)

Table 11.2b. Comparative reflexive style

| Gender* | Reflexive style | | | | |
	Unreflective % (N)	Communicative % (N)	Autonomous % (N)	Fully % (N)	TOTAL % (N)
Male	33% (32)	12% (12)	22% (21)	33% (32)	100% (97)
Female	19% (15)	34% (27)	17% (14)	30% (24)	100% (80)

*$\alpha < .005$

but, again, in ways that might have been expected. With the standard raised for autonomous reflexivity, the percentages of fully reflexives drops among both men and women. Now, comparatively, approximately equal percentages of men and women are fully reflexive or reflect only autonomously. Again, it seems that autonomous reflexivity may be more basic than communicative reflexivity. That judgement is supported by the fact that almost none of our subjects answered 'Never' when asked how often they found themselves in silent conversation with themselves. To be a human person, it seems, is to carry on internal conversations with oneself.

In other respects, when we move from absolute to comparative reflexive style, men and women redistribute differently. Because in absolute terms more men than women tend to reflect only autonomously, when the standard for high autonomous reflexivity is raised, many more men than women become relatively unreflexive. Conversely, as it becomes harder to rate high on autonomous reflexivity, many more women than men become exclusively communicative reflexives.

The picture that begins to emerge from the comparison of absolute and relative reflexive styles is that women tend to have an extra form of reflexivity – the communicative style – of which men less frequently avail themselves. The question then is whether this added register of reflexivity makes any difference. Is it immaterial, in other words, the manner in which one reflects or does the communicative style afford advantages not enjoyed by purely autonomous reflexivity?

A more specific question is how the various reflexive styles considered so far relate to meta-reflexivity. It will be recalled from the methods section that meta-reflexivty was measured by asking people whether they reflected on their emotions and on what matters most in life. They were asked whether they engaged in such reflection, first, in their own minds and, second, with family or friends. Thus, two separate measures of meta-reflexivity were created, one reflecting an autonomous style of reflexivity and the other a communicative form.

Table 11.3 shows the relation between reflexive style and the two forms of meta-reflexivity. The first important finding shows up in the marginals. Some 41 per cent of the sample engage in autonomous meta-reflection and an even larger percentage – 45 per cent – engage in a communicative form of meta-reflection. It is thus clear that meta-reflection should not be tied in style to autonomous reflexivity alone.

Second, it is striking how strongly related reflexive style is with the manner of meta-reflexivity. The non-reflexives and communicative reflexives are less than half as likely as autonomous or full reflexives to engage in the autonomous form of meta-reflexivity. The disparities are even greater for the communicative forms of reflexivity. Almost three quarters of the communicatives and the full reflexives engage in the communicative form of meta-reflexivity. In contrast, only 10 per cent of the non-reflexives and 17 per cent of the autonomous reflexives engage in communicative meta-reflexivity.

Finally, it turns out that in our sample women exhibited more meta-reflexivity than men. Unsurprisingly, women certainly exhibited more communicative meta-reflection than men. Whereas only 34 per cent of men scored high on

Table 11.3 Comparative reflexive style and meta-reflexivity

Table 11.3a. Autonomous meta-reflexivity*

	Unreflexive % (N)	Communicative reflexive % (N)	Autonomous reflexive % (N)	Fully reflexive % (N)	TOTAL % (N)
LO	78% (36)	74% (29)	53% (18)	37% (21)	57%(104)
HI	22% (10)	26% (10)	47% (16)	63% (36)	43% (72)
TOTAL	100% (46)	100% (39)	100% (34)	100% (57)	

*$\alpha < .001$

Table 11.3b. Communicative meta-reflexivity

	Unreflexive % (N)	Communicative reflexive % (N)	Autonomous reflexive % (N)	Fully reflexive % (N)	TOTAL % (N)
LO	81% (38)	42% (16)	74% (26)	32% (18)	59% (98)
HI	19% (9)	58% (22)	26% (9)	68% (39)	41% (79)
TOTAL	100% (47)	100% (38)	100% (35)	100% (57)	

*$\alpha < .001$

communicative meta-reflection, 54 per cent of the women did ($\alpha = .005$). More surprising, however, is that even autonomously, the women were more meta-reflexive than the men. Whereas, again, only 34 per cent of the men exhibited autonomous meta-reflection, 49 per cent of the women did ($\alpha = .023$). Given these results, it is perhaps also unsurprising that the women more than the men say they dwell long and hard on how they fall short of their ideals ($\alpha = .009$); that they think often about the meaning of life ($\alpha = .002$); and that they are religious ($\alpha = .039$).

Conclusion

While we used Archer's approach to reflexivity as our starting point, we ended up framing reflexivity in a different way than Archer. Our approach produced a three dimensional social space that could be seen as having x, y and z axes. Together, the x and y axes identify four different styles of individual reflection: unreflexive, communicative, autonomous or fully reflexive. These are really about the process of reflection; are you reflexive at all? Do you need to communicate with others? Do you reflect fully in your head? Are you fully reflexive, drawing for reflection on both communication with others and self talk? In our model, full reflexives are those who can make major decisions on their own without talking to others but in fact do tend to communicate with others when the situation permits before making a major decision.

An important finding here is that there seem to be some gender differences in the way that people reflect. In particular, while men and women are equally likely to reflect in a more exclusively autonomous way, women are comparatively more likely to reflect in a more exclusively communicative way. Whereas Archer suggests that autonomous reflection is indicative of success in terms of mobility, our data suggest that autonomous reflection may be more basic and an ability to reflect communicatively a more developed skill. This is certainly in line with some other research on gender and the ways many women learn to focus on and become skilful at managing relationships.[2]

Our z axis looked at the content of reflection and whether individuals tended to be meta reflexive or whether their reflections were more instrumental. A major result here is that there does seem to clearly be a category of communicative meta-reflexives. These are people who are primarily communicative in their reflexive style but who also tend to be meta-reflexive. As we pointed out earlier, in Archer's work all meta-reflexives share with autonomous reflexives the tendency to do their reflection in their heads. This result raises some very important questions about meta-reflexivity.

Archer's research on inner speech and reflexivity has an in-depth qualitative component and therefore she is able to think about persons in much more detail than we have been able to. As such, Archer's focus has been more on what Tillich (1951) has referred to as ultimate concerns. Archer, by developing an in-depth relationship with a person, is able to assess some general characteristics of the whole person. This focus is critical for research on inner speech and reflexivity. It is hard for us, on the basis of a survey, to say whether someone is truly autonomous, communicative or fully reflexive. Our research is really only a mapping out of possibilities and tendencies.

On the other hand, our research does hold out promise for a different configuration of patterns of reflection in the United States. We would argue that this would make sense. While we support a focus on the autonomy of the person and personal agency, it is also the case that persons must in fact be shaped by the social context within which they are found. As the United States is a culture and political economy that encourages individuals to multiply their patterns of communication and consumption, it is not surprising that maybe that population is more likely to have a broader mix of patterns of self-reflection. It will require future and more detailed qualitative research to mine the potentialities of the research reported on here, something we hope to do in the near future.

Notes

1 Archer (2007:76–7) is critical of her interlocutors, who suggest there is a relationship between reflexivity and Bernstein's codes. One of her criticisms is that for Bernstein codes are linguistic and reflexivity is much more than just language. Reflexivity is about consciousness and the person and not just a matter of linguistic pattern. And so for Archer 'internal conversation' is much more of a full reflection of the self and not just a matter of linguistic variation. We would certainly agree with Archer in her characterization of the internal conversation. However, we would also quibble a little

bit with the characterization of Bernstein's codes as purely 'linguistic'. It is true that in places Bernstein calls the codes 'linguistic codes' but he also says they are not like dialect but really more about styles of interaction. So restricted and elaborated codes are about the way language is used. As such, comparing the codes to Archer's forms of reflection seems like a fair task. But it is also the case that they involve specific issues of vocabulary and are more linguistic than Archer's forms of reflection, and so the comparison is limited.

What does seem to be important in the comparison is the implications for class and class mobility. Bernstein was one of the early sociologists of education identifying mechanisms for why working class kids did not do as well in school as their middle class counterparts and why they were more likely to not go on in schooling and remaining working class. Archer is sceptical of the kind of position that sociologists like Bernstein take up, seeing in this work a determinism operating.

In a very different voice Archer points out that the communicative reflexive may be located in the working class, and the individual's desire to work through life choices with friends and family may explain why this individual does not move up and out of the working class. But this is rather a choice, given a set of structural possibilities, not a determinism. Further, as she herself points out, this does not explain why a larger percentage of working class individuals become autonomous reflexives and do go on to more middle class lives.

We can agree with Archer that perhaps this is just a matter of agency – some individual choice – but also maybe it too is linked to class (or another aspect of structure) in some more subtle way. Perhaps the difference in life choice is not determined, but influenced by being part of a different fraction of the working class. And it is possible to even redeem thinkers like Bernstein not by seeing Bernstein's codes as a determining system, but rather as a set of structural pressures that could be responded to differently by different individuals. Perhaps Archer's notion of reflexivity could explain why one group of working class individuals seem constrained by a set of structural conditions and another group is not. These are things that still need to be explored through further research.

2 But again we would hasten to add that as our sample was drawn from university students, this may affect in some important ways the patterns we are seeing. We have fewer traditionally working class individuals who are tied to kith and kin through communicative reflection in the way that Archer saw in her sample.

References

Appadurai, Arjun, 1949 *Modernity at Large: Cultural Dimensions of Globalization.* Minneapolis, Minn: University of Minnesota Press.

Archer, Margaret S. 2003 *Structure, Agency and the Internal Conversation.* Cambridge: Cambridge University Press.

——. 2007 *Making Our Way Through the World.* Cambridge: Cambridge University Press.

——. forthcoming *Routine, Reflexivity and Realism.*

Bellah, Robert, Richard Madsen, William M. Sullivan, Ann Swidler, and Stephen M. Tipton 1985 *Habits of the Heart: Individualism and Commitment in American Life.* Berkeley: University of California Press.

Barthes, Roland 1974 *S/Z.* Translated by Richard Miller; pref. by Richard Howard. New York: Hill and Wang,

Bernstein, Basil B. 1971 *Class, Codes and Control.* London, Routledge and K. Paul.

——. 2000. *Pedagogy, Symbolic Control, and Identity Theory, Research, Critique.* Lanham, Md: Rowman & Littlefield, 2000.

Bourdieu, Pierre 1977 *Outline of a Theory of Practice.* Cambridge: Cambridge University Press.

——. 1984 *Distinction: A Social Critique of the Judgement of Taste.* (Translated by Richard Nice.) Cambridge, Mass: Harvard University Press.

——. 1990 *The logic of practice.* Translated by Richard Nice. Stanford, Calif: Stanford University Press.

——. 1991 *Language and Symbolic Power.* Edited and introduced by John B. Thompson; translated by Gino Raymond and Matthew Adamson. Cambridge, Mass: Harvard University Press, c. 1991.

——. 1997 *Pascalian Meditations*, Stanford: Stanford University Press.

——. 1998 *Masculine Domination.* Stanford: Stanford University Press.

Bowles, Samuel and Herbert Gintis 1986 *Democracy and Capitalism: Property, Community, and the Contradictions of Modern Social Thought.* New York: Basic Books.

Burke, P. J. 2003 'Relations Among Multiple Identities.' in P. J. Burke, T. J. Owens, R. T. Serpe, and P. A. Thoits (eds) *Advances in Identity Theory and Research.* New York: Klewer, pp. 195–214.

——. and A. D. Cast 1997 'Stability and Change in the Gender Identities of Newly Married Couples' *Social Psychology Quarterly* 60: 277–90.

Butler, Judith 1990 *Gender Trouble: Feminism and the Subversion of Identity.* New York: Routledge.

Clifford, James, 1945 *The predicament of Culture: Twentieth-Century Ethnography, Literature, and Art.* Cambridge, Mass: Harvard University Press, 1988.

Clausen, John A. 1993 *American Lives: Looking Back at the Children of the Depression.* Berkeley: University of California Press.

Darnton, Robert 1984 *The Great Cat Massacre.* New York: Vintage.

Deleuze, Gilles and Felix Guattari 1987 *A Thousand Plateaus: Capitalism and Schizophrenia.* Minneapolis: University of Minnesota Press.

Derrida, Jacques 1976 *Of Grammatology.* Baltimore: Johns Hopkins University Press.

——. 1978 *Writing and Difference.* Chicago. University of Chicago Press.

Durkheim, Emile 1951 *Suicide.* New York: The Free Press.

Duval, S., and R. A. Wicklund 1972 *A Theory of Objective Self Awareness.* New York: Academic Press.

Elder-Vass, Dave 2007 'Reconciling Archer and Bourdieu', *Sociological Theory*, 25: 4.

Fabian, Johannes 1983 *Time and the Other: How Anthropology Makes Its Object.* New York: Columbia University Press.

Fenigstein, A., M. F. Scheier, and A. H. Boses 1975 'Public and Private Self-Consciousness: Assessment and Theory' *Journal of Consulting and Clinical Psychology* 43: 522–7.

Fleetwood, Steve 2008 'Structure, institutions, agency, habit and reflexive deliberation', *Journal of Institutional Economics*, 4: 2.

Foucault, Michel 1972 *The Archaeology of Knowledge.* London: Tavistock.

——. 1977 *Discipline and Punish.* London: Allen Lane.

Gallup Organization 1990 *World Values Survey.* See USGALLUP.90.WVAL, Q133 on Public Opinion on-Line. University of Connecticut: The Roper Center.

Geertz, Clifford 1995 *After the Fact: Two Countries, Four Decades, One Anthropologist.* Cambridge, Mass. Harvard University Press, 1995.

Giddens, Anthony 1991 *Modernity and Self-Identity: Self and Society in the Late Modern Age.* Stanford: Stanford University Press.

Goffman, Erving 1971 *Relations in Public.* New York: Harper & Row.

James, William 1890 *The Principles of Psychology.* London: Macmillan.

Leary, Mark R. and Nicole R. Buttermore 2003 'The Evolution of the Human Self: Tracing the Natural History of Self-Awareness' *Journal for the Theory of Social Behaviour* 365–404.

Lévi-Strauss, Claude 1966 *The Savage Mind*. Chicago: University of Chicago Press.

Margolis, Joseph 1978 *Persons and Minds*. Dordrecht: D. Reidel.

——. 1987 'Minds, Selves, and Persons' in Joseph Margolis *Science without Unity*. Oxford: Basil Blackwell. pp. 51–100.

Mead, George Herbert 1964 *Mind, Self, and Society*. Chicago: University of Chicago Press.

Morin, Alain. 1991 'Self-Awareness and "Introspective" Private Speech in 6-Year-Old Children' *Psychological Reports* 68: 1299–1306.

——. 2002 'Do You "Self-Reflect: or "Self-Ruminate?"' *Science & Consciousness Review* December (1) http://psych.poona.edu/scr/LN_Dec02/SelfRuminate.htm

Peirce, Charles Sanders 1958 *Collected Papers* (Arthur W. Burks ed.). Cambridge: Belnap Press.

Porpora, Douglas V. 1996 'Heroes, Religion, and Transcendental Metanarratives' *Sociological Forum* 11(2): 209–30.

——. 1997 'The Caterpillar's Question: Contesting Anti-Humanism's Contestations' *Journal for the Theory of Social Behaviour* 27 (2/3): 243–64.

——. 2001 *Landscapes of the Soul: The Loss of Moral Meaning in American Life*. New York: Oxford University Press.

Rosaldo, Renato 1989 *Culture & Truth: The Remaking of Social Analysis*. Boston: Beacon Press.

Sartre, Jean Paul 1956 *Being and Nothingness*. New York: Washington Square Press.

Sayer, Andrew 2009 'Review of *Making our Way through the World*', *Journal of Critical Realism* 8(1): 113–23.

Shumar, Wesley 2003 'The Role of Community and Belonging in Online Learning'. In Marcia Mardis (ed.) *Developing Digital Libraries for K-12 Education*. Syracuse: ERIC.

——. 2004 'Interaction, Imagination and Community Building at the Math Forum Under review for Antonio Dias de Figuiredo and Ana Paula Afonso (eds) *Managing Learning in Virtual Settings: The Role of Context*. Hershey, PA: Idea Group, Inc.

——. and K.A Renninger 2002 'On community building'. In K. A. Renninger and W. Shumar (eds), *Building virtual communities: Learning and change in cyberspace*. New York, NY: Cambridge University Press.

Stets, Jan E. and Chris F. Biga 2003 'Bringing Identity Theory into Environmental Sociology' *Sociological Theory* 21(4): 398–423.

Stewart, Kathleen, 1953 *A Space on the Side of the Road: Cultural Poetics in an 'Other' America*. Princeton: Princeton University Press, c. 1996

Strauss, Claudia and Naomi Quinn 1997 *A Cognitive Theory of Cultural Meaning*. Cambridge: Cambridge University Press.

Taylor, Charles 1982 'Responsibility for Self' in Gary Watson (ed.) *Free Will*. Oxford: Oxford University Press. pp. 111–27.

——. 1989 *Sources of the Self*. Cambridge: Harvard University Press.

Tillich, Paul 1957 *The Dynamics of Faith*. New York: Harper & Row.

Tsushima, T. and P. J. Burke 1999 'Levels, Agency, and Control in the Parent Identity' *Social Psychology Quarterly* 62:173–89.

Weber, Max 1976 *The Protestant Ethic and the Spirit of Capitalism*. New York: Scribners.

Wiley, Norbert 1994 *The Semiotic Self*. Chicago: University of Chicago Press.

Part IV
Reflexivity in production and consumption

12 'Reflexive consumers'

A relational approach to consumption as a social practice

Pablo Garcia-Ruiz and Carlos Rodriguez-Lluesma

Consumption theory should benefit from the concept of 'reflexivity'. To substanti-ate this statement, this chapter firstly presents 'lifestyles' as the *modus vivendi* of consumers who – aware of it or not – have developed 'consumption projects'. We review structuralist and individualist approaches to reveal some of their limita-tions, which derive from the scant attention they give to the relationship between agents and their socio-cultural context. We will argue for the need to study the way in which people take into account the socio-cultural context in which they develop their projects. We then examine a few interesting illustrations that sup-port our claim. As a last step, we discuss how to introduce into consumption studies not only the notion of reflexivity, but also its different modalities. These different reflexive modes would yield different types of 'reflexive consumers', each with its own features, which we propose as a starting point for further research.

Lifestyle as *modus vivendi*

Human reflexivity becomes important as the linkage between concerns, projects and practices. We act in order to promote our concerns, and form projects to advance or to protect what we care about most. It is through our internal conversa-tions that we reflexively define the courses of action conducive to the realization of our ultimate concerns in an appropriate *modus vivendi*. What people seek to do is reflexively defined by reference to the concerns they wish to realize. This means establishing practices, both satisfying to and sustainable by the subject, in an appropriate social environment (Archer 2007, p. 88). Hence, to understand the meaning of those practices it is necessary to grasp the life-projects in which they are embedded, as well as the ultimate concerns that underlie such projects.

The claim we wish to explore is whether this very argument – put to the test by Archer in the context of occupational trajectories – may be useful in better under-standing consumption patterns in our society. To do so, we need to examine:

1 Whether, as a consequence of their own internal conversation, people for-mulate deliberate 'consumption projects'.
2 Whether any relationship exists between such projects, people's ultimate concerns and the practices that shape their *modi vivendi*.

3 What room is left for the exercise of reflexivity in those 'consumption projects', that is, what role is played by the agents' consideration of their relation to their social and cultural context in the formulation and implementation of such projects.

The concept of lifestyle has gained an increasing prominence in the sociology of consumption, becoming a central feature in the study of consumption patterns. The term 'lifestyle' refers, in its clearest meaning, to the set of habits, attitudes and tastes that make up the way of life of an individual or group.

A lifestyle is a set of characteristic behaviours that embody a specific meaning for others, as well as for the agent himself, in a given temporal and spatial context. It tends to mirror the basic values and ideas that agents have of themselves and of those around them. Hence, a lifestyle is a means of forging a sense of self, and of creating cultural symbols that resonate with personal identity (Chaney 1996). Obviously, the natural, technical and social contexts influence the alternatives available to agents, as well as the symbols they can use to express themselves or to communicate with others. As Featherstone holds:

> though [lifestyle] has a more restricted sociological meaning in reference to the distinctive style of life of specific status groups (Weber 1968), within contemporary consumer culture it connotes individuality, self-expression and a stylistic self-consciousness. One's body, clothes, speech, leisure pastimes, eating and drinking preferences, home, car, choice of holidays, etc., are to be regarded as indicators of the individuality of taste and sense of style of the owner/consumer. (Featherstone 1991, p. 83)

Dress, leisure preferences, house, car, vacation choices, and so forth, feature as indicators of the owner/consumer's taste and style.

Shopping decisions may be trivial, as when we choose between two different cola drinks, or when we buy yet another pair of black socks because we are running out of them. Other spending decisions, though, are not so easy or carefree. They require planning, foresight, comparing, audacity, prudence, or calculation: how we dress for a party, our vacation spot, our children's school, our house, and so forth, are examples of decisions that many people deem important due to the consequences that they entail for their lifestyle.

In this respect, we can talk about 'consumption projects', inasmuch as certain spending decisions imply whole courses of action oriented toward the achievement of important goals for the agent and, therefore, require specific processes of discerning, deliberating and dedicating (Archer 2007, p. 20f). Discernment means making forward- and backward-looking comparisons: it is a moment of review, so as to clarify our relationships to our main concerns, in the light of our satisfaction or dissatisfaction with our present situation. Deliberation implies organizing, even if provisionally, our concerns, rehearsing the *modus vivendi* that each of them would entail, as well as listening to the emotional reactions that they prompt in us. Dedication consists in deciding not only whether a particular course of action is worth a candle or seems attractive to us, but also whether or not we are capable of living such a life.

Consumption decisions require discernment, deliberation and dedication insofar as people see them as important in their lives, which seems to be ever more frequently. In our society, lifestyles feature as projects imbued with both ethical and aesthetic significance. People use lifestyles, in some ways, to design themselves (Chaney 1996, p. 108; Lipovetsky 1994; Featherstone 1991; Bauman 2007). Consumption decisions are related to our ultimate concerns not only because of the economic or material resources they require, but also because of their expressive capacity and their potential to achieve desired goals, values and ideals.

Indeed, in our age of 'nascent globalization', the restructuring of the social and cultural context in which we live enhances the capacity to determine one's concerns, as well as to design projects and develop practices to achieve them. Consumption is precisely one of the realms where increased choice and the capacity to design one's courses of action have grown strong.

Further, some authors even point to consumption as the main sphere in our society for the achievement of identity. Featherstone (1991: 86), for example, holds that for many people consumption decisions have turned into 'heroic challenges'. These new heroes of consumption culture get by unaided by habit and tradition, having to:

> make lifestyle a life project and display their individuality and sense of style in the particularity of the assemblage of goods, clothes, practices, experiences, appearance and bodily dispositions they design together into a lifestyle. The modern individual within consumer culture is made conscious that he speaks not only with his clothes, but with his home, furnishings, decoration, car and other activities which are to be read and classified in terms of the presence and absence of taste.

Indeed, the importance of lifestyle decisions grows along with the increasing irrelevance of the social and cultural context for those decisions. Lifestyles are forged as the set of practices that express the projects that people undertake to realize their concerns and goals in the sphere of material culture. Before dubbing individuals as 'heroes of our new consumption culture', however, it is worth examining in more detail the relationship between the people who decide on courses of action and the influence – or lack thereof – of the social and cultural context in which they live.

(Post) modernity's man and social hydraulics in the consumer society

From several perspectives, the sociology of consumption has delved into consumers' habits, manners and patterns, so as to understand their reasons and the causes that explain them. It is evident that social and cultural contexts strongly impinge on lifestyles. But underlining that influence does not exhaust the study of the relationship among people's attitudes and values, the social and cultural contexts in which they live, and their consumption practices. Among other questions, we need to ask ourselves, to what degree are people aware of that relationship, and how do they take it into account when making a decision on this or that course of action?

Many of the theoretical answers put forward in the literature seem to take no account of reflexivity – understood as a real capacity in people – or of its potential consequences on the evolution of consumption patterns. Some of those theories may be labelled as 'deterministic', insofar as they see the meaning of people's projects and practices as dependent on the characteristics of the context, a perspective that Archer (2007:89ff) has termed 'social hydraulics'. On the other hand, further theories seem to ignore the social and cultural context, or simply reject the idea that these contexts may influence consumers' projects and practices in any way. Rational Choice Theory, for example, defines consumption merely at the individual level, as it is basically held to depend on disposable rent and price levels. From this perspective, the meaning of consumption practices is always the same: the maximization of a utility function. This approach – despite its merits in helping analyse the aggregate effects of individual decisions – proves seriously inadequate for understanding the meaning that people bestow on their relationship with material culture. The very concern with lifestyle signals that the consumption and display of goods spills over the narrow concepts of exchange value and instrumental rational calculation.

Classical sociology underlined certain elements frequently glossed over by economists, such as the ceremonial function of goods, and their role in marking social relationships and in demonstrating social position (Sassatelli 2007, pp. 72–3). From this sociological perspective, consumption appears as a relevant space for social competition, rather than for the mere implementation of individual preferences. Colin Campbell summed up the classical perspective in what he names the Veblen-Simmel model (1994, 1987, pp. 49–57). The main assumptions of this model are: a) consumption is an activity geared mainly to the other, in which b) maintaining or improving one's standing features prominently; c) motives underlying consumption are imitative and emulative insofar as the patterns exhibited by superior groups are imitated by those below them in the hierarchy; and d) the elites – intrinsically attracted by novelty – must continuously adopt new fashions and consume new goods so as to stay at the top of the pecking order.

Emulation is proposed in this model, not as a supplement to economic utility, but as a substitute. Indeed, as Veblen argued, 'with the exception of the instinct of self-preservation, the propensity for emulation is probably the strongest and most alert and persistent of the economic motives proper'. In our modern societies, this propensity to emulate 'expresses itself in pecuniary emulation; and this, so far as regards the Western civilized communities of the present, is virtually equivalent to saying that it expresses itself in some form of conspicuous waste' (Veblen 1994, p. 85). Goods are acquired, therefore, not because of their utility for the individual, but because of their symbolic import to others. Those seeing this exhibition may or may not be members of the group (or category) to which one belongs (or would like to join), or members of groups (or categories) from which one would wish to set oneself apart. This is why Simmel wrote that fashion had the two-pronged function of binding a group together and of setting it apart from other social groups (1990 pp. 599–600; 1957).

Inasmuch as consumption objects reveal themselves not only as useful, but as bearers of meaning, they become part of a language. It then becomes necessary for the observer – and also for the user – to find the keys to decipher it. The emulation model, however, has alerted us to the symbolic richness of consumption objects, but it has also reduced our reading of consumption to one logic alone by limiting it to the dynamics of imitation-differentiation.

Structuralist authors such as Bourdieu and Baudrillard have emphasized the syntactic dimension of consumption as a language. For both authors – albeit in different ways – the meaning of consumption practices stems from the social and cultural contexts in which they take place. Agents per se receive only marginal attention, being defenceless against mechanisms that go well beyond their control and understanding.

For Bourdieu, it is the individual's social position that determines consumption decisions. It is not only a matter of purchasing power, but also of taste and of the processes through which tastes are shaped. True, individuals express their preferences and likings for these or those goods, services and experiences. But those preferences are not formed in isolation. Rather, they are expressions of tastes cultivated for generations in social groups that occupy very definite cultural and economic spaces. For Bourdieu consumption patterns arise as a consequence of 'the history of social space as a whole, which determines tastes by the intermediary of the properties inscribed in a position, and notably through the social conditionings associated with particular material conditions of existence and a particular rank in the social structure' (1996, p. 256).

Along these lines, Bourdieu also holds that people's preferences, inclinations, and dispositions are related to, are features of, different social positions:

> Taste classifies and it classifies the classifier. Social subjects, classified by their classifications, distinguish themselves by the distinctions they make, between the beautiful and the ugly, the distinguished and the vulgar, in which their position in the objective classifications is expressed or betrayed. (1979, p. 6)

Dispositions – and, together with them, social positions – manifest themselves both in artistic preferences and in culinary habits, in music and food, painting and sport, literature and hairstyle.

From this perspective, people would choose consumption objects not only on the basis of their prices and expected utilities. They perceive, acquire and display those objects as an expression of their own dispositions and tastes, of what we normally call their lifestyles. But both disposition and taste – that is, one's own lifestyles – depend on a higher-order logic that imposes itself on individuals to reproduce their social differences. Consumers distinguish among objects in order to distinguish themselves. Bourdieu is thereby proposing a refined version of Veblen's reasoning: social differences are not only affirmed, but also reproduced, through consumption (Sassatelli 2007, p. 69; Parmiggiani 1997, pp. 127–32; Erner 2005, p. 167). That is why even those most intimate tastes which seem to be private are in fact traceable to their origin on the social map. Despite efforts to the contrary, the agent always ends up expressing his or her own social condition. The consumer society turns people into docile agents, bound to reproduce their class logics and to perpetuate the system.

In sum, for Bourdieu the meaning of consumption choices is limited to a logic, that of distinction, which suffers from, at least, one problem: its explanation of lifestyles becomes a cliché, a kind of analytical blueprint – increasingly reified and attenuated – of the dominant function of tastes, rather than of those tastes themselves (Alonso 2005, p. 238f). For this theory, agents lack any real relevance in understanding the genesis and meaning of consumption practices as social practices.

Baudrillard concurs with Bourdieu in advancing a logic of differentiation, in the system of objects, which imposes itself in people and determines their choices. This is the unavoidable consequence of an economic system that needs the relentless creation of new needs and wants in order to be able to reproduce itself (1996). As Ritzer (1999: 71) has commented, Baudrillard holds that in the twentieth century capitalism has gradually taken centre stage, pushing aside production, which entailed the parallel transition from the control and exploitation of workers to the control and exploitation of consumers. Consumers are no longer allowed to decide by themselves whether they consume or not, or even how much or what to consume, or how much to spend. Capitalists feel that they need to spend more time, energy and money on influencing – if not controlling – those decisions. This idea features explicitly in Baudrillard's early works, where he writes that consumption is a 'social labour'.

Baudrillard's work denounces how much our lives depend on consumption and objects. Complying with the trends created and imposed by the system amounts to a new form of alienation against which he rebels. In several of his books, Baudrillard (1981, 1996, 1998) attempts to formulate an analysis of the consumer society through the study of the messages borne by objects, by the merchandises that make them up, seeking an explanation for the compulsive character that consumption bears in our society, as well as the consumer's apparently unlimited 'needs', which render the idea of 'use value' obsolete. The instrumental character of objects cannot adequately explain their frenetic exchange. In a post-industrial society objects do not act as tools or merchandise, or as symbols of subjective attitudes or projects. Consumption is defined as a language, but understood only as a communication system governed by the code of social differentiation. Advertising and the media have turned objects into pure signs that fluctuate independently of their usefulness.

Developing some of Roland Barthes' (1957) insights, Baudrillard understands material culture as a system of signs that refer to one another, and which acquire their meaning only in relation to each other. This is precisely the system used by consumers, even though they may not be aware of it. It is not 'need', but 'difference', that now counts as the fundamental category through which to understand consumption. Hence, consumption can no longer be understood by delving into the relationship between the consumer and the specific good he or she is acquiring: Needs are created as elements in the system, not as the relations of a subject to an object (Baudrillard, 1998: 75). The system of objects reflects and reproduces the differences among categories of people and, in turn, these categories are created by the mass media: they amount to simulacra that impose themselves on individuals as referents of meaning.

In our post-industrial society not only production, but also consumption is disciplined and rationalized with an eye to the reproduction of the economic structure, in which people are seen as agents at the mercy of a system of sign-objects. As Ritzer (1999: 185) points out, 'from this perspective the "mall" substitutes the "factory" as the main social structure, and advertising is the new ideology for domination.' It is not people who use objects to build their own messages, but rather they are vehicles for the expression of the differences among objects: their identities are tantamount to consumption patterns determined from the outside.

The meaning of objects changes: the consumption process is no longer based on the satisfaction of existing demand, as classical economics assumed. Now consumption should be understood as a process through which the buyer commits himself to the attempt of creating and maintaining a sense of identity through the display of the goods acquired. But it does not follow from this claim that individuals determine the meanings of the objects they use: which objects contribute to express which identities depends most proximately on the mass media, which dominate the social communication stage.

The ever-changing and ever-growing content of media simulacra impose their own logic on particular individuals. Objects are the only reality that dances to its own tune. They are not co-constituted by subjects but, rather, they constitute those subjects and, in so doing, cancel out any other possibility of meaning. In defining the language of objects as inexorably deterministic, Baudrillard denies the possibility that, in consumption practices, merchandise may change from a sign into a symbol, in such a way that he implicitly considers the appropriation of the object by the individual as a stage in the passive assimilation of meanings assigned to those objects by the system of social differentiation (Parmiggiani 2001, p. 52; Erner, 2005, p. 167). Hence, for Baudrillard (1998: 25), any desire to moderate consumption or to establish a normal web of needs is but an absurd and naïve moralism. The individual no longer counts as a social agent, as a subject who can make symbolic distinctions through her own actions and interpretations.

For Baudrillard's semiotic structuralism, the social logic of consumption is, therefore, a logic of the generation and manipulation of signs. But in this language the master status of the structural dynamics impedes the symbolic nature of objects, which only feature as 'signs.' In this approach, their meaning lies in the structure of that language known as 'consumption', not in the consumers' capacity to bestow meaning upon objects. Communicative intention is reduced to the communication of differences.

But social differences are no longer class differences. In regard to the analysis of consumption, Baudrillard rejects the centrality of the concept of class, since it remains an expression of the previous state of the social system. A consumer society is now an amorphous mass of individuals in search of an identity. As Bourdieu had claimed earlier, 'lifestyle' now substitutes for class as the axis of new identities which individuals achieve – or, more precisely, are ascribed to them – in accordance with their consumption practices. The logic of the system of objects – the logic of distinction or of value – imposes itself on the subject in the same way that social structure imposes itself on individuals.

For post-modern sociologists, a lifestyle bestows a collective identity, but it does not stem from interpersonal relationships. A lifestyle exists only as a simulacrum in the imagination of a group of people. And these people only share their exposure to the influence of mass media. Lifestyles exist if, and only if, the mass media and marketing bestow existence upon them. In consequence, the consumer is an individual with no real ties to a real way of life. His consumption decisions may be swayed by the playful, floating from one lifestyle to another, as someone bearing disposable, provisional identities.

In this framework, consumption would appear as an inherently experimental activity, in which everything has to be tried out. In fact, the consumerist agent fears the prospect of 'missing something', any random enjoyment. As Baudrillard (1998, 102) puts it:

> one never knows whether this or that encounter, this or that experience (spending your holidays in the Canary Islands, tasting eels, visiting the El Prado museum or smoking crack) will end up being a sensation for us. It is not even desires or 'taste', or even a specific inclination to play, but a generalized curiosity prompted by a diffuse obsession; it is the fun-morality, the imperative to have fun, to enjoy all possibilities to the limit, to try out every emotion, to have a great time.

From this perspective, consumption becomes a strictly individual activity. As Bauman has claimed, 'consumption is a thoroughly individual, solitary and, in the end, lonely activity; an activity which is fulfilled by quenching and arousing, assuaging and whipping up a desire which is always a private, and not easily communicable sensation' (2003, p. 53; 2007, p. 106f). Hence, a consumer's society tends to weaken and dissolve social units while fostering the rapid creation of masses as well as their quick disaggregation.

From this point of view, a consumption object isolates and uproots individuals, who become solitary. The system of objects generates distinctions that isolate agents or, at best, assign consumers to a codified social category in which no collective solidarity can take root. For post-modern authors, the subjective experience of consumption amounts to the experience of an individuality under siege by a system of objects that can be enjoyed, but not manipulated.

But, then, what meaning can we find in consumption practices? Apparently, as Christopher Lasch argued, the only way out for the post-modern consumer would be narcissism because once the aspiration – typical in the 60s – to better life in a significant way dissolved into thin air, people have come to believe that what counts is the improvement of one's mind. For example, getting in touch with one's feelings, nurturing oneself on organic products, taking belly dance lessons, or plunging into the Far Eastern seas of wisdom (1980, p. 16f). Other scholars contend that consumption is still the gateway to social position, but not so much because of the quantity and quality of the goods one acquires, but rather because of the freedom of access to more and more diverse goods and experiences. As Bauman puts it, the more freedom of choice one has, and above all the more choice one freely exercises, the higher up one is placed in the social hierarchy, the more public deference and self-esteem one can count on, and the closer one comes to the ideal of the 'good life' (2003, p. 54). The name of the game is not to consume more, but to have the real possibility to do it. For post-modernists, the link between consumption and identity demands it. Once the traditional sources of social identity have been blurred, identity itself turns into a task. Bauman himself points out how 'individualization' consists in transforming human identity from a 'given' into a 'task' (2002, p. 15).

One of the many problems entailed by this post-modern perspective seems central to our argument. If agents' identity no longer derives from structural dimensions, but features as an ever-changeable goal implemented through successive practices – among which consumption practices feature prominently – how should we study consumption practices? They can no longer be understood as a – conspicuous or unconscious – consequence of one's social position. In this context, consumption decisions acquire marked relevance, because they do not appear as routine, dull repetitions of those in a known social position, but as sustained epiphanies of what individuals want to be and to display to others. If the tenets of individualization hold, then consumers are to be regarded – in Featherstone's words – as the 'heroes' of our new consumer society, in which they ceaselessly need to create, reproduce and transform an identity for themselves.

But, what kind of identity is this that appears associated with consumption choices? Following Beck, 'individualization' means that each person's biography breaks free from external determination and becomes the responsibility of personal and internal decisions (Beck 1992, p. 135; Giddens 1991). However, if these decisions – through which the identity construction is determined – amount to narcissistic consumption, which is always changeable, unbounded and alert to the latest new thing, then the identity so acquired can only be an empty one. Those decisions do not construe anything, since their commitments have no content and deliberately ignore their likely consequences (Archer 2007, pp. 36–7). Agents capable of relentless 'self-invention' cannot but ignore their social and cultural context: they reject or neglect the ties binding them to others, and the cultural meanings that give direction to acting and communicating with others. If ties and meanings are ever-changeable, then they are neither ties nor meanings as generally understood. And a 'changed' identity is no more meaningful – for oneself or for others – than that which it precedes or substitutes for it. As Parmiggiani (2002, p. 55) concludes, the post-modern perspective celebrates the erasure of the subject in the identity game, and the playful dimension in consumption is substituted for the tragic in identity formation.

Consumption as a socio-cultural practice

In recent years some authors have focused on the consumers' capacity to create, sustain and develop social ties and cultural meanings (Miller 1978, 1998b; McCracken 1990; Douglas and Isherwood 2007, p. 75f). In so doing they bring to light consumption as a social practice, as well as the consumer as an active social agent. According to these scholars, and contrary to post-modern pessimism, consumption frequently works as a relational factor, not only being embedded in social relations, but also being used to sustain, negotiate and modify interpersonal ties. Mary Douglas and Baron Isherwood put it austerely but expressively, 'Goods are neutral: their uses are social: they can be used as fences or bridges' (1996, p. xv). In that statement these authors underline one of the dimensions of consumption: its capacity to express and establish social relationships. When members in a society regard consumption in this way, it also becomes reasonable to talk about the language of objects: 'as far as keeping a person alive is concerned, food and drink are needed for physical services; but as far as social life is concerned, they are needed for mustering solidarity, attracting support, requiting kindnesses, and this goes for the poor as well as for the rich' (p. xxi). The meaning of goods purchased and displayed goes beyond mere social distinction. People use goods to send messages, express feelings, return favours, prompt envy, and so forth. Consumption has a 'thick' meaning, which reflects the density of social relationships themselves.

To understand consumption as a social practice requires clarifying the influence of cultural, structural and subjective factors. Indeed, understanding the evolution of the meaning of goods implies identifying the structural pressures within which consumers make their decisions, but also the web of cultural references that confer meaning upon communicative intentions, as well as the interpretation and use that people make of them in the implementation of their projects.

The literature offers some illustrative examples of the claim just made. We will first refer to Daniel Miller's (1998) work on how the relational context influences everyday consumption decisions. Then we will comment on some ideas by Francesco Morace (2007), a specialist in global dressing trends, and particularly in the evolution of the meaning of dress within each cultural context of reception.

Miller conducted a one-year ethnography study in a commercial area of North London. The study attempted to gather first-hand information on the consumption habits and practices of ordinary people in ordinary circumstances, as well as on the subjective experience that agents had of such tasks. Miller's conclusions show that 'there exists a normative expectation that most shoppers will subordinate their personal desires to a concern for others, and that this will be legitimated as love' (1998, p. 40).

The reasons prompting people to choose among goods depend on for whom they buy and what they want for them. As Miller puts it, 'Shoppers develop and imagine those social relationships which they most care about through the medium of selecting goods' (p. 5). Among those interviewed by Miller, there were old and young couples, with and without children, single mothers, sweethearts, old people, men and women, who shop with others or by themselves. In almost all of those situations the idea of shopping for others crops up again and again, not so much to please them, but rather to show in deeds how much the shopper cares for them. A housewife, for example, will buy a particular brand or flavour, not only based on what she thinks her significant other wants, but on the basis of her deliberations about what would be beneficial to that individual. In practice, 'the two may be compromised in the form of what she can get the wretched object of love to actually eat!' (p. 108).

Obviously, it is not always love that justifies the purchase, nor do all decisions stem from it. Frequently caprice, tradition, hedonism or a myriad other reasons may explain a particular purchase. But we need to bring to the forefront the existence of normative elements with regard to consumption, which hinge on its relational character. It behoves us to understand consumption not as a solitary, isolating, individualistic activity. Interest in objects, even those one acquires for oneself, stem from the development – rather than the absence – of significant relations. As this author shows too, incapacity to relate to people tends to imply incapacity to relate to things. In an entertaining typological example, he illustrates this relational character of consumption even regarding those goods that one chooses, in principle, for oneself. Although long, Miller's (1998: 2–3) vignette is worth quoting in full:

> Perhaps you are a junior male lecturer and last week you went shopping for clothes. You went to three shops: two chain stores (C&A and Marks & Spencer) and a small independent, more fashionable outlet. Your girlfriend was complaining about your wearing things she felt you shouldn't be seen dead in. The relationship between the two of you was not such that you were going to admit how attached you had become to the admittedly now well worn jeans you had at the time. You are not in the habit of changing during the day, and you tend to meet up after work, so whatever you buy has to do for work also. At work, there are two colleagues on the staff who are better at withering sarcasm than writing papers and don't share the same taste as your girlfriend. You can see a couple of pairs in the independent shop that she might approve, but you can just imagine the response at work. But then anyway would she actually like them – she might hate them. Maybe you should go with her, but then she isn't going to give a toss for your workmates' opinions. OK, it shouldn't really matter very much, and yet it was this that made you spend over an hour between the three shops. And anyway what about yourself – your own taste – shouldn't you have some say? There was a pair you liked, but to be honest it was just the same as those you were out shopping in order to replace. You got really fed up: why are you wasting time when you could be on line looking at the new website? But you really do care about her, and you know this is just the kind of gesture that could make the difference, show her you

really are willing to compromise, to make some commitment to the future sharing of taste. In the end you find a pair in C&A that is a more sober (and frankly a whole lot cheaper) version of the independent shop's pair, and just hope she won't notice the label.

Miller is certainly aware that this proposal runs counter to the bulk of current studies on consumption, both within economics and social or cultural studies. But his ethnography shows that, for most consumers, the purchasing act rarely boils down to a self-regarding act. A clearer understanding of their purchases is gleaned if these are not seen as individualistic (and individualizing) behaviours stemming from the subjectivity of the shopper. The post-modernist discourse of consumption as individualistic hedonism does not tally with what consumers actually do, even though shoppers themselves may know and repeat that discourse.

The consumer is, according to Miller, a 'productive' subject, able to use objects and to infuse them with meaning, as well as to sustain and develop those social relationships they really care about. Consumers are able to appropriate the meaning of objects, and to use them strategically. Their purposes are not determined by their position in social structure, or by an alleged ideological determinism. Rather, understanding consumption projects requires comprehending that a difference obtains between the agent's ultimate concerns and the context in which those concerns are formulated and implemented.

Miller has demonstrated the importance of the social context for consumption projects. At this point, we need to remind ourselves that the social and cultural dimensions to the relational context are analytically separable. Thus, it becomes possible to assert that discursive struggles are socially organized and that social struggles are culturally conditioned. Even more importantly, it becomes possible to specify which is more influential for the other, when, where, and under what conditions (Archer 1995, p. 324).

Morace (2007) has illustrated the dynamics of the cultural context and its influence on people's choices with regard to dress. As a professional *coolhunter*, Morace – together with his team of photographers – has observed different cultural dressing practices and customs in fifty cities around the world. In a nutshell, this author first identifies global trends stemming from such fashion centres as Milan and New York and adopted all over the world. Second, he observes and interprets the different shifts in meaning that fashion objects undergo in interaction with local cultures.

Morace's starting point is that dress – together with other aspects of personal image – is in the process of becoming a language reflecting the person's deepest values and existential choices, rather than a symbol of socio-economic status (p. 20). Because of huge distribution chains, global trends reach all countries and cultures, where they are 'read', interpreted and used by a local audience in accordance with its own cultural references, so as to establish, sustain or develop projects of action in their own social context. Among those global trends Morace points out the following (albeit in rather pompous language):

- 'Hyper memorable': Those objects that remind us of, embody and transmit past stories, moments or ages worth remembering. Illustrations include the success of 'vintage', a preference for bygone dresses or furniture pieces. Objects become 'historic icons' that acquire meaning as long as they are able to withstand the functional requirements of our current world. This trend may express shallow or deep attitudes, such as a love for one's roots (retrospectively recovered), while allowing us to play a masquerade with recognizable cultural references.
- 'Micromega luxury': In its 'macro' aspect, luxury includes the notions of exclusivity, excess, exhibition, the violation of limits set by society and rationality; in its 'micro' aspect, luxury comes about in the acquisition and use of small, everyday glamour objects, materials and craft icons affording originality and experimentation.
- Other trends we will not comment on, for the sake of brevity include: 'Wonder simplification', 'Extra rules', 'Ultra graphic', 'Huge interlace', 'Super material', and 'Massive details'. They all refer to the use and combination of materials, shapes and colors by the most innovative subjects observed, and which seem to have spread to significant groups of their peers.

The second part of the book focuses on the evolution of fashion in the BRIC (Brazil, Russia, India, and China) emerging areas. Comparing and commenting on a series of pictures, Morace analyses the differential uses to which the same trends are put in each of those cultural contexts. Specifically, pictures taken in Moscow evince an ostentatious taste for originality in the sense of singularity of being – or at least, of appearing as – different from the others, not so much because of the price or quality of the outfit, but due to some detail, material, shape or feature symbolizing rejection of the uniformity suffered in the recent past. Luxury – prominent to the extravagant – serves to signal singularity, although it expresses economic and social success as well in that hypercompetitive society. In China, on the other hand, ostentation is embodied in global luxury brands. Their outlets occupy the finest commercial zones and have become the reference defining elegance and prestige. A luxury brand name object – be it a fountain pen, a purse, a car or a pair of shoes – symbolizes social success. This central position of (mostly Western) luxury brands is compatible, however, with pride in their own cultural traditions. The mingling of classically-inspired themes with the proper combinations of colours – red and gold, for example – expresses the symbolic talent of Chinese culture for welcoming the materials and shapes of western brands, while retaining their iconic power.

In both cases Russians and Chinese make evident that they are learning how to use new content in their material culture, which has swept through their countries spurred by massive marketing campaigns run by global distributors. But cultural dynamism does not end there, because the influence does not run in one direction alone. Morace draws our attention also to how the reading of and local reaction to those trends (the very 'genius loci', and its characteristic customs, interpretations, hybridizations and innovations) react back upon global trends. Design centres in

Milan and New York thus become global nodes, receiving signals and creations from those diverse 'genii loci' and then incorporating them into the concepts they distribute in the next round. Logically, some local proposals prove more compatible than others with global trends and thus achieve broader diffusion. At any rate, what seems significant is that they are progressively, more readily at hand for people in other places, with other cultures, who will use them in relation to the projects they will carry out in their own cultural contexts.

Reflexive consumers: some proposals

At the beginning of this chapter we queried whether or not the notion of reflexivity could be applied to consumption. The answer to that question was held to hinge on three points: a) whether consumption decisions were suitable material for an internal conversation; b) whether such internal conversation gave rise to the formulation of 'consumption projects' expressing people's ultimate concerns; and c) whether the influence of the socio-cultural context allowed for the exercise of human reflexivity in the realm of consumption.

Up to this point we have analysed the main tenets pertaining to these topics by some of the most relevant studies in the area of consumer sociology. Through this analysis it has become clear how consumption decisions have come to the forefront of our society. Due both to the sheer number of choices available and to their economic, social, cultural and identity-related consequences, consumption decisions require a growing degree of deliberation, discernment and dedication. And precisely, because of these reasons, consumption practices – especially those bearing more permanent or significant consequences – are perceived as elements of a personal *modus vivendi*; and as such, they are increasingly entering our internal conversation. Furthermore, our decisions frequently fall under sets of practices linked together by a common and specific purpose or meaning, which we could refer to as 'consumption projects'. There remains the task of considering our third question, i.e. to what extent those 'consumption projects' are 'reflexively' defined and implemented by people.

In the previous section we have critically reviewed the main structuralist and individualistic propositions with regard to this point. We reached the conclusion that neither of the two perspectives could satisfactorily account for the relationship between agent and social context. We need an appropriate conceptual tool to study the reciprocal influence between social agents and the cultural and structural dimensions of the social networks in which those agents implement their projects. That tool comes in the form of reflexivity, defined as the capacity humans have to regard themselves in relation to significant others and, therefore, to consider – and, if necessary, modify – projects for courses of action in relation to the social and cultural context which condition – as enablements or constraints – their implementation. Miller's work and Morace's work have been discussed as particularly good examples of this claim.

Hence, we can now respond that it is not only possible, but even necessary to employ and deploy the concept of 'reflexivity', if we wish to develop theories capable of accounting for the reality of consumption as a social practice.

In the first place, the concept of reflexivity brings to the fore the active character of social agents. Against any form of 'social hydraulics', which assumes a
deterministic view of consumption, the notion of reflexivity encourages us to
regard people as champions of their projects. Against the idea that consumers just
assimilate and reproduce behaviour and meanings imposed from the outside, the
reflexive consumer proves able to appropriate objects, infuse them with meaning
and use them to the service of his own projects. The internal conversation makes
us 'active agents', people who can govern themselves to some point, unlike the
'passive agents' to whom things just happen. Being an active agent means that
individuals are able to define and develop their ultimate concerns and priorities:
that is, those internal goods they really care about.

Focusing our analysis on the voluntary character of human action helps overcome the limitation of all versions of the 'oversocialised view of man' – including
'his' post-modernist dissolution – to explain the human capacity to lead a
meaningful life. This general assertion is useful too in considering consumption
practices. Consumers are people, able to organize their practices into projects aiming at implementing their ultimate concerns, the values and goals they care most
about. Agents may fail when choosing practices or be fallible in believing that
such and such a practice will help them lead the life they aspire to, but they are the
creators and main characters in the design and implementation of such lifestyles.
Certainly, this position does not obtain under conditions of complete autonomy
and independence. Consumers construe their own projects under circumstances
not of their own choosing, but rather the ones they find in the natural, cultural
and social contexts in which they live.

The meaning of consumption projects is not determined by external factors, as
structuralism would have it, nor is it volatile and ephemeral, as the imagination
of post-modern individualism would hold. Rather, meaning should be regarded as
a more or less complete and accurate implementation of the consumer's values
and ultimate concerns. Such meaning shares its degree of stability with that of
the commitments it expresses. Together with them, it remains open to successive
interpretations and modes of expression.

Each of the perspectives in the sociology of consumption has privileged one
of its multifarious meanings. Thus, some theories conceptualize the meaning of
consumption decisions and practices as a search for utility maximization, as ostentation, as class distinction, as identity construction, as psychological comfort, as
mere enjoyment, and so forth. In our previous section we have shown that these
viewpoints have been underpinned by reasoning and illustrations, which should
come as no surprise, given that they all embody possible courses of action.

However, the idea we wish to underline is that if, instead of reducing the meaning of consumption to one of its aspects, we link it to the human capacity to create
and pursue projects of action, we will then be in a better position to understand the
dynamics of meaning in consumption practices. In other words: we can understand
the possible meanings mentioned in the paragraph above (including others not
explored here) as particular cases of a more general perspective. The use of objects

remains open not only to a plurality of objective meanings, but also to a variety of subjective intentions. If consumption is a form of language, then we need to bear in mind not only its syntactic, but also its semantic and pragmatic contents. Hence, in their projects consumers enjoy some wiggle room with respect to the influences of the socio-cultural context in which they formulate and revise their own strategies (Sassatelli 2007, p. 76; Douglas 1996). This recursive process of deliberation has nothing to do with cost-benefit analysis. On the contrary, it is suffused with emotion which, tied to our ultimate concerns, provides us with the impetus leading to action or resistance.

Can we, then, understand which courses of action consumers will adopt, as well as the reasons prompting them? Our claim about the reflexive consumer leads us to assert that people take up courses of action that allow them to implement their ultimate concerns in an appropriate *modus vivendi*. We can thus distinguish between the objective meaning uncovered by the researcher and the subjective meaning embodied in the agent's intention. Usually, the former ends up being integrated in the consumer's cultural context. Yet, far from being an independent, more adequate, vision of reality, it quickly becomes one more element the agent considers as meaningful for his or her own action (Miller 1998b, p. 11).

What we seek to do is reflexively defined with reference to the ultimate concerns we wish to see realized, which implies establishing practices at once satisfying to and sustainable by the agents, given their social context. This is the reason why reflexive consumers talk to themselves about their relationships to others and about how they can sustain, transform, improve, eradicate, establish or reinforce those relations through the acquisition and use of consumption objects, be they goods, services or experiences.

Hence, consumers cannot but be 'productive consumers': the meanings of objects are always provisional in the sense that they remain open to the agent's creative work. Active consumers appropriate the meanings of objects so as to build a *modus vivendi* – a lifestyle – meaningful for themselves and for their social context. In contrast to Bauman's and other authors' definition of consumption as a literally and irreversibly individualistic pastime, it is incumbent on us to note its intrinsically relational and intersubjective nature. In this sense, 'lifestyle' becomes an analytical category that provides us with the keys to the codification and interpretation of the messages carried by consumption objects. Thus, the concept of reflexivity facilitates understanding of how consumers live with reference to themselves and to their social context, and how that perception leads them to define and practise a particular lifestyle.

If this reasoning holds, different types of reflexivity give rise to different lifestyles. In other words, the notion of reflexivity can help us understand the diversity of lifestyles, as well as to identify the reasons underpinning them. Archer (2007) has identified four types of reflexive subjects, and has delved into their relationship to different occupational trajectories. Analogously, we can now inquire about the correspondence between modes of reflexivity and consumption styles. In the same way as different modes of reflexivity give rise to differing occupational trajectories, they could also stand behind different consumption decisions and practices. Let us turn to them, to illustrate their relationship to several modalities of consumption.

'Communicative' consumers seek to carry out their deliberations with the aid and approval of others. They prioritize contextual continuity, the upholding of their familial and friendship ties, and primary solidarity over advancement opportunities. Because of this 'elective affinity', they may prove more sensitive to value consumption as their capacity to express and foster integration in the group, imitating and reproducing tastes and styles in their context of origin. In ranking their concerns, they privilege personal ties, to which they subordinate their, to name a few, home buying, vacation, hair-styling or leisure decisions.

'Autonomous' consumers, on the contrary, will tend to seek in their consumption the same social success that they pursue in their occupational lives, defined according to the value hierarchy of their socio-cultural context. They are probably more prone to conspicuous consumption, so as to signal that they have achieved their social goals (or as a means thereto). Their decisions will be more sensitive to fads and trends, especially to those held up as expressions of social ascent. Their desire to emulate those they deem to be in a higher position may guide the bulk of their decisions, as they tend to see consumption as one more means towards the achievement of their career goals. With regard to their lifestyle, they will show more interest in knowing that they have risen as far as they reasonably could than in the approval of their peers or close associates.

'Meta-reflexive' consumers will manifest a stronger proclivity towards making an expressive use of consumption. They frequently assess their own conduct, and would also adopt a critical stance toward consumption, remaining committed to values and attitudes found personally satisfying, sidelining current success criteria and the opinions prevalent amongst those closest to them. In developing a consumption style they would prioritize their commitment to non-materialistic values, even if this decreased their comfort or their savings, if they had any. Meta-reflexive agents might feature as consumers of ecological foods, fair trade goods, members of online communities supporting moral and quasi-moral causes, as well as participants in social movements related to international trade and big multinationals.

Exploring 'fractured' consumers may carry especial importance for the study of consumption. These agents can barely exercise their reflexivity. They behave like passive agents: overwhelmed by the influence of their socio-cultural context, they can hardly organize and delineate plans for themselves. Their lifestyles may suffer from this in several ways. Some of them may find themselves among the ranks of so-called 'fashion victims', compulsive buyers pushed by those false and growing necessities about which Baudrillard wrote. Others, incapable of elaborating consumption projects for themselves, will reject the mere idea of going shopping. The mere possibility of doing so will imply uneasiness and disorientation: they know the marketing messages and the existence of a language of objects, but they don't speak it. They find it difficult to decipher it in others, and even more difficult to speak it themselves.

Growing globalization influences the ordinary exercise of our reflexivity in general, as well as, no doubt, our consumption practices. Among the many consequences of globalization on society we could single out, first, decreasing contextual continuity: fewer and fewer people have relatives or peers at hand to understand them enough to help them complete their deliberations and confirm their decisions (Archer, 2007: 320). And because of this it becomes increasingly difficult to carry out communicative reflexivity, in an accommodating, traditional, repetitive, consumption style. One can seek some social integration or express a sense of belonging through consumption, but that no longer holds as the default option: the agent now needs to exert himself as much as anyone following some other lifestyle. This is the case with 'brand communities' or any other particular group organizing their social life around such shared passions as canal restoration, ballroom dancing, vintage motors, etc. (Muniz and O'Guinn 2001).

Many people who might have been 'communicative' consumers at some other point in time, now seem bound to some other lifestyle, more akin to those of autonomous agents: they follow general patterns but regret not having people around who can provide some orientation and security when making a decision. Maybe because of this, new marketing techniques are on the rise that hinge upon customization and client services, where the point of sale or the brand provide the certainty lost in contextual discontinuity. Those that do not accommodate to the new techniques may well resemble 'fractured' consumers, because, lacking any meaningful references, they withdraw from consumption projects and leave the construction of their own lifestyles in the hands of others.

A second consequence of globalization is that, for the first time in history, the situational logic of opportunity is becoming predominant (Archer 2007, p. 54). The cultural items available have multiplied. International trade has spread acquaintance of local products almost everywhere. Today, not only a privileged few, but most of the population in the developed world, have access to Chinese chrysanthemum tea, Indian cotton, Uruguayan mate, or Swedish reindeer meat. Together with these products from other cultures, we can also have access to what they incorporate: the world views and values, traditions and heritages, ambitions for improvement, emulative reactions or rejection of others. All those elements are at hand, as part of our global culture, with which to enrich, modify or transform our own lifestyles, as Morace has documented. Increasing globalization will augment the salience of alternative values, as an increasing number of possible value-commitments will enhance the possibilities for elaborating and propagating new lifestyles, thereby fostering a still more propitious context for meta-reflexive consumers.

Some interesting topics for discussion open up at this point, such as the relationship between consumption and identity, the diffusion of different forms of reflexivity and its consequences for social and cultural morphogenesis. All these would help to provide analytical histories of the emergence of consumption patterns in our society. But this task lies outside the scope of the present work.

References

Alonso, Luis Enrique, 2005, *La era del consumo*, Madrid, Siglo XXI.

Archer, Margaret S., 1995, *Realist social theory: the morphogenetic approach*, Cambridge, Cambridge University Press.

Archer, Margaret S., 2007, *Making our Way through the World. Human Reflexivity and Social Mobility*, Cambridge University Press.

Barthes, Roland, 1957, *Mythologies*, Paris, Seuil.

Baudrillard, Jean, 1981, *For a critique of the political economy of the sign*, St. Louis, Telos Press.

Baudrillard, Jean, 1996, *The system of objects*, New York, Verso.

Baudrillard, Jean, 1998, *The consumer society*, Thousand Oaks, Ca., Sage.

Bauman, Zygmunt, 2002, 'Foreword', in Beck, U. and Beck-Gernsheim, E., *Individualization*, London, Sage.

Bauman, Zygmunt, 2003, *Work, consumerism and the new poor*, Maidenhead, Open University Press.

Bauman, Zygmunt, 2007, *Consuming life*, Cambridge, Polity Press.

Beck, Ulrich, 1992, *Risk society*, London, Sage.

Beck, Ulrich, and Beck-Gernsheim, Elisabeth, 2002, *Individualization*, London, Sage.

Bourdieu, Pierre, 1979, *Distinction: a social critique of the judgement of taste*, Cambridge, Mass., Harvard University Press.

Bourdieu, Pierre, 1996, *The Rules of Art: Genesis and Structure of the Literary Field*, Cambridge, Polity Press.

Campbell, Colin, 1987, *The Romantic Ethic and the Spirit of Modern Consumerism*, Oxford, Basil Blackwell.

Campbell, Colin, 1994, 'The desire for the new: its nature and social location as presented in theories of fashion and modern consumerism', in Roger Silverstone and Eric Hirsch (eds) *Consuming Technologies: Media and Information in Domestic Spaces*, London, Routledge, pp. 48–66.

Chaney, David, 1996, *Lifestyles*, New York, Routledge.

Douglas, Mary and Isherwood, Baron, 1996, *The world of goods. Towards an anthropology of consumption*, London, Routledge.

Douglas, Mary, 1996, *Thought Styles: critical essays on good taste*, London, Sage

Erner, Guillaume, 2005, *Víctimas de la moda*, Barcelona, Gustavo Gili.

Fabris, Giampaolo, 1995, *Consumatore e mercato*, Milano, Sperling & Kupfer.

Featherstone, Mike, 1991, *Consumer culture and postmodernism*, London, Sage.

Geertz, Clifford, 1973, 'Thick description', in *The Interpretation of Cultures*, New York, Basic Books.

Giddens, Anthony, 1991, *Modernity and self-identity: self and society in the late modern age*, Cambridge, Polity Press.

Hebdige, D., 1981, 'Object as image: the Italian scooter cycle', *Block*, vol. 5, 44–64.

Lasch, Christopher, 1980, *The culture of narcissism: American life in an age of diminishing expectations*, London, Abacus Press.

Lipovetsky, Gilles, 1994, *The empire of fashion: dressing modern democracy*, Princeton, N.J., Princeton University Press.

Maffesoli, Michel, 1996, *The time of the tribes: the decline of individualism in mass society*, London, Sage.

McCracken, Grant, 1990, *Culture and consumption: new approaches to the symbolic character of consumer goods and activities*, Bloomington, Indiana University Press.

Miller, Daniel, 1987, *Material culture and mass consumption*, Oxford, Blackwell.

Miller, Daniel, 1998a, *A Theory of Shopping*, Ithaca, New York, Cornell University Press.

Miller, Daniel, 1998b, *Material Cultures: why some things matter*, Chicago, University of Chicago Press.

Morace, F., 2007, *Real Fashion Trends*, Milano, Libri Scheiwiller.

Muniz, Albert M. and O'Guinn, Thomas, 2001, 'Brand Community', *Journal of Consumer Research*, 27, 412–32.

Parmiggiani, Paola, 1997, *Consumo e identità nella societá contemporanea*, Milano, FrancoAngeli.

Parmiggiani, Paola, 2001, *Consumatori alla ricerca di sé. Percorsi di identità e practiche di consumo*, Milano, FrancoAngeli.

Remaury, Bruno, 2005, *Marcas y relatos. La marca frente al imaginario cultural europeo*, Barcelona, Gustavo Gili.

Ritzer, George, 1999, *Enchanting a disenchanted world: revolutionizing the means of consumption*, Thousand Oaks, Calif., London, Pine Forge Press.

Sassatelli, Roberta, 2007, *Consumer culture*, London, Sage.

Simmel, Georg, 1899–1990, *The philosophy of money*, London, Routledge.

Simmel, G., 1957, 'Fashion', *American Journal of Sociology*, vol. 62, 541–58.

Veblen, Thorstein, 1899–1994, *The theory of the leisure class: an economic study of institutions*, London, Routledge.

Weber, Max, 1968, *Economy and Society: an outline of interpretive sociology*, New York, Bedminster Press.

13 Organizational use of information and communication technology and its impact on reflexivity

Alistair Mutch

Towards the end of *Making Our Way Through the World*, there are observations about the potential impact of both information technology and the multinational enterprise in disturbing the contexts in which reflexivity is practised, with the potential to favour the exercise of autonomous reflexivity in particular (Archer 2007: 320–1). In this contribution I seek to combine these two terms with a view to assessing the impact on reflexivity of the widespread use of information and communication technology (ICT) within organizations, with a particular focus on data intensive applications. I am not concerned with the extra-organizational use of applications such as social networking, important though these might be for reflexivity. The discussion of these is understandable, because their use is publicly exercised, but it can obscure the importance of what Kallinikos (2006) calls the 'deep web', that is, the myriad applications which run within organizations. My focus is on formal work organizations, often of a large and for-profit nature, because that is both where the putative impact is stronger and where more research has been carried out. Much of the discussion relates to managerial and professional staff, often covered under the broad rubric of 'knowledge workers' (Burris 1993). That latter term is notoriously slippery of definition, as is the term 'knowledge' itself (Lyons 1988). Some dimensions of the debate in the organizational studies literature will emerge during the main body of the discussion, but I provide a brief overview of the contending positions in the literature. It is clear from this that most of the work is not developed either from a critical realist perspective or from a concern with reflexivity, but there are useful insights that I believe can be gleaned.

I seek to show that much of the discussion on knowing in organizations has been taken up with the explication of 'tacit', experiential forms of knowing in conditions which would suggest communicative reflexivity. This is a misleading focus, I suggest, and one which obscures much of the practice with ICT, which involves a range of applications all featuring the analysis of extensive data sets in ways that favour the development of more abstract and systemic forms of reasoning, and so may be connected to growth in autonomous reflexivity. I question, however, the degree to which meta-reflexivity may be stimulated. Rather, I suggest, developments in organizational use of ICT and associated practices favour the simulacra of reflexivity, producing what we might term 'splintered reflexivity'.

These observations require further work and the lens provided by modes of reflex-ivity is helpful in framing this. Bringing insights in from the organizational studies literature may help to refine and deepen insights in social theory.

Modes of organizational knowing

There is extensive concern in organizational studies with the topic of 'knowledge management' (for overviews see Hislop 2006 and Mutch 2008). Some of this reflects fashions, both academic and organizational, but it also relates to real shifts in the activities of organizations. There are two contending approaches, with their roots in different disciplines and with different underlying assumptions, neither of which produce entirely satisfactory results. The literature on knowledge management itself tends to emanate from the information systems domain, with a focus on technical solutions and an impoverished conceptualization of social and organizational factors. That on organizational learning is marked by an emphasis on practice-based approaches, often informed by social constructivism. However, there are aspects of both that are insightful and useful in assessing reflexivity, as a brief overview indicates.

Knowledge management often manifested itself within organizations as the use of ICT to store and communicate the working knowledge of organizational members, with a view to profiting from its wider exploitation. Some of these applications, especially in more technical domains, produced a measure of suc-cess, but they often represented little more than a re-badging of systems previously labelled as 'information management'. This induced a degree of scepticism about the whole enterprise, scepticism which was fuelled by the technical focus of much of the literature (Wilson 2002). Much of the mainstream Information System (IS) literature operates with a very impoverished conceptualization of the organization, with little use of the resources of social theory. However, there is a substratum of more critical approaches. Some of these, especially as they relate to technological artefacts themselves, are profoundly influenced by forms of social constructiv-ism, such as actor-network theory (Mutch 2002). Of those accounts that essay an approach to the relationship of agency and structure which is more amenable to a realist position, the most influential social theorist has been Giddens (Jones and Karsten 2008).[1] Use of his work has led to a focus on more flexible forms of technology, with structures in practice shrinking into the background. This means that there is a tendency to neglect the more data intensive applications that we cover in more detail below.

There is a link here in the focus on practice adopted by these more critical IS theorists with that in the literature on organizational learning. This body of work emanates to a greater extent from organizational theory, although it is more influenced by social psychology and anthropology. This has important impacts on the focus upon experiential forms of knowing. Two influences are important here. One, which straddles the two bodies of literature reviewed here, is the highly influential division between 'tacit' and 'explicit' knowledge formulated by Nonaka and Takeuchi (1995) in their work on *The Knowledge Creating Company*. Drawing on studies of innovation and on a particular reading of Polanyi, they suggested that much of the valuable knowledge in organizations lay in the heads of organizational members and could only be drawn out by processes of co-production. This focus has strong parallels with work on learning, which stresses experiential learning based on master-apprentice models (Lave and Wenger 1991; Wenger 1999). Here, too, knowing is not thought to be amenable to rendering in a form which is capable of manipulation by ICT. I review the problems with this approach in more detail below, but one common weakness is that there is almost total neglect of the specificity of ICT. That is, in common with the practice-based approach in the IS literature, there is (if there is consideration at all) a focus on flexible forms of technology such as groupware, intranets and social networking, with profound neglect of some of the applications which, it is argued below, are central to the organizing of contemporary multinational enterprises. Again, if the relationship of agency and structure is considered, it is Giddens who predominates, although there are some limited influences of critical realist and cognate approaches (such as Engstrom's activity theory) (Garvey and Williamson 2002; Blacker 1995).

To develop our consideration of the links between ICT use in organizations and modes of reflexivity, it is necessary first to tackle the question of 'tacit' knowledge. It will be seen that this focus would tend to suggest the continuing importance of communicative reflexivity. A starting point for this assessment is with the notion of 'tacit' itself. As noted above, this widely used (in organizational analysis) term derives from a particular reading of Polyanyi, one which is comprehensively challenged by Tsoukas (2003). He shows that for Polanyi there can be no distinction between tacit and explicit knowledge. If tacit knowledge is that which is not accessible to conscious choice, being embodied in nature, it is profoundly wrapped up in the ability to apply explicit knowledge. Explicit knowledge is that associated with formal educational experiences and is codified in a variety of forms. Tacit knowledge by its nature, argues Tsoukas, is not going to be amenable to conscious recall, and hence will not be available for codification and sharing through the medium of ICT. This seems a convincing critique, but it still leaves the question of whether tacit is a suitable or sole antonym for 'explicit'. Spender (1998) suggests that we use the term 'implicit' for those areas of knowing which are taken for granted but which, once brought to awareness, have the potential to be brought to the surface and expressed in such ways that they might be shared.

Granted this shift towards considering implicit knowledge, another concern is with the way in which focus on this category of organizational knowing, which is undoubtedly of importance, tends to overshadow both more formal bodies of knowledge and structural influences on the formation of knowing. This is particularly the case with the very influential work on situated and experiential learning produced by Lave and Wenger (1991). This work, with its roots in educational psychology and anthropology, takes as its catalyst work with adult learners who are able to produce skilled performances in particular contexts (such as mental arithmetic in specific situations) but are unable to reproduce the same performance in formal settings (such as examinations) (Rogoff and Lave 1984). This led to a focus on the way in which learning occurs through what is termed 'legitimate peripheral participation' in apprenticeship learning. Here, argue Lave and Wenger, learning takes place in 'communities of practice', in which the apprentice moves steadily from the edge of the community to the centre. This is learning by experience, in which learning is as much a matter of learning to have a particular social identity as of content. Indeed, this mode of learning is explicitly set against more formal bodies of learning and knowledge. This line of reasoning has prompted much work which is important for its valorization of the creativity of many often neglected members of organizations. However, it runs the risk of neglecting significant developments in organizations, notably in its neglect of data intensive applications. It may have been observed that the emphasis on contextual continuity and on community, with its shared identities and assumptions, strongly suggests a parallel with the conditions which foster communicative reflexivity (Mutch 2003). However, most of the examples which Lave and Wenger draw upon are from more traditional settings. Their examples, in their much-cited *Situated Learning* (Lave and Wenger 1991) are: Yucatec midwives; Vai and Gola tailors; United States Navy quartermasters; meat cutters; and nondrinking alcoholics. There is a notable lack of examples drawn from large business organizations and no consideration of the impact of ICT (although there is some consideration of these issues in Wenger 1999). This has established a whole tradition of exploration focused on practice-based learning, which tends to neglect both the articulation of such learning with more formal bodies of knowledge and the potential impact of ICT (Gherardi 2006). This means that there is neglect of those developments which, I am now going to argue, would tend to undermine this contextual continuity and, rather, to foster autonomous reflexivity.

Data intensive applications and autonomous reflexivity

My starting point for considering the impact of ICT-enabled data intensive applications in organizations is the work carried out by Zuboff in the 1980s (Zuboff 1988). Based on extensive ethnographic inquiry in paper mills and insurance offices, she suggested that the application of ICT to work processes brought a new potential, one which she labelled 'informate'. Her argument was that traditional forms of automation simply took a manual process and made it more consistent and reliable. By contrast, she suggested that the application of computer technology to automate processes brought with it new potential. This was that, as well as carrying out the process, data would be gathered automatically on the way in which the process was carried out. It was for this potential that she coined the rather ungainly neologism 'informate'. For example, when manually operated valves were replaced by computer activated sensors, not only was the operation carried out more accurately, but the flow of materials could be accurately recorded. From such recordings it would be feasible to relate various input states to the nature of the final product. In a study of a plastics plant which installed a computer process control system, for example, Earl (1994) found that learning about the impact of different parameters on the nature of the final product enabled the company to move from being a volume producer to being a niche producer of specialist plastics.

Zuboff is clear (contrary to some critics: Knights and Murray [1994]) that infor-mate exists as potential rather than being determined by ICT implementation.[2] That is, a number of factors are required to take the data which is automatically recorded and do something with it. One is the need for awareness that the data exists at all and that learning can take place based on its use. This requires a body of knowledge which is different from that traditionally deployed. In the paper mills that Zuboff studied, traditional forms of knowing were based on physical senses, were action-centred and were typically unexplicated. That is, they had been built up through experience in a particular context, thus bearing out the situated learning that Lave and Wenger (1991) focus on. However, Zuboff suggests that to realize the potential embodied in the new bodies of data, operators required what she termed 'intellective skills', meaning:

> a shift away from physical cues, towards sense-making based more exclusively on abstract cues; explicit inferential reasoning used both inductively and deductively; and procedural, systemic thinking (Zuboff 1988: 95).

This means the requirement for more formal bodies of knowledge to help form these characteristics. Thus, in the example Earl (1994) gives, the operators in the plastics plant were not only trained in how the process control system operated, but also attended a local college for education in mathematics and basic physics.

For both Zuboff and Earl, the potential of the data available was only realizable by the interaction with process operators. However, such interaction poses a threat to existing authority structures. At one level, this involves questioning about how local operations fit into the overall working of the organization. As one of Zuboff's manager informants suggests:

> We've never expected them to understand how the plant works, just to oper-ate it. But now if they don't know the theory behind how the plant works, how can we expect them to understand all of the variables in the new computer system and how these variables interact? (Zuboff 1988: 95)

However, this in turn can be seen as representing a challenge to managerial authority. As Zuboff notes

> Questions, in a fundamental way, are inimical to authority. The question val-ues change over tradition, doubt over reverence, fact over faith. The question responds to knowledge and creates new knowledge. The question initiates and reflects learning. The question is incompatible with the unity of imperative control. Yet the question is essential if information is to yield its full value. (Zuboff 1988: 290)

This relationship of forms of knowing to authority structures is one to which we will return. However, these same pressures towards more systemic and abstract forms of reasoning have been observed by others in contemporary work organizations.

In his study of a Fiat car manufacturing plant, for example, Patriotta (2003: 138) notes 'the numbers and messages displayed on electronic boards have important cognitive implications for shopfloor operators. The capacity to read the data displayed on electronic boards and make inferences from them indicates the presence of systemic maps at the cognitive level'. A study of five UK manufacturing plants by Moss Jones (1990: 153) noted that 'Traditional, practical skills are disappearing; new conceptual skills related to information management and to operating in more creative, flexible, less routinized ways are developing'. He noted similar challenges to managerial authority and the need felt by managers to have a more systemic understanding of activities. This focus on the increasingly integrated nature of organizational activities is mirrored in Senge's (1990) advocacy of systems thinking in managerial education. Carroll's study of learning in high-hazard industries suggested 'the need for a broad range of employees with a *system-wide* understanding of the relationships between operations, maintenance, quality and costs' (1998: 714: emphasis in original). His observation was also that data accessibility was central to such efforts. These examples suggest the shifts which might be taking place; the discussion now looks in more detail at the nature and impact of some of these data intensive applications.

For the purpose of this discussion I define ICT as 'technologies for the processing, storage and transmission of digital material, consisting of ensembles of hardware and software with distinctive feature sets allowing for the physical storage and logical representation of different forms of data' (Mutch 2009). One implication of this definition is that we need to be specific about technology; that is, just what combination of levels and features exists in any particular ensemble can have very different impacts on information use. Many of the discussions covered already operate, if they are specific about the technology at all, at the level of user customizable applications running on widely available hardware, such as personal computers. However there is another class of applications which is more specialized in focus but arguably has an equally significant impact on organizational activities. My goal in outlining these applications is not to give a full account of their use, but rather to consider some potential impacts on the exercise of reflexivity. I should note that the literature on which I draw does not have this as its main focus. Rather, two features might be noted. One is that there is much focus on the way in which organizational actors 'work around' the limitations and constraints of such applications (Boudreau and Robey 2005). The other is that there is much focus in the literature on the failure of such applications to meet expectations (Markus 2004). Whilst one can grant the force of many of such observations, it is the case that many are made fairly soon after the implementation of such systems, making it unclear whether we are talking about the absolute failure of the systems themselves or rather failures of implementation. The limited research which takes a more longitudinal perspective suggests that it takes several cycles of use and learning before such systems are stabilized, often with different forms of use from those first envisaged (Leonardi 2007). This might be the reason why observers such as Ackroyd (2002) can suggest that these data intensive applications are at the heart of global enterprise, despite widespread reports of relative failure.

The classes of application I wish to consider are all ones that handle extensive bodies of data, often in a way which purports to overcome existing functional boundaries within organizations (that is, those activities organized around discrete business functions, such as sales or accounting). In manufacturing industries, changes in the nature of products mean that it is essential to record data about states at different stages of manufacture. This is particularly the case in highly regulated environments, where product acceptance is dependent on the presentation of data about the production process. *Product data management* systems are ICT-enabled systems designed to take data from design onwards and carry it with the product through all stages of production. The desired state is that the data created at one stage forms the input for the following stage. In practice, it would appear that such attempts at integration through data raise awareness of occupational boundaries previously taken for granted. For example, in her study of one such system, D'Adderrio (2004) found that design and production engineers attached different meanings to the same data terms, revealing a need for translation between the two sub-divisions of the same occupational group. Such systems might be thought to disrupt taken for granted contexts.

In more service based sectors, such as retailing and financial services, much has been made of *customer relationship management* systems. It has to be admitted here that there is considerable debate about what such systems are, with use of the label ranging from sales force automation (recording the contacts sales representatives have with customers) to systems storing the interactions customers have with organizational web sites (Payne and Frow 2005). However, the underlying approach is the attempt to gain value through the analysis of customer data. Such customer data can be gathered automatically through electronic systems at the point of sale and are seen at their clearest in the customer loyalty systems operated by retailers such as Tesco and Sainsbury (Humby, Hunt and Phillips 2003). Such systems raise important questions about the definition of phenomena such as customers and categories of products and have facilitated important changes in organizational activities which upset previous arrangements. One in particular has been the emergence of the 'category manager' in which those working for suppliers have to think about not only their own product but also its place in its competitor set, thus disrupting traditional boundaries (Emberson *et al.* 2006).

In many types of organization, the desire has been to replace disparate and incompatible systems with a single point of data entry and handling. Emerging from manufacturing systems, and given a boost by the year 2000 problem which saw many ageing systems replaced, *enterprise resource planning* systems (often shortened to enterprise systems) are sold on the premise of overcoming traditional boundaries within organizations. These are highly specialized systems which require considerable change in business processes if they are to be successful. They have been heavily criticized on the grounds that such changes are too radical and expensive. However, there are those who argue that once these initial hurdles have been overcome, organizations are beginning to exploit the data which such systems provide (Davenport and Harris 2007). The notion that there might be one authoritative source of data on organizational performance has proved something of a chimera. The final class of applications to be considered here, the *data ware-house*, is designed to overcome such limitations. This is an extremely specialized application, which sees the extraction of items of data from operational systems to form a single store of data which is then used to report on organizational perform-ance. Such systems are often used in organizations which collect millions of data items in the routine course of business. The most vivid example is that maintained by the US retailer Wal-Mart, which operates the largest civilian database in the world (Westerman 2001; Lichtenstein 2006). This requires highly specialized and very expensive equipment running specialist software.

It is on the basis of the volume of data collected by such applications and the experience of some organizations in seeking to learn from that data that Davenport and Harris (2007) have suggested that 'business analytics' represents a new source of competitive advantage for organizations. This involves the application of ana-lytical techniques, often derived from statistics, to large bodies of data with the aim of discovering relationships, trends or patterns which can then point to new areas of activity. Whilst many of their examples are drawn from industrial or service organizations, they also point to examples from the domain of commercial sports organizations, notably in the United States. Of course, there are many questions over the dimensions of their analysis, but such advocacy tends to confirm some of the trends towards more systemic and abstract modes of thinking, not least in their deployment of bodies of formal mathematical and statistical knowledge.

A common feature of these applications is their attempts to cross traditional boundaries, the boundaries that form the limits of what have been termed epis-temic communities (Knorr-Cetina 1999). That is, much of the focus in the work on organizational knowing has been on relatively bounded occupational commu-nities, in which background assumptions might be created and stabilized through experience, thus fostering communicative reflexivity. ICT-enabled systems which purport to integrate activities across occupational groupings by common defini-tions threaten such conditions. The focus on definitions is an important one, as it is essential for common data use. It means that taken for granted definitions now become open for debate and change, rendering areas of the organization which have been relatively closed off with non-integrated systems open to scrutiny (Stinchcombe 1990). It could be objected that the specialized nature of the appli-cations discussed makes them the province of a rather limited set of users. It would be true to say that direct use of such systems is often far less than use of, say, email, but direct use might not be the most important impact. For it is possible to argue that such systems feed into a broader culture of performance management within organizations, in which more and more people are exposed to the panoply of per-formance indicators and 'balanced scorecards' (Kaplan and Norton 1993). Once the province of relatively few senior managers, 'executive information systems' become translated into 'everybody's information systems' in which the practice of monitoring by key indicators becomes much more widespread, especially amongst the management cadre (Wheeler, Chang and Thomas 1993).

Other technologies are also important here, often in unexpected forms. Many organizations deploy systems by which extracts from the core data systems are taken and electronically communicated to the relevant managers, often using systems like email and intranets. By this means the impact of systems which are not used directly by managers is generalized throughout the organization. This is where we have links with the more familiar desktop systems. Not only are these used as access mechanisms to summaries of the data, by means such as organizational intranets, but the widespread use of technologies such as word processors and the portable document format (pdf) has made it increasingly easy to produce documentation of all types. Thus organizations are awash with strategy papers, departmental newsletters and other forms of communication. The problems of overload which this poses are considered below, but all these forms of ICT-enabled production foster the disruption of previous contextual continuity. One key feature of autonomous reflexivity is argued to be contextual discontinuity; another is the focus on strategic thinking. One final element of ICT-permeated organizations might be the increasing exposure of many more organizational members to the discourse of strategy formulation. The 'strategy as practice' approach in organizational analysis emphasizes the importance of examining mundane practices, such as the consultant facilitated 'away day', in producing organizational strategies (Whittington 2006). It seems plausible to argue that ICT enables, though the relatively easy production and communication of large bodies of data and accompanying analyses, the involvement of many more organizational actors in the discourse of strategy.

This section has argued, therefore, that there seems a *prima facie* case that the organizational use of ICT has in many ways fostered the conditions for the wider exercise of autonomous reflexivity. It does so by challenging the traditional boundaries that have shaped occupational groupings within organizations, in particular by demanding common definitions for data which transcend their conditions of production. Systems for the collection and processing of extensive bodies of data contribute to the creation of a climate of performance management which raises questions about taken-for-granted activities. Such questions are transmitted to an ever greater group of mangers who are encouraged to partake of a discourse of strategic thinking, both as applied to themselves and their organization. Such conditions seem to support the contention that organizational practices foster the development of autonomous reflexives. However, I have said nothing to date of any impact on meta-reflexives. One might imagine that the widespread questioning of organizational arrangements might lead to a much greater questioning of the purpose of organizations themselves and so to forms of meta-reflexivity. In the next section I argue that there are a number of factors which might close down the space for meta-reflexivity and indeed might produce a particular form of autonomous reflexivity.

The limits of organizational reflexivity

Let us take stock of the discussion so far. I have suggested that within organizations there are a number of ICT applications which foster the conditions for autonomous reflexivity. These are data intensive applications, which are capable of capturing, manipulating and analysing large bodies of data captured or produced as a routine part of organizational processes. It might be objected that such systems fail to live up to the expectations which are fostered by their vendors, that they are less effective because of the quality of the data which feeds them, that organizational actors seek to mitigate their effects by 'work arounds', that they are used in practice at tactical rather than strategic decision making level and that the fantasies of those who promote 'business analytics' remain just that. All these objections have their foundations, but they are beside the point when it comes to considering the impact on reflexivity. For such systems disturb existing patterns. As Tsoukas (2004: 178) suggests '… information has potentially reorganizing effects, for, in principle, it enables a system to reflect on it and thus come up with new descriptions of itself, leading to potentially novel patterns of action'. These systems provide such 'information' by crossing existing boundaries and demanding that attention be paid to the definition of existing and taken-for-granted entities, such as 'customer' and 'product'. However, how actors react to such disturbing tendencies remains a matter for investigation, rather than something which can be automatically read off a 'system'. That is, if reflexivity is a personal emergent property, actors can react in a number of ways to the same context, with their mode of reflexivity, shaped by prior contexts, either being confirmed or modified.

Whilst I have argued above that it is likely that the focus on tacit, experiential forms of knowing, which tends to suggest the relatively closed world of the communicative reflexive, is under considerable pressure from the integrative pretensions of these systems, there is some counter evidence of that. In his study of managerial responses to earlier systems, Moss-Jones (1990: 150) observed that 'IT increases the pressure on managers to respond quickly; thus their 'pace' of work is increased and they have less time for reflection'. Of course, to some extent managers may here be drawing on an alternative discourse, that of the fast-moving action-oriented figure. Carroll notes:

> The fixing orientation is consistent with American managers' desires for certainty and action. People are not encouraged to look at the linkages among problems and issues, because it creates a feeling of overwhelming complexity and hopelessness in the face of pressure to do something quickly. (1998: 706)

The degree to which such an orientation is a function of American approaches in particular is a matter for concrete investigation, but the observation does point to some limits on reflexivity. Another means of coping is the use of genres. Orlikowski and Yates (1994: 300) suggest that genres are 'social institutions that both shape and are shaped by individuals' communicative actions'. That is, over time, certain forms of communication, such as the memo and the report, become institutionalized in such a way as to condition and shape forms of communication and thus place limits on reflexivity. They do so by becoming to-hand resources which are taken-for-granted and which reduce the degree of conscious action needed. Certain responses thus become habitual and these responses can carry forward as coping mechanisms for the new torrent of information. A key genre that Kellogg, Orlikowski and Yates (2006) look at in more recent work is the PowerPoint presentation. Achieving a central position in many organizational routines, with no event being complete without its presentation, whether relevant or not, the presentation becomes an object in its own right. In the Web advertising agency that the authors examined, the presentation played a vital role in enabling actors to work across areas of expertise to produce artefacts rapidly:

> here community members make information visible rather than transferring it from one community to another, where they represent their work legibly through a repertoire of project genres rather than translating different meanings to reconcile interpretive differences, and where they assemble work products through a process of juxtaposition, adaptation, and dynamic alignment, rather than engaging in joint transformation. (Kellogg, Orlikowski and Yates 2006: 42)

The genre of 'presentation', especially as inscribed into the form prescribed by one software application, thus made effective performance possible, or at least it enabled the meeting of short term goals. For such presentational devices did not stimulate reflexivity but coping, and while this was successful it engendered contradictions which the authors claimed 'may limit organizational creativity in the long run by suppressing the mutual engagement and occupational friction that can generate creativity' (Kellogg, Orlikowski and Yates 2006: 42). We may, that is, get the impression of reflexivity and yet its opposite in practice. This example suggests a degree of retreat into the boundaries of existing epistemic communities; if we add power into the equation then this retreat is confirmed.

Organizations are sets of roles linked by authority relationships (Reed 1992). Those authority relationships condition the practice of reflexivity. In an interesting account of the use of a sales contact recording system, albeit not one which raised the question of reflexivity directly, Hayes and Walsham (2000) observe two different responses from their sample of sales representatives in a pharmaceutical company. Responding to the visibility which ICT gives to activities, one group of (generally older) representatives retreated into their local enclaves and abstained from participation in discussion forums which were facilitated using ICT. Their response was to hoard their knowledge and share it only with those who shared local assumptions. They rather despised those who did participate, labelling such as 'careerists'. These more career minded reps contributed to the nationally visible discussions, but more with a view to being seen to be doing so, rather than on the basis of the reasoning behind their contributions. Zuboff (1988: 156) refers to this ability of ICT-enabled systems, such as email, to record and preserve details of organizational activities as 'textualization'. The impact is seen in particular in the creation of email debates, where those who realize that visibility can work to their advantage contribute in large measure (Woolgar 2002). In this way, the more strategic actions of certain organizational actors can be encouraged, producing what we might regard as the simulacra of reflexivity.

Authoritative control is not the only way in which power plays out in organizations. We have noted above that functional boundaries can be challenged by enterprise-wide systems. However, another effect can be to consolidate the position of some managerial groupings over others. That is to say, there is considerable evidence of struggle between groups of managers to be regarded as those who best reflect the ultimate needs of the 'owners' of the business (increasingly to be regarded in systemic, rather than personal, terms). Thus, the early years of the twentieth century saw a struggle between engineers and accountants for leading positions in for-profit organizations, a struggle which has played out with different results in different institutional settings (Armstrong 1989). However, a more recent struggle has been that between marketing and other managerial groups, under the label of customer sovereignty. In this struggle, data becomes an important ally. Thus, speaking of customer knowledge in the music recording industry, Negus (1999: 59–60) observes that:

> It informs intra-departmental rivalry to the extent that knowledge of what consumers are doing – and legitimating that knowledge through 'hard' information and verifiable data rather than 'hunches' or 'intuition' – is deployed in struggles for influence and position within the organization.

So it is that marketing departments, once known for their looser approach to questions of data, become enthusiastic champions of data intensive systems such as data warehouses. Once again this produces both the conditions for loosening traditional conceptions of what it takes to be in a particular occupational grouping and so sets up the potential for new forms of reflexivity. The nature of such systems suggests a shift towards an autonomous form of reflexivity, but can we say if they are likely to produce shifts towards meta-reflexivity?

Conclusion

The argument presented above is that shifts in organizational practice may have significant consequences for modes of reflexivity. Against the current of much thinking in studies of organizational learning, I have argued that the widespread deployment of data intensive systems is likely to create the conditions for the wider spread of autonomous forms of reflexivity. This is not just because they permeate a culture of data analysis and 'rational' decision making which tends to favour the strategic and planning aspects so important to autonomous reflexivity, but also because they challenge the traditional boundaries supporting the contextual continuity which supports the communicative reflexive. This is without considering the need for communication across cultural boundaries, which might also disturb embedded assumptions. Just within organizations, the focus on challenging and agreeing definitions, which are needed if data is to be used in an integrated way across an organization, has the capacity to upset patterns of communication. This is not a once and for all practice, and we can see in some of the above discussion some impulses towards preserving local spaces which facilitate communicative encounters. Indeed, much emphasis is placed within large organizations on rec-reating those communities of practice which ICT-facilitated developments have been seen to rip asunder. However, it appears that the organizational use of ICT tends to foster, as Archer suggests, the wider spread of autonomous reflexivity. In this fashion the ideas she presents are a valuable lens through which to view the organizational literature. Further investigations within organizations to examine more closely the specific impacts of the applications on modes of reflexivity we have discussed would be of particular value.

However, this is still to say nothing of meta-reflexivity. One response is that if meta-reflexivity is seen to be about 'reflecting upon one's own acts of reflexivity' then there is encouragement to be found in this through the widespread accept-ance of ideas of reflective practice in organizations, especially in public sector ones (Argyris and Schon 1974; Schon 1987). However, such encouragement comes into sharp conflict with the requirements to maintain an action orientation to deal with the fast pace of organizational activities. This is more likely to produce the impression of reflexivity, what one might term 'splintered reflexivity'. This relates in part to the mediating impacts of genre, as explored above. But going beyond this there is extensive literature on the existence and nature of manage-ment fashion (Newell, Robertson and Swan 2001). That is, there are waves of initiatives within organizations. Many of these contain some interesting kernels of reason, but they are more likely to demand surface conformance, thus produc-ing the ugly and contorted language that so easily falls victim to the satire of *The Office* and other treatments. The place to search for meta-reflexivity, that is, may not be within the organization itself. Rather it is to be found in the interaction of organizational actors with their wider concerns, formulated in their personal projects. Some of these may be limited to the confines of organizational life, but this seems unlikely.

Garvey and Williamson (2002), in an account consciously drawing upon criti-cal realism, present an alternative perspective, one in which they draw upon the concept of 'meta cognition'. This in turn is drawn from the learning literature, where it is positioned as the capacity to 'learn about learning'. In this body of work the focus tends to be on educational interventions by which the skill of learning can be improved by self-conscious reflection about the process. This suggests, for Garvey and Williamson (2002: 16), that 'meta-cognitive capacity is a qual-ity of individual human minds and something that can be nurtured to become a feature of the ways in which organizations of many different kinds can function'. This proposition might appear somewhat optimistic in the light of some of the features of organizations that we have discussed above, but while it seems to have clear parallels with aspects of meta-reflexivity, it also has problems. One is that it is derived from the literature on education which is profoundly influenced by cognitive psychology, with its individualizing tendencies. In addition, much of this literature suggests that while there is a distinction between 'deep' and 'surface' learning (with the former more likely to display the impact of meta cognition) many learners are capable of exercising 'strategic' learning; that is, of adapting their learning styles to particular contexts and subjects. This perhaps suggests something of the instrumentalist approach that characterizes many autonomous reflexives, rather than the reflection on personal projects that meta-reflexives might engage in. Perhaps this line of thinking suggests the need for approaches based on critical realism to tackle the boundary with psychology. It might also suggest that there might be much value in bringing modes of reflexivity as formulated by Archer into the centre of debates within organization studies.

It is here that one has to regret the increasing separation of organizational studies from the wider domain of sociology. The home of organization studies has become, with a few exceptions, the business school, which suggests the potential for an unwelcome narrowing of focus. This has a number of adverse impacts. From within organization studies in general, and the articulation of ICT and organizations in particular, it often appears that social theorists draw broad and sweeping conclusions about the impact of particular organizational changes which would benefit from a more detailed engagement with organizational literature and practice (Jones and Karsten 2008). In the opposite direction, it suggests that organizational scholars need to reconnect with the broader discourse of social science. A focus on modes of reflexivity offers much opportunity for re-establishing these connections.

Notes

1 It would be fair to point out, as Jones and Karsten do, that much of this usage is rather shallow. In many cases it is possible to argue that the operationalization in practice of the relationship between agency and structure bears more similarities to a morphogenetic approach than to Giddens' formulations (Mutch 2005).
2 It is interesting to note that the French Marxist Jean Lojkine (1986) was also noting a similar potential slightly earlier, again drawing upon studies of factory work.

References

Ackroyd, S. (2002) *The organization of business: applying organizational theory to contemporary change*, Oxford: Oxford University Press.
Archer, M. (2007) *Making our way through the world: human reflexivity and social mobility*, Cambridge: Cambridge University Press.
Argyris, C. and Schon, D. (1974) *Theory in practice: increasing professional effectiveness*, London: Jossey-Bass.
Armstrong, P. (1989) 'Management, Labour Process and Agency', *Work, Employment &Society*, 3(3): 307–22.
Blackler, F. (1995) 'Knowledge, knowledge work and organizaations: an overview and interpretation', *Organization Studies*, 16(6): 1021–46.
Boudreau, M., and Robey, D. (2005) 'Enacting integrated information technology', *Organization Science*, 16(1): 3–18.
Burris, B. H. (1993) *Technocracy at Work*, Albany: SUNY.
Carroll, J. (1998) 'Organizational learning activities in high-hazard industries: the logics underlying self-analysis', *Journal of Management Studies*, 35(6): 699–717.
D'Adderio, L. (2004) *Inside the virtual product: how organizations create knowledge through software*, Cheltenham: Edward Elgar.

Davenport, T. and Harris, J. (2007) *Competing on analytics: the new science of winning*, Boston: Harvard Business School Press.

Earl, M. (1994) 'Shorko Films SA', in Ciborra, C. and Jelassi, T. (eds) *Strategic Information Systems, A European Perspective*, 99–112.

Emberson, C. Storey, J., Godsell, J. and Harrison, A. (2006) 'Managing the supply chain using in-store supplier employed merchandisers', *International Journal of Retail & Distribution Management*, 34(6): 467–81.

Garvey, B. and Williamson, B. (2002) *Beyond knowledge management: dialogue, creativity and the corporate curriculum*, Harlow: Pearson.

Gherardi, S. (2006) *Organizational knowledge: the texture of workplace learning*, Oxford: Blackwell.

Hayes, N. and Walsham, G. (2000) 'Safe enclaves, political enclaves and knowledge working', in Pritchard, C., Hull, R., Chumer, M. and Willmott, H. (eds) *Managing knowledge*, Basingstoke: Macmillan 69–87.

Hislop, D. (2005) *Knowledge Management in Organizations*, Oxford: Oxford University Press.

Humby, C., Hunt, T., and Phillips, T. (2003) *Scoring points: how Tesco is winning customer loyalty*, London: Kogan Page.

Jones, M., and Karsten, H. (2008) 'Giddens's structuration theory and information systems research', *MIS Quarterly*, 32(1): 127–57.

Kallinikos, J. (2006) *The consequences of information: institutional implications of technological change*, Cheltenham: Edward Elgar.

Kaplan, R. S. and Norton, D. (1993) 'Putting the balanced scorecard to work', *Harvard Business Review*, 71(5): 134–49.

Kellogg, K., Orlikowski, W. and Yates, J. (2006) 'Life in the trading zone: structuring coordination across boundaries in postbureaucratic organizations', *Organization Science*, 17(1): 22–44.

Knights, D. and Murray, F. (1994) *Managers Divided*, Chichester: Wiley.

Knorr-Cetina, K. (1999) *Epistemic Cultures: How the Sciences Make Knowledge*, Cambridge, MA: Harvard University Press.

Lave, J. and Wenger, E. (1991) *Situated learning: legitimate peripheral participation*, Cambridge: Cambridge University Press.

Leonardi, P. (2007) 'Activating the informational capabilities of information technology for organizational change', *Organization Science*, 18(5): 813–31.

Lichtenstein, N. (2006) *Wal-Mart: the face of twenty-first-century capitalism*, New York: The New Press.

Lojkine, J. (1986) 'From the industrial revolution to the computer revolution: First signs of a new combination of material and human productive forms', *Capital and Class*, 29, 111–29.

Lyons, D. (1988) *The information society: issues and illusions*, Oxford: Polity.

Markus, M. L. (2004) 'Technochange management: using IT to drive organizational change', *Journal of Information Technology*, 19, 3–19.

Moss-Jones, J. (1990) *Automating managers – the implications of information technology for managers*, London: Pinter.

Mutch, A. (2002) 'Actors and networks or agents and structures: a critical realist critique of actor-network theory', *Organization*, 9(3): 477–96.

Mutch, A. (2003) 'Communities of practice and habitus: a critique', *Organization Studies*, 24(3): 383–401.

Mutch, A. (2005) 'Concerns with mutual constitution: a critical realist commentary', *International Journal of Technology and Human Interaction*, 1(3): 60–72.

Mutch, A. (2008) *Managing Information and Knowledge in Organizations*, New York: Routledge.

Mutch, A. (2009) 'Technology, organization and strcture: a morphogentic approach', *Organization Science*, Forthcoming.

Newell, S., Robertson, M. and Swan, J. (2001) 'Management fads and fashions', *Organization*, 8(1): 5–15.

Nonaka, I. and Takeuchi, H. (1995) *The knowledge-creating company: how Japanese companies create the dynamics of innovation*, New York: Oxford University Press.

Orlikowski, W. and Yates, J. (1994) 'Genre repertoire: the structuring of communicative practices in organizations', *Administrative Science Quarterly*, 39, 541–74.

Patriotta, G. (2003) *Organizational knowledge in the making: how firms create, use and institutionalize knowledge*, Oxford: Oxford University Press.

Payne, A. and Frow, P. (2005) 'A strategic framework for customer relationship management', *Journal of Marketing*, 69(4): 167–76.

Reed, M. (1992) *The Sociology of Organizations: Themes, Perspectives and Prospects*, Hemel Hempstead: Harvester Wheatsheaf.

Rogoff, B. and Lave, J. (1984) *Everyday cognition: its development in social context*, Cambridge, Ma.: Harvard.

Schon, D. A. (1987) *Educating the Reflective Practitioner*, San Francisco: Jossey-Bass.

Senge, P. M. (1990) *The fifth discipline: the art and practice of the learning organization*, New York: Doubleday.

Spender, J. (1998) 'The dynamics of individual and organizational knowledge', in C. Eden and J. -C Spender (eds) *Managerial and organizational cognition: theory, methods and research*, London: Sage 13–39.

Stinchcombe, A. (1990) *Information and organizations*, Berkeley: University of California.

Tsoukas, H. (2003) 'Do we really understand tacit knowledge?', in M. Easterby-Smith and M Lyles (eds) *The Blackwell handbook of organizational learning and knowledge management*, Oxford: Blackwell 410–27.

Tsoukas, H. (2004) *Complex knowledge: studies in organizational epistemology*, Oxford: Oxford University Press.

Wenger, E. (1999) *Communities of practice: learning, meaning and identity*, Cambridge: Cambridge University Press.

Westerman, P. (2001) *Data warehousing: using the Wal-Mart model*, San Francisco: Morgan Kaufmann.

Wheeler, F. P., Chang, S. H. and Thomas, R. J. (1993) 'Moving from an Executive Information System to Everyone's Information System: lessons from a case study', *Journal of Information Technology*, 8(3): 177–83.

Whittington, R. (2006) 'Completing the practice turn in strategy research', *Organization Studies*, 27(5): 613–34.

Wilson, T. (2002) 'The nonsense of 'knowledge management'', *Information Research*, 8(10) [available at http://InformationR.net/ir/8-1/paper144.html] paper no. 144.

Woolgar, S. (2002) *Virtual Society? Technology, Cyberbole, Reality*, Oxford: Oxford University Press.

Zuboff, S. (1988) *In the age of the smart machine: the future of work and power*, London: Heinemann.

Index

Entries for figures and tables are in *italic*

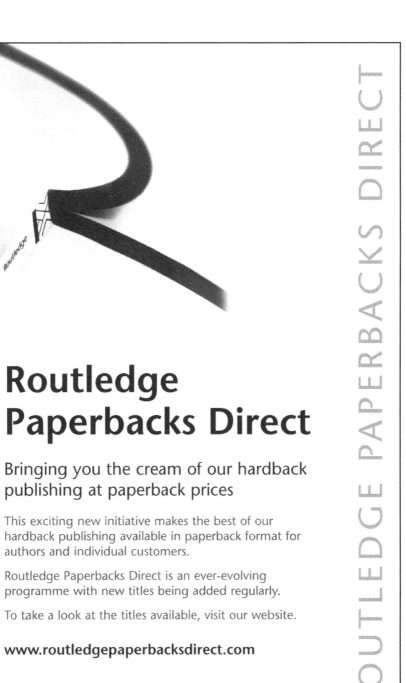

19380445R00160

Printed in Great Britain
by Amazon